History's Memory

History's Memory

∾ WRITING AMERICA'S PAST, 1880–1980

ELLEN FITZPATRICK

HARVARD UNIVERSITY PRESS

Cambridge, Massachusetts, and London, England   2002

Excerpt from "This Pleasing Anxious Being" in *Mayflies: New Poems and Translations,*
copyright © 2000 by Richard Wilbur, reprinted by permission of Harcourt, Inc.

Library of Congress Cataloging-in-Publication Data

Fitzpatrick, Ellen F. (Ellen Frances)
    History's memory : writing America's past, 1880–1980 / Ellen Fitzpatrick.
      p. cm.
    Includes bibliographical references and index.
    ISBN 0-674-00731-X
    1. United States—Historiography.   2. United States—History—Philosophy.
  3. Historiography—Social aspects—United States.   4. Historiography—Political
aspects—United States.   5. Historiography—United States—History—
20th century. I. Title.

E175 .F58 2002
973'07'2—dc21   2002017178

for Revan
and Boo

Contents

Acknowledgments

A book about historical writing and the work of previous scholars must begin with thanks to the many historians whose work has proved so influential to my thinking about this book. It would be impossible—I rather dejectedly admit—to remember them all; many are named in the notes throughout the text. The following deserve mention here for the deep impression their work has left on me: Robert Berkhofer, Paul Buhle, Jacqueline Goggin, John Higham, the late Richard Hofstadter, August Meier, Peter Novick, Dorothy Ross, the late Elliott Rudwick, and Robert Skotheim. I hasten to add that none bear any responsibility for what I took away from their work and some may no doubt wish I had been a more faithful student of their studies on historiography.

This book began many years ago with an invitation from Gary Kulik to present a paper on Caroline Ware at a conference sponsored by the Woodrow Wilson Center. Arthur Kaledin at the Massachusetts Institute of Technology encouraged me to expand on that initial study. I am extremely grateful to have had the opportunity of meeting and interviewing Caroline Ware, and of spending time with her over the conference weekend. She was an extraordinary human being.

The late Merle Curti shared valuable impressions about historical writing with me, as did Oscar Handlin in an early interview. Shirley Leckie generously sent me an early copy of her outstanding biography of Angie Debo and answered several queries, as did Richard Lowitt.

I am grateful for the financial support I received from the Spencer Foundation, Harvard University, and the Ford Foundation. Constance Buchanan at Ford was an especially decisive figure; her encouragement and assistance enabled me to finish the manuscript, as a year of leave provided by the Ford Foundation turned a dream about a completed book into a reality. Maxine Gaddis, also at Ford, and Cindy Corriveau and Jeanne Mitchell, at the University of New Hampshire, were eternally patient with administrative issues, and I wish to thank them here.

Bernard Bailyn provided helpful commentary and made it possible for me to return to the Charles Warren Center when I was teaching at Harvard University. I thank Stephan Thernstrom for his interest in my work and his kindness during the years I spent at Harvard. Aida Donald at Harvard University Press took an early interest in this book, proved unfailingly supportive during the years I worked on it, and helped with a title at the last moment. Joyce Seltzer graciously took the project on when Aida retired and has been a superb editor in every respect. I am grateful to have had the opportunity of working with her, and with her excellent assistant, David Lobenstine. Donna Bouvier oversaw production of the book with uncommon grace and skill.

More than one generation of students provided research assistance in the many years I labored over this manuscript; all did yeoman's work. Thanks to Jessica Dorman, Chris Hilliard, Barbara Keyes, Alexis McCrossen, Eben Miller, Laura Serna, J. Paul Stracco, Marcus Smith, and especially Kevin Ostoyich.

Several friends and colleagues read chapters and prodded me to improve the manuscript. I did what I could and remain extremely indebted to the following for their generosity: Bernard Bailyn, Jacqueline Goggin, Sue Halpern, J. William Harris, Margot Honig, Frederick Hoxie, Anne Janowitz, Morton Keller, David Montgomery, Anne Firor Scott, Theda Skocpol, and anonymous readers at Harvard University Press. Jacqueline Jones provided an insightful reading not only of the whole manuscript but also of its author; her steadfastness has been a gift over many years. Joan Crawford Poser turned her expert editorial hand to two chapters; she and Charles Poser have been sources of encouragement, wisdom, and good cheer. The following friends likewise supported me in countless ways: Catherine Clinton, Steve Come and Ann Lambert, Jeff and Barbara Diefendorf, Rick and

Sabrina Halloran, Alice Kelikian, Jane and Kit Reed, Sara Rimer, Ellen K. Rothman, and Bette White. My family—Maureen, Bob and Evie, Betsy, Mary and Ryan, Jean and Jeff, Brigid, and Bobby—as ever, kept things in perspective and cared for me. My mother did so while providing her own incredible example of what intelligence, steadiness, and love can contribute to a family.

I did not expect Chuck to hang in there to see the end of this book, but he did—faithful companion, occasional typist, and constant source of amusement.

Finally, this book is dedicated to two people whose support has sustained me and whose example—whose courage especially—I have learned from and been deeply moved by.

When will they speak, or stir? They wait for you
To recollect that, while it lived, the past
Was a rushed present, fretful and unsure.

—RICHARD WILBUR, "THIS PLEASING ANXIOUS BEING"

Prologue

One of the most striking intellectual developments in American historical writing during the last thirty years has been the emergence of a "new history" paradigm. Beginning approximately in the mid-1960s and maturing over the next many years, this paradigm has reflected a genuine shift in the ways historians have thought about the American past, written the nation's history, and understood the American experience. Crucial to the model of a "new" history has been the conceptualization of an "old" history, which the new history has held itself very self-consciously in contradistinction to. This notion of an "old" and a "new" history is more than a rhetorical device designed to highlight new advances in historical scholarship. It reflects a way in which American historians have thought about their own past, one that has profoundly shaped historical memory. This book is about that memory and the forces that have shaped its creation for over a century.

As both its enthusiasts and its critics have pointed out, the "new history" that emerged in the 1960s and 1970s owed much to the historical moment in which it took form. It was the tumultuous political context of the 1960s, many have claimed, that in no small part led modern historians to reject long relied upon ways of exploring and understanding the American past. The civil rights movement, the rise of feminism, renewed attention to economic inequality, sweeping critiques of American foreign policy, and the scandals of political corruption were just a few of many political trends of the time that set historians thinking in new ways about the substance, style, and forces that charted the trajectory of American history. For many practitioners of the new history (though by no means for all) those origins represented a wellspring of political commitment and a rich source of intellectual inspiration. Others were less inspired by or sympathetic to the political underpinnings of the new history than they were energized by the opportunity to reexamine, from a new vantage point and with new methodologies, the American past.[1]

Critics have cast the lineage of the new history much more darkly. Indeed, they have sought to discredit the entire project as an undertaking rooted not in historical truth but in political passion, presentism, and ideology. Ironically, however, in doing so they have often affirmed one of the central tenets of the new history: that it was born amid the riotous political conflicts and the social upheaval that accompanied the 1960s—that it was rooted, in short, in relatively recent history.[2]

However one assesses its merits, it is clear that the new history idea soon became a reigning one among American historians. By the 1970s, the existence of an "old" and a "new" history appeared to have itself become a virtual historical axiom. It was then already commonplace for historians to make reference to "the old labor history," the "old political history," and most often simply to a more generalized "old history" when establishing the significance of their own work. The distinction was appealing, for the new history provided not simply a means of sweeping away dusty intellectual remnants of the historian's past; it offered a fresh way of describing an exciting and modern approach to historical inquiry, methodology, and analysis that already seemed well under way. Indeed, the new history afforded a way of understanding what historians had done before and what they might accomplish still.[3]

What was new about the new history? No unified explanation ever became etched in stone. But over time the new history paradigm tended to coalesce around certain fundamentals. It was new, first, in rejecting a long tradition in American historical writing that viewed the past primarily as a story of formal politics and elites. This tradition stretched back to the patrician historians of the nineteenth century and their patriotic and celebratory tales of American history. But it had far more immediate origins as well. The new historians jettisoned what they saw as a post–World War II consensus on the American past that appeared to be the principal project of the World War II generation. That consensus was framed by the political orthodoxies of the Cold War period and was dominated by sweeping theories that stressed the nation's essential liberal character. "Consensus history"—the reigning fashion of the immediate postwar years—saw in the American past a story of the unfolding of liberty, abundance, and equality.

By contrast, the new history of the 1960s and 1970s moved the study of the American past in an entirely fresh direction. It not only found a place in American history for the experience of ordinary men and women; it also stressed the centrality of previously ignored groups to the drama of the American past. Where history had once been written from the top down—that is, by focusing on the determinative behavior of elites—it would now be written from the bottom up, from a foundation built on the lives of common people. As one recent study evocatively described the change: "The social history research of the past twenty years has lifted from obscurity the lives of those who had been swept to the sidelines in the metahistory of progress. It has also pierced the veil of those hidden systems which regulated the flow of opportunities and rewards in the United States, demonstrating how their functioning influenced the personal outcomes of success and failure. Those disinherited from the American heritage had at last found advocates at the bar of historical justice." The new history had, in short, restored the people—the masses—to the history of American society. This was its great leveling project and one, it was claimed, that was badly overdue.[4]

The new history likewise emphasized conflict in American history. Where historians of the post–World War II period had purportedly found consensus in American society, new historians found ample evidence of struggle and of clashes between a wide variety of competing groups. According to the new historians, the "liberal tradition" so celebrated by consensus historians was but one strand—and indeed, not even the dominant one—in a skein of tangled lines that ran through the American past. Competing traditions—radical beliefs, impassioned social movements rooted in penetrating criticisms of American society, a long history of challenges to the hegemony of American industrial capitalism, cultural beliefs that diverged from the common stream—made up the mosaic of American history. Although the United States may have lacked a feudal past, its history was no less fraught with dissension, conflict, and even inequality. There was more to be learned by confronting that complex and variegated history head-on than by explaining it away with sweeping generalizations about American exceptionalism.

The new history placed particular emphasis on social and economic forces as powerful agents of historical change. Not content to locate causality in grand ideas, national character, or vaguely realized notions of shared dreams and ideals, the new history turned a lamp on the engine of history and revealed its workings to be complex, intricate, finely tuned. The distribution of economic resources, the locus of political power, the dynamics of industrial capitalist development, the process of cultural and class formation—these were among the forces that helped shape the contours of American history.

In an effort to get at these trends and to reveal the experience of common men and women, the new history employed novel methodologies. Its tools included quantitative, empirical, and theoretical models borrowed from the social sciences. Indeed, the term "cliometrics" was coined to describe the application of modern quantitative methods—lifted to dazzling technical heights by computers—to research in history.[5]

Even fields such as intellectual history, which seemed rather poorly suited to such empirical methods and to a focus on the history of "ordinary" men and women, felt the impact of the new history. Ideas, the levers of history that nineteenth-century historians cherished for their explanatory value, would be understood in new ways. "Mentalités"—the mental structures individuals and groups created out of their cultural and historical environment, or found themselves saddled with through the workings of history—became a way of reconceptualizing the force of intellectual life. Culture too became the province not only of elites but a way of describing shared values, modes of being, ways of using leisure time that had important class, racial, ethnic, and gendered dimensions.[6]

All this added up, it has often been said, to nothing less than a true intellectual watershed in American historical writing. Indeed, it has been frequently argued that the new history that came to prominence during the 1960s and 1970s had few, if any, precedents in nearly a century of American historical writing. To the extent that precursors existed, the new history tended to locate them in the Progressive era. In the late nineteenth and early twentieth century, a young generation of American historians had also attempted to focus more attention on social and economic factors as decisive in shaping American history. Such a perspective briefly restored conflict to the narrative of American history and made of the past a much more complex and lively tale. The struggle between competing interest groups moved closer to the center as early-twentieth-century historians saw in the past the kind of fierce competition for political power and economic resources that was all too apparent in their own era. Some of the Progressive historians, most notably James Harvey Robinson in his 1912 book *The New History,* had actually made a brief for the importance of the social sciences and their methodologies to the study of history. For this they were applauded by many new historians in the 1960s and thereafter, who looked back with some regard and even a measure of affection at Progressive history.

At the same time, the limits of Progressive era history were often invoked by those who announced the arrival of a new history so as to distinguish further the unique thrust of historical inquiry in the 1960s and 1970s. Progressive historians such as Charles Beard were imaginative, it was said, in exploring the economic underpinnings of American constitutional history. Still, for many Progressive historians the United States remained largely exceptional, removed from the most brutal forms of class conflict that had characterized many European societies. The Progressives' quaint faith in democracy as the linchpin of American society, their firm belief in American exceptionalism, their faith in the likely further advance of liberal capitalism, their reliance on a sometimes crude economic determinism that lacked any well-developed understanding of class relations—all these ideas played a part in limiting the power, the force, and the achievements of Progressive history.

Most notably, the Progressive historians tended to emphasize progress as the underlying motif of American history. When the forces of democracy battled powerful "interests" over the course of American history, the interests might have won, but they continued to face the always-present willingness of Americans to rise against the presence of antidemocratic forces within their society. Finally, new historians in the 1960s and later who looked back at the work of the Progressive historians often sharply criticized it for the absence of any sustained attention to "ordinary" Americans—the working class, the "inarticulate" masses of immigrants, the impoverished, African Americans, women, and countless others whose stories and lives were often lost in American historical writing, even in the Progressive years.[7]

All this changed, it has been said, when a new generation of historians burst on the scene in the 1960s and 1970s. They offered a "radically different perspective on the American past" and thereby "threw into sharp relief the standards of significance which earlier generations of gentlemen scholars had assumed when they concentrated upon statesmen, generals, diplomats, intellectuals, and elite institutions." Indeed, in 1990 the American Historical Association itself sponsored publication of a volume entitled *The New American History* that affirmed the widely shared belief that "in the course of the past twenty years, American history has been remade."[8]

How new, in fact, is this new history? This question has been rarely posed despite all the debate the new history has inspired in contemporary America and all the political passion it has stirred. Few seem to doubt that, whatever its merits, the new history is a product of relatively recent events. However, there is ample reason to think otherwise. For much of the last century, historians have repeatedly concerned themselves with issues and ideas now credited to the "new" history. There has been no linear progression over the course of the twentieth century toward contemporary trends in historical study. But American historical writing has been characterized by persistent efforts and much substantive research on the part of many talented historians, working across a long span of time, to enrich the study of American history in ways that are often thought of as modern.

Casting no doubt on the value, integrity, bracing freshness, or sweeping accomplishments of the new history, this study seeks to place modern historical initiatives within the larger panorama of American historical writing in the twentieth century. It questions the paradigm of "old" and "new" history by suggesting that the political roots of the new history reach back not simply to the 1960s and 1970s but deeper in the American past. The new history carries with it a rich, and politically complex, history of its own, with strong moorings to earlier moments of political turmoil and strife that did much to shape the direction of twentieth-century historical inquiry. This fact has been too often overlooked amid contemporary debate about the writing of American history. It is time now for both those who have celebrated and those who have criticized the new history to themselves "stand at the bar of historical justice" and face the past.

There is, simply put, a way in which the new history paradigm is itself fundamentally ahistorical. Professional historians have been subject to forces that have at times telescoped and distorted historical memory. Political currents, social trends, cultural conflicts, and intellectual upheaval—the very history of the United States in the twentieth century—have been profound determinants of historical tradition and memory. Historians are no more immune to these forces than any other group of Americans. A vulnerability to presentism, however, carries a special and poignant irony when found among historians. It also offers an opportunity to explore the dynamics that have shaped the writing of modern history.

My focus here is largely, though not exclusively, on professional historians. Virtually without exception, I consider books, essays, articles, and reviews on the American past that were published in the discipline's leading journals over a hundred-year period. The historical studies explored herein belonged to the marketplace of ideas most accessible to professional historians. Though some of the scholars who wrote these works were amateur historians, many others taught at prestigious universities, held high office in the major professional organizations, and were leading figures in the discipline. Still others worked on the margins of academic history—at small schools with no graduate students to carry on their legacy or, in some cases, without an academic appointment in any college or university at all. Some who occupied intermediate positions produced serious scholarship but were never remembered as major figures in the historical profession. Regardless of the authors' professional standing, however, the research considered here was known to the discipline and thus achieved a measure of recognition in its own time. It belonged to history's domain. Prestige derived from prominence in the academic profession has often proved evanescent; it would thus be a mistake to confuse academic status with intellectual importance. For over the long run, the work itself remains—even when it has not loomed large in the collective memory of historians.

A reexamination of the long record of scholarly production within the boundaries of the discipline clearly reveals that the creation of historical memory devolves from more than the inherent value of an idea, the currents of politics, or even the trajectory of historical change itself. Writing important history and putting serious scholarly work before the discipline did not necessarily ensure intellectual recognition. Rather, the reward structure of the historical profession, the place of women and African Americans within it, the ways in which a good idea takes hold and wins regard and stature for its creator—these too have been among the many factors that have helped build or erase historical memory. Those who would root the thrust of modern historical writing in the trends of the moment would do well to look closely at such realities. As American higher education expanded so too did ideas about the fitting focus and character of American history. It is tempting to see this as an artifact or an achievement (depending on one's perspective) of relatively recent American history. But in fact for over a century such forces of professional concern and investment have shaped the writing of American history to a greater or lesser extent, and they have influenced the ways in which intellectual preoccupations have been forgotten or remembered.[9]

Looking back from the new history paradigm of the 1960s to the Progressive years, I have tried to sharpen the ways in which some historical work in the Progressive era prefigured the new history of the 1960s and 1970s. There is no need to rewrite the story of Progressive history or to retell the oft-told story of Frederick Jackson Turner, Carl Becker, and Charles Beard—the leading historians of their generation who did so much to enliven the study of American history. There is, however, reason to look more broadly at the historical work undertaken in the Progressive era and to look beyond these four historians, who have essentially become reified as figures who exemplify the entirety of Progressive history. Historical writing at the turn of the century was far richer and more complex than many accounts of Progressive history would suggest.[10]

Rarely do accounts of Progressive history devote more than a sentence—if that—to scholars such as W. E. B. Du Bois and Carter Woodson, for example, who devoted so much energy to advancing African American history in the Progressive years. Nor has much attention been paid to early efforts to examine critically the historical underpinnings of American industrial society. These initiatives belong to Progressive history. It is striking to see how often early-twentieth-century historians invoked the goal of broadening the scope of history to include ordinary working men and women and to deepening the discipline's meaning by advancing social history. By exploring these concerns, I hope to suggest new ways of thinking about the connections between Progressive history and the imperatives of historical writing later in the twentieth century.[11]

The interwar period was a critical time in shaping the new history agenda. The 1920s and 1930s were a pivotal moment, when the events of modern history prompted young American historians to radically rethink the past, to ask new questions of it, and to dramatically enlarge their notions of who mattered in the nation's history and what prompted historical change. Those who came of age during the interwar years were early made aware of the atrocity of total war, the frightening rise of totalitarian regimes, and the cost of crippling economic depression. Those realities, and the response of some talented young historians to them, did much to move the study of American history toward what are commonly seen as modern imperatives. The students of Frederick Jackson Turner, Arthur Schlesinger, and Charles Beard, among others, translated the vague and sometimes poorly realized aspirations of the Progressive historians into an agenda that clearly prefigured the new history that appeared to emerge so freshly and forcefully in the mid-1960s. Indeed, some interwar historians self-consciously sought to write history from the bottom up, to enlarge the scope of the past, to chronicle the lives of the "inarticulate" (the very word was used in 1939), and to employ inventive new methodologies in doing so. Marcus Hansen's work on immigration, Angie Debo's explorations of Native American history, the efforts of Vera Shlakman and Caroline Ware to advance urban and labor history, the young Oscar Handlin's immersion in a deeply research-based social history, Roger Shugg's exploration of class struggle in southern society, to name but a few examples, challenge the fixed paradigm of an "old" and "new" history. Indeed, as one looks at historical writing during the Depression years especially, it is clear that young historians of that era were moved by their historical moment to reexamine the American past in ways that resulted in scholarly concerns remarkably similar to those of their successors in the 1960s and 1970s. The obstacles some of them faced and overcame in doing so deserve respectful scrutiny.

The story of the interwar years is an especially compelling one because it has been so recessed in accounts of American historical writing. In his massive study of the American historical profession's romance with objectivity, *That Noble Dream,* Peter Novick concludes that little came during the interwar period of the Progressive era's much touted call for a new history. The new history "agenda," Novick writes, "hardly advanced beyond programmatic statements." Though some leading new historians "called repeatedly for the expansion of history's domain into such fields as the history of cities, of immigration, of women . . . with a few exceptions the call went unanswered."[12] In fact, however, the exceptions during the interwar years were numerous. When the few "exceptional" historians are moved from the periphery of our historiographical vision to the foreground, the substance and character of American historical writing, simply put, looks different. It gains further complexity and diversity.

Historians have tended to stress the prevalence of relativist perspectives and the dominance of Progressive history in much historical writing during the 1920s and 1930s. But relativism—the conviction that historical truth is contingent on the values, intentions, and experience of historians and the world they inhabited—does not capture the substance, the tone, or the passion of much important work undertaken during the Depression years. Indeed, by its very nature relativism describes a posture, a perspective, and what was for some a burning conviction. It does not reveal, nor is it intended to reveal, the actual content of historical scholarship during the interwar years.[13]

In truth, there was an explicit effort during the 1930s to create an overarching paradigm for a new approach to historical analysis. The 1939 meetings of the American Historical Association were devoted to "the cultural approach to history"—a way of looking at the past not unlike what would emerge with such fanfare thirty years later. Perhaps more than at any other moment in the past century, a radically and profoundly ahistorical disjuncture has tended to sever the strong ties that bind the work of Depression era scholars to the trends of modern history. To rediscover these commonalities does nothing to diminish the achievements of contemporary historians—rather, it embeds these accomplishments in a deeper and richer history.[14]

After assessing some of the compelling themes of interwar historical writing, I explore the fate of such concerns in the period from 1945 to the mid-1960s, when the "new history" emerges. Here the often-invoked dominance of consensus history appears less striking than the many countervailing themes in American historical writing after World War II. There is no question that the United States' experience in World War II, the fate of the European powers, and the extraordinary American position of economic, military, and political strength in the postwar period prompted historians to reexamine the long course of American history. In this context, the determinative effects of abundance, individualism, and political democracy were powerful themes in post–World War II historiography. Deeply influential studies in the 1950s such as Louis Hartz's *The Liberal Tradition in America* (1955), Daniel Boorstin's *The Genius of American Politics* (1953), and David Potter's *People of Plenty* (1954) returned to the theme of American exceptionalism and emphasized what seemed to be a striking harmony, stability, and continuity in the long course of American history. A more quiescent political climate, a much changed perspective on radical movements, a raging cold war, and the return of economic prosperity dovetailed smartly with these concerns.

But what became of the emphasis on class, culture, and community that was so apparent in the 1930s? What of the paradigm for a history that charted the experience of workingmen and -women, that depicted the heavy cost extracted by the advance of American industrial capitalism, that examined the distribution of economic and political power and the fate of the downtrodden within American society? Far from disappearing with the end of the Depression, the eclipse of New Deal liberalism, the onset of the Cold War, and the often pernicious domestic campaigns to root out American communism, the critical thrust of historical writing so apparent in the 1930s remained alive in the work of some historians throughout the 1950s.

At the same time, the antiradicalism of the period took some prisoners among historians, a fact that undoubtedly shaped historical memory of their scholarly work and their standing within the historical profession. Into the haze of consensus history went many countervailing themes and trends that underscore some of the mythic dimensions of that intellectual construct. Important work that ran against the grain of consensus history enriched the field of American history during the 1950s. But that reality was overshadowed by the sweeping interpretations that came to represent the hallmark of the post–World War II period. For it is another rich irony of American historiography that the paradigm of consensus history, which began as a warning to postwar historians of intellectual dangers ahead, wound up fulfilling its own prophesy. Young historians in the 1960s and 1970s, and their harshest critics, often read consensus back into the past and treated it as a fixed description of a historical and intellectual reality.[15]

They may have done so in part because the myth of consensus history served as a straw man that permitted historians to reinvent the past in the 1960s and the 1970s. Each generation of modern historians has, it appears, seen itself as standing on the edge of history—

alive at a unique moment in the history of the nation, determined to use that moment to broaden understanding of the essential "truth" lying at the heart of the nation's history. That conviction has provided much of the passion and lifeblood of modern historical writing. And yet it has also produced a confounding and subtle quality of ahistoricity that has obscured elements of drama and theme that have powerfully, and persistently, shaped the writing of modern American history.

We return, finally, to the paradigm of the "new history"—to its essential strengths and weaknesses as a way of understanding American historical writing in the twentieth century. I do so well aware of the potential pitfalls inherent in any project that locates lacunae in historical memory. I make no claim to remembering all the nuance, richness, and complexity that have been the defining characteristics of so much modern American history. Nor could I feature the literally hundreds of historians who advanced the agenda of a broader history over the twentieth century. Rather, I hope to persuade my readers to take a fresh look at the roots of contemporary history. Historians—of all Americans—have a special obligation to fully historicize their own past. In so doing, they can help frame a more honest and fruitful conversation about the mission of modern history in the twenty-first century. By embracing the full richness of their own past, historians can remind Americans of a compelling reality: recognition of the extraordinary diversity of the American national experience is not an artifact of recent politics; rather, it is embedded in the marrow of modern American history.

CHAPTER ONE

Industrial Society and the Imperatives of Modern History

> History will be better written in the ages to come. The soldier will not take the place he has taken. I do not say that the drum and trumpet history will have gone out; but when the American Historical Association shall assemble in the closing week a hundred years hence, there will be, do not doubt it, gifted writers of the history of the people. . . . We shall have the history of culture, the real history of men and women.
>
> —EDWARD EGGLESTON, PRESIDENTIAL ADDRESS READ AT MEETING OF THE AMERICAN HISTORICAL ASSOCIATION, 1900

It is a common complaint nowadays that American history has become politicized and that the past no longer is studied and understood in its own right. But the same might well have been said of American historical writing over a century ago. Indeed, the founding of the American Historical Association in 1884 was intended to bring together intellectuals and concerned citizens determined to better understand both the contours of history and the state of modern politics. If the venture represented a commitment to intellectual inquiry, it also reflected a wish to master or at least better guide the fast-moving currents of late-nineteenth-century American politics and society.[1]

These goals were changed but not forsaken with the advance of the historical profession in the 1890s. By the time the American Historical Association launched its scholarly journal, the *American Historical Review,* in 1895, a younger generation of historians was helping to redefine the mission of modern history. These scholars, working in modern research universities, holding doctoral degrees in history, committed to academic life, and often conservative in politics, were determined to create a more rigorous, scientific history. They struggled to free the discipline from its explicit ties to contemporary politics. Indeed, the severing of history and political science as fields of

inquiry was an important part of the era's drive toward professionalization. Despite such efforts, however, social and political forces continued to shape the agenda of historical scholarship in the United
States throughout the 1890s.[2]

Especially apparent was the shadow cast by the Civil War, a tragedy
that in the 1890s loomed large in recent memory. The war cast in new
light themes favored by patrician historians earlier in the century and
did much to spur the continued preoccupation with American constitutional history. Scholarly enthusiasm for broad, sweeping interpretations of national history reflected a determination to explain American history in ways that situated the devastating consequences of
sectional conflict in a wider, and more reassuring, framework. The
war and its aftermath had itself become a subject of historical study
by the 1890s, as professional historians parceled out blame for the
bloody conflict and critical, and often deeply racist, studies of Reconstruction appeared.[3]

It would be impossible to confuse the preoccupations of American
historians at the close of the nineteenth century with those of their
successors one hundred years later. The disparities in tone, style, substance, and often political conviction are obvious. American historiography properly records the ways in which the values, attitudes, and
preconceptions displayed in fin de siècle historical scholarship existed
within parameters defined by a moment now lost to American society.
Yet, for all the discontinuity, American historical writing in the 1880s
and 1890s already offered hints of what would become some of the
central imperatives of modern American historiography.

Several themes now familiar to American historians can be easily
detected in the work of professional historians at the close of the nineteenth century. Some research, such as Frederick Jackson Turner's forays into Western and environmental history, has long been acknowledged as vital motifs in "Progressive history." Other scholarship, such
as W. E. B. Du Bois's initial work in African American history, rarely
figure in accounts of the Progressive historians and their legacies.
Studies in social history, women's history, and labor history were also
undertaken in the 1890s. Though such endeavors in no sense constituted dominant trends in American historical writing, neither were
they ignored by professional historians in the late nineteenth century.
In fact, the goal of advancing a more diverse, searching, and sometimes critical perspective on the American past, even when viewed

with disfavor, was itself a subject of lively discussion and impassioned debate in the 1890s. Modern times, some argued, mandated a history that attended more closely to the common people.

It is little wonder such a notion would win favor in the late nineteenth century. By the 1890s, the rapid growth and expansion of American industrial capitalism, the wide reach of urbanization, and the arrival of millions of immigrants had done much to transform American society. There was a great deal to celebrate in the lavish riches, flourishing cities, wondrous technological feats, and expanding communication and transportation networks that characterized modern urban, industrial society. But certainly by the close of the century, many were acutely aware of the costs industrialism had extracted from American society. In the 1890s alone fierce labor conflict, the Populist insurgency, persistent debate about immigration, the Spanish-American War, and the hotly contested election of 1896 unsettled even the most confident observers of the national scene.

For some historians, such upheaval served as an occasion to emphasize how American history affirmed the United States' clear identity as an exceptional society. But even in the late nineteenth century modern social, economic, and most especially political realities intersected with historical writing, resulting in historians' engagement in issues that in retrospect were often viewed as artifacts of the later twentieth century.[4]

Although late-nineteenth-century historians moved slowly and more cautiously than many of their contemporaries in the social sciences, some voiced at least a rhetorical conviction that the mission of modern history needed to be squared with the realities of mass industrial society. In the 1880s and 1890s not many professional historians carved out of their sense of contemporary America an agenda for social history. Nonetheless, even historians who were discomfited by the diversity and unruliness of the "people" appeared aware that modern history needed to account for their experience in American society. Indeed, the voicing of such ideas within the discipline was of sufficient concern to some conservative historians of the time that they felt moved to defend the preeminence of political history.

That sentiment was voiced in the very first essay to appear in the *American Historical Review* when the journal was launched in October 1895. The author, William M. Sloane, had worked closely with the great nineteenth-century patrician historian George Bancroft and shared Bancroft's idealized and romantic notions of American history. But Sloane also claimed some of the distinguishing features of the rising class of professional historians who were about to displace their amateur predecessors. After earning a doctorate in philosophy from the University of Leipzig in 1876, Sloane returned to America to begin his academic career at Princeton. The year after his *AHR* essay appeared, Sloane moved to Columbia University, where he occupied a prestigious chair in history.

Sloane's meditation, "History and Democracy," blended forward-looking and traditional perspectives on the mission of history. He acknowledged that the character of modern society imposed new demands upon the historian to attend to the common people. But he insisted that the evolution of political institutions and the theme of progress were of critical importance in understanding America's historical experience. The result was a rather ambiguous stance that affirmed traditional notions of the past while attending to countervailing trends.[5]

Sloane's recognition of modern concerns deeply informed his understanding of contemporary history. Drawing on evolutionary theories, he took as axiomatic the notion that "contemporary history" was "apparently the most complex conceivable." This was true in part because the unfolding of history led inexorably to progress and the advancement of human society and because historical study had itself become more sophisticated and scientific in recent years. Detailed examination of "epochs" rather than nations commanded the attention of modern historians, whose breadth of vision took in more than "the achievement of heroes." Contemporary history surveyed "the development of civilization," and in so doing it had to account for the "masses of men" who figured so centrally in modern democratic societies.[6]

The centrality of the "masses" to democracy, Sloane stressed, fed demands for a history that moved beyond the province of politics and the behavior of elites. "Mere political history, for example," Sloane explained, "will no longer suffice for a public hungering after information."

The social, industrial, commercial, aesthetic, religious, and moral conditions of the common man are so determinative in our modern life that we now demand some account of them from the history of every period, in order that we may have clear notions of their genesis and development in the past for our guidance in the present. And inasmuch as they so sensibly affect our own politics, we expect the historian to explain how they affected past politics—being loath to believe that they were as unimportant as the tenor of histories written in the past would seem to indicate.

These demands inevitably made the study of the past an undertaking that in fundamental ways was contingent upon current conditions and relative to the historian's place in modern society. "History," Sloane observed, "will not stay written. Every age demands a history written from its own standpoint,—with reference to its own social condition, its thought, its beliefs, and its acquisitions,—and therefore comprehensible to the men who live in it."[7]

At the same time, for Sloane, such ideas had disturbing implications. "We must not go too far," he warned, "in yielding to a popular clamor, nor admit that the weight of the individual in modern life entitles his occupations and beliefs to more than a certain moderate share in the story of the organism to which he belongs." The historian must resist making religion, economics, institutions, or cultural life themselves, rather than their consequences, the focal point of historical study. In the end, "the conduct of the state" and the institutions of government made up "the essential matter of history." Furthermore, the pressure to enlarge the scope of history must be kept within moderate political bounds and not be allowed to give way to extremism. In this sense, intellectual life ran along parallel lines to American democracy, and faced similar dangers. In both settings, if "radical democracy" were allowed to run amok it would inevitably "level down" and "destroy all greatness both in the making and in the writing of history."[8]

Indeed, although Sloane celebrated the virtues of democracy and the achievements of the American people, he displayed deep ambivalence toward the various races and ethnicities that constituted the "masses" in late-nineteenth-century society. Sloane noted that many European governments viewed with disdain the "sludge thrown upon our shores" by innumerable waves of immigration, prejudices he appeared to share. But he criticized the hypocrisy of foreign critics who foisted "the shiftless, stupid, and too often, criminal elements of their populations" onto the United States only to disparage the nation as one full of primitive and brutal people. Too little publicity, Sloane asserted, was given abroad to American reform efforts to counteract such evils—including, presumably, immigration restriction.[9]

At the same time, Sloane expressed confidence in the pluralism of American society and its capacity to endure and even thrive from its diversity. "Mixed races and mixed civilizations have been the most persistent in the history of man. It is a great mistake to suppose that there can be nothing American except it originate from Anglo-Saxon sources on the soil of the United States." Immigrants from countries such as England, Holland, France, Ireland, and Germany had brought sturdy habits and beliefs with them to the United States and thereby helped create vibrant American institutions and traditions. So resilient was the resulting nation that "successive deposits of foreign immigrations"—from origins Sloane appeared to feel less enthusiasm for—were able to be "ploughed under and assimilated" in ways that further strengthened the American democratic experiment. Even the "dreadful system of African slavery," which Sloane viewed as a product of European greed and mercantilism, had been "painfully destroyed, although we wrestle still with the race problems entailed upon us by its creation and abolition." In the mastery of such challenges could be found the great achievements of American democracy.[10]

Sloane thus saw an important and compelling connection between America's identity as a democratic society and the thrust of modern history. The history of a society deeply influenced by science and governed democratically would differ from "what it was in the days which were imaginative and aristocratic or absolutist." A history of "kings, courts, and battles" held no inherently greater interest than one of "presidents, parliaments, and social conditions." So too the "meanest potsherd" might tell a story as absorbing as that revealed by "the greatest statue." How modern historians might balance all the competing demands of history Sloane's essay did not reveal. Nonetheless, this inaugural article in the *American Historical Review* revealed the existence even in the 1890s of the divergent and often contradictory political and intellectual impulses that would shape the writing of modern history.[11]

The lure of a richer and broader history, along with a persistent ambivalence about the masses who made up American industrial society, was also clearly apparent in the work of one of the great architects of the American historical profession, John Franklin Jameson. The first person to earn a doctoral degree in history from Johns Hopkins University, in 1882, Jameson would leave an indelible mark on the field of American history as editor of the *American Historical Review* for over thirty years and as a critical force in the collection of historical materials and manuscripts in the early twentieth century. In his early years as a historian, Jameson had an avid interest in social history and strongly believed that historical study should be enlarged to encompass the "real political history of the masses of the American people." These convictions freely mixed deep-rooted suspicion of the "less articulate classes" (a phrase Jameson used in 1885) with a belief that they deserved some place in the study of modern history. Nonetheless, they drew Jameson in the 1880s and 1890s to the study of such issues as race, labor, and the distribution of economic and political power in American society.[12]

Indeed, Jameson's first important seminar paper at Hopkins, delivered in November 1880, focused on an 1876 political conflict between the British colonial governor and white planters on Barbados that had incited an insurrection by the impoverished black majority. The choice of topic itself was noteworthy. As a young boy, Jameson had visited the West Indies, an experience that no doubt influenced his selection of this graduate-school research project. Herbert Baxter Adams, who then led the training of graduate students in history at Hopkins, encouraged his young scholars to focus their research on "local self-government" and to pursue topics with contemporary political significance. Jameson attempted to fulfill both those aims in his study "The Disturbances in Barbados in 1876." In it, he made use of newspaper accounts detailing the situation of black laborers on Barbados and interviews he conducted with West Indian businessmen.[13]

Jameson's paper recounted the explosive conflict that followed the efforts of the colonial governor of Barbados to persuade the island's political assembly to join a confederation of several West Indian islands. The white planters, who controlled not only the assembly but also much of the land and wealth of the island, fiercely resisted. Slavery on Barbados had been abolished, Jameson noted, but the largely black citizenry lived in overwhelming poverty. When the governor spoke of confederation as a plan designed to improve the lives of black islanders, the recalcitrance of the white planters incited large-scale mob action, the burning of cane fields, looting, and wholesale riots among what Jameson referred to as the "excitable Negroes." The white planters, Jameson dryly observed, "were even more excited, and with great reason." They believed they faced a threat to their economic dominance and "the even more alarming prospect of a negro insurrection, a prospect terrifying under any circumstances, but especially where the colored population outnumbered the white in the proportion of nine to one."[14]

Jameson's essay on Barbados offered little support to the position of the white planters. It nonetheless attempted to extract from their political contest some larger meaning for contemporary society, particularly for nations such as Britain, which administered a large colonial empire, and the United States, which struggled with the tensions of a postemancipation, biracial society. Jameson pointed to the inherent self-interest and distorted political judgment of the privileged white settlers when confronted with British schemes for political confederation. American sensibilities understandably ran toward colonists who were rebelling against the political constraints imposed by Great Britain. But Jameson warned against the tendency to endorse the views of the planters. Even in instances "when they do not form an oligarchy divided from the mass of the population by distinction of race and color," their narrow motives often led them to value independence over "good government."[15]

Further, Jameson stressed that the events in Barbados were also relevant for the insight they offered into the ways in which matters of political economy shaped legislation. There could be little question, he argued, that economic motives governed the political sensibilities of the planters. As Jameson explained:

> The planters held to the comfortable belief that the over-population of the island, the exceedingly low rate of wages, and the consequent degradation and misery of the laboring classes, were inevitable, and that they, as the employing class, had no other duties toward the employed than to profit as much as possible by the advantages given them by the cheapness of labor. Accordingly, the legislature made almost no effort to improve the economic conditions of the laborers, or to reform the well-filled prisons and lunatic hospitals, and in passing a law nominally promoting emigration, practically nullified it by the important exception that no laborers should emigrate.

In taking such a harsh stance, the planters were emboldened by "the narrowest school of English economists," one that permitted the white settlers to view their dominant position on the island as one that flowed naturally from the laws of political economy.[16]

Finally, Jameson underscored what he saw as "the most important inferences to be drawn from the account I have given." These concerned "the government of inferior races." In a postemancipation society several models for governance presented themselves. One was to enfranchise the former slaves—the choice, Jameson noted, made by the Republican Party in the United States during the Reconstruction era. Political power could also remain solely in the hands of the former slaveholders, a feat accomplished in Barbados by the imposition of high property requirements for voting. A third model might permit both former slaveholders and former slaves to vote, while retaining some property requirements that limited the electorate. A final possibility would be temporarily to rescind self-government and establish "as executive a governor impartial to the interests of black and white." In Jamaica, Jameson pointed out, this had been tried after an 1865 revolt with "excellent results."[17]

Jameson's preferences among these four models well illustrate his simultaneous concern about the realities of the economic exploitation of the impoverished Barbadian workers he studied and his discomfort with popular political democracy, particularly in multiracial societies, however much he may have celebrated the ideal of self-government in principle. In the end, of all the political possibilities he identified in Barbados, he favored what he termed "impartial administrative despotism" as the best solution to the island's political difficulties. Full enfranchisement of the former slaves, he noted, "is generally regarded as unwise, though whether in the particular instance of the United States the Republican party did wisely in adopting it, to retain its own supremacy, I do not intend, and indeed do not feel able to discuss." Such an assertion endorsed a belief Jameson likely believed many in his Baltimore audience would share—namely, that it was far from clear whether the former slaves could rise to the occasion of full citizenship. Indeed, the issue was a subject of intense debate among many whites in post-Reconstruction society.[18]

At the same time, Jameson expressed suspicion that the white planters on Barbados could be any better trusted as custodians of political rights and freedom. To protect their political and economic dominance, they had advanced "class legislation" and steadfastly resisted any effort to "consider the claims of the negroes to legislative attention." He was also pessimistic about qualified voting rights as a remedy. Such a system could only work if property, not race, formed the basis of eligibility and if "there were security for fairness of voting." Only administrative government, Jameson believed, would act as a restraint on each race "from oppression of the other" and gradually pave the way for "constitutional government."[19]

Despite his wish to use the Barbados example as a way of highlighting "analogues with many American troubles," Jameson was circumspect in directly invoking recent American history. He made vague references in his paper to "similar conditions and events in our own and other countries" and expressed hope that his historical example might offer lessons for nations that had struggled with the legacy of slavery. But he refrained from explicitly addressing race relations in the United States.

There can be no mistaking Jameson's musing as a first-year graduate student in 1880 with modern historical studies that have attended to the realities of postemancipation American society. His endorsement of "impartial administrative despotism," his reference to "inferior races," his paternalism, his distrust of mass political democracy, his advocacy of property holding as a litmus test for voting rights, and his general ambivalence about the political status of those freed from slavery are more than evident. Such views reflected the sensibilities of many white conservative Gilded Age intellectuals who felt considerable discomfort with the direction of change in post–Civil War society. But those views did not preclude Jameson's making an effort to examine class relationships among the planters and former slaves (albeit on Barbados), to explore the impact of political economy on governance, and to reflect on the ways in which the American experience might be set within a broader historical framework.[20]

Indeed, although Jameson was cautious in invoking contemporary political issues, he emphasized the importance of studying modern history. In 1885, he criticized historians who proclaimed the "utility of historical study on the ground that only the study of the past can enable us to understand the present, and then neglects all that part of the past which is most necessary to an understanding of the present, namely, the immediate past." The neglect of nineteenth-century history stemmed from "timidity and indolence in the presence of new and difficult tasks." Jameson hoped such a view would "speedily become obsolete."[21]

In fact, the most urgent business for scholars of American society, Jameson stressed in 1885, was writing a history that was itself democratic, that reflected the nation's identity as a political democracy. "Where the government is a government of the people, it is essential that the history be the history of the people, that, in fact, the history of a democracy ought not to be an Iliad." But that precisely described the character of much American political history, Jameson lamented. "Our political histories have for the most part been Iliads; they are filled with the deeds of the chieftains 'wise in council,' 'fertile in devices,' 'kings of men,' or even, in a humbler sphere of usefulness, 'good at shouting,' . . . while the rest of the well-greaved Achaians stand in their ranks unnoticed and unsung." Indeed, Jameson argued, there could be no "true history of our nation . . . until we can obtain a correct and exhaustive knowledge of the history of public opinion upon politics, the history of the political views and actions of the average voter."[22]

To get at the place of the "rank and file" (Jameson's words) in shaping the nation's political history required methodological and conceptual innovations that challenged traditional ways of doing political history. Carefully constructed analyses of political movements and public opinion at the state and local level would have to be undertaken because "the average citizen has probably more points of contact with the life of the state government than with that of the central government." The story of American politics, therefore, was as much in "the branches" as "in the trunk."[23]

To pursue such a story would be a daunting task, Jameson warned, for "future historians" exploring local and state politics could not rely only on published local histories, town records, newspapers, state archives, and other official records. Average Americans wrote few letters; newspapers by their nature only gave a very telescoped view of public opinion. Historians needed to dig much deeper: "If they would get down to the real facts of the political history of the people, they must examine the masses of county and town and courts records, and what of private correspondence has been preserved, and leave no stone unturned in the effort to reproduce exhaustively the course of democracy in our country."[24]

Jameson placed great emphasis on local records as a key to writing "the political history of the less articulate classes." Entries detailing "the election of hog-reeves, the seats in the meeting-house, the schoolhouse at the north end, the highway by Dea. Smith's house, the minister's salary and firewood" would provide historians with a treasure trove of information. Indeed, rarely would a historian "get so good a chance to see the non-literary classes thus unconsciously self-registered." Such local affairs might seem "parochial," Jameson admitted, but

> by combining many such data, obtained from different towns, we get a solid basis not only for a description of society at any given time, but for a description of the constitution, or, at any rate, of those numerous departments of human life which are common to social history and to constitutional history. Thus, it is of no especial consequence how the quarrel between the Rev. Mr. Parsons and his parishioners at Amherst as to his salary turned out; but if we have data from a hundred different towns as to the dealings of ministers and parishioners with each other, we have some evidence which will help us to form an opinion as to the position and power of the ministers in society and in the state.

In town records might also be found evidence bearing directly on matters of national political import. His own study of documents from one New England town suggested that the Revolution was, so far as this community was concerned, distinctly a movement of the lower and middle classes.[25]

Jameson's prescient call in 1885 for a rich, archivally based political history, one that traced voter behavior at the local level and made use of local records, diverged sharply from the more elite-focused "traditional" history of his own day. But the young historian had little doubt that such exacting efforts would reap rich intellectual rewards for those bold enough to undertake such an endeavor. "The enormous pains required," he wrote, "will be well rewarded; for, as the result, we shall have at last the history of the people of the United States, written with some recognition of the fact that our national name is plural."[26]

Jameson in the end did not fulfill this large scholarly agenda; nor did he even attempt to do so. In the 1880s and 1890s his explorations of Southern political history, like the work of many national historians of the period, offered sweeping generalizations, that traced in broad strokes the successive advance of democracy. Slavery, for example, with its inherent brutality and horrible and bloody consequences, seemed an inconvenient fact standing in the way of such a narrative. Jameson dealt with it by treating it as an anomaly, albeit a terrible one, with no lasting impact on the evolution of American democracy. Slavery was an "episode," though, Jameson admitted in 1891, "an episode of enormous consequence." "A foreign body had been lodged in our political system and increased and festered," Jameson asserted, "until the acute surgery of Civil War was necessary to remove it." For all that Jameson celebrated the idea of a richer political history, his detailed studies of the South focused in excruciating detail on state constitutional history.[27]

At the same time, even in these dense and detailed studies, Jameson attended to the social and economic forces that shaped American political development. He rooted his discussion of the expansion of Jacksonian democracy, for example, in "rapid economic development." And he offered his conclusion that in the main "it was preeminently one economic interest, that of slavery, which organized in the South a devotion to State Rights and a tendency to united action in their defence." In 1895 he delivered several lectures at Barnard College under the auspices of the Daughters of the American Revolution that could not have failed to shock his audience. In truth, they appeared to surprise him. Jameson chose to consider not only the political roots of the American Revolution, but also its social dimensions, including its impact on the American West and on industry, land ownership, and slavery. Jameson concluded that the American Revolution was, in fact, a "social movement" with effects ranging far beyond the obvious political transformation that came with independence.[28]

In Jameson's 1895 lectures, his remarks on slavery evinced greater complexity than he had displayed in his previous commentary. He stated at the outset that the Revolutionary generation well understood the fundamental clash between their celebration of "American freedom" and their toleration of "American slavery." Nothing could erase the fact of the "glaring contrast between the principles avowed by the men of the Revolution and their acts respecting slavery." He quoted the "striking language" of Patrick Henry's tortured meditation on his relationship to slavery: "Would anyone believe I am the master of slaves of my own purchase! I am drawn along by the general inconvenience of living here without them. I will not, I cannot justify it. However culpable my conduct, I will so far pay my devoir to virtue, as to own the excellence and rectitude of her precepts and lament my want of conformity to them." Like many nineteenth-century historians, Jameson affixed considerable blame for slavery on the British government. But he stressed, too, that "had there been no buyers there could have been no sellers." He offered an unsparing account of the "horrors" of the middle passage while emphasizing the ways in which the conditions of colonial slavery varied significantly. Still, in recounting these details, Jameson noted, "If we reflect upon what, under the best circumstances, must be the results of human bondage, I fear we must think of this commendation as qualified much as Lord Burghley in Queen Elizabeth's time qualified his instructions regarding the torturing of certain prisoners, namely, that it be done 'as tenderly as such a thing may be.'"[29]

The thrust of Jameson's argument was that the debates over independence and liberty had bolstered antislavery sentiment among many, spurred the proliferation of antislavery societies, created legal barriers to the importation of slaves, and ultimately led to some modifications, however inadequate, in laws governing the institution of slavery. He stressed that in some states liberalized manumission laws and outright abolition of slavery were the legacy of the Revolutionary period. But he also emphasized that strong economic incentives among the cotton-producing states bolstered their defense of slavery and created a situation in which "the Gordian knot" that tied the South to the institution of slavery "was sure to be drawn tighter and tighter, till only the sword could loosen it." Jameson's explorations of the social and economic impact of the Revolution, however tentative, marked an important divergence from the nineteenth-century millennial and romantic interpretations advanced by some amateur and nationalist historians. They also departed from the focus of many of Jameson's professional colleagues at the turn of the century—namely, historical studies of early America that lavished attention on British imperial policy and administration.[30]

There is much in Jameson's work that foreshadowed the preoccupations of modern American historical writing. The emphasis on widening the scope of American history, incorporating the common man, advancing social history, pursuing detailed local studies, and uncovering new sources and methods that would document the lives of ordinary people is striking. All would become critical themes in twentieth-century historiography. There can also be little doubt that contemporary politics and the immediate social and historical context did much to influence Jameson's calls for a more deeply researched and broadly conceived American history.

But it would be a mistake to confuse the sensibility that informed

Jameson's notions of American history with that of his successors later in the twentieth century. The politics of late-nineteenth-century America, as Jameson perceived them, gave a particular meaning to his conception of American history as an enterprise that needed to account more fully for ordinary Americans. Even as a young man of modest beginnings, Jameson identified with the American elite. He shared with other historians of his day, and indeed with Mugwumps from various professional and social classes, deep misgivings about the state of American democracy in the 1880s. The corruption endemic to patronage politics alarmed him, as did the "ignorance" of radicals, street corner agitators, and ethnic minorities. In 1882, he confided to his diary his despair on observing a local political rally. "Every political meeting I have attended," he confessed, "has had the same effect, to shatter my rising respect for the people, in their political capacity, and make me despise them."

In the context of the 1880s and 1890s, then, Jameson's call for a history that included the "people" and the "masses" did not carry for him the proletarian meaning historians would often attach to these phrases later in the twentieth century. The "people," for Jameson, were responsible, ordinary Americans of low or middling station. Though he clearly meant to include in the "masses" the diverse populations that he observed were part of late-nineteenth-century American society, he was not advocating the creation of histories that focused on telling the stories of workers and immigrants as oppressed groups within American society. Nor did Jameson offer a romanticized notion of "the people" in acknowledging the importance of the "less articulate classes" to American history. On the contrary, he disparaged mass movements, which he believed threatened American democracy.[31]

The Populists provide a case in point. Jameson described Populism as "a movement on the part of masses hitherto but slightly engaged in politics" that threatened "to put the conduct of our public affairs into the hands of a vast horde of unintelligent farmers." It was hard to miss Jameson's dismay as he observed "the progress of the Farmers' Alliance in the South in our own time." The organization, in Jameson's view, consisted of "a vast mass of ignorant voters" who "rushed forward to overthrow an imaginary tyranny, and to renovate American government, in the interest of ideas crude and half understood, but enthusiastically believed in."[32]

Jameson's notions of a democratic history were meant to sharply distinguish the American experience from the evident hierarchies, social divisions, and political turmoil of European society. In 1891, he argued that "great individuals" were less important in American than in European history because in the United States "natural influences" had had an enormous impact on the evolution of American society. The rise of Jeffersonian democracy and "national self-respect" was a critical part of the Civil War legacy that had diminished the place of "individual persons or groups of persons and their conscious efforts" in American history. These moments in American historical development formed the seedbed for Jameson's notions about a "people's" history.[33]

For young professional historians in the late 1890s, rhetoric about a history of the "masses" did not convey radical politics. But it did mean something different from the expansive invocation of the "people" that nineteenth-century patrician historians such as Bancroft employed to describe how the hand of God worked to shape the course of history. In speaking of the "less articulate classes," many turn-of-the-century historians made reference to mass industrial society. In so doing, they were attending to what they clearly perceived as a much-changed historical context that posed new challenges for those who hoped to understand modern American society. This proved an important impetus to evolving notions of how the "people" might figure in accounts of American history.

The perspective of such historians also reflected a recognition of the ways in which critics of industrial capitalism were expropriating history to make a case for sweeping change in American society. This insurgency played no small part in the increasing rhetoric among some professional historians about the importance of broadening the scope of history. The ideas of the Populists, for instance, which Jameson dismissed as "crude and half understood, but enthusiastically believed in," offered specific remedies meant to redress economic and political inequalities. But they also advanced a particular understanding of American history. The language employed by the Populists often emphasized the ways in which the rise of huge corporations, the economic and political power of financiers, and the exploitation of the "plain people" had betrayed ideals that reached back to the American Revolution and that were being perverted by the recent course of American history. Antimonopolists such as Henry Demarest Lloyd frankly made use of history in their efforts to construct accounts of the ways in which capital accumulation had been built on the backs of small businessmen and ordinary Americans. Henry George's *Progress and Poverty* (1879) rooted advocacy of the single tax on land in a historical interpretation that warned of the threat posed to modern civilization by growing inequality.[34]

There was, in sum, no shortage of popular critics, radical voices, and reform advocates who employed history in their efforts to take the measure of modern American society. While many found ways of restoring, at least theoretically, the ultimate forward trajectory of history to circumstances that appeared to call such optimistic scenarios into question, they nonetheless invoked history as an instrument with which to measure and better understand the character of modern industrial society. For the most radical critics, such as the anarchists, the past often served as a political, rhetorical, and intellectual weapon. Little wonder that William Sloane warned of the dangers posed by extremists who might destroy the very meaning and enterprise of history by "leveling down" its lessons to serve the interests of the aggrieved. Taken together, professional historians' own sense of, and worries about, the current political scene, as well as their awareness of alternative historical visions, prodded at least some to reflect seriously on the need to widen the contours of modern history.

There was yet another source prodding professional historians to attend to the experience of the people at the turn of the century, one that came from quarters far removed from social critics, revolutionaries, and mass political movements. Amateur historians proved to be an important force that moved professional historians to address what William Sloane described as a "popular clamor" for historical studies that surveyed social and cultural trends while making room for individuals and groups that rarely figured in traditional political histories.

It is tempting to see the social and cultural studies pursued by such amateurs as an endeavor that rarely intersected with the American historical profession. But during the late nineteenth century, the boundary lines between amateur and professional historians proved far more porous than they would be subsequently. Innovative work by historians without formal academic training in the field regularly appeared in the pages of the *American Historical Review*, the leading professional journal. Men without doctoral degrees in history likewise rose several times to the presidency of the American Historical

Association. The work of amateur historians was thus widely known within the discipline, and it occupied a visible place among the ever growing body of literature examining the American past from fresh perspectives.

This was especially true of the work of historian John Bach McMaster, who had no advanced degree in history and who pursued an ambitious and inventive intellectual agenda. McMaster made much of his intention in the 1880s to write a sweeping history of the American people that would include "the dress, the occupations, the amusements, the literary canons of the times," among many other social and cultural areas of study. McMaster secured a position as a professor at the University of Pennsylvania only after publishing in 1883 the first volume of the multivolume *History of the People of the United States,* a popular narrative history of post-Revolutionary American society. He nonetheless brought an unusual perspective to his avid interest in American history. His experience, which included assisting in a topographical survey of Civil War battlefields, leading a scientific study of fossils in the Badlands, and obtaining a degree in civil engineering, heightened McMaster's interest in social history. He was also much influenced by his reading of the great British historian Thomas Babington Macaulay, whose *History of England from the Accession of James the Second* incorporated social history into its analysis of changing conditions in English society.[35]

As social history, McMaster's work amassed a wealth of information gleaned in no small part from newspapers, some of which he undoubtedly did not consult firsthand but had located in published compilations. Nonetheless, he provided fresh knowledge about topics ranging from slaves' diet to the impact of technology on American society. Like other national historians of his time, McMaster decried the institution of slavery and the exploitation by southern planters of bondsmen and -women. In describing the behavior of slaveholders during the late eighteenth century, McMaster noted, "Toil was the only thing from which the rich planter abstained. Horse-racing by day and deer-hunting by night, duelling and gambling, made up, with the social festivities of the class to which he belonged, his sole occupation and pleasure."[36]

But McMaster's work was largely a celebration of American society and its triumph over the evils of the past, including slavery. Certainly it greeted cheerfully the impact of industrialism on American society.

There *was* a political agenda in McMaster's efforts to write social history, one that affirmed the essential integrity of American democracy. He hoped his rendition of American history would counter vocal critics whose voices and actions threatened the tranquility of American society in the late nineteenth century. Indeed, McMaster's *History of the People* hewed very closely to fixed notions of American national development that emphasized democracy and progress as unshakable forces propelling American society.[37]

At the same time, McMaster offered little analytical or interpretive form to the facts he amassed, other than the general motifs of progress and moral judgment that underpinned his history. As one historian later noted, "McMaster skillfully regiments his facts upon parade, but they do not march." For all its claims to recount the history of the "people," the volumes offered virtually nothing about farmers, although the America studied by McMaster had never ceased being a rural agrarian society. More, McMaster gravitated back again and again to the secure moorings of traditional political history, so much so that some later historians would dismiss his work as little more than an attempt at social history.[38]

In the 1890s, the limitations of McMaster's approach were apparent even to those who sympathized with his objectives. Jameson believed the "general purpose" of McMaster's multivolume *History of the People of the United States* was "most commendable." The project, "with all its faults," Jameson wrote in 1885, represented a sign that history was moving away from its narrow focus on political history and toward a more deeply engaged initiative to record the history of "the people." But an 1895 review of the fourth volume in the *American Historical Review* poked fun at McMaster's "portly volume"—a not unfair characterization of the latest installment in a series that by 1895 had amounted to four volumes, covering a mere thirty-eight years (1783 to 1821) in 2,400 pages. And yet, for all its weaknesses, McMaster's efforts commanded the attention of professional historians. Whether they applauded or dismissed McMaster's endeavors, the historian's goal of preparing a "people's history" clearly existed within the spectrum of ideas about the proper mandate of modern history.[39]

Another amateur historian whose work explored aspects of everyday experience also received notice from professional historians in the 1890s, even though she belonged to a group much on the margins of academic and scientific history: American women. Alice Morse Earle's innovative and prolific studies of American colonial society were especially intriguing for the emphasis they placed on private life and women's history. Earle, who attended high school and later a boarding school in Boston, had no formal training as a historian. But she grew up in a house of collectors and shared with other members of her family an abiding interest in early American history, material culture, and antiquarianism. *Colonial Dames and Good Wives,* published in 1895, reflected some of the romanticized themes common to nineteenth-century accounts of early American history. Ancestor worship and sentimentality informed Earle's narrative. Earle's work continued a long tradition of historical writing by women that reached back to the early republic.[40]

At the same time, *Colonial Dames and Good Wives* was notable as a work of social history. Alice Earle was exploring issues in 1895 that later twentieth-century social historians would find of great import. The status of widows, the social meanings embedded in charges of "scurrilous talk" against vexatious women, the ways in which contentious behavior invited accusations of witchcraft were all treated by Earle, as were details concerning material culture, private life, and household production among colonial settlers. The book offered little, however, in the way of explicit interpretation. And Earle provided no theoretical rationale for her focus on social history in *Colonial Dames.*

But her 1899 history of colonial childhood, *Child Life in Colonial Days,* began a bit more reflectively. It was, she noted, "indeed curious how little is told of child life in history" given the current interest in "child study." Children rarely figured in historical narratives of any era. That fact made it difficult to "make comparisons or note progress." The latter theme figured centrally in Earle's account of colonial childhood. For Earle emphasized that early American history was replete with examples of "tenderness and affection in the family"; young people fared much better in the colonies, she asserted, than in seventeenth-century England. Earle explored their lives in chapters on children's toys, books, and prevailing notions of manners, among other topics. Yet somewhat whimsically, Earle tied her intellectual efforts to the close of the nineteenth century. She spoke of the history of childhood in colonial years as a balm for "our tired century."[41]

Although Earle's reception by the public was most enthusiastic, reaction was more measured among the historical profession. Nonetheless her books were regularly reviewed in the *American Historical Review,* as were the works of other popular historians. In 1895, William Sloane announced in the very first issue of the *American Historical Review* the journal's book review policy: "the amount of notice should as far as possible be indicative of the relative values of the volumes named." Virtually all studies in American history written by women were relegated to the "minor notices" section of the journal in the 1890s.[42]

Earle was often an exception, in part because at least some historians saw in her work modern, not antiquarian, trends in the writing of history. In 1899, a review for the *American Historical Review* tied Earle's *Home Life in Colonial Days* to "the new method of writing history, adopted by Green, McMaster, Fiske and others." This method, the reviewer asserted, "has taken hold of the popular imagination and aroused a degree of enthusiasm for what might be called the social side of life, never exhibited before." The new demand called for "a more adequate literary interpretation of the real life of the olden time." Mrs. Earle, the reviewer reported, "has happily caught this spirit, and with excellent judgment has taken the tide at the flood, and availed herself both of the newly-gathered materials and of the quickened public taste, and with rare industry has associated her name permanently with this engaging field in American history." In 1900 patrician historian William Weeden offered more sparing praise; he characterized *Child Life in Colonial Days* as a "a necessary adjunct of history."[43]

Adjunct or not, the advance of social history by some amateur historians continued apace in the late nineteenth century. But it turned an important corner with the work of Edward Eggleston in the 1890s. Like McMaster and Earle, Eggleston was an amateur historian who believed that progress ordered the evolution of American history. But he also resembled the new professional historians in his emphasis on the importance of science to the methodology of history. Most of all, Eggleston pressed beyond amateur and many scientific historians in analyzing the impact of shifting social, economic, and political forces on the shaping of American society. Eggleston's success in doing so, his dynamic sense of history, and his outspoken assertions about its imperatives led to enormous recognition among professional and amateur historians alike. His election to the vice-presidency of the American Historical Association in 1898 and his subsequent elevation to the presidency of the association in 1900 attested to the regard in which he was held. Indeed, though Edward Eggleston has been largely neglected in American historiography, he was one of the most important figures in the effort to advance a more variegated, less celebratory, and more expansive American history. This was so in part because his scholarship provided a model of what might be included within the province of history. But it was also because he derived from his experience as a historian a theoretical principle he offered to his colleagues as the objective of modern history. In 1900, he would call it "the new history."[44]

Like McMaster, Eggleston brought an unusual set of life experiences to his study of the past that no doubt contributed to his interest in social history. Raised in a small town in Indiana, he became an avid abolitionist (so he later claimed) after observing slavery firsthand at an uncle's Virginia plantation. Before the age of twenty, Eggleston had explored the American frontier, like McMaster partly by assisting a surveying team and also by driving oxen across the prairie. As a young man he labored on a farm, where he took part in chores critical to household maintenance, including making soap and rending lard from slaughtered animals. (Perhaps his familiarity with the hardships of farm life contributed to Eggleston's Populist sympathies in the early 1890s, short-lived though they proved to be.) After riding circuit as an itinerant preacher in the late 1850s, the future historian settled in Minnesota, where he preached, sold bibles, and embarked on unsuccessful ventures as a soap manufacturer and a real estate investor, until he finally turned his hand to writing.

He began as an author mainly of children's books and occasional pieces, though by 1870 several essays written in a realist style depicting the horrific conditions in jails and the abusive treatment of the insane had earned Eggleston a place on the editorial board of *The Independent*. For much of the 1870s, Eggleston turned out novels of the Midwest, including the wildly popular *Hoosier School-Master* (1871). With his daughter he wrote several volumes as part of a series entitled Famous American Indians, for which he consulted sources in colonial history.

The first volume, *Tecumseh and the Shawnee Prophet* (1878), mixed romanticized notions of Native Americans with prevailing ideas about the savagery of the tribes and their misplaced attempts to retain their claims to land usurped by white settlement—themes hardly unknown to the period. The Egglestons spoke in admiring terms of the Shawnee leader whom the would-be historian described as a "genius." Tecumseh, though a "savage," proved to be a "a shrewd diplomatist, a great commander, a persuasive orator, a statesman, and a man of indomitable patience, brilliant courage, and wonderful power of gaining and holding the allegiance of his followers." He was a patriot, however "mistaken" his patriotism might be. Unfortunately, however, Tecumseh put his extraordinary qualities to the losing purpose of forging a powerful Indian confederacy that was doomed to defeat. "All dreams of perpetuating savage life in opposition to civilization are futile," the Egglestons emphasized. Nor was it even "desirable that a savage race which spreads itself thinly in squalid hunting bands should possess a fertile country capable of supporting a hundred times as many people in the comfort and enlightenment of civilization." Such ideas reflected widespread assumptions among white Americans in the late nineteenth century. But while the Egglestons attributed to "savagery" the atrocities carried out by the Shawnees, they also noted, as did some of their contemporaries, that white settlers also displayed cruelty and brutality in their conflicts with the tribes. "In too many instances," the father and daughter wrote, "the white men, in the bitter struggles of 'the dark and bloody ground' easily forgot their civilization, and fell into the cruelty, bad faith, and revengefulness of savages." In the main, however, the book enthusiastically endorsed federal policy toward Native Americans and white efforts to subdue the tribes along the shifting frontier.[45]

By 1880, Eggleston's initial forays into historical research had solidified his decision to devote the next decade of his life to writing a history of the United States. He believed it was a task for which he was especially well suited, for, he claimed, "I have known colonial life, having been among people of different manners and dialect. I can imagine in the colonies the same collision and the same contact with Indian life." European intellectual influences also shaped his ambition. Eggleston was much impressed by French historian Augustin Thierry's efforts to capture the tenor of medieval society and, in doing so, to tell "the history of the people." The third chapter of Macaulay's *History of England* dazzled Eggleston as it had McMaster. As Eggleston later wrote:

It begins with taxes and revenues; the customs and revenue lists of the princes are much elaborated and are not very interesting. But by degrees he draws near to manners, and he draws near to London. The picture of old London, turned over and over in his mind in those long walks Macaulay is said to have made through every street of the metropolis, is a wonderful piece of history. It is worth the whole history beside. And nobody ever dreamed before that such a subject was in the province of history. . . . It is so particular, so minute, so extraordinary.

The prospect of fulfilling such ambitious aims exhilarated Eggleston. To his daughter he enthused of his planned history: "I am ripe for it. Everything in my life seems to have prepared me for it."[46]

There was no greater cure for his high spirits than immersion in this daunting task. In fact, although Eggleston was only forty-three years old at the time he began his research, he was in poor health—a state that the project he undertook did little to improve. He explored records and manuscripts in historical societies, state archives, the Library of Congress, the British Museum and Public Record Office, and the Bibliothèque Nationale to construct his history of colonial society, the first of several planned studies. By 1894, he complained to his daughter of the toll his scholarly labors were exacting: "Poor history! no one man's life is long enough for it, certainly not the life of a sickish man like myself with a dozen other irons and no wealth to come and go on."[47]

Nonetheless in 1896 the first volume of Eggleston's work appeared, *The Beginners of a Nation: A History of the Source and Rise of the Earliest English Settlements in America with Special Reference to the Life and Character of the People.* The title, unwieldy though it was, expressed Eggleston's "distinctive purpose." The book offered, he explained, "the culture history of the United States in the period of English domination." His goal was to "give an insight into the life and character of the people." Such an undertaking explicitly took issue with romanticized notions of English settlement, though Eggleston hardly abandoned all such sentiments. The book traced the often-told tale of the founding of the English colonies in North America. But *The Beginners of a Nation* was quickly recognized for its unusual effort to explore this theme by attending to social history while never entirely abandoning the traditional political narrative or the familiar organization around specific colonies.[48]

Indeed, the critical perspective Eggleston brought to the verities of colonial history received much notice, and for good reason. Eggleston viewed colonization as a dynamic process, and his intent, he confided, was to offer not "the usual account of all the events attending early colonization; it is rather a history in which the succession of cause and effect is the main topic." The origins of the English settlers, the forces that shaped migration, and the society they constructed once in North America formed the decisive focus of his study. Most notably, Eggleston warned his readers that he could not treat "the founders of the little settlements . . . otherwise than unreverently." This was not simply because he found fault with English settlers and some of their leaders, though at times he most assuredly did. Rather, the kind of history he offered aimed to replace exalted Pilgrims and Puritans with real human beings, sentimental tales with an analysis based in rich primary sources. As Eggleston explained:

> Here are no forefathers or foremothers, but simply English men and women of the seventeenth century, with the faults and fanatacisms as well as the virtues of their age. I have disregarded that convention which makes it obligatory for a writer of American history to explain that intolerance in the first settlers was not just like other intolerance, and that their cruelty and injustice were justifiable under the circumstances. This walking backward to throw a mantle over the nakedness of ancestors may be admirable as an example of diluvian piety, but it is none the less reprehensible in the writing of history.[49]

Although *The Beginners of a Nation* traversed much familiar ground, the book made ample use of Eggleston's extensive research in primary source materials. More, his skeptical tone imparted to Eggleston's narrative history a fresh and inventive quality. "The history of American exploration is a story of delusion and mistake," Eggleston began as he described the preconceptions English settlers brought with them to the New World. The "enterprises" they planned in the New World were "brilliant in conception, but in the execution" of them, Eggleston concluded, "there was often a lack of foresight and practical wisdom."[50]

Indeed, it was the critical tone of the study that diverged most sharply from nineteenth-century romanticized notions of British colonization. When Eggleston took the measure of the age in which the white colonists lived, he found much that was wanting. For example, his discussion of Indian-white relationships, while recounting the brutal attacks on white settlers, also described instances where the white settlers themselves displayed great cruelty and savagery. In a footnote he offered gruesome details about the "revengeful wantonness" inflicted upon Indians at Jamestown by settlers in retaliation for an attack on the fragile colony. And in describing the aftermath of a 1622 Indian massacre of whites in Virginia, Eggleston wrote, "the settlers even emulated, if they did not surpass, the treachery of the Indians."[51]

Such judgments were intertwined with attention to the impact of society, culture, religion, and mental outlook on colonial settlement. These factors played an especially significant part in Eggleston's account of the disastrous Jamestown settlement. His devastating portrait began with a judgment of the English colonizers: "Those who shaped the destinies of the colony had left little undone that inventive stupidity could suggest to assure the failure of the enterprise." A poor appreciation of nature, evident first in locating the settlement on "a malarial peninsula," the corruption and "incompetent management in the London Company," a scarcity of tradesmen, a surfeit of lazy gentlemen, an absence of women ("a colony of bachelors can hardly found a state"), and an economic organization that at first failed to build in incentives for work were only a few of the factors that set the colony on its ill-begotten course. Though Eggleston lionized Captain John Smith, he used his primary source materials to depict not only the challenges of colonization but the foolhardiness, greed, and incompetence of the colonizers as well as the social and economic roots of their misfortunes in Virginia.[52]

Heaping such criticism on the failed Jamestown settlement was one thing; it was another to view the Puritan migration and the colonies established by New England's founders irreverently. Of Puritanism, Eggleston wrote simply: "Its government and its very religion were barbarous." The religious intolerance of the Puritans especially offended Eggleston, and he employed that theme to highlight the "centrifugal force" that held together the Massachusetts Bay Colony. "Dislike as we may the principles on which uniformity was enforced, we must admire the forehanded statesmanship of the Massachusetts leaders in strangling religious disturbances at birth, as Pharaoh's midwives did infant Hebrews." His rendition of the Antinomian controversy was notable for its sympathetic treatment of Anne Hutchinson. Hutchinson, Eggleston argued, "was a woman cursed with a natural gift for leadership in an age that had no place for such women." Indeed, he praised the female dissenter as a "brilliant" woman who "almost alone of the religionists of her time . . . translated her devotion into philanthropic exertion."[53]

The controversy Hutchinson's heretical views precipitated, and her later trial before the General Court and banishment from Massachusetts, Eggleston wrote, "lets in much light upon the character of the age and the nature of Puritanism." His conclusions were hardly flattering. The historian bitterly condemned the intolerance of the Puritan divines and questioned the very integrity and morality of the colony's elite by recounting their atrocious response to the stillbirths experienced by two dissenting women, Mary Dyer and Hutchinson. John Winthrop and John Cotton saw the hand of God in the anguish of these women and used their tragedies to warn of religious heresy. Of Hutchinson's "maternal misfortune" and its aftermath, Eggleston wrote, "the wild reports that were circulated regarding this event are not fit to be printed even in a note." The tales spread by Cotton "were worse than pathological" and revealed a kind of depravity. "We are now peering," Eggleston solemnly wrote, "into the abyss of seventeenth-century credulity." Of Winthrop and Cotton he wrote: "Here are a grave ruler and divine once eminent at the university, and now renowned in England and in America, wallowing in a squalid superstition in comparison with which the divination of a Roman haruspex is dignified." But Eggleston did not cast such behavior as entirely a matter of premodern magical thinking. Rather, he rooted his analysis in the social, political, intellectual, and institutional forces that governed early American society.[54]

Criticisms of Puritan intolerance were hardly unprecedented in nineteenth-century American intellectual life and letters, but Eggleston's fusion of social and political history, his iconoclasm, and his emphasis on the wide range of motives inspiring colonization diverged from the interests of leading American colonial historians in the 1890s. Herbert Levi Osgood, then immersed in his study of British imperial administration and constitutional development in the American colonies, acknowledged Eggleston's innovative approach. In an 1897 review of *The Beginners of a Nation* for the *American Historical Review*, Osgood dismissed much of the material Eggleston amassed as previously understood. "But the spirit in which the material of this book has been wrought out and presented," Osgood wrote, "is far superior to that usually attained. The author has put ancestor-worship, sectionalism and partisanship beneath his feet. His treatment of men and events is realistic. He has striven to know and to depict men as they were. He has not allowed later events to distort his vision of the beginning of things English on this continent. He says that he has not been able to treat the early settlers otherwise than unreverently. . . . This, of itself, is a great achievement." [55]

Acknowledging the "leveling" sentiment that Sloane and others had detected among some Americans, Osgood concluded that "we have reached a time when a broad and impartial treatment of our early history is possible, and when such treatment in many quarters is actually in demand. The success with which Mr. Eggleston has met this demand constitutes, in the opinion of the reviewer, the highest merit . . . of his work." Certainly reviewers in the popular press seized upon what they variously viewed as the merit or disgrace of Eggleston's message. Their response not only mirrored the popularity among some late-nineteenth-century Americans of criticisms of Puritanism, it reflected the ways in which others extracted political implications from the rendering of remote colonial history. A San Francisco newspaper gathered the following from Eggleston's book: "It turns out these ancestors were very common. There was hardly a streak of blue blood through them all." The *Baltimore Sun* expressed disgruntlement: "We all agree that the first settlers of Virginia were a thriftless lot, but no one has pictured them as quite as worthless as Mr. Eggleston." [56]

Eggleston himself scarcely paused amid the attention awarded *The Beginners of a Nation*. He plunged headlong into the second volume of his people's history, an extraordinary book that would be published in 1900 with the title *The Transit of Civilization: From England to America in the Seventeenth Century*. In sometimes stunning prose, remarkable for its imagination and beauty, Eggleston sought to explain "the complex states of knowing and thinking, of feeling and passion," of seeing the world as it was understood "by the man of the seventeenth century." The title of the first chapter—"The Mental Outfit of the Colonists"—captured perfectly Eggleston's belief that it was essential to enter the world of seventeenth-century colonists to grasp their experience. [57]

The results were impressive. Far more than in *The Beginners of a Nation*, Eggleston set aside the familiar political narrative of early American history to examine culture, folkways, and ideas. A chapter on medical "notions" sketched a history of medicine in the seventeenth century impressive for its detailed description of scientific theories and remedies. Efforts to adapt the English language to the settlers' extraordinary new surroundings led to a fascinating Eggleston disquisition on "Mother-English, folklore, and literature." Manners, customs, education, and land use and distribution also received attention.

The flavor of the book, though impossible to capture with a single example, can perhaps be gathered from Eggleston's explication of labor. He wrote sympathetically of the indentured servants "who had been bound for a long term before leaving England, and were treated as a recognized species of property." Many in the southern colonies were convicts and other undesirables cast out of England; their cruel treatment, as he described it, was appalling. It was, Eggleston wrote, "an age of flogging." The introduction of slavery into the colonies took place, Eggleston stressed, to satisfy the need for labor as staple crop production progressed in the southern colonies. The English saw "no repugnance . . . to the enslavement of blacks, who were not only pagans, but so different in appearance as to seem to be another species, not entitled to human consideration."[58]

Economic reliance on slaves led to innumerable rationalizations for bondage—though "for nearly sixty years after the beginning of negro slavery here, there seems to have been no scruple or question about it." By denying black bondsmen had souls, many English settlers could remain untroubled by the institution of slavery. The hypocrisy of New England settlers was again Eggleston's target. The Puritans lacked the sensibilities of those Quakers who first spoke out against slavery. "Refusing to participate with 'man-stealers,' the textual conscience of the Massachusetts forefathers did not shrink from selling Indians captured in war into chattel slavery, or from buying slaves who appeared to have come into bondage otherwise than by downright kidnapping." Indeed, by ending *The Transit of Civilization* with American slavery Eggleston upset notions that might equate history and progress. "So closed the seventeenth century," Eggleston concluded. "The progress in humanity had been very slight. The number of bond servants was constantly increasing; the black tide of African slavery was ever swelling. No voice worthy of the name was yet heard in protest."[59]

The Transit of Civilization tested the patience of some critics, who felt Eggleston had gone too far in trampling on sacred truths and veering away from the proper terrain of history. In the *American Historical Review* literary critic Barrett Wendell, a biographer of Cotton Mather, characterized the study, with its unorthodox themes and unusual data, as "confused." Further, he upbraided Eggleston for his unsympathetic portrait of the English colonists' religious worldview. "They had their errors," Wendell wrote, "but their widest error seems less than that of a modern historian who finds in the majesty of their Divinity even a tinge of mockery." For all its faults the book did, Wendell admitted, point "the way to a kind of American history which in time may flood our past with revivifying light." Colonial historian Charles Andrews was not so sure. He had little to say about the social history Eggleston had offered other than characterizing the entire effort as "a kaleidoscopic assortment of notes, lengthy, discursive and often bewildering."[60]

By the time these reviews had appeared, Eggleston was dying. He was so ill in December of 1900, shortly before *The Transit of Civilization* appeared, that he could not read his presidential address at the American Historical Association meetings. Finishing the book itself had taken heroic effort—"I can not go on writing long with sleep so broken," he told his daughter—and he knew he would not live to write another volume. But though he would contribute nothing further to its realization, Eggleston's parting message to the historical profession was that the time had come for a "new history." He exhorted his colleagues to set aside politics and explore "culture history."[61]

Eggleston voiced pointed suspicions of political history. "Never was a falser thing said," Eggleston wrote in 1899 as he prepared his address, "than that history is dead politics and politics living history. Some things are false and some things perniciously false. This is one of the latter kind." Politics was part of history, but, Eggleston warned, "it often sails under false colors, and it will deceive the historian unless he is exceedingly vigilant." To follow elections and leaders, to mix history and patriotism, was to miss the roots of change: "Look for its origins among the people," Eggleston said of the American Revolution. Nor could a focus on "military affairs" fulfill the mandate of modern history. War was "exciting" and it mattered, "but the scene has been so often repeated, the subject has become trite." Further, when historians focused on battle "we . . . cover our pages with gore."[62]

Though ill, worn out by his labors, and saddened by his declining powers, Eggleston used his presidential address to portray historical study at a crossroads and to reassure his colleagues that progress remained a powerful leitmotif even in a revivified modern history. "History," he wrote, "is the great prophylactic against pessimism." He explained, "There never was a bad, in the five progressive centuries, that was not preceded by a worse. Our working people live from hand to mouth; in the eighteenth century and in England it was from half empty hand to starving mouth. Never was the race better suited than in this nineteenth century—this twentieth century on the very verge of which we stand." In many ways such sentiments echoed nineteenth-century views that equated history with progress. But Eggleston had also done much to encourage a history that was cut free from what he viewed as the stranglehold of traditional political history.[63]

Explicit debate about the proper scope of American history, the work of amateur historians such as John Bach McMaster, Alice Morse Earle, and Edward Eggleston to name but a few, the perspective of no less a professional historian than John Franklin Jameson—all these things suggest that the notion of a history that attended to social history and the "less articulate" existed in the intellectual world of American historians in the 1890s. Equally important were the specific studies individual scholars undertook to advance that goal, without much fanfare and often with little professional recognition. No more compelling example can be offered than that of W. E. B. Du Bois, the first African American to earn a doctorate in history.

Du Bois's early life appeared removed from the worst manifestations of racial oppression in post-Reconstruction American society. In the rural white community of Great Barrington, Massachusetts, where only a small number of black families lived, Du Bois later recalled, "the color line was manifest," but it was "not absolutely drawn." As a young boy, Du Bois earned much praise for his brilliance as a student. He made the acquaintance of the local historian, who made an impression on the young scholar, as did a visit to a grandfather in New Bedford, who later left Du Bois extraordinary personal diaries that helped Du Bois better understand his family's history. During high school, Du Bois saved quarters from after-school work to purchase, one volume at a time, Macaulay's *History of England*. He also wrote short pieces for the *Springfield Union* and the *New York Globe*, the latter newspaper founded by African American writer Timothy Fortune. By the time he was fifteen, Du Bois had assumed the role of commentator on items of local interest and national significance. He so impressed his high school principal that the man urged him to go to college.[64]

Du Bois began his undergraduate studies at Fisk University in Tennessee. His exposure to the south, particularly during summer sojourns as a teacher in rural black schools, shaped Du Bois's intellectual and emotional life in ways that would soon find expression in his profound meditations on race in American society. Meantime, after graduating from Fisk in 1888, he began study at Harvard, where he took history courses from Edward Channing and Albert Bushnell Hart. But an early magnet was the philosophy department, where Du Bois studied under George Santayana, Josiah Royce, and William James. As he had throughout his young life, Du Bois earned recognition for his great intelligence; when he graduated from Harvard cum laude in 1890, he was one of just a few students selected to offer an oration at commencement.[65]

Du Bois's brief speech, "Jefferson Davis as a Representative of Civilization," interwove history and philosophy. His remarks on the Confederate president offered a sardonic commentary on the Teutonic theory of history that Albert Hart still advanced in the 1880s. Rather than tracing the roots of American institutions to England and then Germany, the graduating senior offered his own rendition of the course of history. "The Teutonic," Du Bois explained, "met civilization and crushed it. The Negro met civilization and was crushed by it." Using Davis as a Teutonic antihero, Du Bois made reference to a civilization that moved ahead by dominating others, even killing when necessary, and that depended on the submission and "ruin" of one race for the triumph of another. He urged his largely white audience to remember the "Thou"—black Americans—whose voices had been stilled and whose identities had been forgotten by the "overwhelming sense of the I." The speech achieved much favorable notice—no doubt in part because Du Bois softened his most penetrating criticisms by affirming some racial truths of the day and by stressing moderation.[66]

By the time he graduated from Harvard, Du Bois had decided he wanted to earn a Ph.D. in social science in the hope that he could use his knowledge to advance "the social and economic rise of the Negro people." He undertook further course work with historians Hart and Channing as well as with political economist Frank Taussig. Although he would reject many of the political views of his professors, he profited especially from Hart's emphasis on the importance of undertaking careful research in primary sources. And, as promised, he turned the skills he was acquiring to the history of African Americans. Du Bois's early essays pointed to the economic motives that shaped the dynamics of slavery and the vital role the slave trade had played in replenishing the system of slave labor, even after it had been outlawed.[67]

During two years abroad (1892–1894), with a fellowship supporting his study at Berlin, Du Bois gained exposure to the German historical school through his work with Gustav von Schmoller and Adolph Wagner, two bright stars in the German intellectual firmament. Du Bois's studies at Berlin not only enriched his understanding of political economy but also enlarged his perspective on American history. His German thesis examined the "large and small-scale system of agriculture" in the southern United States between 1840 and 1890. Du Bois's professors were impressed with his work, and only bureaucratic obstacles prevented the young scholar from earning a German doctorate. Du Bois returned to the United States and began teaching at Wilberforce University in Ohio. He finished his Harvard dissertation during his first year at Wilberforce, earning his doctoral degree in 1895.[68]

With Hart's support, Du Bois's dissertation was selected as the first volume in the Harvard Historical Studies series. Published in 1896, *The Suppression of the African Slave Trade to the United States, 1638–1870* amassed an extensive array of primary source material that ranged from congressional documents, census reports, and legal decisions to "personal narratives." His aim, Du Bois wrote with what was very likely false modesty, was to make "a small contribution to the scientific study of slavery and the American Negro." In fact, the book offered a wealth of detail about the slave trade.[69]

In his preface, Du Bois warned that while the legal research he offered was "nearly complete; on the other hand, facts and statistics bearing on the economic side of the study have been difficult to find, and my conclusions are consequently liable to modification from this source." That word of caution proved prophetic. Du Bois's interpretation that the North colluded with the South after the 1808 federal ban on slave importations and thereby ensured the continual growth of the American slave labor force would be disproved by historians later in the twentieth century. Nonetheless several aspects of the book anticipated future directions in slave historiography, most especially its emphasis on the economics of slavery.[70]

Du Bois bluntly described the material motives he believed underlay the colonial and revolutionary generation's treatment of slavery.

> We must face the fact that this problem arose principally from the cupidity and carelessness of our ancestors. It was the plain duty of the colonies to crush the trade and the system in its infancy: they preferred to enrich themselves on its profits . . . there never was a time in the history of America when the system had slighter economic, political, and moral justification than in 1787; and yet with this real, existent, growing evil before their eyes, a bargain largely of dollars and cents was allowed to open the highway that led straight to the Civil War.

Less interested in the dynamics of plantation slavery once established than in its colonial origins and its progression during the nineteenth century, Du Bois nonetheless devoted considerable attention to "the rise of the cotton kingdom" as a crucial factor in shaping American slavery. As he explained it, "the history of slavery and the slave-trade after 1820 must be read in the light of the industrial revolution through which the civilized world passed in the first half of the nineteenth century." For so long, Du Bois argued, Southern slavery had been understood by historians "from the ethical and social standpoint that we are apt to forget its close and indissoluble connection with the world's cotton market." Late in life, Du Bois would issue an "Apologia" for his thesis in which he criticized his failure to develop a full (and presumably Marxist) economic analysis of slavery. But in 1896, his perspective was striking.[71]

Also notable was Du Bois's assessment of the intellectual and moral implications of historical research on slavery. The institution of slavery could not be explained within a romantic and idealized theory of American history. "It is neither profitable nor in accordance with scientific truth," Du Bois sternly instructed his readers, "to consider that whatever the constitutional fathers did was right, or that slavery was a plague sent from God and fated to be eliminated in due time." Indeed, Du Bois called into question the very qualities of independence, autonomy, and determination many nineteenth-century historians viewed as the very core of American national character.[72]

Instead, the history of slavery suggested that "each generation sought to shift its load upon the next."

One cannot, to be sure, demand of whole nations exceptional moral foresight and heroism; but a certain hard common-sense in facing the complicated phenomena of political life must be expected in every progressive people. In some respect we as a nation seem to lack this; we have the somewhat inchoate idea that we are not destined to be harassed with great social questions, and that even if we are, and fail to answer them, the fault is with the question and not with us.

Du Bois shared with some nationalist historians the moral didacticism common to the age. In addition, his idealism, though trammeled, was nonetheless apparent in the 1890s as he spoke of Americans as a "progressive people." Nonetheless, for Du Bois the past seemed very much alive in turn-of-the-century America. The greatest lesson of the story he had told, he concluded, was "that it behooves nations as well as men to do things at the very moment when they ought to be done."[73]

Although this latter message was waved aside, an otherwise long and respectful review of Du Bois's book appeared in the *American Historical Review* in 1897. The anonymous critic especially seized upon Du Bois's discussion of the "cotton kingdom" as among the "most interesting chapters in the book." Du Bois had, the reviewer noted, undertaken "an immense amount of faithful and diligent work in gathering the sources from many directions." In the end, *The Suppression of the African Slave-Trade* was judged "a valuable review of an important subject."[74]

Du Bois's work in African American history stood out in the context of American historical writing in the 1890s for its harsh critique of slavery, its emphasis on economics, its enormous store of information, and its challenge to romantic narratives of American history. The study was hardly unknown nor its significance unrecognized among professional historians at the turn of the twentieth century. Thus, amid the many who sifted through the ruins of the Civil War and the bitter legacy it left to American society was an African American historian, highly trained, honored with fellowships, a participant in professional meetings, recognized in leading journals for his originality—however little he would later be remembered in the sweeping studies of American historiography.

The same fate certainly did not befall Frederick Jackson Turner, who within a few years of delivering his address "The Significance of the

Frontier in American History" at the 1893 Chicago World's Fair would become one of the most famous historians in American history. Turner's focus on the West, his theory about the evolution of American democracy, and the imposing agenda he sketched out for future generations not only offered exciting and innovative ways of looking at the American past; they also spoke to critical realities in the America of the 1890s. The disappearance of the frontier captured the imagination of many Americans because it so well described the very visible changes they observed taking place with the advance of modern society. The convergence of an inspired idea and a remarkable historical moment made Turner and his thesis perhaps the most discussed subjects in a century of American historiography.[75]

Yet another Turner essay, published in 1891 in a local Wisconsin journal and far less commented on than his subsequent paper, demonstrates well the ways in which Turner shared a sense with other young historians of his time that the turn of the twentieth century constituted a pivotal moment for those who would write the history of American society. Like virtually every generation that followed, he contrasted his agenda with that of his intellectual forebears. "To a whole school of writers, among whom we find some of the great historians of our time," Turner observed in "The Significance of History" in 1891, "history is the study of politics." Noting the enormous attention lavished on "the evolution of political institutions," Turner likened such historians to biologists who studied "seed, bud, blossom, and fruit."[76]

A new trend was unfolding, Turner reported, in the writing of history. For an "increasing class of historians . . . history is the study of the economic growth of the people." Invoking European intellectuals, Turner reported that such innovative thinkers believed that "property, the distribution of wealth, the social conditions of the people, are the underlying and determining factors to be studied." Their perspective offered an entirely new vantage point for historians. "Viewed from this position, the past is filled with new meaning. The focal point of modern interest is the fourth estate, the great mass of the people." To examine the history of the people was to attend to the "tragedy" as well as the triumphal moments in the history of a society; for such accounts would have to tell "of the degraded tillers of the soil, toiling that others might dream, the slavery that rendered possible the 'glory that was Greece,' the serfdom into which decayed the 'grandeur that was Rome'—these as well demand their annals. Far oftener than has yet been shown have these underlying economic facts affecting the breadwinners of the nation been the secret of the nation's rise or fall, by the side of which much that has passed as history is the merest frippery."[77]

Indeed, Turner explicitly connected what he believed was a new imperative in historical writing to the prevailing conditions of contemporary society. Economic questions mattered most in the study of history, he argued, because modern society was the "age of machinery, of the factory system . . . of socialistic inquiry." Since the present had evolved from the past, both past and present must always stay within the vantage point of scholars and students of history. Turner explained the relationship this way: "The antiquarian strives to bring back the past for the sake of the past; the historian strives to show the present to itself by revealing its origin from the past. The goal of the antiquarian is the dead past; the goal of the historian is the living present." No aspect of modern society could be understood apart from another, given the complexity and interconnectedness of modern society. In endorsing such a view, Turner insisted that diverging elements of American society, including religion, politics, art, and economics, belonged within the purview of historical studies.[78]

Given such a wide expanse, students of history needed to recognize the impossibility of finding the realities of the past in "standard ultimate histories. In the nature of the case this is impossible." Indeed, given the inclusiveness of history, those who would study the past needed to develop entirely new ways of exploring and writing history. History was "not shut up in a book." It was to be found in everything from "mounds," "customs," and languages, to a "chipped flint, a spearhead, a piece of pottery, a pyramid, a picture, a poem, a coliseum, or a coin." Several decades later, in 1923, Turner would observe that "this tendency" to study history "from the bottom up" was "marked in men of Western origins whether they are now in Western or Eastern institutions." His comment accurately reflected the sensibility, if not necessarily in each case the origins, of historians such as McMaster and Eggleston, who brought to the study of history a broad consciousness of the American interior—its prairie, plains, and heartland.[79]

Yet mixed into Turner's ideas about a new scope and mandate for history were familiar nineteenth-century themes that stressed the continuity and unity of history. In this, Turner perfectly captured the paradoxical quality of much turn-of-the-century historical writing. Though many historians believed modern history needed to better reflect the character of modern industrial society, few wanted to abandon entirely the sense of cohesion, progress, and idealism that had informed so many previous accounts of the evolution of American society. It was not at all clear how studies of economy, race, private life, oppression, and inequality could be integrated into a narrative of American history. The questions would persist as the nation entered the twentieth century.

CHAPTER TWO

Advancing a Progressive New History

> The present has hitherto been the willing victim of the past; the time has now come when it should turn on the past and exploit it in the interests of advance. The "New History" is escaping from the limitations formerly imposed upon the study of the past. It will come in time consciously to meet our daily needs; it will avail itself of all those discoveries that are being made about mankind by anthropologists, economists, psychologists, and sociologists. . . . It is inevitable that history should be involved in this revolutionary process.
>
> —JAMES HARVEY ROBINSON, *THE NEW HISTORY* (1912)

During the first two decades of the twentieth century, American historical writing developed in ways that reflected scholars' determined effort to enlarge the scope of the past and to cast light on the state of modern American society. Some influential historians, such as Charles Beard, constructed sweeping interpretations of American history that found in the past the roots of conflicts liberal Progressive reformers had located in modern industrial society. Others, such as Frederick Jackson Turner, mounted ever more frank arguments for the necessity of a deeply research-based social history. Even those who disagreed seemed alarmed at the advance being made by social and economic history and by new interpretations that challenged revered notions of American national history.[1]

Perhaps more notable were the painstaking, detailed studies undertaken by historians who eschewed the broader debate and set to work carrying out the mandate for a history that emphasized social and economic facets of American society, often in an effort to illuminate the contemporary scene. Research that attended to the powerful impact of economic forces in shaping historical change, that explored the influence of the physical environment on social and economic development, that shifted the locus of attention from the East to the

American West and Southwest, and that examined the fate of African Americans surfaced in books and articles during the early twentieth century. Indeed, under the determined leadership of Carter Woodson, a journal devoted to African American history, *The Journal of Negro History,* appeared in 1916.

By modern professional standards, the volume of such work may seem meager, its tone tentative and ill formed, its generalities hopelessly outmoded, its practitioners often lacking a sense of collective identity. But an emphasis on disconnectedness would be misleading. The intellectual concerns of scholars in the early twentieth century were not so distant from their successors later in the century. If the political views of historians working in the Progressive era often diverged dramatically from those who would follow, contemporary politics deeply informed the questions they asked about American history. If the Progressive era's sense of the past reflected a social and historical context far removed from that of the later twentieth century, that context played no less a role in inspiring American historians to redefine the field of history. In the early twentieth century, some American historians rebelled against the perceived constraints of political history. They set off to explore what they considered to be entirely new lines of inquiry into the history of American society. In so doing, they helped set an agenda for American historical writing in the twentieth century. Indeed, when weighed against a historiographical tradition that has increasingly tended to narrow the scope of "Progressive history," the varieties and complexities of early-twentieth-century historical writing are striking.[2]

The Progressive era also gave rise to an explicit "new history" paradigm—a development that crystallized many of the paradoxes that would be inherent to the redefining of historical study throughout the twentieth century. The new history paradigm was most widely disseminated in Columbia University professor James Harvey Robinson's 1912 collection of essays, *The New History.* But as Robinson himself made clear, the volume simply served to summarize trends and weigh in on one side of a debate that had already preoccupied the discipline of history. Nonetheless the formal unveiling of the new history paradigm constituted an important milestone in early-twentieth-century historiography. It not only shaped prevailing notions of where historians had been and where they should be going; it also reflected the ways in which contemporary politics and society were helping to set an agenda for American history.

The new history paradigm of the Progressive years resembled in significant ways subsequent calls for a new history. First, as later such paradigms would do, it offered a critique of traditional historical study, rooting the imperatives of contemporary history in the state of modern society. It boldly made the case for what it claimed were unprecedented departures in historical inquiry, emphasizing especially the importance of widening the scope of historical study to account for the determinative effects of economy and society. It made much of the importance of writing the history of "common" men and women, as opposed to brilliant statesmen, skillful politicians, and valiant warriors. Perhaps most notably, it offered a brief for the use of the social science disciplines as essential tools in the historian's quest to better understand the past. In all these ways, and many more, the new paradigm derived much of its impetus from the vibrant social, political, and intellectual context of the Progressive years.[3]

But in its very efforts to reconfigure historical study to meet what it saw as the unprecedented demands of the historical moment, the early-twentieth-century new history paradigm reflected a subtle but no less apparent ahistoricity. Much could be said, of course, for the argument that modern industrialism had created conditions and posed problems previously unseen in American history. Historians who were sensitive to these changes made a good case that the dynamics of modern society required historians to think in new ways about the forces that had shaped the American past. At the same time, the stress the new history paradigm placed on the uniqueness of modern history tended to work against a fully historicized vision of the American past. Certainly it emphasized the ways in which contemporary historical scholarship had no real precedents. Indeed, as imaginative historians worked indefatigably to uncover the roots of contemporary society, they often couched their endeavor in terms that emphasized its discontinuity with the past. In this respect, too, the Progressive years would foreshadow the trends of the later twentieth century.

Among the most important themes around which Progressive era history would coalesce were the ways in which economy determined the evolution of American society. Few aspects of Progressive historiography have received more attention than the sweeping and often deterministic economic interpretations advanced during the early twentieth century. It is little wonder that historians of the Progressive generation would gravitate toward economic explanations of American history. In their own lifetimes, they had witnessed the nation's transformation from a rural agrarian to a modern industrial society. Many scholars raised in quiet farming communities experienced these changes firsthand. Moreover, the persistent social, economic, and political problems of modern American industrial society had given rise by the late nineteenth century to persistent criticisms of existing institutions; many of the harshest complaints focused on the consequences of an unfettered laissez-faire economy to industrial workers, the urban poor, immigrants, and even Americans of modest means.

These realities infused historical writing of the early twentieth century, giving rise first to stark economic interpretations of American history. No historian became more famous during (or after) the Progressive era for tracing the dominance of economic forces in America's present to its distant past than Charles Beard. Beard's name became virtually synonymous with the economic interpretation of American history. His *Economic Interpretation of the Constitution of the United States* (1913) long stood as one of the most controversial and well-known monographs in American history. Beard took his inspiration from the reform climate of the Progressive years, with its antimonopoly critique, its open suspicion of centralized power, and its fears that the unchecked power of industrial capitalism might ruin the essence of American democracy. At the same time his work captured much of the idealism and faith in progress that would sustain liberal visions of history and democracy in the twentieth century.[4]

Well before Beard's 1913 book, however, economic interpretations of American national development had become an increasingly important theme in American historiography. The historical perspective that informed *An Economic Interpretation of the Constitution* was very much part of a zeitgeist that was energizing historical research. By the early twentieth century, work of distinction was being produced by scholars who strongly subscribed to the notion that economic forces shaped in fundamental ways the evolution of American society. Indeed, crucial to shaping Beard's own interpretation was the work of one of his professors at Columbia University, political economist E. R. A. (Edwin Robert Anderson) Seligman.[5]

Seligman was most influential in providing a theoretical blueprint for historians in 1902 that Beard, among others, would follow. An influential and well respected member of the Gilded Age generation of political economists, Seligman rebelled against the political conservatism of classical political economy in favor of a historicized economics. He hoped to set in context the dynamics of modern industrial American capitalism in order to find solutions to the pressing problems of the modern industrial age. Seligman's stress on the ethical dimensions of reform and his vision of enlightened social and economic change vexed some conservative historians. Nonetheless, his early work on the history of taxation earned praise from even his critics for its theoretical and historical soundness. As one skeptic noted in an 1896 issue of the *American Historical Review,* "American representatives of that 'historical school of economics' much discussed in this country some ten years ago have made, as a rule, but slight use of history in their published works. To this rule Mr. Seligman is an exception."[6]

Seligman's 1902 book *The Economic Interpretation of History* (a compendium of essays previously published in 1901 in the *Political Science Quarterly*) proved enormously influential in providing a way of framing economic interpretations of the American past. He offered a theory of historical development that borrowed central intellectual constructs from Marxism without endorsing socialism. Seligman pointed out that Marx's theory of history had not been fully studied in America despite the fact "there has been no more original, no more powerful, and no more acute intellect in the entire history of economic science." As he sought to introduce Americans to European Marxian ideas, the political economist paid special attention to Marx's philosophy. In the end, Seligman offered historians a way of squaring economic interpretations of social development with a liberal vision that emphasized progress, the importance of collective action, the goal of economic equality, and the persistence of individualism.[7]

Perhaps most revealing, Seligman set his efforts to develop an economic theory of historical development in the context of contemporary efforts to redefine the study of history itself. In recent years, he explained to his readers in 1902, "the conception of history has been broadened until it is now well recognized that political history is only one phase of that wider activity which includes all the phenomena of social life. If the term 'politics' is used in the common but narrow sense of constitutional and diplomatic relations, then to repeat the familiar dictum, 'History is past politics,' is to utter a half-truth, in lamentable disregard of these newer ideas." The rejection of politics as the engine of historical change posed, Seligman argued, a "profound and far reaching question." If "the history of mankind is the history of man in society, and therefore social history in the broadest sense" what were "the fundamental causes of this social development?"[8]

The answer for Seligman was that economic forces drove historical change. It was Marx's great insight, Seligman argued, that social relations were derived from economic conditions and realities. To understand historical "transformations in the structure of society" one needed to look at changes in the means of production and the shifting relationship of various classes to the prevailing economic order. The economic interpretation of history did not focus on material forces to the exclusion of all others, Seligman stressed. Rather, it held only that economic relations exerted "a preponderant influence in shaping the progress of society." This had been true throughout human history, Seligman maintained, though he expressed his hope that it would "tend to become less and less true of the future"—presumably because industrial capitalism would create material prosperity and abundance on a heretofore unseen scale. Only when "the mass of the people shall live as do to-day its noblest members," Seligman explained, would economic factors lose their crucial explanatory power in history.[9]

Seligman exhorted historians to "search below the surface" and take up the "fascinating and immeasurably more complicated" task of exploring the economic forces that underlay historical change. "Wherever we turn in the maze of recent historical investigation," he marveled, "we are confronted by the overwhelming importance attached by the younger and abler scholars to the economic factor in political and social progress." The "great-man theory of history" was giving way in the face of a new understanding of economy and society, one that "Marx and his followers first emphasized in a brilliant and striking way." Indeed, Seligman argued that the economic interpretation of history was itself responsible "for turning men's minds to the consideration of the social factor in history." The more historians attended to economy, the more they would inevitably find themselves writing the social history that flowed from the economic relations of the past.[10]

The immediate political context clearly and indeed explicitly informed Seligman's exhortation that historical research needed to attend to social and economic history. In an address before the American Historical Association in the winter of 1902, for example, Seligman noted that in contemporary American society "economic impulses are everywhere discernible. By fully recognizing the influence of economic striving and conditions in the past one is better enabled to appreciate the meaning of the present and to look forward hopefully to the future." A year later, in another speech before the AHA, Seligman stressed the importance of applying "sound social principle to the solution of the pressing problems of the day."[11]

At the same time, Seligman's fusion of an economic analysis of the American past with an idealized vision of its future did much to take the sting out of his brief to historians. The nation's "present prosperity," he reassured his audience in 1902, would be unlikely to crumble into "decadence" in large part because economic conditions would not permit the rebirth of slavery, industrial capitalism would increase abundance, and enlightened public opinion would safeguard democracy. Even so, not all historians were reassured. A 1903 review of *The Economic Interpretation of History* published in the *American Historical Review* warned historians to be skeptical "about the value of any attempt, such as this of Marx and his school, to find the causes of historical change in any particular succession of phenomena, to say nothing of its feasibility." The reviewer nonetheless found reason to praise Seligman's "complete and able exposition of the most instructive and interesting theory of social dynamics . . . the book must be regarded as a distinct contribution to the philosophical side of historical literature."[12]

Yet economic interpretations of American history were not so easily relegated to the realm of historical philosophy in the early twentieth century. On the contrary, joint sessions held between the American Economic Association and the American Historical Association in the first few years of the twentieth century insured continued intellectual interchange between economists and historians, however much they might disagree. As would be true throughout the early twentieth century, some economists pressed the case for social and labor history and in so doing prodded historians to think more expansively. At a 1903 session of the American Historical Association on "industrial history" Carroll D. Wright, chief of the Carnegie Institution's economics division, described the outlines of a sweeping project that aimed to draft an economic history of the United States. The study would focus on eleven lines of inquiry, ranging from agriculture, population and immigration, manufacturing, and finance to "the labor movement," "industrial organization," and "social legislation, including provident institutions, insurance, and poor laws." In addition, the enterprise would tap the talents of some seventy-five specialists, most of whom were economists because, as one noted pointedly, "the historians have as yet taken so little interest in the writing of economic history." In smaller regional associations, other scholars reported on research detailing the impact of economy on various topics in American history. Also in 1903, a gathering of historians in Champaign, Illinois, heard University of Chicago professor and Harvard Ph.D. Joseph Warren expound on the origins of Shays' Rebellion. The professor's talk "dealt chiefly with the causes of the insurrection," which, Warren revealed, "were economic rather than political."[13]

In truth, early-twentieth-century research in economic history outside the discipline of history generated valuable studies of the history of American industrial society, including some of the first academic work in American labor history. A good deal of this research was inspired by contemporary concerns about persistent conflict between labor and capital as well as by the horrific conditions endured by many industrial workers in the United States. Certainly these themes figured prominently in the scholarship of University of Chicago political economist Edith Abbott, who in 1906 began publishing the results of her research on the history of women industrial workers. Her 1908 book *Women in Industry* traced the long history of women's work for wages from the colonial period to the modern age. It soon became recognized as the most important study in women's economic history ever published in the United States.[14]

American labor history earned its greatest legitimacy as a field of intellectual inquiry through the efforts of economist John R. Commons. In 1909 Commons published *American Shoemakers, 1648–1895,* in which he linked changes in the concerns, work patterns, and labor consciousness of shoeworkers to the historical evolution of American economy. Another Commons work published that year, *Horace Greeley and the Working Class Origins of the Republican Party,* explored the impact of social forces and economic conditions on nineteenth-century political history. Indeed, Commons credited workers with having a powerful impact on the development of the

Republican Party. From this early work, Commons went on to compile an expansive account of American labor history. Between 1900 and 1911, he oversaw the compilation of a voluminous documentary history of American labor in the Progressive era, which included contributions from Southern historian Ulrich B. Phillips as well as several economic historians. Commons also devoted his energies to constructing a multivolume history of American labor underwritten by the Carnegie Institution in the early twentieth century.[15]

Not all labor history sprang from liberal sympathies with workingmen. In fact, one of the first articles on American labor history published in the *American Historical Review* told a bloody tale that emphasized the viciousness of an effort at labor organizing. Amateur historian James Ford Rhodes in 1910 depicted the story of the Molly Maguires as one that reflected not only completely unjustifiable violence but also the deficiencies of the Irish as an ethnic group. These miners of Irish origins, who used force and intimidation to advance the cause of labor in the Anthracite coal regions, displayed, according to Rhodes, the intrinsic Irish hostility to government and their unique capacity for drunkenness and violence. English, Scotch, and Welsh immigrants, Rhodes maintained, "shrank from such a society with horror"; but the Mollies flourished among the Irish until the rule of law ultimately vanquished their threats and wrongdoing.[16]

Still, early-twentieth-century interest in labor history commonly sprang from more liberal political allegiances. Reformers outside the academy, for instance, disseminated historical research as a means of shaping public opinion and mobilizing public support for an array of policy changes. The Pittsburgh Survey, the work of the United States Industrial Commission, and the various studies undertaken by social settlements such as Hull House frequently employed a historical perspective on the problems they detailed. In so doing, they generated much valuable data in American social and economic history.[17]

The work of Commons and that of his contemporaries inside and outside the academy cannot be mistaken for the "new labor history" of our own time. As his critics have shown, much of Commons's work bolstered sweeping theories of American exceptionalism, stressing the ways in which the actions and organization of American workers were driven not by class consciousness but by market forces particular to the United States. Over time, Commons fixed his attention on and increasingly directed many of his hopes toward trade unionism.

Edith Abbott proved remarkable for her attention to unskilled workers and to the role of gender in labor history. But more often, liberal
academic intellectuals and reformers sought to minimize the structural forces impeding American workers within the modern capitalist
economy. For many, socialism lurked as a threat in the background—
ill suited to American conditions, bizarrely out of place in American
society.

At the same time, early-twentieth-century historical research on
industrial society foreshadowed in some ways concerns that would
animate historians later in the century. Although the political wellspring of early- and late-twentieth-century history came from different sources, there was no mistaking the passions that inspired the
work of Progressive era historians who attended to work and economy. The political preoccupations of the Progressive era everywhere
informed early-twentieth-century efforts to explore the history of
American labor. Convinced that inequality, class conflict, and the degradation of labor threatened American democracy, some scholars
worked vigorously to mine new source materials and to ask new questions about the American past. For Commons and other scholars of
his day, labor and economy were as central to the study of American
history as political institutions had been to historians of an earlier
day.[18]

While their work may at times seem arid and crude by today's standards, the political convictions and research of some of these early-
twentieth-century scholars convey a sense that they were breaking
through the crust of an outmoded, sterile, and even reactionary history. For these writers made a place in American history for the men
and women who carried the burden of America's advancing industrial economy. This was an intellectual development of no small significance given the hostility to labor apparent among many elites in
the early twentieth century and given the thrust of much nineteenth-
century historiography.

The effort to uncover the economic roots of American history received an enormous boost from Frederick Jackson Turner, who continued in the early years of the twentieth century to offer both rhetorical and practical support for innovative work in social and economic
history. Moving away from the broad synthetic essays that had earned
him acclaim, Turner set to work demonstrating how economic and
social forces had shaped American institutions and had given rise to

sectional differences that would have profound effects on the nation's political history. These themes figured centrally in Turner's contribution to the American Nation series, *The Rise of the New West, 1819–1829* (1906).[19]

The series stemmed from an 1899 decision by the American Historical Association to sponsor a multivolume history of the United States that would incorporate recent work in the field. "Personal, social and economic factors are to enter in," the Association announced, "as well as political." Due in no small part to the indefatigable efforts of the series editor, Albert Bushnell Hart, all planned twenty-six volumes of the American Nation series appeared between 1904 and 1908. Hart's introduction to the series revealed some of the discomfort the Harvard professor felt with the various subcurrents in modern historical writing. On the one hand, Hart stressed, the series would be "a consecutive history" organized chronologically, rooted in fact, crafted with attention to national themes, attentive to "the personalities who have stood forth as leaders and as seers," and mindful of the progress that guided American national development over the centuries. At the same time, "This is not intended to be simply a political or constitutional history: it must include the social life of the people, their religion, their literature, and their schools. It must include their economic life, occupations, labor systems, and organizations of capital." In the end, despite Hart's stated intentions, much of the series focused on political history. National development served as its central intellectual construct.[20]

Given these preoccupations, Turner's *Rise of the New West* seemed the most fresh and innovative volume in the series. Turner made good on the promise to explore the social, political, and economic forces that shaped American society by tracing the development of the western regions of the country. The project soon assumed nightmarish proportions for Turner, who found writing difficult. He amassed enormous piles of data and was flooded with detail on such things as tariff and land policy, manufacturing, internal improvements, roll call votes, newspaper editorials, as well as numerous other source materials documenting the history of the states in the region.

Amid all this came constant prods from Hart to keep on schedule and deliver a manuscript on deadline, something that Turner could scarcely contemplate doing. After granting a two-month reprieve in the summer of 1905, Hart warned Turner he would have to work nonstop—"but I do not see why young fellows like you need vacations," he grumbled. "I am 'pegging away' at my volume for the Hart series," Turner miserably reported to a friend, "and have a profound respect for a man who has a volume behind him." In the end, Turner was grateful that Hart managed to extract the volume from him. In a letter to Max Farrand written after *The Rise of the New West* had been submitted, the Wisconsin professor and fishing enthusiast praised his editor. "One thing I do owe to Hart, and that is the steadfast way in which he has worked the reel and finally landed the MS. It's a poor sucker instead of a trout, but it fought like the devil against coming to the landing net—it looked so much more like a trout in the water that it was really a pity to bring it to the surface—but he did it nobly." The enormous praise and recognition afforded the book soon affirmed Turner's sense of accomplishment.[21]

Early in 1906, Turner published two articles in the *American Historical Review* from his forthcoming book *The Rise of the New West* that gave readers a good sense of the thrust of the larger work. The first article, "The Colonization of the West, 1820–1830," repeated many of the themes laid out in his famous essay on the frontier. In creating typologies to describe the pioneers who had migrated west, Turner repeated some of his now-familiar mythic notions of the American frontiersman. But in detailing the dynamics of frontier settlement, he did not treat the settlers as an undifferentiated mass. Rather, he noted their divergent opportunities for land acquisition and economic advancement, differences he found to be rooted in class. Turner similarly offered a penetrating economic assessment of sectional differences in the United States. His essay concluded with the statement "These are the economic conditions that assist in understanding the political attitude of Western leaders in our period." A subsequent article, "The South, 1820–1830," placed the cotton trade at the center of Turner's interpretation of Southern society. "Never in history, perhaps," he claimed, "was an economic force more influential upon the life of a people." Indeed, in his 1906 article Turner claimed, "No better illustration of the influence of economic interests upon political ideas can be found than in the history of cotton culture and slavery in these important years. . . . Sectional economic interests had dominated the political philosophy of the greatest Southern statesman since Jefferson, and the South had entered on the long struggle that culminated in the Civil War."[22]

Half a century later, critics would take on the sizable task of dismantling Turner's romanticized portrait of the West. Turner's blindness to the brutality of the Indian removal, his apparent insensitivity to the violence that underlay the conquest of what he blithely characterized as "free land," and his naïve assumptions that westward settlement embodied American virtue and formed a crucible for democracy led to a general repudiation of Turner's ideas. Unfortunately, the sweeping generalizations that made Turner's work so accessible and memorable made it easy for his critics to overlook the many complexities in his scholarship. Turner's effort to unravel the social and economic forces that shaped the evolution of American society constituted, in its own time, a bold repudiation of the dominance of political history.[23]

The effort to accent economic forces in American history received another boost in 1906, when Ulrich B. Phillips published a major essay in the *American Historical Review* on slavery. Phillips shared with other young historians the belief that political history could not begin to grasp the complicated dimensions of nineteenth-century history. But he would also demonstrate the conservative political ends to which economic interpretations of history could be used. Although a graduate student at Columbia of William Dunning, the leading expert on Reconstruction politics, Phillips turned early to the study of economic and social facets of Southern history. He took courses with E. R. A. Seligman and was much inspired by Turner, with whom he had studied briefly in 1898. After writing a dissertation on antebellum politics entitled *Georgia and State Rights,* Phillips turned his attention to plantation slavery. Before long, he had become the major figure in American slave historiography.[24]

Phillips's early essays on the economics of slavery demonstrated the skills that catapulted him to such fame. His 1906 essay "The Origin and Growth of the Southern Black Belts" was an extraordinary piece of work by several measures. Although many American historians had turned their attention to slavery, no one had as yet immersed himself in archival materials and manuscripts in the same way as had Phillips. He drew on plantation records, census data, letters, travelers' accounts, tax records, and other sources to construct his analysis of slavery. In fact, Phillips's essay on the Southern black belt was the first article in American history published by the *American Historical Review* to offer graphs along with its narrative.[25]

Phillips's work was also notable for its rigorous, if flawed, efforts to analyze the economic and social dynamics, rather than the moral implications and political consequences, of American slavery. "The present study," Phillips explained, "is concerned with the tendency of slavery as a system of essentially capitalistic industry to concentrate wealth, such as there was, within the hands of a single economic class and within certain distinctive geographical areas." Phillips traced the spread of plantation slavery within the South, its routinization, division of labor, and maintenance through patterns of landholding and class formation among the planters.[26]

For Phillips, slavery was an "economic burden" that retarded industrialization, discouraged agricultural diversity, and sapped the South of too much capital. But it was far more than a labor system. According to Phillips, a culture of slavery held masters and slaves in a mutual relationship that defied rational economic forces. Over time, profitability became less important than the maintenance of a social and economic institution that had become a way of life for the planter class. With the publication of his book *American Negro Slavery* in 1918, Phillips would offer a richly detailed account of plantation slavery that argued "it was less a business than a life." These ideas ironically would long continue to inform much important work on slavery despite the fact that by the 1960s Phillips had become for many the very archetype of the racist white historian whose work constituted an apology for slaveholding. Eugene Genovese was unusually forthright in describing the importance of Phillips's work to the field of slave historiography.[27]

Throughout his work, Phillips's insulting and demeaning characterizations of African Americans fairly dripped with contempt for what he clearly believed was an inferior, "stupid," and dull race. Such racist commentary, and Phillips's evident sympathy for the ruling planter class, demonstrated that the economic approach to history could coexist just as comfortably with reactionary politics as with liberal reform ideals. But in both cases, there could be little doubt that modern historical writing reflected the social conflict and varying political sensibilities of early-twentieth-century society.[28]

Those who admired the innovative efforts of young historians to advance economic interpretations of American history thus had much to celebrate as the first decade of the twentieth century neared its end. But critics of the new approaches were not lacking. In 1908 Yale professor George Burton Adams used the occasion of his presidential address before the American Historical Association to deliver a bitter jeremiad against the incursion of the social sciences into the field of history. Ostensibly Adams's foes were social scientists from disciplines newly emergent in the late nineteenth century who concerned themselves "with the same facts of the past which it is our business to study." Political science, sociology, geography, economics, and social psychology, according to Adams, laid claim to history without demonstrating any deference to its empirical methods, its intellectual demands, or its moral sensibilities. "Certainly their attitude towards traditional history has not been that of dutiful children towards a parent," Adams complained.[29]

In fact, however, at least some of Adams's pique reflected his displeasure that insufficient regard was being shown for *political* history. Indeed, to differentiate social scientists who masqueraded as historians from professionally trained historians he invoked the term "political historians" for the latter group. "After three-quarters of a century of practically undisputed possession of our great field of study," Adams argued, "during which the achievements of the political historian have won the admiration and applause of the world, our right to the field is now called in question, our methods, our results and our ideals are assailed, and we are being thrown upon the defensive at many points." In laying out the hostile "lines of attack" on history, Adams displayed absolute contempt for the discipline of sociology. "Let me hasten to relieve your minds of the apprehension that I am going to try to tell you what is the field of the sociologist," he reassured his listeners. "He is indeed lord of an uncharted domain, and I have no intention of attempting to supply him with a chart." But Adams seemed far more deeply concerned about the increasing influence of economics on history.[30]

Here Adams clearly felt troubled by the risks and benefits historians might accrue from their attention to economy. Though he maintained that "the historian of the old school, the traditional historian, has no more valuable ally than the economic historian," he drew a sharp distinction between inquiry and interpretation, fact and theory. As Adams put it, "there is a great difference between economic history and that which calls itself the economic interpretation of history." There could be little doubt that Adams had in mind E. R. A. Seligman and his students. Indeed, when his paper was later published in the *Ameri-*

can Historical Review, Adams referred readers in a footnote to Seligman's *Economic Interpretation of History* "as giving a very clear idea of the ideas and aims of one portion of the new movement in the field of history."[31]

Adams acknowledged the great strides made by scholars who conducted research into economic history. "So far-reaching have been the discoveries . . . so profound the influences whose operation he has uncovered, so satisfactory the explanations which he offers, that it is not strange if many have found here the final explanation of history." Indeed, Adams avowed: "The economic interpretation of history has come to be a standard formula, and the explanation offered is in form complete." What troubled Adams about such approaches, however, was "the controlling influence of the imagination in the new history in comparison with the stricter scientific faculties." Fact and scientific research on the past were being subordinated, in Adams's view, to a relentless pursuit of theories and laws that made of history "the orderly progression of mankind to a definite end." Such an object to Adams seemed a repudiation of the true scientific spirit of history.[32]

In 1908 Adams warned his audience that these trends were not passing fancies. "You will have seen, by this time, I am sure," Adams explained, "that in my opinion this allied attack upon the field of history by the five divisions whose advance I have briefly sketched is not an affair of the moment, but formidable in character and likely to last at least one swing of the pendulum of time." The social sciences would continue to lay claim to history and influence the discipline, Adams believed, precisely because "the new interpretation of history brings us too much that is convincing. . . . Its contribution to a better understanding of our problems is already too valuable, we are ourselves too clearly conscious in these later days of the tangled network of influences we are striving to unravel." The only road ahead was for younger historians to "unite the old and the new" and to sustain the primacy of empirical research as an end in itself for history. "The field of the historian is, and must long remain," Adams insisted, "the discovery and recording of what actually happened." One day when the pendulum had swung back, Adams ventured, older historians would find their adherence to scientific methods, research, and traditional historical ideals vindicated.[33]

Two years later Frederick Jackson Turner offered an eloquent defense of the new directions being pursued in American history in *his* presidential address at the American Historical Association's meeting in Indianapolis. His speech, later published as "Social Forces in American History," brilliantly captured the imperatives that had informed much innovative new work in early-twentieth-century history—so much so that it deserves to be seen as something of a second Turner thesis, one that fused the rise of modern industrial society to the need for a reconfigured approach to the study and writing of history.

Yet in his effort to champion this ideal, Turner revealed the many contradictory strands in the emerging "new history." There was first the simultaneous and somewhat paradoxical search for the roots of American social and economic development and the insistence on the uniqueness of contemporary society. "The transformations through which the United States is passing in our own day," Turner asserted, "are so profound, so far-reaching, that it is hardly an exaggeration to say that we are witnessing the birth of a new nation in America." Turner compared the "revolution" produced by the rise of modern industrial society to such events as the founding of the Republic and the Civil War and Reconstruction in describing its transforming impact on American society.[34]

Further, the sweeping changes in modern industrial society provided a rationale for Turner's now familiar insistence that the scope of history be widened—a view he sharpened and elaborated upon in his 1910 presidential speech. "The times are so close at hand," Turner explained, "that the relations between events and tendencies force themselves upon our attention. We must deal with the connections of geography, industrial growth, politics and government. With these we must take into consideration the changing social composition, the inherited beliefs and habitual attitude of the masses of the people, the psychology of the nation and of the separate sections, as well as of the leaders." For Turner, American history was "chiefly concerned with social forces, shaping and reshaping under the conditions of a nation changing as it adjusts to its environment." Certainly this aim had informed Turner's own scholarship in American history.[35]

The Progressive critique of American society also surfaced in Turner's remarks about the current state and the mandate of American history. The nation's cities were filled with impoverished immigrants "of alien nationality." Turner enthusiastically praised the luxury and progress industrialism had brought to the nation and to "masters of industry." But he also stressed that the concentration of capital in the hands of a few and the shrinking opportunities for individuals to compete for national resources challenged traditional "pioneer" values and ideals. "Colossal private fortunes have arisen. No longer is the per capita wealth of the nation a real index to the prosperity of the average man. . . . The self-made man has become, in popular speech, the coal baron, the steel king, the oil king, the cattle king, the railroad magnate, the master of high finance, the monarch of trusts. The world has never before seen such huge fortunes exercising combined control over the economic life of a people." The political consequences of such sweeping economic changes, Turner asserted, could be readily seen in contemporary society. "Federal activity" designed to limit corporate privilege and protect the well-being of the people had grown exponentially. Where American democracy had once been safeguarded by free land, "the present finds itself engaged in the task of readjusting its old ideals to new conditions and is turning increasingly to government to safeguard its traditional democracy." Socialism and electoral reforms gathered adherents, Turner claimed, because they were "efforts to find substitutes for that former safeguard of democracy, the disappearing free lands. They are the sequence to the extinction of the frontier."[36]

The joining of past and present led Turner to endorse the notion that intellectual gains could be reaped from the political currents that continually fed the study of history. Here too the presentism of Turner's appeal emerged forcefully. Historians should attend to the current state of American society because it provided the context through which national development could be most clearly seen. "If recent history, then, gives new meaning to past events . . . it is important to study the present and the recent past, not only for themselves but also as the source of new hypotheses, new lines of inquiry, new criteria of the perspective of the remoter past." The whole framework of American history might well be altered when historians brought a consciousness of contemporary society and politics to their work. "Minor political parties and reform agitations" would perhaps emerge not as "side eddies" but as "concealed entrances to the main current." Indeed, Turner argued, it was possible to "trace the contest between the capitalist and the democratic pioneer from the earliest colonial days." Turner called on his colleagues to "rework our history from the new points of view afforded by the present." Far from mandating a history removed from politics, Turner rooted the very enterprise of historical research and study in the political matrix of the Progressive era.[37]

This mission led Turner to a final exhortation to his colleagues: namely, to use the tools of social science to advance the study of history. To reduce history to a search for facts was to pursue a will-o'-the-wisp. Facts, Turner maintained, were not "planted on the solid ground of fixed conditions." Their significance could be derived only when set against the "deeper-seated movements of the age." The very elusiveness of the past, its complexity, and its dynamic character required historians to use every intellectual means available, especially the insights of economists, political scientists, psychologists, geographers, "students of the literature, of art, of religion." Indeed, Turner urged his colleagues to train themselves in their "sister subjects" to better expropriate social science methodologies.[38]

The clashing messages of Adams's and Turner's presidential speeches reveal the very real tensions that characterized historical writing in the early years of the twentieth century. Some conservative historians clearly felt the discipline was under assault from young scholars who advanced economic interpretations of American history. A powerful defense of these initiatives had been mounted by one of the most creative historians of the early twentieth century. By the time Charles Beard burst on the scene, the ideas underlying his focus on economic forces as determinants of American national development were being openly debated by American historians.

No one succeeded more brilliantly in bringing the conversation before the public than Charles Beard, whose work popularized the economic interpretation of American history. Beard carried to his work a deep immersion in the reform enthusiasm of the Progressive years, and for this reason alone he well exemplified the spirit of much Progressive era history. Born to well-placed and liberal parents, educated in Quaker schools, Beard began his study of history at DePauw University, where his early learning focused on English constitutional history. Though in his senior year he was already writing short pieces that looked skeptically at the U.S. constitution, he fully absorbed his professors' belief in the Teutonic origins of American democracy. During graduate studies at Oxford in the late 1890s, Beard continued to pursue his studies in English political history.

But it was his experiences outside the classroom that seemed destined to have the larger impact on Beard's reading of American history. Shortly after arriving at Oxford, he joined forces with another American to establish Ruskin Hall, an educational institution for workingmen. The venture reflected Beard's belief in the importance of nurturing education and leadership among members of the working class as both a means of uplift and a means of access to political power. Before long Ruskin Hall developed an Extension Division, which Beard took charge of. He traveled through the industrial towns of England, lecturing to unions and other gatherings of working-people. In these talks, he exhorted his audience to seize control of their future through education and other forms of self-improvement. His exposure to industrial workers and their grim surroundings inspired an early Beard treatise, *The Industrial Revolution* (1901). Though the book stressed the transforming impact of industrialization on modern society, it also described in idealistic terms the potential of harnessing industry and technology so as to advance progress for all humanity.[39]

In 1902 Charles Beard and his wife, Mary, a classmate from DePauw, a feminist, and a participant in many Ruskin Hall activities, returned to the United States and enrolled in graduate school at Columbia University. Charles Beard quickly gravitated to Seligman; James Harvey Robinson, who was then teaching European social and intellectual history; and Frank Goodnow, a liberal progressive whose expertise was in administrative law and government. By 1904 Beard had won a faculty appointment in the department of history. His close association with Robinson led in 1908 to a collaboration entitled *The Development of Modern Europe* (1907–1908), which laid claim to the mandate of modern history. "In preparing the volume in hand," the two wrote, "the writers have consistently subordinated the past to the present. It has been their ever-conscious aim to enable the reader to catch up with his own times; to read intelligently the foreign news in the morning paper." Although the authors claimed they had devoted "much less space to purely political and military events than has commonly been assigned to them in histories of the nineteenth century" in favor of the "more fundamental economic matters," in fact the work devolved mostly around political history.[40]

Beard also wrote and lectured widely on American politics and history in the early years of his career. In these activities, Seligman's influence on Beard's teaching and intellectual development was especially apparent. Beard's first important work in American history, *An Eco-*

nomic Interpretation of the Constitution (1913), advanced the case that economic factors exerted enormous power in the evolution of American political institutions. Applying Seligman's theories about economic forces as fundamental to the development of virtually all social and political development, as well as Goodnow's thesis that law was socially constructed, Beard sought to uncover the true origins of the American framework for political democracy.[41]

With this book Beard intended to make a frontal assault on some of the most cherished truths in American political history. He later explained his approach to a student: "The thing to do is to lay a mine, store it with nitro, and then let it off in such a fashion that it rips the bowels out of something important, making it impossible for the fools to travel that way any more." In this instance, the "something important" was the United States Constitution. Beard attacked the assumption that the ideas embodied in the Constitution stemmed from the "people" without reference to class or economic interest. Slaves, women, indentured servants, and those who did not own property were all people, Beard pointed out; but they had no real voice in framing the instruments of political democracy.[42]

More pointedly, Beard made the case that the men who sought a revision of the Articles of Confederation and those who later attended the Constitutional Convention in 1787 were pursuing the interests of their own class. Poring over documents from the Treasury Department, Beard assessed the economic status of the fifty-five delegates. He found that many had been deeply involved in mercantile activities, manufacturing, and land speculation. The majority, he noted, had held public securities—at least, they did in 1790 (a date his critics would seize upon subsequently). Virtually none were small farmers or artisans. They were, in short, strongly motivated to create a document favorable to their shared economic interests, one that prevented the states from interfering with the obligations of contract and from issuing paper money and that permitted the federal government to raise money to pay the public debt. Beard stressed that these were overwhelmingly the concerns of mercantile and manufacturing, rather than agrarian, groups.[43]

The battle for ratification in the states broke down, Beard claimed, along similar lines. The latter point had previously been raised in the 1890s by Orin Libby, a student of Turner's. Animated by the Populist movement as well as by his mentor's ideas, Libby had traced the geographical patterns of the vote over ratification, noting the resistance of poor farmers and debtors in some of the interior regions of the country. In both its thesis and in its quantitative approach, this was imaginative work which brought, one observer noted, "the study of American political and constitutional history down from the clouds and set it firmly on the ground." Turner considered Libby's work brilliant and pressed hard for his graduate student to be included on the program of the 1893 American Historical Association meeting in Chicago. Turner had already agreed to read a paper at that meeting, but he was determined that Libby's work also be given a hearing. When the program chair said no, Turner asked whether the chairman might then "kindly put it in the place of my own paper on the 'Significance of the Frontier in American History.'" Libby failed to get a place on the program that year, but he soon earned recognition for his innovative research. Beard made ample use of Libby's findings, pushing them far beyond what Libby himself believed were logical conclusions.[44]

Although Beard stressed that the framers were not evil men but were simply molded by their environment to pursue their best interests, *An Economic Interpretation of the Constitution* soon set off a public firestorm, fueled by what many believed was Beard's contempt for the great patriots whose intellectual labors served as the very bedrock of American democracy. One Ohio newspaper reported Beard's findings under the headline: "SCAVENGERS, HYENA-LIKE, DESECRATE THE GRAVES OF THE DEAD PATRIOTS WE REVERE." The story below the headline denounced the book's "filthy lies and rotten aspersions."[45]

Professional historians responded in a more measured tone, familiar as they were with economic determinist interpretations of American history. But many took issue with Beard's methods and findings. Chicago professor Andrew C. McLaughlin, a leading expert on constitutional history, dwelt on the deficiencies of Beard's approach (without ever mentioning his name) in his 1914 presidential address before the AHA. "Many of us are even now looking out upon the field of constitutional history as a branch and only a branch of economic history," McLaughlin observed. But he went on to warn his colleagues of the wolf that masqueraded in the sheep's clothing of such new historical initiatives. "One can find no fault with the desire to trace the development of economic conditions, or with the wish to see how economic forces have played through political institutions or toyed with constitutions and parties. . . . The ever present danger is the old one—the temptation to find in the past the present, not simply conditions out of which the present came, and to find just what we expect to find and not the almost infinite variety of motive and interest." What was for McLaughlin an alarming intrusion of present into past, however, represented for other early-twentieth-century historians an exciting opportunity.[46]

Undeterred by criticism of his work, Beard repeated and expanded much of his argument in his 1915 study, *Economic Origins of Jeffersonian Democracy*. Perhaps to bolster his claims, he began the book with an epigram: Turner's claim that "we may trace the contest between the capitalist and the democratic pioneer from the earliest colonial days." On the next page, Beard invoked the name of Carl Becker, whom he described as "one of the most brilliant of the younger historians in the United States." Professor Becker, Beard explained, "has prophesied that American history will shortly be rewritten along economic lines." The book that followed was "intended to be a modest contribution to the fulfillment of that prophecy."[47]

The book offered a sweeping interpretation of Jeffersonian democracy that does not suggest "modesty." Beard attempted to recast the whole battle between Jeffersonian Republicanism and Federalism as a clash between agrarianism and capitalism. The lines of economic interests that ran through the debate over the Constitution persisted into the early Republic, according to Beard. In the end, Beard charged Jeffersonian democracy with being something of a sham. It did not fundamentally alter the Constitution forged by the Federalists; it "simply meant the possession of the federal government by the agrarian masses led by an aristocracy of slave-owning planters, and the theoretical repudiation of the right to use the Government for the benefit of any capitalistic groups, fiscal, banking, or manufacturing."[48]

Beard's work, and the attention it received, bolstered the confidence of many students of American economic history. Indeed, as professional economists appeared to evince ever less allegiance to history, professional historians laid claim to economic history and trumpeted their new dominance in the field. In 1913, Guy Callender contrasted the enormous enthusiasm for economic history among American historians at the 1912 AHA meeting with "the lack of it among members of the Economic Association. Topics in economic history found no place upon their programme. Their meetings were devoted entirely to the discussion of current problems and no one showed the slightest disposition to approach those problems from an historical point of view or to look to history for any light upon them." By 1916, one scholar predicted what he viewed as the inevitable direction of American historical writing:

> How far strictly economic influences have directed the course of our political history will always be variously judged by different students, but increasing research will probably add to our present estimate of their effect. Many literary historians, and most readers of history, are so attracted by the personality of leaders and statesmen, by broad expressions of national policy, and by the dramatic episodes of the country's tragedies and triumphs, that they neglect the dry commonplaces of business annals. But leaders and statesmen attain power and prominence, and national policies acquire meaning, through consulting that material welfare which is recorded in market quotations and ledger balances, and even the moral enthusiasm and heroic sacrifices of national crises are inspired remotely or immediately by economic causes.

Those who preferred to avoid polemics about the future of history simply worked to advance the case by conducting research that they believed demonstrated the economic determinants of American political history.[49]

Beard also helped justify the increasing scholarly attention to recent American history. In 1914, he published a textbook entitled *Contemporary American History, 1877–1913,* designed to enable students and "general readers" to better grasp contemporary debates in American society. The book surveyed the recent past, focusing on topics such as "the development of capitalism," "imperialism," "the campaign of 1896," and, perhaps most remarkably, "the restoration of white dominion in the South." It depicted the struggle of the American working class and its fate within the capitalist economy. Beard clearly both admired the achievements and abhorred the costs of America's industrial revolution. But whatever his views, he made no attempt to disguise the fact that his political convictions drove his narrative of modern American history.

Those political convictions reflected many of the paradoxes of liberal thought in the early twentieth century. In his chapter "The Restoration of White Dominion in the South," for example, Beard described the disfranchisement of African Americans and the rise of segregation in the post–Civil War period. As Beard forcefully explained it:

The whites in the South were even less willing to submit to anything approaching social equality with the negro than they were to accept political equality. Discriminations against the negro in schools, inns, theaters, churches, and other public places had been common in the North both before and after the Civil War, and had received judicial sanction; and it may well be imagined that the southern masters were in no mood, after the War, to be put on the same social plane as their former slaves, and the poor whites were naturally proud of their only possession—a white skin.

Northern politicians showed no appetite for protecting the civil rights of African Americans as time went on. The only hope for "permanent advance of the race must be built on substantial elements of power in the race itself . . . in the development of intellectual and economic power on its own account." But Beard's stress on the economic and political barriers placed in the path of racial advancement broke down under the weight of the historian's own prejudices. One serious obstacle to progress, Beard noted, were nagging doubts about "the innate capacity of colored masses to throw off the shiftlessness and indifference to high standards of life."[50]

Contemporary American History reflected Beard's continued belief that beneath the surface of political conflict and debate lay clashing economic interests and the struggle for power among various classes in American society. The book also unabashedly embraced the notion that historians could analyze recent events as clearly as the remote past. It is hard to imagine that the charge of being presentist could have meant much to Beard. For he insisted, as did so many early-twentieth-century historians, that contemporary politics and society gave meaning to the past. In a passage that no doubt carried a double meaning for those who attacked his work on American constitutional history, Beard wrote: "It is showing no disrespect to our ancestors to be as much interested in our age as they were in theirs; and the doctrine that we can know more about Andrew Jackson whom we have not seen than about Theodore Roosevelt whom we have seen is a pernicious psychological error."[51]

The various economic interpretations of American history advanced during the Progressive era represented only one facet of a broader effort to enlarge the scope of historical research and writing. Among the most innovative studies were early forays into environmental history. Western history was, of course, the central dimension of this endeavor. But research on climate, geography, and the broader ways in which nature shaped American society, politics, and economy extended beyond the terrain of western history. Taken together, early-twentieth-century studies in western and environmental history were important facets of the larger effort to redefine American history.

One of the most ambitious efforts to pursue an environmental interpretation of American history came from a woman, Ellen Churchill Semple. Born to a wealthy Kentucky family, Semple belonged to the first generation of college-educated women in America. She matriculated at Vassar College when she was fifteen years old and graduated as valedictorian four years later. During postcollegiate travels through Europe, she learned of the work of Friedrich Ratzel, the leading German anthropo-geographer. After reading his work and schooling herself in the social sciences, she earned a master's degree in history from Vassar. By then, she had decided to study with Ratzel at the University of Leipzig, despite that university's prohibition against women earning advanced degrees. She traveled to Germany in 1891 and secured an arrangement whereby she was permitted to sit in the room adjacent to Ratzel's lecture hall and listen to him through an open door. Of Ratzel's some five hundred students, Semple was his first and only female student. She also soon earned a reputation as the most brilliant of Ratzel's students.[52]

Certainly Ratzel's influence on Semple proved lasting. Ratzel's work concentrated on the ways in which environment shaped human history. Drawn especially to comparative study, Ratzel had toured the United States in the mid-1870s and was captivated by what he learned of American westward expansion. The United States example, he believed, resembled mass migration in other societies, though he credited the American pioneers for their extraordinary skill in subduing the land and turning it to their own ends. Turner appears to have been unaware of Ratzel's work when the Wisconsin historian laid out his thesis about the American frontier. And despite their mutual interest in the role of land and sectional differences, they reached some conflicting conclusions about the trajectory of national history.[53]

Semple applied Ratzel's theories about the force of environment to the study of American society. After returning to Kentucky, she camped out among settlers in the Kentucky highlands and examined the ways in which their geographical isolation shaped their life experience. Her penchant for travel and independent research did not lend itself to a traditional academic career, even if the profession had been more hospitable to women. She taught one term every other year at the University of Chicago from 1906 to 1924, when she joined the graduate division of geography at Clark University. Her first scholarly article, "The Influence of the Appalachian Barrier upon Colonial History," appeared in 1897. It was followed in 1901 by "The Anglo-Saxons of the Kentucky Mountains," an essay that summarized her fieldwork and that won her enormous attention.[54]

In 1903, Semple published a sweeping synthetic work, *American History and Its Geographic Conditions*. She began, in the style of so many historians of her generation, with a most revealing epigraph: "So much is certain: history lies not near but in nature." Her book made the natural environment the central determinant of American history. In chapters on the early colonies, the westward movement, the War of 1812 and the development of sea power, the Civil War, immigration and industrialization, and the rise of cities, among other topics, American rivers and streams, prairies, mountains, and valleys served as the touchstone for the evolution of American society. "Civilization is at bottom an economic fact," Semple claimed, "at top an ethical fact. Beneath the economic lie the geographical conditions, and these in the last analysis are factors in the formation of ethical standards." Semple attempted to demonstrate these convictions with detailed analyses of every region of the country, making ample use of impressively detailed and carefully drawn maps.[55]

The approach often led Semple to reductionist explanations for crucial epochs and events in American history. Her commentary on the Civil War provides an apt example. Slavery, Semple maintained, was "primarily a question of climate and soil, a question of rich alluvial valley and fertile coast-land plain, with a warm, moist, enervating climate, versus rough mountain upland and glaciated prairie or coast, with a colder, harsher but more bracing climate." Once New England discovered that its "boulder-strewn soil" made its economy ill suited to slavery, it "took the lead in the crusade against it." The South defended slavery on economic and moral grounds largely because its climate and geography made the system profitable. Sectional conflict arose from "differences in climate and soil," Semple claimed; Union and Confederate sympathies could be traced within the border states along topographical lines. In her own native state of Kentucky, Semple argued, political loyalties broke down along geographical lines, with aristocratic planters in the Bluegrass siding with the confederacy and "the non-slaveholding population in the rough uplands of the Cumberland Plateau" having no use for plantation slavery in its "sterile hillside farms, pathless forests, and roadless valleys."[56]

Like Turner, Semple placed enormous importance on the United States' vast expanse of free land in explaining its history. She spoke of the frontier as a great democratizing force, one that tended to erase class differences, speed assimilation, and encourage "vigor, enterprise, and independence." Semple also resembled Turner in her conceptualization of unsettled terrain as those lands not yet tamed by white pioneers. As Semple put it, the first white Europeans to travel into the interior were "the first genuine Americans."[57]

Native Americans figured primarily as "savages" who posed a terrifying and often violent obstacle to white settlement. At the same time, Semple did allow that white incursions into their land were what had made the Indian "the natural foe of the settler." Further, she stressed that the presence of Indians in the interior could not help but change the character, social organization, and way of life of white pioneers. "A frontier," Semple explained, "is never a line but always a shifting zone of assimilation, where an amalgamation of races, manners, institutions, and morals, more or less complete, takes place." In the presence of Indians and the wilderness, the white settler "yielded himself" and waged against Indians "a war of extermination, with all its savage features of ambush and scalping, and all its brutalizing effects." Even here, however, Semple attributed the brutality to the transfer of culture from the Indians to whites on the frontier.[58]

Like so much Progressive era history, Semple's 1903 study reflected in no small degree prevailing political currents at the turn of the century. Her discussion of history and geography took as axiomatic the belief that the United States needed to expand its borders to ensure ample markets and to strengthen its stature internationally. Concerned about the contraction of arable land within the interior of the United States, Semple urged the adoption of a "recently proposed scheme of a national system of irrigation" in the Far West. She also looked to Mexico and Latin America as fertile grounds for American capitalism.[59]

But if the nation's location on the opposite side of the Atlantic Ocean from Europe had been a chief determinant of its past history, Semple predicted that "the most important geographical fact in lend-ing a distinctive character to [its] future history will probably be [its] location on the Pacific opposite Asia." Asia represented the last great maritime frontier. And the gains made in the Philippines during the Spanish-American war, Semple asserted, served as a "signal" that pointed to America's destiny. The geography of the United States, its abundant natural resources, and its burgeoning industrial economy had positioned the country to be a "pacific ocean power"—one that could stand preeminent in the world economy. Far from seeing any of these potentialities as a troubling sign of American imperialism, Semple greeted them enthusiastically. The nationalist fervor that had captivated so many Americans at the beginning of the twentieth century informed her sense of American history.[60]

Semple's extreme emphasis on geographical forces as determinants of American history soon set off a fierce controversy among her colleagues in the field of American history. The book received a polite, if rather condescending, review, from Albert Bushnell Hart in a 1904 issue of the *American Historical Review*. Hart reviewed Semple's work with a book by Albert Brigham, a professor of geology at Colgate, grandly entitled *Geographic Influences in American History*. Acknowledging the importance of both studies, Hart readily conceded that historians needed to pay closer attention to geography: "Though geography is well known to be the handmaid of history, their relations are too little noticed by experts in either subject." Semple's book, Hart offered, was "larger, more ambitious, and more distinctly historical" than Brigham's. But in comparing the two, Hart concluded that Brigham's study "is the work of an expert scientific man"; Semple's he found to be "much less precise and authoritative."[61]

A year later a more pointed critique of the kind of historical work Semple's study exemplified appeared in an essay by Alfred Lloyd entitled "History and Materialism." Lloyd's essay suggests that scholarship on nature and the environment was of sufficient interest among members of the profession that it merited questioning as an undertaking. Lloyd asked:

> Is history losing its human character and interest? Is it becoming more and more a natural science, a mere record of natural causes and effects, less and less a story, artistic and dramatic, of what men and nations by dint of the will and might and coursing blood within them have now and again achieved? Is it no longer a humanity? . . . Some people have detected such changes as these, and certainly the historian's growing em-

phasis on material conditions, on climate, geographical location, natural resources, and the like, would give color to the idea, while his resort to prosaic minutiae of all sorts, to statistics and to psychological laws, that seem human only through the accidents of association, would greatly deepen the color already given.

Lloyd argued that the danger of historical materialism lay in its tendency to select one facet of existence and treat it as the central determinant of all human history.[62]

That sentiment surfaced often in challenges to some of the new approaches to history being advanced in the early twentieth century. Certainly it was raised repeatedly in connection with Semple's work, and became the focus of an extended debate at the December 1907 meeting of the American Historical Association in Madison, Wisconsin. At a session called "The Relation of Geography and History" chaired by Frederick Jackson Turner, Semple delivered a paper entitled "Geographical Location as a Factor in History," which maintained that "the location of a country is the supreme geographical fact in its history." That aroused the ire of Professor George Burr of Cornell, who charged Semple with being insufficiently attentive to the role of individuals in making history. In fact, as can be seen from the following extract, Burr could not accept Semple's basic thesis that the environment was the main determinant of American history:

> When Miss Semple tells us that "the most important geographical fact in the past history of the United States has been their location on the Atlantic opposite Europe" we are in danger of forgetting that she speaks, not of a condition, but of an achievement—for what has made the story of the colonists other than that of the aborigines is not geographical position, but their European birth and training, their ships and their compass, the friends they left behind and the habits which engendered their trade. To impute action or causation, influence or control, to things which are inert is a figure of speech which gives vigor to style, but which always involves a fallacy; and when to nature is imputed what is planned and achieved by man, the sufferer from the fallacy is history.

Semple defended her view vigorously, as did other attendees. Ulrich B. Phillips displayed maps that showed, he claimed, a correlation between voting patterns in the 1848 presidential contest and plantation slavery. He claimed that his maps sustained the correlation between history and geography. In addition, Orin Libby's paper explored the ways in which physiography had influenced Native American patterns of existence and white settlement in North Dakota.[63]

The interest in region, environment, and geography received a boost at the same AHA meeting when the Mississippi Valley Historical Association (MVHA) was formed. Its creation reflected the enormous growth of interest in western history. Though Turner had done much to inspire such lines of inquiry, his ideas struck a responsive cord among many because they challenged the hegemony of the East as the foundation of American society. The founding of the MVHA followed the proliferation of state historical societies throughout the Midwest and indefatigable attempts by local archivists to gather the materials that would permit studies of their states and localities. These trends—a growing consciousness of region and efforts to compile a record of state historical identity—were taking place at a time when nationalizing influences seemed in many ways to overshadow localities. At the same time, the growing interdependence of the American industrial economy sharpened a sense of regionalism. Undoubtedly nostalgia for a simpler past inspired preservationists, whose work provided a wealth of material for professional historians. The changing makeup of the historical profession also clearly influenced the growing interest in Western history: many of the most innovative scholars working in the field hailed from the South and the Midwest.

Whatever the cause, western history as a field of study became a growth industry within the historical profession in the early twentieth century. At the 1907 AHA meetings, admittedly held on Turner's home ground in Wisconsin, seven papers on the West were delivered. Subsequent meetings kept up the pace. By 1914, a specialized scholarly journal, the *Mississippi Valley Historical Review* (later renamed the *Journal of American History*) provided a venue for countless essays, articles, book reviews, notes, and comments on topics ranging from the fur trade to "settlement and development of the lead and zinc mining region" in Illinois to "the rise of sport."[64]

It took some time for western history—which to some early-twentieth-century scholars seemed to mean Ohio—to extend its reach to the Southwest. As early as 1901 an unsigned review (penned in fact by editor John Franklin Jameson) appeared in the *American Historical Review* that made note of this neglect. Assessing the merits and weaknesses of a recent book by Albert Bushnell Hart, Jameson charged:

A more serious criticism might be based upon the lack of pieces illustrating the character and condition of the Southwest. The author is abundantly alive to the importance of the West in his scheme, but it is practically the Northwest alone which is in his mind's eye. . . . We dwell upon this thought because it is distinctly the habit of historical scholars, more especially of Northern historical scholars, not to consider the western expansion of this portion of our population in anything like the same way as that in which they view the western expansion of the North.[65]

Among those who took up the challenge of broadening the expanse of western history was Frederic Paxson, a talented scholar who took Turner's place at Wisconsin when the latter left for Harvard in 1910. Paxson's "The Cow Country" (1916) described the development of the cattle drive from Texas to Nebraska, Wyoming, and Dakota in the post–Civil War period. His detailed account emphasized how wire fencing, enclosure, and increasing government regulation influenced the trade. The cowboy, Paxson noted, "was created by his trade." Describing the background of the drivers and the culture that arose around their often romanticized world, he noted that the ballads they "improvised on the border . . . are a genuine contribution to American folk literature."[66]

In terms that reflected the political mood of his time, Paxson centered his analysis around the fierce competition that developed in the cattle industry. Cattlemen, railroad men, and meat packers battled fiercely, Paxson maintained, for the profits of the cattle trade. He depicted the cattlemen as hopelessly outflanked by the meat packers, who, he claimed, had "the same advantage in ownership of plant and conveyance that the Standard Oil Company had over the producers of crude petroleum during the same years. It was in vain that the cowmen tried to combine." The conclusion offered perhaps Paxson's most prescient comment on this chapter in western history. He described not only the disappearance of the cow towns, but also the rising interest in a world that was fading from memory. As Paxson put it:

Between 1885 and 1887 all these forces came to a focus, and the cow country that had bred them ceased to be. The open range was blocked by occupation so that the long drive was no longer possible. Cattle quarantines completed the obstructions begun by the farmers. The greed of stockmen that had led to their illegal enclosures had forced effective intervention by the government to break them up and to end the period of unregulated free grass, while the beef industry, with its impetus derived from the cow country, had started new forces that continue to touch American life on many sides. The packing and dressed beef consolidations had come to stay; barbed wire was on the road to monopolistic consolidation in a huge trust; railroad regulation had become more acceptable because of the abuses that had been revealed . . . and the Wild West had received clear recognition as one of the most valuable assets of American life and literature.

Indeed, the passage touched on one of the subtle ironies of Western history. Like so much early-twentieth-century history, it used the present as a compass that charted the past and in so doing located a path for contemporary history.[67]

Amid all the work on western history, however, precious little of it focused on Native American history. References to Native Americans surfaced most often in accounts of westward expansion, where tribes were often depicted as inconvenient barriers to white settlement. Some studies focused on public policy toward Native Americans. In addition, Philip Bruce's *Economic History of Virginia in the Seventeenth Century* devoted roughly one hundred pages to a discussion of Indians, half devoted to the "Indian economy," though here too Bruce's prejudices were amply evident.[68]

At the beginning of the twentieth century, efforts to deepen the study of Native American history appeared. Ethnographic studies by anthropologists extended the reach of western history further into the Southwest. Among historians, the first important and sustained scholarly work in the field of Native American history began to appear under the authorship of Annie Heloise Abel.[69]

Born in England in 1873, Abel grew up in Kansas, where her parents had emigrated when she was eleven years old. While attending the University of Kansas as an undergraduate and then as a graduate student in history, she became interested in the fate of Native Americans. She earned her master's degree in 1900 for a thesis entitled "Indian Reservations in Kansas and the Extinguishment of Their Title." She entered Yale University in 1903; two years later she had earned a doctorate for her dissertation "The History of Events Resulting in Indian Consolidation West of the Mississippi." The work made extensive use of documents from the Indian Records Office and nearly instantly won her wide professional recognition. The American Historical Association awarded Abel the Justin Winsor prize for her thesis in 1906, the same year she joined the faculty in history at Goucher

College. She remained at Goucher until 1914, when she left to become a professor of history at Smith College. Over her career, Abel published almost a dozen books in Native American history, a body of work that "placed her," in the words of Francis Prucha, "in the top rank of American historians of her generation." Most of her studies focused on the Civil War period, though among her works was a massive three-volume study entitled *The Slaveholding Indians* (1915–1925).[70]

Even in the earliest stages of her career, Abel's work quickly captured the attention of professional historians. There was, of course, the Winsor prize and the subsequent publication of her thesis. In 1908, she delivered a paper at the AHA on efforts to establish an Indian state in the hundred years between 1778 and 1878. In this paper she explored various steps and missteps in federal policy but also gave some agency to the Indians themselves, explaining their responses to the political maneuvering. In 1910, Abel's essay "The Indians in the Civil War" appeared in the *American Historical Review*.[71]

The 1910 essay revealed the suppleness of Abel's mind and the way in which her approach diverged so markedly from many other previous historians in making sense of the Native American experience. In the piece, Abel asked how some Native American tribes in the Indian Territory who at first proclaimed their neutrality in the Civil War had become drawn into siding with the secessionists. The answers to the question lay, Abel asserted, in the chicanery of white Southern officials in the Indian Territory; the vulnerability of the Five Civilized Tribes geographically; the aggressive recruitment efforts of Confederate sympathizers and military officials; and, in the case of two tribes, the Native Americans' own self-interest as slaveholders. Abel detailed the divisions among Indian tribes over secession and argued that half-breeds were far more likely to support the Confederacy than the full-blooded Indians in tribes such as the Creeks.

Although the article evinced signs of prejudice and paternalism, its tone was strikingly different from that adopted by most professional historians at the time. Abel's sympathetic posture toward the Five Civilized Tribes came through clearly. The Civil War, Abel maintained, extracted an enormous toll from the tribes. In describing the war's aftermath, Abel wrote: "For years and years, it was a sad picture of charred dwellings, broken fences, unstocked homesteads, and woe-begone people that presented itself to the white squatters who thronged into the Indian Territory during the Reconstruction Period.

Many of these invaders were under the impression that the Indians had forfeited all their rights under treaties by their advocacy of secession, and they were themselves resolved to lose no time in profiting by the circumstance."[72]

More remarkable was Abel's attempt to understand events from the perspective of the tribes themselves. In her work, Native Americans emerged as more than threatening figures impeding white civilization from advancement. She described the differences among and within tribes, contrasting the perspective of the Native Americans with that of the white officials and settlers who attempted to govern, despoil, or remove them. Abel's emphasis on the interaction between Native Americans and whites reflected a tendency in traditional historiography that historians of recent years have condemned for its ethnocentrism, among other things. At the same time, Abel's research represented a determined effort to add complexity to the familiar tale of Indian and white encounters on the frontier. In this sense, Abel's work gives evidence of the multiple currents that enlivened the field of early-twentieth-century western history—however much Abel herself is overlooked in subsequent accounts of American historiography.[73]

The various early-twentieth-century initiatives to broaden study of the American past converged, in some respects, in social history. Progressive era social historians undertook some of the most important work in western and environmental history. In addition, they often combined their study of social forces, as in the case of Turner, with an exploration of economic variables. They not only brought subjects and groups that had once figured relatively little in historical writing to the center; they did so in an interpretive and analytic style that went far beyond the efforts of antiquarians and amateur historians. Progressive era social history may have lacked the volume and depth that would accompany the explosion of the field in later years. Nonetheless, it anticipated in important ways many of the concerns that would animate historians throughout the twentieth century.

As would be true of virtually all efforts to enlarge the scope of historical study, however, social history received its fair share of criticism from those who sought to uphold the authority of "traditional" history. Critics detected the scent of contemporary politics in the questions posed by some early-twentieth-century social historians. Furthermore, they bristled at the social historians' reliance on new forms of data, including (most infuriatingly) statistics and census records, which seemed to erase human agency in favor of aggregates when explaining the trends of history. Such debates reflected, in part, competing scholarly efforts to claim the intellectual and even political high ground in defining the future of American history.

The suspicions aroused by social history surfaced in response to an innovative study in urban history by Adna Weber entitled *The Growth of Cities in the Nineteenth Century: A Study in Statistics*. Undertaken as a dissertation at Columbia University, where Weber was a graduate student in economics and social science, the work was published in 1899 as part of a Columbia University series in history, economics, and public law. Weber's book surveyed the rise of cities with an eye toward understanding the factors that spurred urbanization and the consequences of urban growth for modern societies. One third of the book was didactic—it explored "tendencies and remedies." Ambitious in its comparative approach, the study surveyed cities (defined by Weber as places with more than 10,000 inhabitants) in both the United States and western Europe. It emphasized industrial growth as a central force in spurring urbanization.

Weber's impressive use of census records and statistics earned the book recognition for its methodological "care and skill" and for "the wide sweep of figures embracing nearly all civilized countries." At the same time, statistician Walter Willcox found fault with Weber's study as history. In an 1899 review written for the *American Historical Review*, Willcox asserted, "[T]he great difficulty with all such statistical works as the present is that they are not strictly speaking books. A book is a work of art, it has unity and progress." Weber's study, for all its value, was "a good compend, not a book."[74]

Albert Bushnell Hart similarly criticized the increasing obsession with research and investigation for its deadening effect on historical imagination. "The basis of history is human nature . . . and therefore history must include the study of persons," Hart explained. For Hart "the heroic, the startling, the extraordinary are fairly the prize of the historian, who must always seek to sound the depths and measure the heights of national life." At the same time, he acknowledged that "history includes also the ordinary commonplace experiences of mankind; hence economic and social history have made a place for themselves alongside the narratives of political events." Yet however much Hart both in principle and in fact supported the new initiative, he seemed troubled about social history's threat to traditional history.[75]

Theodore Roosevelt expressed the same sense of ambivalence in his

1912 presidential address before the American Historical Association, delivered after the publication of James Harvey Robinson's *The New History*. With soaring rhetoric and a clear affection for narrative history, Roosevelt expounded on the literary demands of history. Careful and detailed historical research was necessary for the advance of history, Roosevelt asserted, but those demands did not diminish the importance of narrative. "Men without literary power" might well be able to make important contributions to history. "My only protest," Roosevelt explained, "is against those who believe that the extension of the activities of the most competent mason and most energetic contractor will supply the lack of great architects." Indeed, Roosevelt's remarks to historians echoed his earlier charge to muckrakers that they should put more "sky" into their exposés of corruption in American society. As Roosevelt put it: "Those who wish history to be treated as a purely utilitarian science often decry the recital of the mighty deeds of the past, the deeds which always have aroused, and for a long period to come are likely to arouse, most interest. These men say that we should study not the unusual but the usual. They say that we profit most by laborious research into the drab monotony of the ordinary, rather than by fixing our eyes on the purple patches that break it."[76]

Roosevelt insisted that historical imagination was as important to social historians as to those who studied traditional political history. And he strongly endorsed the necessity to write history that attended to "the actual lives of the men and women who live on ranches or work in factories." According to Roosevelt, the "common" people deserved a central place in the annals of American history.

> The great historian must be able to paint for us the life of the plain people, the ordinary men and women, of the time of which he writes. . . . [He] will in as full measure as possible present to us the every-day life of the men and women of the age which he describes. Nothing that tells of this life will come amiss to him. The instruments of their labor and the weapons of their warfare, the wills that they wrote, the bargains that they made, and the songs that they sang when they feasted and made love; he must use them all. He must tell us of the toil of the ordinary man in ordinary times, and of the play by which that ordinary toil was broken.

But, like Hart, Roosevelt could not relinquish his equally strong belief that extraordinary times and leaders remained the very lifeblood of history. "Many modern writers," Roosevelt complained, had "gone to the opposite extreme" in valorizing plain people. Perhaps he was thinking of his own future historical legacy as he exhorted historians to remember the transforming moments when great achievement meant the difference between "whether the nation shall walk in the glory of the morning or in the gloom of spiritual death."[77]

Defenders of social history, statistics, and the ordinary were also quick to mount the stump in the early twentieth century. In his 1905 presidential address before the AHA, amateur social historian John Bach McMaster laid out an agenda for historical research that stressed the importance of painstaking work in social history. Four years later, Dr. Joseph Hill, an official from the Census Bureau, offered a paper at the convention entitled "The Use of Census Materials in American Economic and Social History." Hill suggested that historians might reap rich rewards from research into "the vast statistical data" stored at the Bureau. Discussion at another session that year focused on the "historical uses of American newspapers." An archivist instructed the assembled scholars that newspaper advertisements proved particularly revealing since they offered data on everything from "the costumes, characteristics, and status of runaway servants and slaves" to "the fortunes and vogue of lottery projects." Even among colonial historians, still much under the sway of the Imperial school, mention was made that "the social history of the Revolutionary period is an especially unworked field, wherein the religious changes, the results of the changes in land tenure, the amelioration of the criminal code, are much in need of study."[78]

An early effort to graft some of the ideas infusing early-twentieth-century social history onto political history came from Carl Becker. A student first of Frederick Jackson Turner and reform economist Richard Ely at Wisconsin, Becker went on to Columbia to study with James Harvey Robinson and colonialist Herbert Osgood. Although he finished his degree at Wisconsin, his work reflected an amalgamation of the varying interests of his professors and most of all the wonderful subtlety, imagination, and felicity as a writer that would secure Becker's reputation as a historian.[79]

Becker's early work explored the class dimensions of the American Revolution. Focusing on New York, he unraveled the forces that shaped the emergence of revolutionary politics and strategies. "The Revolution," Becker maintained in a 1901 essay and later in *The History of Political Parties in the Province of New York* (1909), "was the culmination in theory, and in fact to a considerable extent, at least in New York, of the effort of the masses to pull down authority from the top and place it upon the ground. In theory and in practice the masses, for the time being, got vital control of the business of governing." Becker credited "the masses" of New York workers with propelling the Revolution in part out of their quest to wrench economic and political power from provincial elites. A little less than a decade later, Arthur Schlesinger, who had studied with Osgood and Beard at Columbia, would examine the economic motives that fed American merchants' opposition to British colonial policy. Never very far below the surface of these interpretations were Progressive era notions about the economic and social forces that drove political history.[80]

Early-twentieth-century studies of immigration, though small in number, were mostly feeble attempts at social history. A few strove to enrich the story of the nation's social fabric by breaking away from the traditional emphasis on early Anglo-Saxon migrations. But those who did often displayed a sense of chauvinism or pique at the treatment of a particular ethnic group in American society. These undercurrents were apparent in 1910, when American historians at the AHA meeting held a session entitled "Ethnic Elements in the History of the United States." The choice of topic appeared to reflect a recognition of the importance of research on immigration and ethnicity. But the papers lacked the breadth, imagination, and analysis of other scholarly efforts in the growing field of social history. A professor from the University of Illinois, for example, made a brief for the importance of studying German immigrants and criticized the "constant habit of assuming the Anglo-Saxon to have been always the typical American, all others 'foreigners'" as a misapprehension that "could only lead to a distorted view of our history." But his overriding wish was to demonstrate German contributions to a "higher" American culture. Similarly a paper on Dutch immigration seemed designed to restore status to what the author believed was a neglected ethnic group. Even a slightly more substantive essay in a 1910 issue of the *American Historical Review* on Scandinavian immigration was peppered with bigoted references to "gambling gypsies, Chinese coolies, Mexican peons," and "recruits from the proletariat of the south or west of Europe" by way of contrast to the hardworking, and presumably superior, Swedes and Norwegians.[81]

To the extent that liberal Progressive reformers pressed for more sympathetic treatment of the masses of new immigrants from Southern and Eastern Europe, there was precious little evidence of that sentiment in the historical profession. As was the case with labor history, however, some early-twentieth-century studies of immigration conducted by scholars in other social science disciplines as well as by liberal reformers and commissions outside the academy included a strong historical dimension in their analyses. They more often invoked the past to explain the harsh conditions immigrants had long suffered in their homelands and the political oppression, economic deprivation, and quest for freedom that spurred migration. History served in such instances to bolster demands that American society attend to the needs of the foreign born and demonstrate compassion in dealing with the daunting problems they faced in American industrial society. Over time the historical profession would better reflect the ethnic and religious diversity of the American people. And when it did, more penetrating and thoughtful studies of immigration would surface.

The fact that work on women's historical experience took place largely outside the academic discipline of history during the Progressive era also reflected the lack of diversity among practitioners in the field. Although some settlement workers, liberal reformers, and women social scientists advanced historical knowledge of women, few professional historians devoted their energies to that endeavor. Moreover, books about, and often by, women continued to be relegated to the "Notes and News" or "Minor Notices" section of the *American Historical Review.* While it is true that many of these works were carried on by amateur historians, lack of professional training did not provide a similar bar for male amateur historians, who routinely were allowed to publish articles and reviews in the prestigious journal.[82]

Even so, when women wrote about the American past they seemed to gravitate to social history. In a review published in the "Minor Notices" section of the *American Historical Review* in 1900, the editor made note of a new book by Sara Robinson entitled *Kansas: Its Interior and Exterior Life.* In Robinson's rendition of western history, cattle drivers and the romance of the frontier constituted only one part of the narrative. "The book," the reviewer explained, "also gives us an interesting picture of social and domestic life in the territory, of the limitations and discomforts which accompanied it and of the good nature and heroism with which they were met." A rare female address before the American Historical Association occurred in 1915, when muckraking journalist Ida Tarbell delivered a paper entitled "The Education of the American Woman in the First Half of the Nineteenth Century." Tarbell described the early female academies, the work of Emma Willard, Mary Lyon, and Catherine Beecher, and the beginnings of coeducation at Antioch and Oberlin.[83]

One fascinating hint of future research came with the publication of Carl Fish's "Social Relief in the Northwest during the Civil War" in 1917. Fish had studied with J. Franklin Jameson at Brown as an undergraduate and then wrote a dissertation on the civil service as a graduate student in history at Harvard. He spent virtually his entire academic career at the University of Wisconsin, where he emphasized social history in his teaching. His remarkable 1917 essay traced the awarding of allowances to the dependents of Civil War soldiers. Although Fish did not cast the essay in these terms, he incorporated gender into his analysis of Civil War pensions. The voices of individual impoverished women are heard, largely through Fish's intensive examination of private letters and government war records. Further, Fish linked the Civil War pension issue to increasing pressure to develop state welfare measures. "There is no evidence of the socialized state," Fish concluded, "though many things were being done which seem to characterize the socialized state." His work clearly anticipates the concerns many subsequent scholars would display as they examined the roots of American social welfare measures.[84]

If the historical experience of American women found no real institutional base within the historical profession in the early twentieth century, African American history was another story. Although slavery and Reconstruction continued to be major subjects of study, relatively little of this work attempted to examine historical realities from the perspective of African Americans. Indeed, outwardly racist essays were published in the *American Historical Review* in the early twentieth century, including one by a planter turned amateur historian who endorsed the importance of economic analysis of slavery while blaming the slaves for the conditions of antebellum slavery and for the continued "backwardness" of the South in the postemancipation era. Historiographical debates over slavery, the Civil War, and Reconstruction demonstrated the degree to which the searing conflicts of the nineteenth century shaped the preoccupations of historians in the early twentieth century. The wide influence of historians such as William Dunning, who viewed Reconstruction as a "tragic era" in American history, further ensured that such interpretations would persist well into the twentieth century.[85]

There were important challenges, however, to these ways of looking at slavery and its aftermath in the Progressive era. Du Bois confronted the racism and vulgarity of some historical work on African American history. Indeed, he took on Ulrich B. Phillips and became perhaps the latter's harshest critic among professional historians. A 1918 Du Bois review of Phillips's *American Negro Slavery* published in *The American Political Science Review* eviscerated the book and its pretensions as history. "This book," Du Bois wrote, is "a defense of American slavery—a defense of an institution which was at best a mistake and at worst a crime—made in a day when we need sharp and implacable judgment against collective wrongdoing by cultured and courteous men." Du Bois exposed a glaring weakness that Phillips's book shared with most early-twentieth-century treatments of plantation slavery: "The Negro as a responsible human being has no place in the book." He continued, "A history of slavery would ordinarily deal largely with slaves and their point of view, while this book deals chiefly with the economics of slaveholders and is without exception from their point of view."[86]

Nearly ten years earlier Du Bois had courageously taken on the leading figures of Reconstruction historiography at the 1909 meeting of the American Historical Association in New York. The session was entitled "Reconstruction and Race-Relations since the Civil War"; Dunning was to deliver a paper, as was Du Bois. At the last moment Du Bois was almost forced to withdraw because he lacked the funds to travel from Atlanta, where he held an appointment at Atlanta University. Albert Bushnell Hart intervened, however, and Du Bois made it to New York.[87]

At the meeting Du Bois ventured a radical reconfiguration of the history of Reconstruction. He boldly suggested that Reconstruction had actually had some benefits. Rather than being "the prime cause of the misfortunes of that period," black voters and legislators had actually made lasting contributions to the regeneration of the South. He emphasized black support for an expansion of public education, political reforms, and more extensive charitable institutions. And he noted the persistence of many provisions in Reconstruction constitutions long after the end of "negro rule." Du Bois courageously told his audience, "Paint the 'carpet-bag' governments and negro rule as black as may be, the fact remains that the essence of the revolution which the overturning of the negro governments made was to put these black men and their friends out of power. . . . Practically the whole new growth of the South has been accomplished under laws which black men helped to frame thirty years ago. I know of no greater compliment to negro suffrage."[88]

A heated—at least by the gentlemanly standards of the historical profession—discussion apparently followed. Ulrich B. Phillips, who was seated in the audience during Du Bois's speech, suggested "the need for recognizing on the one hand the wide variety of types of negroes (and indeed also of Southern white men) and on the other hand the norm." Du Bois's presentation was published a year later in the *American Historical Review,* but it would be some twenty-five years before he would issue his sweeping study, *Black Reconstruction* (1934). The genesis of that work was apparent in his 1909 challenge to Reconstruction historiography.[89]

Early-twentieth-century white historians published a few books and articles that attempted to explore little-covered facets of slavery. An 1896 article in the *American Historical Review* by Wilbur Siebert must have impressed readers for the approximately 2,500 oral histories the author claimed he had undertaken with abolitionists or their associates who worked on the Underground Railroad. Siebert began the study as a graduate student in history at Harvard University, where he labored on a broad study of the antislavery movement. In tracing the paths of fugitive slaves out of the South, Siebert's text for his 1896 essay was accompanied by detailed maps; he emphasized the importance of mining untapped source materials in examining the slave experience. Marcus Jernegan used legal and church records for his article "Slavery and Conversion in the American Colonies" in a 1916 issue of the *American Historical Review.* Jernegan examined the various arguments employed to rationalize slavery over the centuries. He pointed to competing desires among the colonists, with some religious leaders seeking to convert slaves to Christianity and slaveholders hoping to prevent conversion so as to better protect their economic investment. Jernegan described planters who felt that permitting slaves to worship might interfere with work on Sunday (which was customary on many large plantations) and inspire mis-guided and even dangerous notions of equality among the bondsmen and -women.[90]

At the same time, Jernegan's essay was filled with casual references to the mental deficiencies of slaves and sympathetic understanding of the distaste many whites felt when they contemplated common wor-ship with African Americans. The earliest slaves, Jernegan main-tained, resembled "savages of the lowest types . . . quite different in appearance and character from the negro of the present generation, so much changed by infusion of white blood and contact with a Chris-tian civilization."[91]

Some black intellectuals outside the profession of history offered a different viewpoint. They crafted texts that made the case for African American history as an essential component of any truly national his-tory. Benjamin Brawley, a graduate of Morehouse who had pursued graduate studies for a time with William E. Dodd at the University of Chicago before becoming a professor of English at Morehouse and then Howard, wrote a popular *Short History of the Negro People,* published in 1913. A more scholarly study published by Richard Wright, Jr., in 1912 joined the enterprise of African American history to economic approaches to American history. While studying for his Ph.D. in sociology from the University of Pennsylvania, Wright gravi-tated toward historical questions and analysis. His dissertation, en-titled *The Negro in Pennsylvania: A Study in Economic History,* proved to be Wright's last venture in the field of history. He became a well-respected minister for the African Methodist Episcopal church and a frequent writer on an array of public issues.[92]

For the sheer institutional foundation he provided for the study of African American history in the early twentieth century, however, no one rivaled Carter Woodson. The son of slaves, the second African American to earn a Ph.D. in history (Du Bois was the first), Woodson struggled long and hard to advance the field of African American his-tory. He attended high school at the age of twenty after working in West Virginia as a coal miner. He went on to college at Berea in Ken-tucky, where he graduated in 1903. From Berea, he returned home to work as a teacher in the black community. The Civil War remained a lively topic of conversation among his father and other Civil War vet-erans; their discussions apparently deepened Woodson's appreciation for drama and the lasting importance of history.[93]

After the Spanish-American War, Woodson joined other Americans in teaching in the Philippines. A trip around the world and a stint studying history in Paris followed. From there, Woodson traveled to the University of Chicago, where he began graduate work in European history and in 1908 earned a master's degree for a thesis on French diplomatic history. His interests, however, were moving toward American history, and he chose to attend Harvard for his Ph.D. As an African American graduate student at Harvard, Woodson later said he endured humiliating treatment from at least one of his instructors. Edward Channing appeared to bait his student with gratuitous remarks about black people and their nonexistent history, including the assertion that "Crispus Attucks and his companions" were but "idlers who happened to be among those who were throwing missiles at the British soldiers in Boston." Channing expressed amusement at the idea that "the incident [was] an important contribution to the independence of this country." Woodson fought back, but ultimately chose Albert Bushnell Hart as his dissertation adviser. Woodson's thesis on secession in West Virginia won approval only with great difficulty. Hart and Channing turned the first submission back, and only the intervention of Frederick Jackson Turner appears to have secured Woodson's thesis eventual approval. Another humiliating setback followed, when Woodson became the only graduate student among sixteen to fail the special exam in American history. He passed the second time around and finally in 1912 earned his doctoral degree. Little wonder Woodson would later say bitterly that "it took him twenty years to recover from the education he received at Harvard."[94]

Although Woodson had trouble getting his thesis published, largely because Charles Ambler's book *Sectionalism in Virginia* appeared to scoop him, his *Education of the Negro prior to 1861* appeared to favorable reviews in 1915. Somehow Woodson had managed to prepare this study while writing his thesis, dealing with the obstacles in the path of his graduation from Harvard, and teaching high school full time in Washington, D.C. In the summer of 1915, Woodson also decided to establish a group that would advance the study of African American history. The Association for the Study of Negro Life and History would tap the support of educators and philanthropists. But it remained the brainchild of Carter Woodson, who borrowed against his own life insurance policy to finance the first printing of *Journal of Negro History*—the periodical that would be crucial to the association's mission.[95]

The *Journal* became the major venue for black scholars seeking to publish their work in the field of African American history. Furthermore, for the first time a scholarly historical journal not only printed but emphasized work on the black experience. The work of many white historians also found a welcome place in the *Journal*. In addition, women scholars, white and black, received a much warmer reception than they had apparently found when submitting their work to other scholarly periodicals. Annie Heloise Abel, for instance, published some of her work on Native American history in the *Journal* with Woodson's encouragement.[96]

Some early articles in the *Journal* adopted a didactic style that emphasized African American achievements. Woodson also printed some polemics, including an extraordinary speech given in 1917 by George Wells Parker before the Omaha Philosophical Society. The speech laid out many of the ideas that have been echoed since in the notion of a "Black Athena." Entitled "The African Origin of the Grecian Civilization," Parker's speech challenged the notion that "the greatest civilization the world has ever known was pre-eminently Aryan." Parker recounted an international debate that he claimed had been raging since 1884 challenging the notion that Caucasians deserved credit for Greek civilization. Drawing on the work of geographers, classical texts, and archaeologists, Parker asserted that Greek civilization was "the civilization of an African people." Indeed, he upbraided historians for failing to face the facts:

> Before closing I wish again to enforce the fact that the ferment creating the wonderful Grecian civilization was preeminently the ferment of African blood. Take all the archaeological facts of the last fifty years and read them up or down, across or diagonally, inside and out, and this fact rises into your mind like a Banquo that will not down. Historians may distort truth and rob the African race of its historical position, but facts are everywhere throwing open the secret closets of nations and exposing ethnic skeletons that laugh and jest at our racial vanities.

Parker went on to suggest that the Renaissance was also rooted in the "contact between feudal Europe and African Mohammedism."[97]

Not surprisingly given its aims, the *Journal of Negro History* devoted much of its attention to social history. Although some early articles emphasized black achievement, the array of topics covered, the chronological periods surveyed, and the interdisciplinary methods employed surpassed that of the mainstream historical journals by a wide margin. Essays on the history of black migration, Nat Turner's rebellion, the slave trade, black physicians, black service in the Revolution, black folkways, and historiography represent just a few of the subjects covered in the *Journal*'s first few years. At the same time, the *Journal* mirrored the *American Historical Review* in providing sections for documents, notes, and book reviews as well as reports of the proceedings of the Association for the Study of Negro Life and History.

In one respect, the *Journal of Negro History* seemed to reflect both an enthusiasm for and an ambivalence toward efforts in the early twentieth century to highlight the history of common people. In January 1918, Woodson inaugurated a new section entitled "Some Undistinguished Negroes." In fact, the short tales selected from magazines, newspaper clippings, and the occasional oral history recounted the stories of extraordinary human beings whose courage, wisdom, and determination were clearly intended to inspire readers. Woodson was also aware of a tension in Progressive era American historiography: historians' tendency to seek a harsh view of the past without abandoning a vision of the future that emphasized progress.

It would be fair to see the publication of James Harvey Robinson's *The New History* in 1912 as something of an afterthought. Virtually all of the essays in the book save one had been published previously— the first, "The New History," in 1900. In addition, the case Robinson made in his book for the expansion of history's domain scarcely needed to be made by 1912. That initiative had been under way, in theory if not in practice, for at least two decades.

Robinson's book did provide a convenient target and a rallying point for critics of the new trends in American historiography. In the aftermath of its publication, several lions of the profession rose to defend traditional political history or to temper the boisterous enthusiasm among younger historians for the "new history." But few took issue with the central tenet of the new historians: that Americans of their generation had lived through a profound sea change in their society. What traditional historians questioned was the idea that the present necessitated a wholly new approach to the past, one that devalued great statesmen, noble ideas, and indeed politics and law, all of which had once been conceived as being the heart of history. The battle among historians, in essence, was over historicity.

Native Americans and the Moral Compass of History

> Every schoolboy knows that from the settlement of Jamestown to the 1870s Indian warfare was a perpetual accompaniment of American pioneering, but the second stage in dispossessing the Indians is not so generally and romantically known. The age of military conquest was succeeded by the age of economic absorption, when the long rifle of the frontiersman was displaced by the legislative enactment and court decree of the legal exploiter, and the lease, mortgage, and deed of the land shark. . . . The orgy of exploitation that resulted is almost beyond belief. . . . Even as a real estate transaction this transfer of property would have attracted wide attention, but the Indians had been forced to accept the perilous gift of American citizenship and they were despoiled individually under the forms of existing law; hence no writer of American history devotes even a sentence to their wrongs.
>
> —ANGIE DEBO, *AND STILL THE WATERS RUN* (1940)

Demarcated on either side by carnage and destruction on a scale heretofore unimaginable, the years between World War I and World War II ushered in an extraordinarily vital period in American historical writing. This was the time when the bold ideals and ambitious plans of the Progressive era "new history" came of age, most notably in the enormous efflorescence of work in American social history. The 1920s and 1930s modernized historical inquiry, moving it in directions that contemporary historians often see as the harvest of late-twentieth-century politics and society.

The scholarship of historians during the interwar period is all the more remarkable for the ways in which it has often been trivialized, overlooked, or ignored in the subsequent collective memory of the historical profession. The work of innovative interwar historians provides an important—if largely concealed—bridge connecting the aspirations of Progressive era historians to the preoccupations of much

contemporary history. The links are apparent in the questions historians of the 1920s and 1930s asked about the American past, in the
groups they sought to examine and the categories they privileged, in
the sources they deployed, and in the complex and often conflict-
driven interpretations of society, politics, and economy they advanced.

Imaginative interwar historians pioneered in using an amazing array of sources ranging from plantation and church records, vital statistics and census data, trial transcripts and probate accounts to oral
histories, tax lists, maps, and long-ignored government documents.
These materials were necessary in historical accounts that focused on
such matters as race, religion, cities, the environment, migration, class
formation, and a host of similar concerns. New research strategies
were likewise mandated by scholarship that made a place for workers, Native Americans, African Americans, immigrants, women, and
other groups who had only rarely figured in historical accounts. Finally, many interwar historians advanced sharply critical, and often
highly politicized, interpretations of the American past. They did not
always do so from ideological vantage points that would be shared by,
or even recognizable to, their successors later in the twentieth century.
In the context of their own time, however, some scholars were as determined to use their historical moment to invigorate understanding
of the past and to influence in some fashion the politics of the present
as were the generations who succeeded them.

It is not surprising that the 1920s and 1930s would give rise to such
intellectual imperatives. The historical moment alone thwarted those
who sought scholarly isolation. Historians who lived through the period, and who sought to work within it, experienced along with their
contemporaries a harrowing series of events that upset the most honored truths and the most relied-upon ways of making sense of the
world. Despite the prosperity the 1920s brought to many middle-class
Americans, the decade forced a confrontation with the horrific realities of modern warfare as it had been waged during World War I, and
with the profound pessimism the failure to secure peace had ushered
in. The twenties likewise gave rise to fierce cultural tensions and a
sense of unease among many Americans, as old values and revered
traditions seemed to wobble in the face of modernist trends. After the
1920s came a decade of economic suffering, searing for many and dis-

orienting even for those most protected from the ravages of poverty, dependence, unemployment, homelessness, and the rootlessness imposed by the Great Depression. By the late 1930s, the march of fascism abroad, the seemingly immovable wall of American isolationism, and the widening sphere of global conflict served to heighten Americans' fear and anxiety. In such a context, history became a weapon of war, a way toward reform, ballast in the futile search for stability—or so it functioned for many interwar historians. Scholarly pursuits were infused with politics and political passion, despite the strong adherence of most historians to the professional creed of scientific objectivity.

Historians had no unified response to the cataclysmic events of the 1920s and 1930s. Indeed, the interwar period is notable for the way in which historians articulated explicit, and frequently extreme, positions on a range of historical events and controversies. Savagely racist, and deeply revisionist, even radical, accounts of Reconstruction, for example, were advanced during the period and published virtually simultaneously in the professional journals—occasionally in the same issue. Though late-twentieth-century historians have emphasized the reactionary quality of much "traditional" history in the early twentieth century, particularly on topics such as Reconstruction, an emphatic counternarrative began to take shape during the 1920s and 1930s. Entire subfields—the history of the South, slavery, the Civil War, and Reconstruction, most notably—were riven with dissension as competing voices sought to capture the essential meaning of the American national experience. The result was a spirited, if sometimes chaotic and often contradictory, conversation among disputants searching for the moral as much as the intellectual and political high ground.

Judging by the salience of the old history–new history paradigm, later generations of historians have been easily tempted to smooth away such rough edges and to assume that the interwar years largely carried forward orthodox historical writing with its emphasis on political history, great actors, and events, its essential political conservatism, and its stress on the triumph of liberal democracy. A few exceptions to the rule have been much remarked upon—most notably, various economic interpretations of the American past produced or influenced by Charles Beard, as well as the ambitious series of books on American social history published under the aegis of Arthur

Schlesinger and Dixon Ryan Fox. Entitled *A History of American Life* (1927–1948), these twelve volumes were praised in their own time, and have been since, as honorable attempts to broaden the reach of historical study. But they were also criticized by contemporaries and subsequent historians for being largely devoid of interpretive power and weighed down by a surfeit of facts that led the reader nowhere of great importance. Such a verdict seemed to stand for all interwar historical writing that moved beyond political and constitutional history—noble goals, failed achievements, empty of any ideological authority.[1]

When a wider range of work is considered and a broader spectrum of historians is placed at the center of American historiography, however, the character of interwar historical writing takes on a much different aspect. The unity of thought and purpose that allegedly existed among historians seems more an ex post facto construct than an apt description of historical study in the 1920s and 1930s. In fact, during the interwar years, a great many presumed orthodoxies faced persistent challenge within the historical profession. The intellectual ferment created by iconoclastic historians was both apparent and real. Further, the accomplishments in social history were broad and deep. Many scholars challenged the fundamental leitmotif advanced by students of the American past who equated historical change with progress and the advance of liberal democracy. They pointed instead to a darker, more sobering view of the trajectory of American history.

Perhaps nowhere was this shift more visible than in historical writing on Native Americans during the interwar years. The history of Native Americans was particularly ripe for reexamination, given the enormous energy scholars were devoting to the frontier, the largely blind eye historians had traditionally turned toward the story of America's indigenous people, and the early forays historians such as Annie Abel had made during the Progressive years. Increased scholarly attention to Native American history during the interwar years thus provides a compelling example of the ways in which the shifting historical moment created an opening for the beginning of a redefinition of a field and engagement in an important intellectual and political realignment.

Much, but by no means all, of the interest in Native American history came from scholars who found their way to native peoples by means of their preoccupation with "larger" issues such as English colonization, the origins and dynamics of the fur trade, the evolution of the South, white settlement of the frontier, and the administrative issues raised by imperial and federal policy toward the tribes. There was an exterior quality to historical work on Native Americans during the 1920s and 1930s that differed profoundly from later efforts to understand the interior experience of native peoples. Many interwar historians tended to focus their analysis on ancillary issues, emphasizing the structural dimensions that shaped Native American experience. These historians were far less interested than their successors in the centrality of Native American experience and identity in its own right. Nor, given these preoccupations, did Native American history emerge as a well-populated subdiscipline among historians during the interwar period, despite the fact that some scholars identified themselves as historians of Native American history. Nevertheless, scholarly work on Native Americans did advance significantly in these decades, in ways that reveal a great deal about the political passions, intellectual preoccupations, and moral burdens of modern history in the twentieth century.

The Native American–white encounter served as the overarching focus of study in Native American history during the interwar years, as it does at the start of the twenty-first century. It was difficult even for the least attuned historian to ignore North America's indigenous peoples in recounting the story of America's founding. In fact, several nineteenth-century romantic historians devoted great energy to describing Indians, though often in highly Eurocentric ways and with little understanding of the complexities of the native peoples, their lives, and the price they had paid for their encounter with white settlers. Although a few exceptions to the traditional narrative appeared in the first two decades of the twentieth century, the 1920s and 1930s brought a rediscovery of Native Americans in ways that added greater complexity to historical scholarship.[2]

The ever-expanding parameters of literature on the history of the frontier provided an intellectual framework for early work on the history of Native Americans—a fact historians recognized as early as 1921. The program of the Mississippi Valley Historical Association that year "evinced a homogeneity in its diversity," according to its reporting secretary, for including a panel "dealing first with the red men" and "then with the pioneers of the revolutionary epoch" as well as "the trans-Mississippi pioneers." So a published account of the meeting described an Ohio State University scholar's paper on the history of Mohegan Indians.[3]

In 1928, William MacLeod, who held a Ph.D. in sociology from the University of Pennsylvania but who was drawn to the study of history and anthropology, explicitly joined the agenda of Turnernian history to scholarship on Native Americans. He introduced his ambitious study *The American Indian Frontier* as "an essay in the 'New History.'" "Every frontier has two sides," MacLeod observed, in introducing his book as "the first attempt at an analysis of American frontier history made particularly from the viewpoint of the Indian side of the frontier development." In fact, MacLeod's wide-ranging survey of Indians from pre-Columbian times forward adopted an early-twentieth-century anthropological voice deeply accented with ethnocentricities, which frequently defeated MacLeod's stated intention to reveal the "Indian side" of the frontier story.[4]

MacLeod's work nonetheless represented a significant departure in historical perspectives on native peoples. Although a firm adherent to assimilationist models of acculturation, MacLeod worked hard to examine the cultural dimensions of Native American society and to animate Indians as complex men and women with distinct traditions, tribal structures, and belief systems. He devoted particular attention to the religious practices of Native Americans, including peyote use among tribal Indians on reservations from the 1890s to the early twentieth century. Plains Indians considered peyote use consistent with their Christian beliefs. It provided a means of enhancing religious experience, according to MacLeod, who narrated these elements of Native American life with notable equilibrium.[5]

The scholar abandoned his disinterested stance, however, in assessing white behavior and motivation. In a chapter entitled "The Origin of Hate: Race Prejudice in North and Latin America," MacLeod described "the frontiersman's policy" toward Native Americans as "extermination." From the seventeenth century to the nineteenth, he wrote, government officials colluded with white settlers in this approach to Native Americans, whether through "beneficent" policies that seemed to speed the demise of Indians or through neglect and "watchful waiting" for their eventual disappearance. Such a bald assessment of white motives signaled a conspicuous divergence from a frontier history that had largely obscured American Indians or that had celebrated their annihilation. For this reason alone, *The American Indian Frontier,* despite its deficiencies, marked a striking shift.[6]

Conspicuous among the small, but growing, number of scholars who attended to Native Americans during the 1920s and 1930s were Southern historians. Their attention to the subject evolved from multiple concerns. For early American historians who focused on the South, inquiry into Native American history formed part of a broader research agenda that aimed to extend the story of colonial settlement beyond the geographic boundaries of New England. Certainly this was the aim of Alfred Morrison, who offered in a 1921 issue of the *William and Mary Quarterly* the first installment of what he hoped would be a much larger and "close" investigation of the Southern Indian trade. (Morrison did not live to complete the study.)

Morrison's interests and sympathies centered on the English settlers and the ways in which they had succeeded in establishing a profitable relationship with various tribes. He largely denied Native Americans an active role in shaping their history and that of white settlers. However, his work struck a tone that would grow more insistent in subsequent interwar historiography—namely, that white-native encounters were far more complex than previous historical accounts had allowed. Of the Indian trade, Morrison claimed that it was "a shifting business at best." Indeed, he approvingly quoted John Rolfe's observation that the Indians seemed to "have mortgaged their whole country" to pay for wheat and corn, giving rise to a range of tensions that shaped the history of both sides forever. "Here were the difficult questions arisen of deed and deed of trust," Morrison wrote, "among a people holding the land by tribe as it pleased them, and as they could." Morrison insisted that as early as 1616 it was obvious that "the red indwellers were beginning to be in pawn"—a passive construction of Native American experience and a prospect that did not seem to trouble him excessively. Morrison nonetheless clearly believed that the dynamics of white-Indian relationships deserved a central place in the narrative of early American history. Two years later the *William and Mary Quarterly* advanced this theme a bit further by printing in one of its issues "Some References to Indians in Colonial Virginia"—a collection of seventeenth-century documents including court records, deeds, and probate accounts that illustrated various contacts between Indians and white settlers and that gave some voice to both participants.[7]

Other historians of the American South found their way to Native Americans in their eagerness to bring Southern history within the parameters of Turner's still dominant "frontier history" by demonstrating the centrality of the Southern frontier to the larger narrative of American history. For them, Native Americans appeared to represent an unwelcome, but nonetheless important, element in a comprehensive narrative about the social evolution of the region. A 1923 essay in the *American Historical Review,* for example, told the story of the "South Carolina Up Country at the End of the Eighteenth Century" by reference to the tribes who inhabited the South Carolina interior. D. Huger Bacot's was a tale of the "Indian peril," of the "war-whoop, the tomahawk, and the scalping knife," and of the ultimate "retirement of the red man." Bacot echoed familiar themes in American historical writing as he invoked both the military valor of the Cherokees and Catawba and their inevitable defeat by the advancing line of white "civilization." "Much more could be written to depict the prowess of the Catawbas," Bacot concluded, "yet by the end of the eighteenth century they were a weak and degenerate people, numbering hardly sixty warriors, addicted to drunkenness, and living in small villages surrounded by whites."[8]

A more discerning version of the white–Native American encounter emerged in the work of Southern historians who used extensive manuscript materials to challenge the depiction of impotent tribes crumbling in the face of white advancement. In a preface to a collection entitled "Documents Regarding Indian Affairs in the Lower Mississippi Valley, 1771–1772" published in 1926, David Bjork described the attempts by English and Spanish settlers to "win the allegiance of the Indians." Bjork, translating and reprinting documents he located in the Archivo General de Indias in Seville, attempted to demonstrate the command exerted by the Native Americans. "Unlike hungry fishes," Bjork emphasized, "the Indians did not thoughtlessly go for the bait, but were always guarding their own interests"—in this instance by attempting to form alliances with both sets of white settlers, much to the frustration of the two European powers.[9]

The themes of Southern trade, colonial ambition, and tribal identity were joined in 1929 by Verner Crane, a professor of history at Brown University, who produced the first thorough overview of the Southern Indian trade in *The Southern Frontier, 1670–1732.* Crane made a case in meticulous detail for the centrality of Indian trade in shaping the Colonial South and in determining the torturous hierarchy among the Europeans who struggled for dominance along the Southern frontier. Both themes earned the praise of reviewers, who especially lauded the book for illuminating the dynamics of "English imperialism" and the fundamental importance to American history of the Carolina frontier. Crane's emphasis was Eurocentric but the Creeks, Cherokees, Chickasaws, and Choctaws emerged as crucial forces in his narrative.[10]

Studies of eighteenth-century British imperial administration in the Southern colonies likewise spurred further historical inquiry into Native Americans. Such accounts frequently depicted white Europeans as moving Indians like chessmen into various power relationships with dominant colonial rulers. Yet they also reflected at least an emerging awareness of the ways in which Native Americans pursued their own interests, exerted power, and thereby influenced the course of history. These themes surfaced in the treatment by several historians of John Stuart's tenure as British superintendent of the Southern Indian department during the Revolutionary era. Perhaps the lure of this chapter in colonial history could be traced to the ingredients of alleged British perfidy, a brutal Cherokee assault on white settlers, and elaborate trading between agents and Indians—all amid the backdrop of incessant political tensions among various colonial officials.

Indeed, the story of Stuart's role in the Southern Indian department provoked some historical revisionism that turned on the question of what underlay Indian behavior toward white settlers. At a 1929 meeting of the Mississippi Valley Historical Association, and in a later essay that expanded his scholarly presentation, University of Tennessee professor Philip Hamer sought to dispute previous American historians who had charged the British superintendent with orchestrating the Cherokee attack on white settlers in the summer of 1776. That interpretation rendered Native Americans as dupes rather than as shrewd agents acting on behalf of their own interests. Using documents from the British Public Record Office, Hamer argued that the violence could be traced to the provocations of whites who had built forts along the Indian frontier, had threatened to invade Cherokee territory, and had stirred up the "hatred and fear" of the indigenous people "chiefly by encroachments upon Indian lands." In this context, the Cherokee attack appeared as a rational response to white incursions against native people.

A similar theme surfaced in John Richard Alden's 1944 study of Stuart's administration entitled *John Stuart and the Southern Colonial Frontier*. A student of Verner Crane's who had gone on to become a productive teacher and scholar of early American history, Alden sought to extend his teacher's work on the relationship between English settlers and Native Americans; the book carried the ambitious, though somewhat misleading, subtitle *A Study of Indian Relations, War, Trade, and Land Problems in the Southern Wilderness, 1754–1775*. Alden's account lavished praise on Stuart as a benevolent administrator who enjoyed considerable success in maintaining peace among white settlers and Indians despite, as one reviewer noted, "the avarice and incorrigibility of English traders, the bickerings and jealousies of colonial governors, and the machinations of French and Spanish agents in the Indian country." Alden, another reviewer claimed, "knows his Indians by individual name as well as by tribe"— a tribute that reflected the historian's efforts at least to make of the native peoples not some unvariegated threatening mass but distinct tribes with their own histories. Still, though Native Americans figured in histories such as Alden's, they often remained shadowy figures in the drama of Southern history, lacking independent agency and substance as historical actors.[11]

At the same time, the moral compass employed by some interwar historians of the South pointed increasingly to white depravity and manipulation as a prominent theme in Indian-settler relationships. As early as 1920 Charles Ambler, a prominent historian of the American South, described Annie Heloise Abel's study *The American Indian as Participant in the Civil War* as "largely a narrative of jealousies and rivalries, interspersed with accounts of drunkenness and incompetency"—and he was referring to white Union and Confederate officers. The latter did little, Ambler noted, to "inspire confidence and enthusiasm in their Indian allies." He dismissed the tribes, however, as "poor soldiers" who did little to assist the Confederacy despite their loyalty to the secessionists. "They refused to subject themselves to drill and discipline," he explained. "They did not hesitate to intrigue with the enemy; and they were constantly reverting to the most revolting practices of savage warfare." Yet he also described the Indians as deeply loyal to "home and country," determined to safeguard their lands from scoundrels driven by land hunger. Indeed, he reserved his harshest criticism, agreeing here with Abel, for "the supremely selfish character of the Indian alliances on the part of those who coveted their lands and used the Indians incidentally to fight their battles."[12]

This judgment was echoed by some historians of the interwar period concerned with the lives of missionaries who worked among Native Americans. Among this group was Frank Klingberg, who earned his Ph.D. from Yale University with a dissertation on the British antislavery movement. Later a professor at UCLA, Klingberg was interested in a range of issues, from women's rights to the fate of African Americans in the Southern colonies. In 1939 Klingberg's research on eighteenth-century missionaries along the South Carolina frontier led him to note how impressed Protestant missionaries were with the intelligence and decency of native peoples. The evangelists soon discovered that "the greatest obstacle . . . in the way of Christianization was the conduct of the whites." Indeed, Klingberg argued that "the white man's ruthlessness and evil effects upon the native" had been a persistent theme in missionary accounts "beginning with the age of discovery." And he approvingly repeated the opinion of an anonymous "distinguished American scholar" who asserted: "The impact of the whites, in their wide-fronted folk migration, swept the Indian westward and disintegrated his civilization. The inadequate internal cohesion of the Indian tribe and something in the nobility of his nature made it easy for the white man to bore within for commercial purposes with destructive results."

Such an interpretation simultaneously exalted and debased Native Americans by attributing to them an inherently virtuous character and an equally apparent cultural weakness that left the tribes vulnerable to victimization. Yet Klingberg perceptively reversed standard notions of white-Indian relationships when he recounted the missionaries' graphic accounts of white traders' "cruelty and injustice" toward Indians and the missionaries' equally pronounced tendency to create a "cult of the noble savage." Further, Klingberg observed that the missionaries' efforts at religious conversion among the Indians "represented imperial as well as Protestant" zeal, as was apparent in the rivalries that developed with Catholic groups in Spanish and French territories who were also attempting to convert the Indians. In the end, Klingberg stressed, "the Indian was in the position of a migratory buffer state, with the long-armed tentacles of rival fur and other traders from the three powers pulling the tribes apart either by actual kidnapping or by means of internal fratricidal conflict." Again, such an interpretation portrayed Native American peoples as largely passive even as it sought to illuminate the forces that shaped their experience.[13]

By the late 1930s, the growing influence of ethnography and anthropology led some historians of the South away from narratives emphasizing victimization toward more probing inquiries into the ethnohistory of various tribes—though the two perspectives were hardly mutually exclusive. The professional history journals had long made space for reviews of books on American ethnology. Now other signs of interest in anthropological perspectives on native peoples began to appear. In 1939 the Southern Historical Association featured a panel on Southern Indians that examined cultural dimensions of Native American history. A researcher from the Alabama State Archives offered a paper entitled "The Contribution of the American Indian to the Culture of the South" in which he argued that "southern pioneer life entirely and modern rural life to a considerable extent" was derived from Native American agricultural, material, and cultural influences. From the "thatched interwoven fences of the rural South" to the southern diet, this scholar averred, "many other Indian customs were not only handed down but have been accepted and continue to be a part of our economic life." During the same session, a scholar from the University of Tennessee reported on archaeological findings that traced the origins and impact of the tribes who had first inhabited the Tennessee region. A final scholarly presentation, "Sequoyah's Contribution to Cherokee Culture," examined the impact of Sequoyah's alphabet on the Cherokee.[14]

A similar effort to join ethnography to historical research appeared in two 1943 articles published in the *William and Mary Quarterly*. In these and subsequent essays, anthropologist Maurice Mook urged historians and anthropologists to use the documentary record of early America to advance a more complete and accurate understanding of Native American life and culture in the East. Although the English colonists, Mook admitted, "were too ethnocentric to allow themselves to become absorbed in cultural patterns other than their own," their firsthand accounts of contacts with Indians contained a wealth of data that cast new light on native peoples and customs, from diet and ecology to politics and gender relations. Mook paid particular attention to the sexual division of labor among the Virginia Indians, finding ample evidence in primary sources given the apparent English fascination with Indian women.[15]

Although one of the most extensive historical studies of southern Indians came from the pen of an amateur historian during the interwar period, it attracted the attention of professional historians, perhaps because it sought to incorporate such ethnographic perspectives. Chapman Milling's 1940 survey of South Carolinian tribes, *Red Carolinians,* made use of public records, journals, account books, and legal documents as well as a range of scholarly studies undertaken by historians, anthropologists, and ethnographers to detail virtually every tribe that had passed through the Carolinas. In so doing, Milling crafted a book that exemplified a theme of much interwar era historical work on southern Indians. It offered an opportunity to portray the South as a multiracial society in ways that moved the narrative of southern history away from a singular focus on the agonies of American slavery and the traumas of the Civil War era.

Milling's sensitivity to the racial dimensions of his subject was evident. The author noted the singular relevance of his subject given "what is now taking place in other parts of the world"—where a "racial minority" was striving for equality. "The modern Indian, where he has been granted his rights," Milling observed, "is an American citizen of whom his country is justly proud. And where he has reached his finest development, he is usually found to be a member of one of those tribes which a century ago were deemed unworthy to remain on the same side of the Mississippi with the Anglo-Saxon." That Milling's frame of reference appeared to be global struggles against colonialism rather than the more immediate realities of segregation in his native South Carolina was revealing of Milling's myopic view of such racial advancement.[16]

For there can be little doubt that Milling shared some of the prevailing racial orthodoxies and preoccupations of his era. His account began with a discussion of the physical characteristics of Carolina's Indians that concentrated on skin color—not red nor true vermilion but reddish brown, he noted. He dismissed "mixed-bloods of doubtful stock" in categorizing the few extant Indians remaining in the Carolinas. And he joined the themes of "amalgamation and deterioration" in discussing the disappearance of the tribes. Shot through with sweeping generalizations and various cultural stereotypes, Milling nonetheless recognized and carefully catalogued the extraordinary diversity among the Carolinian native peoples. In this, he both acknowledged and celebrated the rich racial, ethnic, and cultural roots that linked the modern South to its progenitors.[17]

Although the despoiling and annihilation of native peoples in the South hardly made for an uplifting story, white southern historians such as Milling seemed to find a nobility in Native American history that differed qualitatively from much of the prevailing (white) scholarly view of the African American experience. Milling earnestly detailed the depredations of whites against Indians and placed the judgment of history against those who attempted to defraud and render powerless South Carolina's indigenous people. Yet in so doing, he paradoxically located in Native Americans an unexplored and admirable dimension of southern history.

For Milling, the inevitability of the "catastrophe" that he believed resulted when "the strivings" of "primitive man" were pitted against "civilized man" may have softened the edge and elevated the history he told from the realm of raw exploitation and naked conquest to grand tragedy. The "contributions" Native peoples made to southern society and culture were invoked to add texture and even romance to the portrait of the region's origins. Finally, the story of Carolina's Indians joined the history of the South to the national narrative rather than isolating the region for its peculiarities and its aberrant historical trajectory. As one southern historian complained, in 1936, of longstanding views of the region's history: "The West was discovered by Turner and exploited by his disciples, colonial history was re-written on the basis of facts rather than patriotism, but the South remained neglected as a sort of Bad Lands of 'rebellion' whose history could have no significance except as a warning." Ironically, regionalism thus functioned both as an ideal and an irrelevance in the work of several southern historians on Native Americans. The various southern tribes epitomized traits of courage, imagination, and commitment to land and people, among their many gifts. And yet the sin that tainted whites who engineered the dispossession of the Indians knew no strict regional boundaries. In a book review written for the *American Historical Review,* Angie Debo, herself a distinguished historian of Native Americans, praised Chapman Milling's work for tracing with "admirable detachment" each Carolinian tribe "to its eventual extinction," bare survival, or removal to reservations. In this sense, it was an American as much as a southern story.[18]

Like white Southern historians, African American historians also found in the narrative of Indian experience telling features of America's identity as a multiracial society. They proved far less neutral, however, in their assessment of Native American history. For these scholars, the story of the white-Indian encounter offered a useful parallel to African American history—one demonstrating that racial hierarchies in American society were historically constructed.

Indeed, such early work on African Americans and Native Americans sought to destabilize the established categories of race by demonstrating extensive contacts between blacks and Indians. The mixing of bloodlines between the two groups, these historians suggested, challenged the division between black and white that formed the basis of segregation in American society. In 1920, Carter Woodson described "the relations of Negroes and Indians" as "one of the longest unwritten chapters in the history of the United States." Using Massachusetts as a case study, Woodson argued in the *Journal of Negro History* that "there was extensive miscegenation" between African Americans and Indians in the Commonwealth beginning in the mid-seventeenth century. Indians who had been "neglected," "scantily provided for," "offered few opportunities for mental, moral, or religious improvement," and treated as wards of the state developed "into a state within a state." Some African Americans sought refuge among them, according to Woodson, preferring even "the hard life among the Indians to the whiffs and scorns of race prejudice in the seats of Christian civilization." Race mixing among whites, African Americans, and Indians had created over several generations individuals who could not be easily categorized as red or white or black—an issue with important implications as Massachusetts sought to address the legal status of Indians, including guardianship and property rights in the 1860s and 1870s.

Relying on an 1861 survey of Massachusetts tribes, census records, and other public documents, Woodson advanced an interpretation of black-Indian relations that endorsed assimilationist models of racial amalgamation and that underscored the dominance of black-white racial categories in American society. He attributed to African Americans an important role in creating a "melting pot in which the Indians were remade and introduced to American life as whites and blacks." In this way he suggested that African Americans had played a part in the uplift of Native Americans. Yet his research also attempted to reveal the porous boundaries that existed even within the strict racial hierarchies of black and white. Woodson thus sought to problematize the delimiting of political and legal rights according to such distinctions.[19]

During the 1930s, Kenneth Porter extended Woodson's inquiry by examining the various historical forces that brought Indians and African Americans into close contact. A white man who was raised in a small Kansas town, Porter earned a Ph.D. in history at Harvard in 1936 for a dissertation on John Jacob Astor. But well before that, he had established himself as an avid student and frequent writer on African American history, a subject that competed with his attention to business history. Porter's deep interest in African American history was shaped in part by his abolitionist grandfather and his mother, who grew up in Nicodemus, Kansas, and claimed Exodusters, post-Reconstruction black migrants to the state, among her circle of friends. Porter was acquainted with African Americans who claimed Indian blood—a fact that probably also spurred his interest in racial origins and identity. But the young historian also brought powerful political convictions to his study of African Americans and Indians. Porter led a protest against segregation while he was a student at Presbyterian sponsored Sterling College in Kansas and participated in protest actions against the Ku Klux Klan during the 1920s. An outspoken Socialist who joined the party in 1932, he published a collection of poems during the Depression entitled *Christ in the Breadline* (1932).[20]

In exploring the relationship between African and Native Americans, Porter took as his point of departure anthropologist Melville Herskovits's conclusion that many African Americans rightly "claimed partial American Indian ancestry." Such roots were entirely explicable, according to Porter, given the multiple points of connection between Indians and slaves from the discovery period onward. The ties between "these two exploited races, both of which had been deprived of their land by the white man" did not, however, evolve "solely or even principally by any feeling that as members of the darker races they were natural allies." In fact, Porter observed, during the Colonial era, "Negroes were not guiltless of ill-treating Indians"; they sometimes sided with whites during the Indian wars, died at the hands of Native Americans in these violent battles, and were occasionally captured and held as prisoners by tribes.[21]

Still, Porter's examination of slaveholding tribes and the Indian removal emphasized the complexities of black-Indian relationships in ways that served to minimize enmity between the races and to lay stress on the structural forces that governed the behavior of each group. "In the absence of the white man and the white man's racial attitudes," Porter asserted, "the relations between the two races . . . were usually friendly, as was also the case when individuals of these races found themselves united by the bonds of a common servitude." Porter stressed the intermixture of black and Indian blood in part to challenge biologically determinist arguments that alleged African American inferiority and to cast doubt on the racial categories employed to separate blacks and whites. The racial makeup of both Indians and blacks had been modified to such an extent, Porter argued, as to create "a new race which might, perhaps, for want of a better term, be called 'Aframerindian.'"[22]

An anonymous reviewer of a book on Native American history pursued the point in a 1934 issue of the *Journal of Negro History*. While praising Thomas Christensen's book *The Historic Trail of the American Indians* (1934) for acknowledging the interconnections between blacks and Indians, the reviewer upbraided the author for his racist description of Latin American history. "The author cannot get away from the usual American method of trying to pick out Negroes in South American countries," the reviewer complained. "There are no Negroes as such in the Latin American Republics." Though acknowledging that citizens existed in Latin American republics who were black, brown, mestizo, and pure Latin, the reviewer insisted that that fact should not be confused with the segregated society that existed in North America:

> It is a misrepresentation of the social order in Latin America for Americans to write books on that country in such a vein. Reading what they have to say about Indians and mulattoes in that section, our prejudiced and traducing Americans would naturally wonder whether they provide separate schools, turn those classes away from hotels or force them to ride in jimcrow cars. This very style of writing also leaves the erroneous impression that in matters industrial and commercial the races may be separate as they are in the United States with the white man wringing his bread from the sweat of the poor Negro serf's brow or starving him out in the bread line when he is no longer needed for menial service. This sort of condition which is peculiar to the Nordic element in the United States does not exist in Latin America.

This searing critique (complete with its own racial insult) sought to locate a fundamental hypocrisy in white historical perspectives on

Native Americans: that the racial composition of society should be detailed while the institutional edifice that had been constructed around such racial differences should be ignored.[23]

Two historians of the interwar period located another irony in white and black perspectives on Native American history. Chapman Milling and Kenneth Porter both independently noted the strivings of whites and blacks in contemporary America to claim Indian heritage. In *Red Carolinians,* Milling described the appearance of Indian societies in Oklahoma—a phenomenon that had led to "wealthy club-women . . . searching records to verify the dimmest tradition of Indian blood that they may join. A fair-haired gentleman who more nearly resembles a Viking will declare that he is, in fact, a Choctaw." Surely few such white men and women would have similarly sought to exaggerate blood ties to African Americans. Porter observed an equally strong wish to assert Native American lineage among African Americans. "It is well known," he explained, "to anyone who is personally acquainted with any considerable number of the Negro race in this country that, while the possession of those characteristics which can only come through a proportion of white blood is tacitly admitted to be an advantage, white ancestry is not regarded as a subject for overt pride, but rather a matter to be passed over in discreet silence, like the inheritance of tainted wealth. On the other hand, an Indian ancestor is a distinction to be trumpeted abroad from the housetops." These historians appeared less conscious of their own wish to expropriate Native American history for intellectual and political purposes. Their attraction to the subject reflected an effort to contextualize a deeper preoccupation with region, race, social origins, and the ways in which these forces had shaped the dynamics of American history and the contours of modern social problems.[24]

The concerns of southern and African American historians were two factors that spurred new exploration of Native American history; historians' reaction to the immediate social and economic crises of the interwar period was a third reason for the growing attention to the subject. The political valences of the Depression era stirred a reconsideration of the white-Indian encounter amid fresh awareness of the struggles and isolation of impoverished rural dwellers, the depletion of natural resources in the United States, and the stress imposed on and sustained by those who made their living from the land. Scenes of Americans dispossessed of their land, their farms, their material goods, their life savings, and their dignity and of natural resources ravaged by disasters cast the story of the Native Americans' removal in an anguishing new light. While more than one generation of historians had constructed a triumphant narrative of white settlers advancing across the American frontier largely untroubled by the catastrophic losses sustained by Native Americans, a focus on those losses surfaced with increasing frequency during the 1930s.

Government public land policy, a theme of no small importance to historians of the American West and a matter of great political significance during the Depression era, served as a frequent entry point for reflection on Native Americans. During the 1930s, federal policy effectively ended homesteading and sought to bring more public land under governmental administrative oversight. These actions, and the larger concern over the suffering of rural people, intensified interest in the historic underpinnings of the struggle between private individuals on the one hand, and various economic and political interest groups over the public domain on the other. One result was a far less romantic vision of the frontier than that promulgated by Frederick Jackson Turner; this vantage point provided the opportunity for a new look at the fate of Native Americans.

Paul Gates, a liberal historian who trained with Frederick Merk (Turner's successor at Harvard) and served in the Agricultural Adjustment Administration during the New Deal before accepting an appointment as professor of history at Cornell, led the way in exploring the history of western land policy. Indeed, Gates leveled a hard blow to the Turner thesis in the 1930s when he challenged the premise that white settlement of western lands exemplified the advance of democracy. In a 1936 essay published in the *American Historical Review,* Gates disparaged "the halo of political and economic significance" that historians and economists had placed above the Homestead Law of 1862. He pointed readers instead to the persistent trend toward "land monopolization" that underlay the nation's allegedly democratic land policy. Far from revolutionizing the land system by distributing public lands to families willing to settle the frontier, Gates argued, the Homestead Act did very little to democratize land use. On the contrary, his research indicated that "the Homestead Law did not end the auction system or cash sales, as is generally assumed, that speculation and land monopolization continued after its adoption as widely as before, and within as well as without the law, that actual homesteading was generally confined to the less desirable lands distant from railroad lines, and that farm tenancy developed in frontier communities in many instances as a result of the monopolization of the land." In making his case, Gates pointed to Indian land treaties that had bilked Native Americans out of their territory while fattening the coffers of the railroads and other speculators. Yet in voicing discontent with the sale of public lands on the Great Plains to robber barons, Gates initially made fewer references to the mistreatment of Indians than to the swindling of white squatters.[25]

Two years later, however, Gates harshly criticized the expropriation of Indian land—a theme that would grow more insistent in much of his subsequent scholarship. A 1937 study of Indian land tenure provoked a sharp rebuke from Gates, who judged J. P. Kinney's *A Continent Lost—A Civilization Won* "not quite" a whitewash, but very close to it. "The influence of the railroads, the lumber, mining, and cattle companies, the local chambers of commerce, the land speculators, Indian traders, contractors, squatters, and homesteaders is not appreciated," Gates complained, "nor is the corruption, fraud, and chicanery which characterized the administration of Indian affairs from the time of Pierce to Cleveland recognized." The Indian land grab came to exemplify for Gates the rank exploitation, unchecked corruption, and naked greed that accompanied the disposal of land along the frontier. He directly tied the rise of land tenancy, rural poverty, and agricultural debt in Depression-era America to such historical underpinnings.[26]

Historian Randolph Downes shared Gates's interest in linking contemporary political realities to history. In one article for the *Mississippi Valley Historical Review,* he verged on presentism in tracing the roots of New Deal Indian policy to 1920s reform initiatives. At the same time, Downes was unusual in his early call for a more Indian-centered history. In his review of J. P. Kinney's work on land tenure, the University of Pittsburgh professor joined Gates in disparaging the book, but went on to assert that "the author's treatment is that of the administrator and not that of the social historian. Seldom does the Indian speak, but always does the commissioner of Indian affairs." Downes further insisted, "No true understanding of the Indian land problem can ever be conveyed without the presentation of a thorough analysis of the Indian civilization, its communal values, and the difficulty of changing those values into individualistic ones."[27]

But the cultural analysis Downes called for was not fully realized in Downes's own work, nor in that of several other scholars who pursued yet another intersection between New Deal policies and their historical underpinnings. The reconfiguration of federal policy toward Native Americans during the New Deal drew the attention of several historians to the long relationship between the federal government and the tribes, one that reached back to the earliest years of the Republic.

Downes himself focused on the initial stages of government oversight of Indian affairs in late-eighteenth-century Georgia. At this early juncture, the federal stance toward Indians in Georgia was "rather benevolent," according to Downes. In part this was so because the United States initially stood in a relatively weak position vis-à-vis the Creek nation despite success in ratifying the 1790 treaty of New York (which "did not reflect credit upon the United States"). Creek repudiation of the treaty, as well as violent incursions against white settlements on the Cumberland frontier, set the stage for war. Yet the United States' preoccupation with Indian wars in the Northwest forestalled a military advance against Georgia's Creeks. "Thus a war that was to crush the Indians on one frontier," Downes observed, "meant peace for the Creek and a postponement of their day of disaster." Still, in Downes's account the Creeks emerged as savvy agents of their own interests who cooperated with the U.S. government to preserve their land and hunting grounds from the incursion of Georgian "land robbers and game butchers." The federal presence, according to Downes, held the rapaciousness of the state in check and brokered peace on the Georgia frontier.[28]

For Robert Cotterill, a southern historian, the story of federal oversight of Indian affairs was far more dispiriting. Cotterill could not be confused with most contemporary historians in his ethnocentric views of Native Americans and his easy endorsement of white efforts to "civilize" the tribes, who, he noted, represented a "barrier to southern expansion." Yet in 1933 Cotterill described in harsh terms the flagrant abuses and defrauding of Native Americans perpetrated in the name of the United States government.[29]

The most obvious consequence of federal Indian management between 1789 and 1825, Cotterill asserted, was the catastrophic decline of Native American land holdings and the advancing Indian removal to the West. The Indians who remained in the South were, Cotterill observed, "mere tenants at will. Their domain was alienated, their power had vanished, and their independence was little more than legal fiction." Responsibility for this outcome was laid largely at the feet of the United States government and various federal officials. Cotterill described John Calhoun, Monroe's Secretary of War and hence senior official for Indian affairs, as one who "apparently construed his duty to mean the removal of the Indians by fair means or foul and the securing of their lands for the white men." "Such notorious Indian baiters as Andrew Jackson" and various Southern governors abetted Calhoun, Cotterill charged. The Indian treaties in which land was ceded were based on "force, fraud, and chicanery," and in the larger moral accounting, little credit was owed to the United States, which had doggedly pursued the dispossession and removal of native peoples. Cotterill's essay, published in the *Mississippi Valley Historical Review*, essentially charged the United States with deliberately engineering the destruction of Native Americans as a culturally distinct people. "It is," he concluded, "impossible to balance the account of injuries and benefits." He added, "The outstanding fact was that the southern Indian had practically ceased to exist as an Indian. Possibly despite high-sounding avowals of altruistic motives this was what was hoped for from the beginning. In its very nature Indian management meant Indian spoliation." This was a theme that Cotterill was still advancing nearly ten years later with even greater ferocity. His passion flowed in part, no doubt, from Cotterill's deep sympathies for the "Old South," fully voiced in a 1936 book of the same name that judged slaves as basically content in their oppression even as it bitterly condemned the treatment of Native Americans. Cotterill's equally well rooted suspicions of federal power were likewise evident in his dogmatizing about secession and Southern nationalism.[30]

Other iconoclastic historians of the interwar period who scrutinized the legacy of federal policy regarding Native Americans were equally critical of the federal government. But their hostility seemed less derived from apprehensions about the misuse of federal power per se than from the incompetence and corruption they ascribed to various political interest groups and government agents. These historians gave particularly close scrutiny to the allotment system imposed by the Dawes Severalty Act (1887).

The Dawes Act, which provided in part for the dissolution of tribal holdings in favor of individual land allotments, embodied fundamental late-nineteenth-century assimilationist ideals. Its net result for Native American tribes, however, was catastrophic, as some 90 million acres of land were ultimately lost. During the New Deal, the government finally ended the allotment plan as part of a broad effort to reform federal Indian policy. The Indian Reorganization Act of 1934 made possible some limited tribal self-government and various forms of federal assistance even though it did not entirely succeed in realizing the goals of John Collier, then Commissioner of Indian Affairs and a determined advocate of Indian "regeneration" rather than forced assimilation. But the 1934 act did mark a new era in Indian-government relations, one that ended a devastating period in Native American—and American—history.

For several historians, the shift in federal policy served as a marker that underscored the need to recast past efforts to address "the Indian problem." During the 1930s and 1940s, most professional historians who surveyed the record weighed in largely on the side of Native Americans even though their research acknowledged the complex motives and forces that shaped Indian-government relationships throughout American history. They made of the story no simple morality play, but their ultimate conclusions decisively shifted the moral balance of historical research from a celebration of white conquest to a requiem for the values of equity and decency in American democracy.

Even before the resurgence of New Deal concern with Native Americans, some historians had detected and criticized the emerging moral gravamen of scholarly work on Indians. A book review published in a 1921 issue of the *Mississippi Valley Historical Review* warned that "from the strictly historical standpoint, the reader should remember we are now in the era of apotheosis of the Indian. Our ancestors underestimated and, as a rule vilified him; but in the recoil, present-day writers usually go to the other extreme." The complaint was echoed a few years later by another critic who likewise objected to the excessive space devoted to the "Sioux outbreak of 1862" in a history of Minnesota. While the book's author offered a "fresh treatment" that succeeded in conveying "the Indian point of view," he erred, the reviewer charged, in dwelling upon the Indian war and its consequences. Despite such grumbling, however, interest in Native American history only accelerated, and with it came an ever more sharply drawn calculus of white misdeeds and Indian suffering. By

1938, a reviewer could summarize the findings of a study of the Bannock Indian War as "the usual violated treaty and white encroachment."[31]

Certainly the modern scholarly temperament was apparent in one of the most compelling studies of government-Indian relations, Loring Priest's *Uncle Sam's Stepchildren: The Reformation of United States Indian Policy, 1865–1887*, published in 1942. Priest began his research in 1931 as a Ph.D. candidate at Harvard University, like Paul Gates under the direction of Frederick Merk. He hoped to explore the history of government-Indian affairs in the period between the Civil War and the passage of the Dawes Severalty Act, in part to add context to sweeping New Deal changes in federal policy. Before he had finished his research, Priest observed, the Roosevelt administration "had wiped" the Dawes Act "from the statute books after bitter attacks which made analysis of the reasons for its adoption even more desirable." Of his 1942 work he wrote, "The following account in many ways repeats the debates of today. Because of current disagreements, particular effort has been made to fulfill the historian's obligation to discuss controversial issues impartially." Of the "millions of words" written about Native Americans, Priest asserted, few had been expended on the vital topic of federal policy toward the tribes. Instead, the Rutgers historian noted, "only strange tribal customs, bloodshed, robbery, and hate have been considered sufficiently exciting to merit attention." This characterization was not, of course, true even in the 1930s, when Priest began his research. But in yielding to the historian's ever-present temptation to overstate his innovation, Priest took a relatively modest liberty. *Uncle Sam's Stepchildren* was indeed a fresh, careful, and frank assessment of two decades of Indian "reform."[32]

Priest rooted his analysis in what he saw as fundamental cultural conflict between two different racial groups. "Experience could not have molded people with more variable tastes and traditions than the Indian and the settler," he wrote. "The white man's concept of individual ownership was as alien to the red man as the Indian's communal practices were to Europeans." The historical record revealed, Priest asserted, "three centuries of abuse" that Native Americans steadfastly resisted but ultimately fell victim to, in part because of "the superior number and equipment of their rivals" and the relentless military, economic, legal, and political pressure whites exerted against the tribes. "Few people in the history of the world," Priest explained, "have suffered so long or so severely as the American Indian."[33]

In focusing on white strategies to address the "Indian problem" in the years following the Civil War, Priest narrated a history of failed policies ranging from concentration (an attempt to relocate tribes to specific areas of little value to the railroads and white settlers) to the proposed transfer of administrative authority from one branch of the federal government (the Interior) to another (the War Department). Priest likewise lumped together in this list of losses the disappointing performance of the Board of Indian Commissioners, created in 1869 to examine and recommend reforms regarding Indian affairs, and the federally sanctioned use of churches to nominate Indian agents, a plan that sought to ensure honesty among such officials but instead revealed the enormous fractiousness among American religious denominations. Despite this dismal record, Priest considered the rising interest in Indian affairs a hopeful sign in the period 1865–1880 and saw it as a necessary stage in the evolution of more enlightened federal policy.

The most incisive analysis advanced by *Uncle Sam's Stepchildren* focused on the late-nineteenth-century dismantlement of long-standing features of government policy on Native Americans. Here Priest saw through the chaos of late-nineteenth-century political jockeying to grasp the critical institutional factors that were embedded in reform initiatives. Federal abandonment of the treaty system in favor of direct legislation, reform of government annuity distributions for Indians (including attempts to institute the equivalent of a workfare system), and increased congressional expenditures for Indian education heralded a new epoch in federal oversight of Native Americans. Each measure, Priest emphasized, came with a complex array of costs and benefits.

Indeed, Priest stressed that a coercive and complicated drive for assimilation undergirded the entire reform agenda. Christian humanitarians who expressed sympathy for the plight of Native Americans argued that Indians would survive only if they abandoned everything that made them a culturally distinct people and civilization. As Priest baldly explained the reformers' position:

The only way to overcome racial antipathies, they maintained, was to eliminate the hostility produced by contrasting ways of life. As wholesale extinction of the red men would be the inevitable outcome of any fight to retain native customs, destruction of all practices marking the Indians as a separate race seemed advisable even though many perished in the process. The dictates of civilization might seem harsh; but with fifty million whites facing only a quarter million Indians, nothing was to be gained by ignoring them. To save the individual Indian, the race must be destroyed. In spite of efforts to create an impression that their position was a result of compassion for the Indian, most champions of assimilation supported the policy because they believed no feature of Indian life was worth preserving.

In this conclusion, Priest echoed the views of Robert Cotterill and those of several other interwar historians who boldly equated Indian removal and reform with extermination.[34]

The Dawes Severalty Act, for Priest, represented the culmination of a confused, contradictory, and ultimately unsatisfactory government response to Native Americans. "Most friends of the measure were more interested in securing Indian land," Priest observed, "than in establishing a just policy for the control of Indian affairs." The historian traced the clashing motives of competing interest groups as Congress considered land allotment and citizenship provisions. Neither policy came without costs for Native Americans, who lost crucial government protection in the reform stampede toward tribal dissolution. In a nation that rejected various forms of universal social provision for its citizens, Native Americans at least maintained the possibilities of indispensable federal assistance as long as they retained their independent status. Such an argument accented the importance of the state in safeguarding the rights of native peoples—an ideological position very much in tune with New Deal liberalism.[35]

Yet for all of Priest's insight into the rapaciousness and condescension of those who advanced the reform of Indian policy, he shared their paternalistic attitude toward Native Americans, whom he compared to African Americans after emancipation in being poorly prepared for the rights and responsibilities of American citizenship. It is perhaps for this reason that Priest ultimately judged the architects of late-nineteenth-century Indian reform rather generously as citizens often animated by idealism and betrayed by the misapplication of their principles. The best among these reformers had at least sought to advance through specific legislative action "America's first systematic effort to provide for Indian welfare." That the program they enacted proved "disastrous," Priest suggested, ought to serve as a reminder of the possible pitfalls inherent in New Deal Indian reform measures. A move back toward isolation carried considerable risk to Native Americans, who confronted "the unenviable choice of returning to tribal life or breaking from their race." Priest endorsed instead an approach that would balance individual land ownership with "racial preservation by careful government administration." What such a program would entail he left unspecified. But he clearly envisaged the cultural survival of Native Americans in an environment that encouraged economic advancement for individuals as well as federal assistance for native peoples as a distinct people. It was a position very much in tune with the moderate thrust of the New Deal reform agenda.[36]

For all its insight into the tragic story of Indian treatment by the federal government, *Uncle Sam's Stepchildren* still belonged to a long tradition in historical writing that viewed Native American history from the outside looking in. Interpretations that stressed white atrocities and Indian victimization, however sympathetic, missed a crucial dimension of Native American history—a sense of Indians themselves. This remained an elusive theme for most historians of the interwar era, many of whom relied on government documents to trace the experience of the tribes. Still, the period gave rise to some powerful exceptions to this rule, as scholars began to recognize and rectify a fundamental imbalance in the narrative of Native American history. None rose more fully to the challenge than Angie Debo. Indeed, Debo exemplifies another crucial factor in the rising historical interest in Native American history during the interwar years. In this instance, the life history, curiosity, imagination, and daring of an individual historian converged with shifting intellectual trends, generational change, and a vibrant historical moment to redraw the boundaries of scholarly inquiry.

Deprived throughout almost her entire life as a historian of the various privileges an academic appointment would have conferred, Debo labored in painful isolation amid discouraging circumstances for the better part of sixty years to reveal the ways in which Native Americans experienced and made their own history. She began to chronicle the history of Native Americans in the 1930s; by 1945 she had produced three path-breaking books. Hundreds of articles and several other major works followed, including a full-scale biography of

Geronimo published in 1976, when Debo was nearly ninety years old. By then, Native American history had emerged as a field in its own right, with growing recognition from the American historical profession. Few traced its roots back as far as the 1930s to the pioneering efforts of Angie Debo. Yet the connections were deep and unmistakable.

Born on January 30, 1890—"the very date of my birth is the date of the closing of the frontier," she later recalled—Angie Debo was the daughter of homesteaders who fled the Kansas prairie in 1899 for the Oklahoma territory amid falling farm prices, rising tenancy, and drought. Debo spent much of the rest of her life in Marshall, Oklahoma, where her parents established their farm. Although she had hoped to catch a glimpse of Indians as her family made their way from Kansas to Oklahoma in a covered wagon, all she could see were homesteaders. "Indian territory," she would remember, "was farther away from the experience of Homesteaders than any part of the world is now. All I knew about Indians is what I read in public school."[37]

Public school offered precious little, however, to students such as Debo, who wanted to do more than "mark time on the farm." Her early education was acquired in a one-room schoolhouse that was in session only a few months a year. Debo's successful completion of common school ended any opportunity for further study—at least for a while. She waited for four years until Marshall provided a one-year high school, which Debo attended in 1906, traveling three and a half miles on horseback to do so. After that year, she later recalled, she "waited around some more. There was no library, no magazines, and only the one book our parents managed to buy for each of us children as a Christmas present." Finally, in 1910 Marshall opened a four-year high school, which Debo attended; she graduated with the first class of seniors in 1913. By then she was twenty-three years old and had been a schoolteacher herself for seven years. Two more years of teaching in rural areas followed; in 1915 Debo went on to study history, first at the University of Oklahoma, where she earned a bachelor's degree in 1918, and later at the University of Chicago, where she was awarded a master's degree in 1924 for a thesis on American diplomatic history.[38]

Debo's experience at the University of Chicago rocked the young historian's sense of her place in the world as she confronted what felt like insurmountable barriers to further professional success. As a graduate student, Debo thrived in the rigorous intellectual community that existed at Chicago and felt no hint at first of the prejudice that would soon obstruct her career. But this cosmopolitan environment turned provincial as graduation neared and the university's students sought teaching positions in academic institutions. Some thirty colleges and universities turned to Chicago's history department in search of suitable young professors. Yet as Debo recalled, "twenty-nine of them said that they wouldn't take a woman under any circumstances. One of them preferred a man. They would take a woman if they couldn't get a man. One of the thirty. It hit all of us pretty hard." For all her struggles to acquire learning, Debo was ill prepared for the sex discrimination that pervaded the academic profession, and the discipline of history, in the 1920s. "The history field," she began to feel, "was closed and shut and barred against women. There wasn't anything at all that a woman could do to enter it."

Debo's discouraging sense of the academic profession contained more than a kernel of truth. Academic appointments for women historians at coeducational institutions, though not entirely unavailable, were indeed few and far between. Women's colleges and teacher training schools proved more welcoming to female scholars, but they imposed heavy demands on faculty that made them less than appealing to ambitious graduate students who wanted to combine teaching with a scholarly career. The confrontation with such realities appeared to carry a particularly sharp sting for women who had enjoyed great approbation as graduate students, as had Debo, whose master's thesis was quickly published in the Smith College Studies in History series. At the age of ninety, Debo still vividly recalled how devastated she was by her encounter with such prejudice in the academy. "It was a terrible shock to me," she remembered. She could not recall feeling marginalized as a student, nor did she feel singled out for criticism of her work. "Whatever discrimination I have had," she explained, "was in getting a position in a history department at a college or university."[39]

After leaving Chicago, Debo did manage to land an academic position in the history department of West Texas State Teachers College on the Panhandle: she taught in a high school that was affiliated with the school. She also began to pursue a course of study at the University of Oklahoma toward a Ph.D. Perhaps Debo believed that another advanced degree would brighten her prospects for a scholarly career and lift her over the hurdles imposed by sex discrimination in the academic job market. Whatever her motives, she chose Edward Everett Dale as her mentor at Oklahoma, a decision that led her to Native American history.[40]

Dale had earned a Ph.D. at Harvard under the tutelage of Frederick Jackson Turner in 1922, a fact that underscores the profound personal influence that Turner and his student and successor Frederick Merk had on the intellectual substance of Native American history. By legitimizing social history that took the West and the frontier as worthy subjects of study, these two historians deeply influenced their students, who extended their professors' mandate into entirely fresh fields of inquiry. The lines connecting interwar historians who wrote about Native Americans repeatedly lead back to Turner or Merk, in some cases to both. Despite, or perhaps because, of the inadequacies of their own perspectives on American Indians, these two scholars in a very real sense left a deep imprint on the study of Native Americans.

As a young graduate student Dale came to view his adopted state of Oklahoma as an extraordinary setting for unique research on the history of the American West. He wrote his dissertation on the history of cattle ranching in Oklahoma, a subject he had learned something about firsthand as a range rider on the Texas Panhandle. Dale devoted his entire scholarly career to research on Oklahoma, much of it focused on cattlemen and Indians. Far from encouraging an antiquarian perspective on local history, he instructed his students to view the history of Oklahoma as a rare opportunity to examine in microcosm sweeping trends that had transformed American society. Unlike the slow evolution that gradually altered the national landscape over the centuries, cataclysmic change occurred in Oklahoma within the lifetime of a single generation. That fact made the state an especially rewarding laboratory for historical research. The rich cache of untapped sources available in Oklahoma only heightened Dale's belief in the value for young historians of such regional study.[41]

Although Dale largely subscribed to Turner's equation of frontier settlement with the advance of democracy, the Oklahoma professor early took a keen interest in Native American history. He wrote his senior thesis at the University of Oklahoma on the location of Indian tribes in Oklahoma and his master's thesis at Harvard on white settlement in the territory. Debo once accused Dale of seeing the frontier as a "heroic epic." He ignored "the predatory forces that warped its creative urge," perhaps because the professor had "the naive, unconscious imperialism of the pioneer who went out into the wilderness with the innocent intention of owning it all." But over time, Debo allowed, Dale came to see better "that American expansion was indeed a *mixed* story of sordidness and heroism." An invitation from the Institute for Government Research to join a small group of experts in surveying the living conditions of Native Americans in 1926–1927 at the behest of the Department of the Interior may have deepened such sympathies in Dale. After months of travel through reservations across the country, the group issued what became known as the Meriam Report, a stark depiction of the appalling circumstances in which most American Indians were living in the early twentieth century. The study described infant mortality rates that were twice the national average and a similarly soaring incidence of disease, illiteracy, and poverty.[42]

Dale's exposure to these realities likely sharpened his perception of the need for broader research in the field of Native American history. When Debo was searching for a dissertation topic, it was Dale who pointed her to a superb collection of manuscript records held by the University of Oklahoma detailing the Acts of the Choctaw nation. He suggested that Debo write a history of the tribe in the post–Civil War period; the idea resonated with Debo, in part perhaps because she saw an unusual opportunity to make a place for herself in a field largely untouched by leading scholars in American history. "All I wanted," Debo later remembered of these years, "was to have a chance to create something instead of just wasting my life. And I simply had to build my career in fields where I did have a chance. And I could rise and I had a fair field and no favors."[43]

Debo was likewise influenced by Grant Foreman, an archivist and scholar who came to Oklahoma in 1899 as a field worker for the Dawes Commission and remained to become an avid student of the Five Civilized Tribes (the Cherokees, Choctaws, Seminoles, Chickasaws, and Creeks). Foreman's exhaustive efforts to locate and preserve archival material on Native Americans proved especially important to young scholars such as Debo who would do so much to advance the field. Foreman himself, though not a professional historian, wrote several books on Native American history and provided a model of how one could advance a scholarly field outside the academy. He did much of the spadework in tracing the removal of the five tribes, scholarship so sound, in Debo's opinion, that contemporary Creeks she later interviewed for her own research largely confirmed his account of their experience. Foreman's deep empathy for Native Americans infused his work, leading some to dismiss it as sentimentality. Debo, however, credited Foreman and his wife, Carolyn, likewise a historian of Oklahoma, with "pointing the way" toward a more Indian-centered history.[44]

Debo proceeded from these various influences to write a landmark history of the Choctaw Republic as her dissertation, unusual not only in the wealth of new material she amassed but in her effort to grant historical agency to native peoples. In Debo's work, Native Americans emerged as authentic men and women who struggled to preserve their culture, land, and institutions in the face of the relentless incursion by whites. Debo's dissertation was the result of a prodigious research effort, one that took her from Muskogee to Washington, D.C., and from barely examined tribal government manuscripts to court records, census statistics, elections returns, interviews with surviving Choctaws, and painstaking perusal of Indian newspapers. Her aim throughout was to record "the history of this gifted people, who maintained for so long a distinct social and political existence in the midst of a crowding alien population." Although the chronological focus of the study forced careful inquiry into the attenuation of tribal autonomy, the incursion of whites, and the complex relationships between the Choctaw Republic and the United States, Debo diverged from many historians in never losing her focus on the tribe itself and the complexities of the Choctaw experience.

Her skill in achieving this goal derived not only from Debo's steadfast concern with the Choctaws as a people and her willingness to hunt down a wide range of manuscript materials, but also from her deftness in interweaving social, economic, and political history. Debo also brought to her study of Native American history a larger interpretive framework constructed in part from her previous study of American diplomatic history. Debo came away from her training in that field with an acute awareness of imperialism as a historical force. This was not, of course, an inevitable consequence of inquiry into the history of American foreign policy, and not all students of the field shared Debo's sensitivity. Debo, however, was inclined to see in the experience of Native Americans a confrontation with white imperial power with all the coercion and dehumanization that accompanied aggressive expansionism.[45]

The book that resulted from Debo's dissertation, *The Rise and Fall of the Choctaw Republic* (1934) thus constituted a departure of singular importance from the narratives of victimization that characterized so much Native American history. The Choctaws, to be sure, suffered at the hands of white settlers in Debo's historical account, but they came alive as active participants and shapers of their own destiny. This theme surfaced early, as Debo traced the fateful Choctaw alliance with the Confederacy during the Civil War, a compact that devolved from a reasoned, if ultimately catastrophic, tribal assessment of strategic interests. Debo also depicted the Choctaws as shrewd players in a complex game of negotiation with the United States government during Reconstruction, as they initially preserved the unity of the Choctaw nation even as they lost some land and their slaves in the bargain. Despite enormous economic pressure, ushered in first by the arrival of the railroads and then by the spread of coal mining, the Choctaws managed to maintain significant tribal autonomy for a generation, even amid a steady flow of white immigrants. But in the 1890s, carefully constructed bulwarks against white encroachment on tribal land, institutions, and authority began to fall in ways that ultimately led to what Debo characterized as "surrender" and "dissolution."

Debo's careful analysis of class stratification within the tribe was one of most notable features of her study. Here she revealed a deep interest in the structural forces that shaped inequality and in the human costs extracted from capital accumulation. Neither reality was far removed from Depression-era Oklahoma, where rural men and women endured terrible impoverishment. Debo observed that the Choctaws kept alive a tradition, backed by law, of common land ownership. Yet even in this circumstance, some members of the tribe managed to enrich themselves while many other poorer Choctaws "lived such a hand-to-mouth existence that a crop shortage always threatened them with starvation." In the post–Civil War period, wealthier Indians relied on white and black tenant labor to farm their land, thereby advancing a system of agriculture common throughout the postwar South and of course still evident in the Oklahoma Debo inhabited in the 1930s.[46]

Debo joined her consideration of economy to politics in a lengthy section of the book that explored the political characteristics of the Choctaw Republic. To manage their increasingly complex web of economic interests, the tribe passed new laws and expanded their political institutions in the late nineteenth century to safeguard the integrity of the tribe. The Choctaw constitution reflected Anglo-American influences and stipulated executive, judicial, and legislative branches of government as well as a bill of rights. Indeed, the tribe enjoyed an "active political life," according to Debo, who found in the history of the Choctaw "the influence of many able personalities." According to Debo, full-blooded Choctaws seemed most drawn to political activism while "intermarried citizens and mixed bloods usually devoted themselves to money making, though they sometimes sought to manipulate the elections from the background." The political history of the Republic, in Debo's rendition, while largely orderly, reflected all the tumult of late-nineteenth-century American civic life. This was especially so in 1892 when Progressive Party loyalists and National Party enthusiasts came to blows over a close election. With each side accusing the other of corruption, feeling ran so high that several Nationals resorted to political assassination in an effort to wrest power from the Progressives. In an ironic twist, the principal chief, or governor, called in the U.S. Indian agent and the cavalry to restore order.

Debo's close examination of the ties between Indians and the federal government gave her an opportunity to stress the determined efforts of the Choctaw to preserve their independence while wresting whatever concessions they could from the United States. The Choctaw demonstrated shrewd political sense in tactical moves, ranging from their explicit attempt to influence the appointment of particular Indian agents to their resolute exertions on behalf of fair treaty terms. They possessed, Debo argued, "remarkable ability as diplomats and constitutional lawyers."[47]

But such skills ultimately were no match for the federal onslaught against tribal power in the 1890s. Massive white migration into the Choctaw Republic created a situation in which the tribe ran a minority government and controlled lands that white settlers coveted. The Five Civilized Tribes had been exempted from the Dawes Severalty Act. But from the time of that legislation (1887) forward, the writing was on the wall, and the tribes knew it. When the Choctaws resisted even the appointment of the Dawes Commission, charged in 1893 with negotiating terms with the Five Civilized Tribes for tribal land holdings, the United States held out the threat of even more draconian action. An internal political struggle within the Choctaw Republic ensued, with full bloods who opposed the Dawes plan losing control to those who favored cooperation. Eventually, the federal government managed to liquidate the tribe's estate, abrogating treaties when necessary; most vestiges of tribal government were likewise erased. Thus the Choctaw ceased to exist as an independent nation. Although such a judgment dovetailed with popular conceptions of the "disappearing red man," Debo was well aware that Native Americans remained a visible and vital presence despite the onslaught they had endured. What they, and America, lost, Debo maintained, was independence and power—a fact that deserved to be stated in the starkest and most brutal terms available to a historian.

In tracing the melancholy path toward what she concluded was virtual extinction, Debo emphasized the ways in which the Choctaw confronted a "more numerous and aggressive race." Indeed, she expressed deep pessimism that any more positive outcome could have emerged from the white-Indian encounter. As Oklahoma became a state, and the Choctaws' identity became fused with "the composite citizenship of the newest of American commonwealths," the tribe "had reached the goal that they had unwittingly chosen as their ultimate destiny when they had first set their feet upon the white man's road." Although Debo measured her tone, she clearly judged the outcome a tragic loss of an extraordinary people. In making this case, the book, like much of Debo's subsequent work, tried to find a balance point—one that set the resolve and power of Native Americans against the imperial force brought down upon them. She sought to give Native Americans historical agency without minimizing the oppressive force exerted against them. All the while a deeper intention led Debo to humanize and bring to life the richness of the Choctaw people and their nation.[48]

That Debo succeeded in this goal was evident from the response to her dissertation. Despite Debo's marginal status within the hierarchy of the academic profession, *The Rise and Fall of the Choctaw Republic* received great acclaim from American historians on its publication by the University of Oklahoma Press in 1934. A year later, the American Historical Association awarded Debo the Dunning Prize, an honor bestowed annually for the best book in American history. Laudatory reviews appeared in the professional journals, including one penned by Annie Abel, who remarked that "the narrative is most illuminating and instructive and, to American national pride, not at all flattering." Another reviewer made special note of Debo's "sympathy and a realization of the vital problems of the Choctaw." Interestingly, both the *American Historical Review* and the *Mississippi Valley Historical Review* assigned the book to women for review—a move justified by the prominence of Abel in the field of Native American history, but perhaps also indicative of the gender dynamics of the profession.[49]

Despite such great recognition, Debo remained alone as a scholar—a fact that apparently did little to dampen her resolve or commitment to Native American history. As soon as she finished *The Rise and Fall of the Choctaw Republic,* she began work on a sequel that would explore the fate of the Five Civilized Tribes in eastern Oklahoma as tribal government came to an end and the allotment system was put into place. Work on this book constituted one of the great challenges of Debo's life. She claimed to have never anticipated when she began her research what she would stumble upon: "that all of eastern Oklahoma was dominated by a criminal conspiracy to cheat the Indians out of their property and that corrupted the legislature also." It was not the story that her mentor, Edward Everett Dale, expected her to tell, either, when he enlisted the support of the Commissioner of Indian Affairs in permitting Debo access to long-buried government documents. In the book that emerged from her research, *And Still the Waters Run* (1940), Debo advanced a crushing analysis of the corruption, moral depravity, and criminal activity that underlay white administration and execution of the allotment policy.[50]

Sharpening both the language and force of her argument from her initial book on the Choctaws, Debo began her new study with a blunt assessment of the Dawes Commission. She traced the years of tribal negotiations, when the commission issued countless misleading reports describing conditions among the Five Civilized Tribes. Among other problems, it emphasized the Indians' mistreatment of white settlers and the economic inequality among members of various tribes, which left some Indians wealthy and others impoverished. Debo noted that most students of Native American history relied on the commission's reports as evidence. But the reports, Debo asserted, were worthless as factual descriptions of Native American society. "They are no more objective," Debo asserted, "than the manifestoes issued by the average government before entering upon a war of conquest."⁵¹

Debo's invocation of imperial ambitions, so reminiscent of her earlier work on the Choctaws, was joined in her new study to a powerful antimonopoly argument. Debo insisted that "land hunger," rather than concern for "the poor Indian" and white victims of violence, lay at the root of posturing by the Dawes Commission. The commission could have made a "fairly good case" out of its plans to terminate tribal rule and claim possession to Indian lands if it had couched its argument against the Five Civilized Tribes in terms of "manifest destiny" or the rights of a majority to oppress a minority. But, she observed, "civilized men have seldom been willing to state their motives so baldly." Instead, in a position riddled with hypocrisy, the commission criticized the small number of Indians who had amassed some wealth while others lived in "abject poverty." Such an assertion held "the Indians to abstract and ideal rather than comparative standards," Debo observed, for Choctaw and Creek tribal policy went much farther toward "preventing land monopoly than any law ever passed by an American state." Commission charges of corruption among tribal governments were also laughable, the historian ruefully commented. Given "subsequent developments in Oklahoma," the tribes were no "more dishonest than the state government that supplanted them."⁵²

Debo acknowledged the difficult task that faced the Dawes Commission in assessing the value of Indian land and carrying out the allotment policy once terms were agreed upon. But the entire process exacted an awful price in "human suffering." Furthermore, incompetent federal administration of this massive project—bad enough in itself for Native Americans who were losing territory and nation—created enormous opportunities for graft among white federal and state officials, settlers, land speculators, and a host of other villains—among them some well-respected Oklahomans. Using office files from the Department of the Interior's Indian Territory Division, the Commissioner of Indian Affairs, the Secretary of the Interior, and the Superintendent for the Five Civilized Tribes, among countless other sources, Debo exposed the web of political patronage and corruption that permeated administration of the new Indian allotment policy. She devoted considerable attention to the long record of Indian resistance (including an entire chapter entitled "The Voice of the Indian Territory") and throughout her narrative demonstrated at every turn the perspectives and strategies of various tribes and individual Native Americans. She distinguished herself from "oversentimental defenders of the Indians" by detailing the range of motives, actions, and responses among the Five Civilized Tribes; but there could be no doubt that Debo viewed their miscalculations and mistakes as relatively minor in the greater moral quotient embedded in her historical analysis.

Indeed, if "the devil is in the details," Debo's research uncovered many Satans. As she examined the allotment policy, and found document after document full of appalling evidence, Debo began to see the outlines of an "orgy of plunder and exploitation probably unprecedented in American history." From 1898, when the Curtis Act imposed an end to tribal government and allotment began, tribal funds dwindled under federal management, and there was no proper accounting of expenditures. The conclusion was unmistakable from the federal record: Indians themselves had carried the largest costs involved in "closing out" their nations. Through leases and sales, many fraudulent, Native Americans lost control over most of their allotted lands. While not all suffered equally, "all classes of Indians" ultimately lost. "The wealthy," Debo explained, "were reduced to the common level through the loss of their excess holdings. . . . the humbler citizens were in a state of extreme destitution." Those who refused to accept their allotment wound up in the very worst condition—living in constant fear of being uprooted from their dwellings and left homeless when whites succeeded in wresting control over their allotments.[53]

All of this took place amid a boom atmosphere stoked by the discovery of oil in the Indian Territory in 1897 and the excitement over Oklahoma's statehood in 1907. The stakes were high, with oil and gas leases, abundant land, and mineral rights in play. Many whites proudly identified themselves as "grafters"—a term that become synonymous with one who dealt in Indian lands. They employed a perverse range of tactics—both intricate and effective—in fleecing the tribes. Very few of their misdeeds were lost on Debo.[54]

While other scholars bemoaned such depredations by whites against Native Americans, Debo differed from them in constructing a chain of evidence that implicated specific individuals—businessmen, land officials, real estate agents, and politicians. She named names and carefully showed in microcosm a phenomenon that had resulted in a vast swindle of Native Americans. The fraud, she maintained, was relatively mild—at least comparatively speaking—under federal authority. Soon after Oklahoma became a state, however, new federal legislation removed crucial restrictions on the sale and conveyance of land allotments, including those attached to the land rights of minors. This created fresh opportunities for fraud that "reputable" Oklahomans aggressively sought and quickly exploited.

Among those who engaged in a "battle for the spoils" were various white religious figures. Far from elaborating the romantic version of American Protestantism that undergirded so much American history, Debo specified the ways in which preachers and churches participated in the vandalizing of Native Americans. The Five Civilized Tribes were especially vulnerable to entreaties from organized Protestantism, Debo recounted, because they had long before converted to Christianity and embraced Protestantism "with deep mystical feeling and a strong sense of moral obligation and family and group solidarity." Presbyterian, Baptist, and Methodist churches dotted even the most remote Indian settlements. In the 1920s, an Oklahoma college run by the American Baptist Missionary Society "began to clutch at the property of oil-rich Indians." The Commissioner of Indian Affairs endorsed the effort, "apparently," Debo observed, because he "thought Indian money might as well be diverted from its usual channels of waste and spoliation and used for a good purpose." A million dollars of Indian funds in cash or trust eventually found its way into the school's coffers. Soon "the Baptists began to solicit contributions too eagerly," and a cozy relationship between the Indian Office and the Baptists was cemented.[55]

Far from attributing her findings to the particularities of Oklahoma, Debo insisted that what happened in that state could not be separated from the larger history of the nation. As she put it: "It should not be necessary to point out that Oklahomans are no worse than their neighbors, for this is only one episode—although the most dramatic episode—in a process that constitutes an unrecorded chapter in the history of every American frontier. But the reaction of this process upon the ideals and standards of successive frontier communities is a factor in the formation of the American character that should no longer be disregarded by students of social institutions." In effect, Debo offered a reverse Turner thesis—one that joined the advance of the frontier with the diminution of democratic values and the emergence of a destructive American character.[56]

Work on *And Still the Waters Run* profoundly demoralized Debo. Sitting in the basement of the Interior Department building for months, the historian sorted through bundles of documents "tied in the red tape . . . and I would untie those bundles, you know, and take notes." Debo spent "weeks—months at the Five Tribes agency over in Muskogee. I'd begin to find out more things and they got worse all the time." She later recalled that the time she spent doing her research for *And Still the Waters Run* was "the most unhappy experience of my life." She felt that "everything" she "touched was slimy." As the scope of the malfeasance widened, and names and faces became attached to the calumny, anxiety began to mingle with distaste. "When I knew what they did and what honest people who had tried to check it were up against, I had a feeling of fear as I went through those dark corridors and basements and so on. I just had a feeling of fear." The grafters, Debo had discovered, were "among the leaders of Oklahoma society in 1934 at the time I wrote this. And their deeds, their achievements were on the front page of all the Oklahoma newspapers. And the social activities of their wives were on the society page." Still, Debo believed it was a story that had to be told. She settled down in 1936 to turn her research into a coherent narrative.[57]

Little wonder that Debo would later describe the writing process as a nightmare of worry and frustration. "I enjoy writing a book just as a galley slave enjoyed rowing, and this one was *worst* of all," she later said of *And Still the Waters Run*. The summer of 1936 continued the record heat and drought that afflicted Oklahoma, and much of the rest of the nation, during the Great Depression. "While I was typing," Debo remembered, "the perspiration used to just run in streams down my face and body." After finishing each chapter, Debo would read her work to her mother. Her mother's response was also dispiriting. "She would say, 'Nobody will ever publish that book.'" There was ample reason for such pessimism.[58]

Debo submitted *And Still the Waters Run* to the fledgling University of Oklahoma Press in July 1936. The Press had demonstrated its commitment to the field of Native American history early in the 1930s by starting a series entitled "The Civilization of the American Indian." Even so, Joseph Brandt, the young editor of the Press, quickly recognized Debo's manuscript as "one of the most valuable books ever offered the University Press." But he also foresaw the firestorm its publication might set off. In a letter to Debo, Brandt acknowledged that "there will be some tough problems, I can see, with some of the grafters still living, and if the book passes our readers, I can see that the Wailing Wall of Jerusalem will not have a monopoly on tears." Brandt solicited Commissioner of Indian Affairs John Collier's opinion of Debo's manuscript. Collier in turn passed the book on to D'Arcy McNickle, then Collier's assistant and a mixed-blood Indian, a writer on Native American affairs, and a novelist. McNickle attested that "nothing quite so ambitious has been attempted. Indian history has been so neglected by serious students and so overrun by sentimentalists and free-lance commentators of various stripes and colors that it is a real joy to come across a work of such competence." Brandt solicited still another opinion, this time from a law professor at Oklahoma, who warned of the likelihood that libel suits would be filed if the press proceeded. Yet the work, Floyd Wright attested, was a "masterpiece" and well worth the risk involved in publication. Further consideration by the president of the university, however, resulted in the cancellation of Debo's contract. In reaching his decision, the Oklahoma president relied in part on the advice of a professor in the history department, who Debo apparently believed was her mentor, Edward Everett Dale. In fact, another historian—Morris Wardell—was the one who advised against publication, citing concerns of retaliation by prominent donors against the university. Wardell was, he confessed, "afraid of the book."[59]

Deeply discouraged, Debo returned to her life in Marshall and began the search for another publisher. She later remembered: "This frontier area was so remote from educational institutions and the knowledge of such things that I was sort of buried there. The fact that I had done good work didn't count very much. That was a period in which I had plenty to discourage me. I had no resources of any kind." But she found her way, in part through two New Deal projects. In 1937, she served as an editor and interviewer for the Works Progress Administration Indian-Pioneer History Project, directed by Grant Foreman and designed to record the history of Oklahoma's earliest settlers. Three years later, Debo accepted a position as director of Oklahoma's Federal Writers Project, for which she supervised preparation of a guidebook on Oklahoma. Although Debo herself wrote the chapter on the history of Oklahoma, another text was substituted when the book was eventually published—even though it carried her name. The censorship seems unsurprising, given that Debo's original chapter began with the sentence "Oklahoma came early under the white man's imperial ambitions." The chapter that was published, by contrast, described the land as "vacant."[60]

Amid all these activities, and despite financial hardship and her discouraging experience with *And Still the Waters Run,* Debo continued her scholarship on Native American history. The Social Science Research Council had provided some funding for her work on that book, and she now turned again to the SSRC, with success, for support for another study—this one on the Creek Indians. Finally, in 1940, Princeton University Press issued *And Still the Waters Run,* largely thanks to its new head, Joseph Brandt, who left the University of Oklahoma Press the year after the university rejected Debo's manuscript.[61]

The book was instantly recognized as a remarkable achievement. Grant Foreman wrote in the *Mississippi Valley Historical Review* that the study was a "devastating indictment"—"one of the most comprehensive and convincing" he had ever read. As Foreman explained, "it is not an indictment only of the people first attracted to the Indian country that is now Oklahoma to exploit the immigrant Indians . . . but it is an indictment of the white race, for the reader will recall similar exploitation in every state where the interests of the whites conflicted with those of the Indians." A review in the *Journal of Southern History* echoed this appraisal, noting that "Miss Debo is all the more devastating because of her complete objectivity."[62]

The delay in the publication of *And Still the Waters Run* meant that Debo's study of the Creeks appeared just a year later. Observing that "standard historians" had never accurately told the history of the tribe, Debo suggested that whites had much to learn about their own history from a consideration of these Native Americans. As she had done with the Choctaws, Debo sought to tell the story of the Creeks in their own terms. She did so, one reviewer observed, "with deep sympathy" and, as another historian noted, "always looking through Indian eyes and writing largely from Indian sources." Entitled *The Road to Disappearance* (1941), the book carried an apt title not only for a work on the Creek nation but also for Debo's near fate as a historian.[63]

For all the intellectual dominance of Frederick Jackson Turner's vision of the American frontier, the interwar years brought a lively reconsideration of one of the most crucial and ill-conceived dimensions of romanticized visions of Western history and frontier building. A fresh perspective on Native American history emerged from a great many sources, including the hesitant forays of early American historians, the ambitious striving of southern and African American historians, the hard-nosed criticism leveled by scholars sympathetic to New Deal liberal reform initiatives, and the penetrating research pursued by historians surrounded by the suffering visible everywhere in Depression-era Oklahoma. With their strong moral valences and powerful political convictions, however contradictory their various ideological allegiances, interwar historians pointed the way to a more modern and complex reading of the narrative of American history, even if many later overlooked these compelling origins.

CHAPTER FOUR

History, Class, and Culture between the World Wars

As Louis Adamic has pointed out, it is to Ellis Island rather than to Plymouth Rock that a great part of the American people trace their history in America. More people have died in industrial accidents than in subduing the wilderness and fighting the Revolution. It is these people rather than the frontiersmen who constitute the real historical background and the heroic tradition of the mass of urban Americans. . . . In the still unexplored history of the nondominant cultural groups of the industrial cities lies the story of an emerging industrial culture that represents the dynamic cultural frontier of modern America.

—CAROLINE F. WARE, *THE CULTURAL APPROACH TO HISTORY* (1940)

In the 1920s and 1930s many young historians reinvigorated efforts to unravel how the "inarticulate"—America's workingpeople and those at the bottom of the social and economic hierarchy—had experienced American society and shaped its history. Such an agenda resonated in profound ways with the social, political, and economic realities that existed in the United States during the period. New scholarship that attended to the "masses" surfaced initially among economic historians interested in the rise of American industrial capitalism and the processes that had fueled the country's economic boom. Even amid the prosperity of the 1920s, some historians uncovered a darker theme within this triumphant story—the cost paid by those whose labor fueled the surging industrial economy.

The Great Depression greatly accelerated these trends in historical writing. Mass industrial unemployment, depressed wages, the downward spiraling of the industrial and agricultural economy, pervasive and visible poverty in rural and urban areas, and a resurgence of labor activism supported the authority and fueled the passions of those historians intent on advancing a sharper and more somber version of the American past. While only a few adopted explicitly Marxian models to explain the persistence of poverty and inequality, many turned their attention to class as a fundamental determinant of experience in American society. They often joined that interest to a deep engagement in the history of cultural patterns, habits of life, and community. In such accounts, women, African Americans, immigrants, the poor, and other previously overlooked groups became central players in the drama of American history.

Class divisions likewise surfaced as a theme in the work of several young historians of the American South. Determined to deepen understanding of that region's social and economic history, these scholars resembled, in some respects, the literary "southern agrarians" who rose to prominence in the 1930s. Like the poets and writers who boldly challenged parochial images of the South, these historians struggled to advance a richer and more textured understanding of southern history—one that probed culture, tradition, and the deep roots of inequality. But unlike the literary movement, theirs was less a defense of the South than a reimagination of its elements and character. In focusing on the deep divisions among whites of disparate means—most notably, rich landowners and impoverished tenant farmers—these scholars accented issues of class and so crystallized inequality that existed beyond the South's glaring racial hierarchy. Such a perspective complicated southern history, which had largely turned around slavery, secession, the Civil War, and the legacy of Reconstruction.[1]

Largely set adrift from the inclusive theoretical framework of Marxism, the studies of historians in the 1920s and 1930s may seem most notable to today's historians for an absence of interpretive force and analytical rigor, a quaint affection for local communities, and a failure to cohere as a body of work with sharply defined boundaries. They lack, too, the broad synthetic force of the sweeping, if overreaching, interpretations advanced by Turner and Beard during the Progressive years. Rather, the work of Depression-era scholars more often foreshadowed the carefully detailed and meticulously researched monographic studies that came to define the more fully professionalized, academic history of the mid-twentieth century. Yet such a perspective misses the significance of much new interwar scholarship, which drew inspiration from prevailing social and political realities and, in fact, had a far-reaching legacy.

Interwar historians themselves suffered from no false modesty. They were acutely aware of their importance and of the determinative power of their unique historical moment. By 1940, several leading scholars believed that their work had reaped such a rich intellectual harvest that they were redefining the very nature of historical study. Like the historians who had preceded them in the Progressive era and those who would succeed them in the 1960s, many devalued the history advanced by their elders—in this case, the "new history" of the early twentieth century. In 1939, some boldly claimed to have invented an entirely new frame of historical inquiry: what they called the "cultural" approach to history. Their passions, their hubris, their trumpeting of yet another "new history" mixed the brew of historical scholarship in the 1920s and 1930s.

Among the earliest interwar studies examining the lives of "ordinary" Americans were those that focused on labor history. During the Progressive era, John Commons and his students had done much to advance an institutional approach to labor that focused on specific trade unions and industries. That endeavor continued during the 1920s and 1930s with the publication of Commons's massive four-volume *History of Labor in the United States* (1918–1935), an impressive survey of the evolution of organized labor and the ways in which liberal democracy created a uniquely American story. With this work, Commons and his students helped legitimize labor history as a field worthy of scholarly inquiry.

The institutional orientation of early labor history would come under harsh criticism in the 1960s and 1970s for its neglect of race, gender, class formation, culture, ethnicity, and the ways in which skilled *and* unskilled workers adjusted to or resisted modern capitalist development. Yet some historians of the interwar period cared very much about these dimensions of labor history. Their approach may have prompted them to examine workers within the structural parameters of particular industries. But it did not foreclose attention to the wide range of forces that shaped workers' experience and to the dynamic forces that drove labor history. In addition, some scholars of the period pursued their interest in labor through complex studies of factory towns, racial hierarchies, class relations, political alliances, and the cultural underpinnings of working-class life over the long course of

American history. In exploring such themes, they not only deepened understanding of American social and economic development, they also challenged elite-driven historical narratives.[2]

This was especially true of two studies that appeared in the 1920s, written by authors who shared a last name but no patrimony. Norman Ware and Caroline Ware demonstrated how the institutional approach could accommodate a rich and nuanced exploration of workingpeople. Both composed pioneering works in American labor history that began as dissertations; each won the prestigious Hart, Schaffner, and Marx Prize for the best book on an economic subject in a given year. Norman Ware's *The Industrial Worker, 1840–1860* (1924) set its sights on the shoemakers, textile workers, iron puddlers, and various other laborers who made possible America's industrial revolution. Caroline Ware's focus in *The Early New England Cotton Manufacture* (1931) was on early industrial capitalism and how the textile industry transformed antebellum New England.

Norman Ware's perspective on industrial workers reflected two intellectual affinities that would inform much interwar labor history. One was the ability to imagine the lives of ordinary people and to insist that those who had been largely invisible in national history were in fact central to America's social and economic development. Ware noted the ever-present temptation of historians to feature elites as he called for a redefinition of scholarly inquiry. As he explained it: "One may fix attention upon the condition, activities, and ideas of the dominant group, or one may attempt to uncover the workings of those that were submerged or being submerged. The annals of the poor are short, but seldom simple. They are short, not because they are uninteresting, but because the poor are inarticulate."[3]

Ware's attempt to make visible the submerged was deeply bound up in a second aspect of his identity: his leftist political sympathies. Born a Canadian, Ware pursued graduate studies in economics at the University of Chicago, where he earned a Ph.D. in 1913, only to return to Canada that same year to serve as head of the University Settlement in Toronto. Before long, he returned to the United States, where he pursued an academic career. Ware remained engaged in public life and worked during the New Deal as an economist for the newly formed Social Security Board.

From these catalysts came a fresh approach to labor history that viewed workers less as cogs in the industrial machinery than as active shapers of their own destiny. Indeed, Norman Ware redefined scholarly imperatives by stressing the human dimensions of industrialization. Industrial development, Ware observed, worked two vast changes: one altered the way in which goods were produced and the other reconfigured social relations. Economists and historians, Ware noted, had closely studied the former. But few scholars bothered to measure either industrialism's impact on workers or labor's response to early-nineteenth-century changes in the American economy. The ways in which industrial capitalism had attenuated the "sovereignty" of workingpeople was for Ware the very heart of the story of American social and labor history.[4]

Ware maintained that "capitalist production" and the new "discipline" it imposed on working Americans had ushered in a historical change of monumental significance. The factory system eroded the economic *and* social status of industrial workers, who lost not only control over the conditions of their work and their wages but also their personal autonomy. Speaking from the vantage point of the early 1920s, Ware noted that many viewed such upheaval as momentary pain confined to the distant past and offset by subsequent prosperity. But "a temporary maladjustment," Ware observed, "lasting over one's working lifetime is sufficiently permanent for the one concerned." Furthermore, even if gains and losses balanced out from the "calm standpoint of history," the variables were not equivalent. "No comfort gains" compensated for the loss "of status and independence" endured by working-class Americans.[5]

During the years bounded by the depression of 1837–1839 and the Civil War, the march of industrial capitalism transformed the lives of workingpeople, spreading pervasive discontent and spawning efforts to address "the degradation of the worker." Many found an outlet for their frustration in the extraordinary range of reform activities that flourished during the antebellum period. From the agitation for a ten-hour day in the 1840s and utopian movements such as Fourierism to the militant trade unionism evident among some skilled workers in the 1850s, the American landscape reflected, in Ware's view, a large-scale contest with industrialism.[6]

Ware drew a sharp distinction between the romantic reformers of the 1840s, who sought to restore an agrarian past with its independent yeomen and "community of interest" among employers and workingpeople, and the pragmatic labor activists of the 1850s. "Workers," as opposed to "reformers," came to accept, by the 1850s, the permanence of industrial society and the opposing interests that divided capital from labor. "Transcendental" reformers, on the other hand, never grasped that the fundamental divisions imposed by the rise of the new industrial system were permanent. They sought escape to a simpler time that no longer existed; they lionized a "downtrodden not an upstanding worker" for whom they sought to speak with passion, authority, and paternalism. John R. Commons had depicted Horace Greeley, for example, as "the Tribune of the People, the spokesman of their discontent, the champion of their nostrums. He drew the line only at spirit rappings and free love." Ware ridiculed that characterization.

> It is difficult to say who are intended by "the people" in this characterization. Not the industrial worker surely. He had no "nostrums," had never heard of free love, and had no interest in spirit rappings. Greeley was the spokesman of the industrial workers to the extent that he told of their condition—though even in this he usually avoided the subject of factory labor—gave them good advice and interested himself in philanthropic schemes for their deliverance. Much of his advice to the worker could be briefly summed up: "Don't strike. Don't drink. Save your money and start in business for yourself." This was good advice no doubt but it hardly entitled the giver to the resounding title "Tribune of the People."

What Ware missed in reformers such as Greeley—and in the work of other historians, it appeared—was the "authentic voice of the worker."[7]

Ware acknowledged that historians searching for the genuine convictions of labor faced the challenge of hearing very faint voices. Workers' newspapers, organizations, and the writing of "workingmen editors" offered some clues to the industrial workers' perspective. Close examination of such sources would reveal a "temper" that was not "humanitarian" but cold-eyed in its penetrating understanding of capital's war on labor. Ware reserved his praise for such labor militants, especially those who honed their critique of industrialism and focused through strikes and trade unionism on aggressively improving the material status of workingpeople. Although their drive to improve wages and hours focused on "special classes of workers," the labor movement pursued a "realistic" and pragmatic quest, however disappointing its achievements.[8]

This stress on the agency of workingpeople received special emphasis in Ware's 1929 study of the Knights of Labor, *The Labor Movement in the United States, 1860–1895: A Study of Democracy.* The Knights, in Ware's depiction, exemplified a genuine and powerful drive to achieve solidarity among America's diverse producing class. By reaching out to women and farmers, through boycotts and their cooperative vision, the Knights created "the most imposing labor organization this country has ever known." Ware forcefully rejected the conclusions of other historians who had asserted that the Knights' failure and the triumph of the American Federation of Labor were inevitable. He observed: "It is always a mistake to write history, as it were, *post facto,* to look at the American labor movement through the eyes of the American Federation of Labor."[9]

Ware's deep interest in the "mental attitudes of the workers" as a topic of "primary significance," when coupled with his radical perspective on class relations, made *The Industrial Worker* and *The Labor Movement in the United States, 1860–1895* historical studies of unusual intellectual significance. Although other commentators and critics had sought to understand labor throughout the late nineteenth and early twentieth century, they were often highly critical of workers. Certainly few historians shared Ware's interest in penetrating the experience of labor from such a respectful and egalitarian standpoint. More, while many well appreciated the broad implications of America's evolution from a rural, agrarian society to an emerging industrial economy, Ware rooted that transformation in a quasi-Marxian analysis. He traced the inherent clash between the interests of labor and capital to historical changes that had deprived workers of control over the conditions of their own labor. When the "wage" came to define the relationship between capital and labor instead of the "price" set by craftsmen who sold a product rather than their own labor power, alienated labor was the inevitable consequence.[10]

Ware likewise anticipated subsequent generations of historians in his attention to gender as a factor in industrial relations. He detailed the conditions of women workers in a variety of trades, noting particularly the exploitation they endured in the form of wage discrimination. He described the "Waltham system" of company boardinghouses employed by early-nineteenth-century textile manufacturers as "puritanical paternalism." While intended as a way of protecting women factory workers, such a system easily lent itself to "very effective and harmful despotism." The labor activism of female factory operatives likewise figured prominently in Ware's account. He traced the growing militancy of textile operatives in Lowell to the mill girls' dawning perception that they constituted a "degraded" and "permanent factory population"—a status that reflected the deterioration of working conditions in the mills.[11]

Gender also formed an important element of Caroline Ware's *The Early New England Cotton Manufacture* (1931), which began as a dissertation at Harvard University in 1925 and reflected Ware's deep interest in working-class Americans. Born to a prominent New England family in 1899, educated at the elite Winsor School in Boston and later at Vassar College, Ware evinced sensitivity even as a young girl to class and ethnic divisions. Both were apparent in the geographical configurations of her local neighborhood in Brookline. The Wares lived at "the top of the hill," where professionals and businessmen, mostly Republican and Protestant, resided. At "the bottom of the hill" settled "artisans and the laboring people . . . Irish and Catholic, with very few exceptions." A long tradition of family civic activism, as well as high parental expectations, would do much to ensure that such perceptions would inform Caroline Ware's perspective on American history.[12]

As an undergraduate at Vassar in 1916, Ware gravitated to the study of history and to the classes of Professor Lucy Salmon. A devoted adherent to the early-twentieth-century "new history" idea, Salmon stressed the centrality of social history. One could uncover important historical truths "in a back yard," according to Salmon, whose 1897 study *Domestic Service* constituted an unusual effort to examine female household labor from a historical perspective. Through Salmon, Ware came to envision history as a discipline in which labor, cultural patterns, everyday life, and gender stood as matters of intellectual substance.[13]

Caroline Ware's participation in labor education after her graduation from Vassar in 1920 likewise proved instrumental in shaping her commitment to exploring labor history. While teaching at a private school for girls in Bryn Mawr, Pennsylvania, Ware learned that a summer school for women factory workers was being established at the nearby women's college. She joined the faculty of the Bryn Mawr

Summer School for Women Workers in Industry in the summer of 1922.

Like much worker's education during this period, the Bryn Mawr School blended idealistic and pragmatic intentions. It aimed to give women industrial workers a taste of a liberal arts education. But it also hoped to advance the labor movement by encouraging activism through the nurturance of articulate and well-versed worker-citizens. Trade unionism, while never explicitly endorsed by the school, remained an ever-present theme in the Bryn Mawr experiment—so much so that the political mobilization and organizing that it inspired ultimately claimed the school when wealthy donors concluded that the College was actively encouraging strikes, labor resistance, and agitation. Ware stood squarely behind defining the school's mission in terms that encouraged such activism. "The School," she insisted, "should be directed toward giving both the organized and unorganized as thorough a knowledge of the labor movement and of the necessity of trade unions as possible in eight weeks." Faculty ought to "make a point of the emphasizing the necessity of organizing," and if the school should hold back officially from endorsing trade unionism, the summer institute "should not hesitate to do so" if ever asked directly to take a public stand.[14]

After teaching at Bryn Mawr, Ware spent a year at Oxford University studying economic history before enrolling in the Ph.D. program at Harvard in the fall of 1923. She managed to get "under the wire" before Frederick Jackson Turner's retirement and took the frontier historian's famous seminar for graduate students. Turner's emphasis on social history and on region as a crucial element of social and economic development, and his support for historical research on "common people" as vital forces in shaping national currents deeply impressed Ware.[15]

Ware departed from tradition in choosing anthropology as her outside field of study, a rebellion carefully noted by her classmate Merle Curti because it was such an unusual departure from the typical graduate student's choice of economics or political science. Although disappointed by Harvard's emphasis on physical anthropology, Ware viewed the discipline as a useful corrective to history's tendency to view the past statically and by means of Western values and assumptions. Ware's exposure to anthropology supported her subsequent efforts to integrate culture into historical analysis.[16]

It was economic historian Edwin Gay, however, who first gave practical shape to Ware's emerging, though imprecise, ideals about the proper focus of historical study. A student of German political economists Adolf Wagner and Gustav Schmoller, Gay told his students that "economic truths were not absolute but relative to time and place." He took a particular interest in the history of "industrial processes," a concern that led him to encourage Ware to focus on the early stages of industrialization in her dissertation, just as he had directed another talented female student, Blanche Hazard, to a history of the Massachusetts boot and shoe industry. Although Ware had hoped to undertake a study of African American workers, Gay expressed doubt that sufficient source material would be available. Instead, he suggested she examine the papers of the Boston Manufacturing Company, just then acquired by the Harvard Business School's Baker Library. "And so I took a look at it," Ware later recalled, "and it was rich material."[17]

Ware conceptualized her study of cotton manufacturing as a case study in the history of industrialization. She viewed her in-depth history as a way of illuminating forces vital to modern America but obscured by the overwhelming complexity of contemporary industrial society. The first half of *The Early New England Cotton Manufacture* focused on technological change, capital accumulation, labor recruitment, and the corporate organization that introduced the United States to the industrial revolution through transformations in cotton production. Events in antebellum New England, Ware argued, set "the pattern for the industrial developments of modern times," including elements of economic life unique to the American context as well as "the exploitation of labor" universal in the factory system. Ware drew on an enormous and rich base of source material, including stockholders' papers, business ledgers, wage books, company store accounts, personal letters, labor circulars, travelers' sketches, and newspapers.[18]

Many of the themes Ware explored in *The Early New England Cotton Manufacture* have become so much a part of the collective wisdom of American historians on early industrial development as to appear commonplace from the vantage point of contemporary historians. She carefully analyzed the forces that encouraged and retarded industrial capitalist development in nineteenth-century America and accounted for its regional concentration in New England. She praised the "American genius" for organization and the force of "Yankee ingenuity" for its role in spurring mercantile activity and overcoming obstacles ranging from low demand, scarce labor, and some weaknesses in capital markets to outright hostility to industrial manufacturing. And she placed great emphasis on the merchant capitalists' use of women as a labor force in the early factories. All of these elements, Ware asserted, "made the first American factories quite different from those of other countries."[19]

But Ware's was not a tale of American exceptionalism that found in the peculiar national context a triumph that set the United States outside the confines of the sordid history of industrialization all too apparent in European countries. As she explained it: "Everywhere, the factory tends to reach out for the cheapest and most docile labor and that which has fewest traditions of craftsmanship and pay; everywhere, it tends toward the exploitation of the worker and his subordination to the machine with which he cooperates under the direction of the master; everywhere, it means concentration of population at the scene of group labor." Initially, in America, the pressing need for labor, continuing high return on agricultural pursuits, and wide availability of land "checked" the worst abuses of the factory system and "retarded" the inevitable degradation of wages and working conditions.[20]

Indeed, Ware argued that merchant capitalists were forced to recruit a "higher type" of labor than the unskilled, desperate workers that filled the English cotton mills. Young women, more readily spared from agricultural work, formed the nucleus of the labor force in New England. They migrated from outlying farms to work in factories and lived in boardinghouses especially created to ensure that the women fell "under regulations strict enough to satisfy even the puritan Yankee farmers." The system permitted the recruitment and retention of a labor force free from the vagaries present in many local communities.[21]

The women textile workers also benefited initially from decent wages, the chance to earn income, and independence from home and family. Ware stressed that a variety of motives drew the Yankee farm women to factory work; she likewise emphasized the mobility of the labor force as workers rotated in and out of the factories, moved by personal circumstance and the dynamics of the industry. Ware did not so much romanticize the mill girls as betray her admiration for their grit and independence. Yet she coolly appraised the opportunities the factories afforded the female operatives—terms that initially compared favorably with other forms of employment available to women.[22]

Over time, however, increasing competition transformed cotton manufacturing. The relatively benign, if paternalistic, conditions of the early years, Ware maintained, gave way to speedups and wage cuts as textile manufacturers struggled to shave labor costs and preserve profit margins. Ware spoke sympathetically of the mill owners who faced enormous economic pressures. Still, she traced in unsparing detail a precipitous decline in the fortunes of labor—one that began with wage cuts in the 1830s and that led ultimately to the existence by 1860 of a permanent, degraded class of factory workers—many of them Irish immigrants. The "tyranny of the corporations" evinced itself in the harsh tactics deployed in the face of growing labor militancy. "On the whole," Ware concluded, "the terms of employment reduced the mill workers before 1860 to a status which planters, in retaliation for criticisms of their own system, could well liken to that of slaves." Industrial workers who earned low wages, worked long hours, and depended deeply upon the benevolence of mill owners bore little resemblance to the independent labor so celebrated in the early days of the factory system.[23]

Caroline Ware devoted considerable attention (as did Norman Ware, whom she cited often) to the rise of "class consciousness" among industrial workers. As "the cotton manufacturers became exploiters of labor" and "the first to put the stamp of social degradation on factory labor in America," they fueled labor militancy among factory operatives. Ultimately, however, workers' mobilization could not defeat the forces arrayed against them. The recalcitrance of manufacturers coupled with American resistance to corporate regulation, a strong adherence to laissez-faire, and deep suspicion of government regulation placed enormous obstacles in the way of the labor movement. In addition, the changing ethnic composition of the workforce fractured attempts at labor solidarity. Irish workers came to the mills from "conditions of abject poverty," wrote Ware. "Preoccupied with the problems of adjustment growing out of a transfer from one country to another, wrenched from a peasant status and turned into machine tenders, they were in no position to scrutinize the problems of the worker in industry." Like Norman Ware, she concluded with a pessimistic assessment of organized labor's achievements in the antebellum period.[24]

Ware emphasized that despite such failures the history of early industrialization carried enormous relevance for contemporary American society. Cotton manufacture introduced to the United States "the prototype of the big modern corporation" with all the advantages and costs attendant on new forms of business organization. Corporate "giants" achieved economies of scale, fueled and met consumer demand, stoked the engine of manufacturing, and contributed to the productivity of region and nation. Yet such successes raised fundamental questions about economic equality, the conditions of labor, and the exercise of political power in modern American society. Ware expressed grave concerns about the fate of workers and the threat to democratic institutions posed by unchecked and dominant industrial organizations. Despite her admiration for the business acumen of powerful industrialists and the many benefits that accrued from industrialization, she warned that the economic transformation that began in antebellum New England had led ultimately to "a new alignment of classes and a wider gulf between rich and poor" than Americans had known before.[25]

That divide was both deeper and more lasting under industrial capitalism, Ware maintained, than in other economic systems. The new industrial titans had amassed enormous wealth and power, thereby wielding unprecedented "control over the lives of working men and over the resources of the nation." Furthermore, the modern industrialist was distinct in holding his "wealth in mobile form, he could detach it from himself, from any place or any calling and make it work." A new "giant"—the huge industrial corporation—had appeared in "the community whom others served and feared," Ware noted, suggesting that such untrammeled corporate power posed a threat to democratic institutions. Early-nineteenth-century New Englanders confronted what turned out to be a fundamental and lasting problem: "Could political democracy encompass industrial autocracy, could it harbor a working class and moneyed power and survive?" The answer, Ware wrote in a conclusion written before the 1929 crash, "still lies in the future."[26]

The tone of skepticism (at best) and pessimism (at worst) in Ware's assessment of industrial capitalism provoked the criticism of one reviewer. Delmar Leighton of Harvard University challenged in a 1931 issue of the *American Economic Review* Ware's preoccupation with the exploitation of factory operatives and the "unwarranted" profits others accrued from their labor. "It is, perhaps, too much to ask what would have constituted a 'reasonable return' under the conditions then prevailing," Leighton averred. "But it seems fair to question the justification for the prominent use of the undefined word 'exploitation' in this book. To show that the relative status of workers in a particular industry declines is not to prove the presence of exploitation. The objection is based not on any doubt that the factory system raised serious social problems . . . but on the dark cloud of suspicion which this vague word casts over a situation which needs calm analysis of conflicting forces." Leighton suggested that scholars focus on market conditions that affected supply and demand in sorting out "who, if any, are doing the exploiting."[27]

Norman Ware's effort to examine the social and cultural dimensions of industrial capitalism had similarly failed to persuade a reviewer—in this case, for the *Political Science Quarterly*. In 1925, University of Illinois professor Gordon Watkins questioned Ware's emphasis on the psychological toll the degradation of labor extracted from industrial workers. Yet he also praised Ware for demonstrating that capitalism constituted the "truly radical force, ruthlessly destroying the liberties and conveniences of an older and slower-moving economic order." The advance of industrial capitalism "meant subordination to soulless machines and the rigid discipline of factory life"— facts that carried important implications for modern political economy. "Our approach to economic problems," Watkins concluded, "will be clarified considerably if we can recognize this revolutionary role of capitalistic industry."[28]

Like Leighton, Watkins came down hard on even the hint of socialist sympathies. Whatever its toll on workers, capitalism had been "far more real and effective," Watkins stressed, "than revolutionary socialism." Indeed, this invocation of socialism for the purposes of invidious comparison reflected a persistent theme in American intellectual life, especially acute in the post–World War I period, that frequently colored responses to new research in labor history. The criticism implicit, and sometimes explicit, in histories of American industrial development such as the Wares' inspired a spirited defense of American capitalism among scholars such as Watkins. Academics sympathetic to organized labor similarly raised the bugaboo of socialism in making their case for trade unionism. These historians sought to add luster to the workers' associations they studied by contrasting the moderate, pragmatic aims of American unions with radical European labor initiatives.

A 1920 *Mississippi Valley Historical Review* commentary on Samuel Orth's history of organized labor reflected both concerns. University of Minnesota professor Lester Burrell Shippee criticized Orth's personal bias toward trade unions, for which he seemed, Shippee wrote, to cherish "an especially tender feeling." Still, Shippee quoted with apparent approval Orth's conclusions that the AFL's "earnest and constructive" methods stood in contrast to the "amorphous, inefficient, irresponsible Socialism which has made Russia a lurid warning and Prussia a word of scorn." Thus even the most tentative assays into class analysis appeared to incite a vigorous defense of moderate reform and American capitalism in the 1920s.[29]

Such responses reflected a broader discomfort in the 1920s among scholars who detected in fresh work on American labor history an unwelcome attempt to trace the roots of contemporary social, political, and economic problems to a longer history of class conflict. A 1923 contribution to the *American Historical Review,* for instance, took sharp exception to a suggestion by John R. Commons and his associates that the Workingmen's Party derived its strongest support from urban industrial workers in 1830s Massachusetts. "There is danger in examining the events of an earlier period under the strong light of modern concepts, that the picture may become distorted," Arthur Darling complained. Labor activism in Massachusetts did not prove the existence of a "helpless and immobile industrial class." On the contrary, the Workingmen's Party tapped the support of a broad range of laboring people, most of them "plain country folk" who inhabited rural areas of the commonwealth.

The fiery rhetoric of workingmen's associations, Darling admitted, conjured up lurid scenes for contemporary Americans. But in fact, he insisted, "no distinct laboring class" existed in the 1830s. Farmers, mechanics, and a huge variety of "day-laborers" took umbrage at the privileges enjoyed by the wealthy, urban classes but they should not be confused with a class-conscious cadre of urban industrial workers or a "proletariat." Whatever the merits of Darling's argument, he registered a strong objection to what he viewed as an unwelcome attempt at class analysis. Ironically, labor historians of the 1960s and 1970s would later chastise Commons and his students for insufficient attention to class struggle.[30]

Despite such criticism, other historians of the 1920s evinced considerable sympathy for the incisive work of labor historians and their forceful challenge to time-worn verities. Elinor Pancoast credited Norman Ware with proving in *The Industrial Worker* that the United States had not escaped the degradation of labor that accompanied English industrialization, despite suggestions among other scholars that the West provided a safety valve that freed America from such realities. "Ware does us another great service," Pancoast noted in her 1927 *Journal of Political Economy* review, "by emphasizing the workers'-protest movements of the period, as over against the agitation inspired by intellectuals." Historians have for "too long," Pancoast insisted, allowed the "transcendentalist reformers" of the 1840s to "occupy the center of the stage." There could be no question, after reading Ware's account, "that the labor movement of the period was a reality" equally deserving of such intellectual attention. Columbia University economic historian Carter Goodrich, in a 1925 review of a book on labor disputes and the federal government, extended Pancoast's view in asserting that the book under review did not go far enough in detailing the obstacles labor faced in its attempts to organize. Among the highest bars the labor movement confronted, Goodrich argued, was callous treatment by the federal government, often rendered through federal injunctions against striking workers and by means of hostile Supreme Court decisions.[31]

As historians of the 1920s turned their attention to what was for them modern history—the period from Reconstruction onward—calls for social and cultural histories that attended to labor surfaced increasingly in professional journals and conferences. Ella Lonn, a historian at Goucher College, urged her colleagues in the American Historical Association in 1921 to undertake detailed histories of the South between 1877 and 1890 that focused, among other topics, on "the emergence of a labor problem." That very year a paper delivered at the Agricultural History Society, which met in conjunction with the AHA, examined North Carolina's post–Civil War "transition from wage labor" to sharecropping.[32]

Responses to the eighth volume of James Ford Rhodes's *History of the United States,* covering the period 1877–1896, revealed the rising interest in modern social and labor history. Social and labor history accommodated, of course, a range of political sensibilities. Southern historian David Thomas questioned the moral gravamen and intellectual thrust of Rhodes's assessment of post-Reconstruction history. Rhodes, he argued, overworked some topics and devoted insufficient attention to others, a tendency that appeared to especially rankle Thomas when Rhodes turned his attention to labor history. Rhodes's obsession with violence in the labor movement offended Thomas, as did the author's preoccupation with political history. There was no excuse for such lapses in a work of modern history. As Thomas commented in a 1920 issue of the *Mississippi Valley Historical Review:*

> The Molly Maguires can hardly be said to have exercised any very profound influence on the course of politics, yet they receive thirty-two pages, while the profound unrest which led to the creation of [an] interstate commerce commission is given scant attention. The Maguires may have been cutthroats, but what about the economic conditions which played a part in producing them? The personal affairs of General Grant are hardly as important today as the movement of population and the settlement of the west. The mistakes of the Knights of Labor are made to stand out in bold relief, but what of the causes of unrest?

In an unusual ad hominem attack, Thomas acidly observed that Rhodes's neglect of such topics reflected the author's privileged life experience. "Perhaps we should not be surprised that one who abandoned business to write history," Thomas ventured, "should not be greatly exercised over the giant strides of business during this period in its march to the conquest and subjugation of the nation."[33]

Such criticism provided only a thin veneer for Thomas's own political convictions. His brief for labor evolved from a profound sympathy with southern agrarian interests—a loyalty apparent when Thomas unfavorably contrasted Rhodes's superficial "treatment of industrial unrest" with the attention a previous volume in the series lavished on slavery. Revealingly, another historian sympathetic to the South located similar deficiencies in Rhodes's attempt at social history. Lester Shippee found fault with Rhodes's entire multivolume study for its neglect of Turnerian insights into the importance of the West. But Shippee's championing of the "new history" in this instance represented less a brief for social history than an attack on Rhodes's "northern point of view." Shippee contemptuously noted that Rhodes "saw in slavery a great moral evil which had corrupted the greater portion of a whole society." Such ridicule revealed that for historians such as Shippee, Turnerian history offered a welcome opportunity to bury criticism of slavery and the South in an expansive interpretation of American development that ironically both diminished sectional conflict (North versus South) and privileged the West.[34]

African American historians also found ample reason to criticize sweeping narrative accounts such as Rhodes's for methodological and interpretive deficiencies. Yet they found Rhodes's neglect of social history troubling for rather different reasons than white southern historians. A 1920 *Journal of Negro History* review of Rhodes's magnum opus observed that "the author pays very little attention to the Negro except as he leaves the impression that the race was justly deprived of the suffrage and of holding office." The critic especially bristled at Rhodes's assertion that "making the Negro a citizen was a failure." Rhodes's negative verdict on Reconstruction was premature at best, according to the reviewer, for no one could yet "say whether we shall finally obtain more good than bad results." An inability to see beyond present conditions and to think historically about the recent past blinded Rhodes's "knowledge of human affairs."[35]

A bitter 1923 review of a subsequent Rhodes study of the McKinley and Roosevelt administrations probably authored by Carter Woodson, similarly dismissed Rhodes's inattention to "social and economic questions," noting that "from the point of view of modern historiography, the book cannot be seriously considered as a very valuable work on American history." The emphasis on politics and "chieftains" did little to reveal "the meaning of the forces" that had reshaped American history within "the last generation." Indeed, for this historian, Rhodes's inattention to race made the book especially disappointing. But for a few brief references to notable African Americans, "the race does not figure in this history," the reviewer bluntly concluded. Such a lapse was entirely unacceptable in any modern account of late-nineteenth-century America. "After reading this volume, one who has not lived in this country would be surprised to come here and learn that we have such a large group of citizens about whom so much was said and to whom so much was meted out during this stormy period." Thus did the *Journal of Negro History* note and challenge in the 1920s the connection between elite-centered political histories and the historical erasure of the African American experience.[36]

The plastic quality of Turner's vision of American history lent itself to various political and intellectual purposes in the 1920s and 1930s. If some viewed Turner's approach as a useful means of deflecting attention from Southern moral lapses and the history of racial inequality, others reached the opposite conclusion through similar means. For historians such as Carter Woodson, modern history, with its Turnerian emphasis on social history and economic development, provided an opportunity for accenting the importance of race and African American history to the national experience. Still others of Turner's disciples used their teacher's example in the service of a narrative of American historical development that emphasized the experience of ethnic minorities.

Among the latter group was Marcus Hansen, a talented historian of American immigration whose career was cut short by his untimely death at the age of forty-six. Descended from Danish and Norwegian immigrants, Hansen began his work on migration while a graduate student of Turner's at Harvard University; he earned his Ph.D. in 1924, in the same cohort as Caroline Ware and Merle Curti. Hansen emphasized the centrality of immigration and labor to American history and called for social and cultural studies that detailed the life of immigrant industrial workers. "Community activities demand research," Hansen insisted in 1927. "Every-day life in Boston and Milwaukee and a score of other foreign 'capitals' should be described. The sociology of the hundred-and-sixty-acre farm is as worthy of investigation as that of the ante-bellum plantation. What amusements, festivals, commercial and social habits prevailed? . . . Did each race manifest a characteristic attitude towards social problems such as temperance and Sunday observance?" In examining the lives of urban immigrant populations, Hansen stressed the importance of carefully exploring labor history. "An analysis should be made of the labor policy of canals and railroads . . . the recruiting of men, labor conditions, and the preservation of order," Hansen argued. For all the fascination with the gold rush and the settlement of the far west, Hansen observed, "the history of a 'shanty town' may be as rich in primitive self-government as any mining gulch in California and marks the first participation of its inhabitants in American democracy." Hansen's own work in immigration history would do much to advance his objectives.[37]

Early work on the migration of African Americans similarly located an urban frontier every bit as worthy of study to historians concerned with social history as the West. Carter Woodson surveyed an entire century of black migration in one of the first studies to apply Turnerian models of expansion and settlement along the frontier to African Americans. Woodson located the roots of black migration in the racial and economic hierarchy of the South—one that left African Americans subjugated and impoverished.[38]

Henderson H. Donald, an African American graduate student at Yale University, honed Woodson's theme in 1921, when he published a close analysis of the Great Migration using Labor department records and census data. A student of William Graham Sumner, Donald found in the black migration evidence for Social Darwinist theories of natural selection. African Americans chose "flight" as a means of survival amid the inhospitable social, economic, and political environment of the South. Among the many "adversities" facing black men and women in the South, Donald viewed three as particularly decisive. Migration devolved from the "racial prejudice" blacks confronted as part of their daily experience in the South. It was further spurred by natural disasters, such as flooding, the boll weevil, and the repeated crop failures that ensued. Finally, it stemmed from the pervasive "economic and social disadvantages in the form of unjust farming conditions, wretchedly low wages, lynchings, segregation, injustice in the courts, poor housing, poor schools" that African Americans endured. The lure of industrial jobs during the World War I period provided a powerful magnet North for African Americans seeking to escape these injustices.[39]

But Donald warned blacks that formidable obstacles confronted the "rank and file" who traveled out of the South in their quest for advancement. Their welcome in the North was itself contingent on the need for labor. As Henderson explained: "The North wants the Negro, but to a limited extent only. It is glad to have him, but only so far as he can be of use to it in its industries. It is not at all disposed to invite and welcome him within its confines merely for the sake of enabling him to escape his unfortunate situation in the South. This is seen, to some extent, in the somewhat changed attitude on the part of certain employers toward Negro labor. It is reported that with the signing of the Armistice the barriers of race were again set up in industry." The prospects for African Americans in the North would largely be determined, Henderson argued, by the exigencies of the labor market. If foreign immigration continued to provide a competing pool of white labor, African Americans would confront powerful constraints on their economic mobility and would be "forced almost wholly into those lines of work which are very menial, often irregular, and poorly remunerative." Even without competition from foreign labor, blacks faced uncertain economic chances given the erratic nature of the industrial economy. Finally, Donald stressed that economic advancement strongly turned around "the extent to which Negroes are actually given effective membership in the unions." Donald emphasized the burdens migration imposed upon African Americans as well as rising racial tensions in northern cities, which had resulted in riots in east St. Louis and Chicago in 1917 and 1919.[40]

The economic origins of racial conflict surfaced repeatedly in 1920s historical studies of free black northern labor. Arnett Lindsay's 1921 essay "The Economic Condition of the Negroes of New York prior to 1861" argued that free African Americans suffered from de facto segregation in the labor market. Irish and German labor advanced in the trades at the expense of free blacks, who found it very difficult to overcome the prejudices of white employers for white labor. Lindsay noted that one advocate of colonization even employed the disgraceful realities of such discrimination in an attempt to persuade free blacks "that they could not finally succeed in the struggle in competition with the white laborers and would be crowded out of the higher pursuits of labor." Still, Lindsay took pains to emphasize the progress many free African Americans had made in the trades and professions in antebellum New York. Their history of advancement, Lindsay suggested, disputed southern apologists for slavery, who unfavorably compared the conditions of free labor to bound in the antebellum period.[41]

Other historians of the African American experience focused their attention on servitude in the interests of adding complexity to the prevailing understanding of black labor history. Slavery, they insisted, did not represent the sum total of the race's history of work in America. In a 1923 essay, T. R. Davis explored black servitude in colonial America, which, he argued, often predated slavery. Gradually the terms of service were extended to perpetuity, partially to offset the decline of white indentured servants and to meet the need for a steady, reliable supply of labor. "The Negro servant was held," Davis observed, "whenever the occasion demanded and the opportunity presented itself."[42]

Political scientist Elizabeth Ross Haynes narrated the modern counterpart to this story in a study of black domestic servants published in a 1923 issue of the *Journal of Negro History.* Drawing on statistics from the U.S. Department of Labor, her own survey of employment agencies, and data gathered from the report of the U.S. Industrial Commission, Haynes closely examined the labor patterns, wage levels, working conditions, and gender ratio among black domestic servants in various American cities. African Americans, she noted, were greatly overrepresented among the ranks of domestic servants from 1870 to 1900, with black women especially prominent among such workers. Despite finding some improvement over the thirty-year period, Haynes emphasized the difficulties African Americans faced as domestic servants. Their wages, Haynes concluded, lagged behind "any other occupation or industry except agriculture," while their hours remained longer than for laborers in many other occupations. Haynes's conclusions meshed well with the extensive early-twentieth-century literature on domestic service produced by social analysts and critics who were worried about the declining pool of household workers. Still Haynes's scholarly work on black domestic service reflected a broader interest among African American historians in the multifaceted nature of black labor history.[43]

During the 1920s some scholars took pains to analyze slavery as a labor system, emphasizing variations in the institution by region and economic activity. Kathleen Bruce, a graduate student of Edward Channing's at Harvard and in the later 1920s a professor of history at William and Mary College, focused her attention on slave labor in the Virginia iron industry. In a narrative laced with appallingly racist commentary on African Americans, Bruce's work explored the ways in which slave labor met the particular demands of fledgling Southern industrial capitalists. Among the advantages an "ironmaster" enjoyed in using slave labor were "the master's easy control of negro slaves engaged in an occupation personally congenial; in his ability to avoid sudden fluctuations in labor costs; in the physical aptitude of the colored men for furnace work which, therefore, ensured steadiness of labor; and in the cheapness of slave as compared with white labor." There was, as well, little threat of strikes "in a slave-holding community."

Bruce painted a rather bucolic picture of "the life of these antebellum colored iron workers." Yet she took pains to detail not only the economic forces and labor discipline prevalent in the ironworks but also working-class life, including diet and leisure activities, among the black ironworkers. In this way, Bruce's work, with all its limitations, represented some effort to arrive at a more complex view of slavery as a labor system. With that short turn of the intellectual kaleidoscope, the familiar pieces of nineteenth-century American history—slavery, the Old South, sectional differences—fell apart and then together in ways that offered hints of new historical perspectives on old themes.[44]

In sum, even before the Great Depression, many historians exhibited a consciousness of labor that led to some of the first careful studies of working-class Americans, of the culture of work, and of the impact of industrial development on labor and on class relations. Although the work of these historians lacked the broad sweep of interpretation that gave the writings of Turner and Beard so much vitality and force, it closely resembled the painstaking, detailed, and archive-based research that would give the discipline of history its modern cast. During the 1930s, politics would hone that edge, as new research initiatives on the history of America's "ordinary" men and women and on the impoverished assumed a special urgency.

The field of southern history became a proving ground for new historiographical endeavors in the 1930s. This field might have seemed an unlikely locus for innovative work on class, community, and culture, given the dominance of a rigid historical narrative that revolved around well-worn and deeply ideological interpretations that sought to defend the region. Young historians of the South keenly felt the weight of that historical consensus, one that "proclaimed," as C. Vann Woodward explained it, "the enduring and fundamentally unbroken unity, solidarity, and continuity of Southern history."[45]

Wrenching themes of slavery, sectional conflict, racial oppression, and inequality—all of them culminating in the chaos of the Civil War—permeated Southern history. In the hands of influential southern historians these tragedies had been transmogrified into a narrative that stressed the benign character of slavery, the glories of the Lost Cause, the utter moral and political bankruptcy of the Reconstruction Era, and the possibilities of a redeemed South rising on a foundation of reconciliation and the restoration of order. As one critic observed in a 1930 issue of the *Journal of Negro History:* "Certain evils of modern life furnish the impulse to an easy romantic escape in dreams to a pleasanter past. Young men of the South, keen of mind, having set themselves up as 'liberals,' after having learned the most advanced technique, now use that technique for the buttressing of ancient prejudices." The result was "a host of books glorifying the South and debasing the North," a project that amounted to a genre of "unhistoric history."[46]

Despite the intellectual dominance of this brand of southern history, important crosscurrents ran during the early twentieth century that would inspire younger scholars to envision a different way of understanding the past. The southern literary renaissance of the 1930s, itself a product of shifting social and political tides, powerfully inspired historians such as Woodward, who found little zest in the traditional narrative of southern history. As local writers and novelists such as William Faulkner, Erskine Caldwell, Ellen Glasgow, Thomas Wolfe, and Allen Tate searched to capture the region's elusive but compelling essence, they fixed their gaze on dark themes of conflict and tragedy and the complicated human relationships that formed beneath the surface and formal bonds of community. They captured in poetry and prose the enigmatic personalities that gave localities their distinctive flavor. Religion, race, and rural life often framed their tales in ways that evoked a sense of the deep roots of southern regionalism. These were seductive themes for historians who wanted to breathe life into the hardened shell of southern history, however subtle and genteel their initial efforts to challenge the style and substance of their elders' historical orthodoxies.

Also compelling was the work of southern social scientists such as Howard Odum and Rupert Vance, who made regionalism the very core of new sociological inquiry into the making of the modern South. (Both men encouraged C. Vann Woodward in his early days as a graduate student.) From an ever-growing academic empire at the University of North Carolina in Chapel Hill, well supported by the Social Science Research Council, Odum encouraged carefully detailed "descriptive studies" of southern communities, social problems, and folk habits that might result in a coherent "regional portraiture" of the South. The initiative reflected Odum's exposure to Boasian anthropology as well as his determination to bring the South into the realm of modern academic social scientific research. The importance of race, rural life, and labor relations to the social, cultural, and economic dynamics of the region received special emphasis.

The result was an impressive body of work, especially during the Depression era. Odum's *Southern Regions of the United States* (1936) demonstrated the potential intellectual rewards of painstaking research on regional development. Rupert Vance, Odum's assistant at Carolina, followed suit with important studies, including a 1929 survey, *Human Factors in Cotton Culture,* and the influential *Human Geography of the South* (1932), which linked landscape and region to cultural patterns. In his book on the cotton culture, Vance portrayed, as the *Journal of Negro History* put it, "the perniciousness of the old regime, of which the disastrous economic harvest has not yet been reaped. He studies closely what our commentators have inhumanely neglected; the drastic life of the poor whites and the Negroes in the cotton fields." Vance's cold, hard stare at the realities of rural life and cotton cultivation sharply distinguished his perspective from the Nashville agrarians, whose attack on industrialism and defense of the South were summarized in the famous 1930 polemic *I'll Take My Stand.*[47]

The twelve writers who contributed to the volume, Vance asserted, were "neo-Confederates" who offered a "new apologetic" for the old South in the guise of a "passionate attack upon mass production, the industrial way of life, and its ideals of service and progress." Vance excoriated the Southerners' attempts to romanticize rural life and the cotton culture. As he expressed it: "To lead a return to the agrarian tradition in the South is to lead a return to the abyss. Around the cultivation of cotton is grouped a large class comparable to the poorest peasants of Europe. No culture worthy of permanence can be built on these three million poverty stricken farmer-families." Vance and Odum instead urged a realistic assessment of the high price paid by the South for its "unbalanced agrarian economy" and "moribund cotton system." Both men called for, and sought to provide, a rich and nuanced understanding of southern society—one that balanced an appreciation of the region with a forthright determination to address its legacy of social and economic inequality.[48]

The issue of inequality underscored the importance of the contemporary moment to the reinvigoration of southern intellectual life during the Depression. The economic crisis, natural disasters, and agricultural downturns of the decade broke the backs of rural people and flooded the consciences of those who observed the burdens borne by "common people." The promise raised by New Deal reform initiatives, however inadequately fulfilled, similarly lent a sense of urgency to new scholarly endeavors that examined labor, rural life, and poverty in the backcountry. Odum dedicated himself to ensuring that his research and that of his compatriots would inform government planning at the local, state, and federal level. His vision of a research-driven Council on Southern Regional Development reflected not only personal ambition but also broader aspirations for social and economic betterment that grew more pressing in the face of the ravages visited upon the South during the Depression years.

If one was a person of any sensitivity, C. Vann Woodward later recollected, one could not travel the South during this period and overlook the suffering. As Woodward explained the process of his own education: "To read about conditions is one thing, to confront them first hand another. One could read all about the Great Depression at the time and did so daily—the failures, foreclosures, bankruptcies, and shutdowns; the soaring unemployment, the breadlines, the homeless, the hungry, the army of transients, the Hooverville shanty towns, the Dust Bowl. But what did cotton at 4.6 cents a pound and sugar at 3 cents and 25 percent unemployment actually mean in human terms to the millions most affected? One way to find out, a way rarely taken by the college bred, was to go and see." Woodward did so in 1935 while working for a New Deal agency surveying poverty in rural Georgia. As he traveled back roads and peered into the crude dwellings of sharecroppers, he came "face to face with people in conditions that made a mockery of my prescribed questions and embarrassed me for asking them." Confronted with "all the misery and hunger and despair," Woodward saw the full weight of the Great Depression. Later when he read James Agee and Walker Evans's portrait of rural sharecroppers, *Let Us Now Praise Famous Men,* he felt its truth "in the pit of my stomach"—he had seen it all in rural Georgia in the shacks of poor men and women.[49]

Even before the Great Depression, the fate of poor whites in the South had become a subject of growing interest to southern historians, who puzzled over the political and economic dynamics that shaped relationships among classes within the dominant racial group. Why didn't class tensions create a larger rift between white slaveholders and whites too impoverished to profit from the peculiar institution? As early as 1857, Hinton Rowan Helper raised this question in his meditation *The Impending Crisis of the South.* Helper advanced an analysis of the nineteenth-century South that emphasized class conflict and called on nonslaveholding whites to overthrow "the planting oligarchy" that oppressed their class interests. As U. B. Phillips later summarized it, Helper hoped to see "class war upon a double front, to humble the 'lords of the lash' and then to destroy the 'black and bi-colored caitiffs' who cumbered the white man's world" by exterminating, if necessary, black men and women.[50]

In 1925, Harvard-trained historian Paul Buck reinvoked Helper's views in an *American Historical Review* essay that sought to understand the "life, attitude and social significance of the most wretched portion" of antebellum Southern society—impoverished whites— without endorsing Helper's extreme racism. Still, Buck claimed in his essay that "the poor whites of the ante-bellum South were at the very bottom of society"—a stunning assertion given the existence of slavery. Buck wondered what "congeries of complex interests" kept impoverished southern whites from "the development of a class consciousness that could be directed against the institution of slavery."[51]

He found his answer in the illiteracy, poor health, limited economic opportunities, and marginal status of the rural whites who existed on the fringes of the plantation system. Although Buck's assessment was liberally salted with disparaging comments about poor whites, he emphasized the social and economic determinants of their lowly status. Noting recent scientific findings that linked the widespread phenomenon of clay eating among poor white Southerners to advanced hookworm disease, Buck concluded that the malady was common in the antebellum period and left indigent whites in a "weakened" mental and physical condition.[52]

Economic marginalization cemented this degraded status. The dominance of slavery made free labor "superfluous," according to Buck, leaving impoverished whites consigned "to a life of uselessness so far as productive society was concerned." Planters preferred the labor of black slaves to that of free whites because the latter "might leave their jobs at any time and because it was impossible to drive them." Whites who were "simple in mind and attitude" accepted the system out of passivity, ignorance, and the dubious privilege of enhancing their own status by standing on the shoulders of enslaved African Americans.[53]

Indeed, nonslaveholding whites exhibited a "groping classconsciousness," Buck argued, in their "radical attachment to the institution of slavery." By allying themselves with the planter aristocracy through the medium of white supremacy, they escaped what seemed a greater threat—"the possible emancipation of the despised negro" with its prospect of even more threatening "social and economic dangers." For Buck, only an industrialized South with the prospect of employment in manufacturing held the promise of providing whites with a pathway out of poverty and helplessness. In the interim, the conditions they endured left destitute whites vulnerable to a particular brand of "popular democracy" that played to their prejudices.[54]

The interplay of class, race, and politics received much more sustained and critical scrutiny in the work of Paul Lewinson in the 1930s. Lewinson began his career as a professor at Ohio State and later Swarthmore, but left the academy in 1935 to work at the National Archives, where he remained for the next twenty-five years until his retirement. His 1932 study *Race, Class, and Party: A History of Negro Suffrage and White Politics in the South* traced the process of black disfranchisement in the post–Civil War era. For a brief moment, the agrarian movement heightened white interest in a political alliance with black voters. Ultimately, however, "political niggerism" triumphed as Democrats restored party power and unity, in part by means of race baiting. The systematic elimination of competing voices, Lewinson argued, was eventually achieved through widespread constraints on black voting. Lewinson charged both Democratic and Republican politicians with advancing "lily-whitism" and retarding through such political terrorism the social and economic advancement of African Americans.[55]

C. Vann Woodward cut a different swath through what he viewed as a New South historical orthodoxy that featured "progress, prosperity, peace, consensus, white solidarity, black contentment, sectional reconciliation, and the overarching themes of unity, continuity, and nationalism." He found in the Georgia Populist rebel Tom Watson a way to leave none "of these shibboleths unchallenged." Watson's story accented the great hardships borne by rural southern farmers whose grievances inspired an impassioned political revolt in the last two decades of the nineteenth century. *This* New South was one marked by "crass and materialistic essentials" and "included class favoritism, subservience to wealth, and indifference to growing impoverishment of the countryside." The enemies, not the saviors, in Woodward's drama of Georgia politics were "the rising class of industrial capitalists."[56]

Woodward was particularly drawn to the complex place that race occupied in the story of Watson and southern Populism. In a 1938 essay for the *Journal of Southern History* entitled "Tom Watson and the Negro in Agrarian Politics" and in his book *Tom Watson: Agrarian Rebel* published the same year, Woodward portrayed Watson as unusually daring in his efforts to build alliances between black and white southern farmers. Georgia's political elite, dominated by industrialists, pandered to racial fears among whites as a way of securing unity among white voters. In stark language, Woodward depicted this tactic and the larger political struggle as deeply rooted in class relations. The industrialists demanded, Woodward argued, "strict subordination of class conflict in the South in the interest of the *status quo* of a business man's regime identified in the popular mind with white supremacy."[57]

As representative of the Farmers' Alliance, Watson challenged such demands for "racial solidarity" and the submersion of agrarian interests. He boldly appealed to black farmers as he sought to build the People's Party by emphasizing the organization's opposition to lynching, to the Ku Klux Klan, to the convict lease system, and to disfranchisement, though he maintained his opposition to "social" race mixing. The People's Party, in Watson's vision, would "recruit its ranks from the farmers of all classes and both races and from the working class of both races in the cities." Thousands of African Americans warmly responded, thronging to the rallies of the People's Party and mobilizing for the cause of Populism despite the ever-present danger of personal attack and violence. According to Woodward, "never before or since have the two races in the South come so close together politically."[58]

Woodward's depiction of Watson as a heroic figure, animated by a genuine concern for African American and white farmers, devolved in no small measure from the historian's insistence that Watson overcame, for a time, the obstacle of race because he stood as a valiant warrior against "industrial capitalism." Although that assertion would eventually earn Woodward a good deal of criticism, it reflected a deeper desire to imagine Populism as a struggle on the part of the "Southern masses of both races against industrial capitalism." The People's Party crusade represented a moment, Woodward argued in the midst of the Great Depression, of extraordinary possibility. As he expressed it, "Here was a foundation of political realism upon which some more enduring structure of economic democracy might have been constructed. The destruction of that foundation constitutes a tragic chapter in Southern history." In depicting southern farmers as engaged in an "ancient feud with industrial capitalism," Woodward borrowed liberally from the agrarian temperament even as he attempted to address the difficult issue of race that other white southern historians so frequently side-stepped.[59]

Woodward's effort to portray the class dimensions of Populism also reflected the rough-hewn radicalism common among some young historians during the Great Depression. Economic interpretations of historical change were hardly new to the 1930s, but they gained force for many amid the conditions prevalent during the Depression. "Several approaches and ideologies to which I had been exposed competed for dominance in my own interpretation," Woodward explained of his work on Tom Watson. "Prominent among them were those of the Agrarians, the Marxists, the Liberals, and ideas associated with the name of Charles Beard." These strains of thought mingled with personal experience to shape Woodward's political alliances.

As a young man growing up in Arkansas he became aware early of the Ku Klux Klan and observed, on one occasion, local members assembling for a lynching. He gravitated toward liberal circles while a college student in Atlanta, traveled through Weimar Germany and the Soviet Union in the early 1930s, and became deeply involved in the defense of Angelo Herndon, an African American communist and labor organizer prosecuted for "insurrection." The Communist Party vigorously supported Herndon, a fact that apparently did not deter Woodward from participating actively in the campaign to spare him. In fact, Woodward's circle of friends and associates in New York (where he studied for a master's degree at Columbia in 1932), Atlanta, and then Chapel Hill included many liberals, radicals, and various other dissidents. These associations, as well as his intellectual attraction to economic interpretation, shaped his outlook on Watson and the class-based roots of Populism.[60]

Yet Watson proved a difficult figure for the young Woodward to lionize in the end. Left with the challenge of explaining Watson's evolution to virulent racist later in his career, his biographer stressed the agrarian leader's bitter disappointment at the defeat of Populism, his frustration that everywhere in the South victory ran up against the racial "stumbling block," and his own growing wealth as a planter. Watson, Woodward claimed, remained blind to the implications of rising tenancy in the South and chose instead to equate "tenancy, landlessness, and dependency with the Negro." In so doing, he avoided acknowledging the deep divisions that fractured southern farmers while preserving his own class interests. Woodward later acknowledged his error in overstating Watson's racial enlightenment, but explained that his flattering portrait derived in part from the historical context in which he found himself working. The book, he noted, was written from the perspective "of the 1930s, when blacks had long been thoroughly disfranchised and depoliticized and no white Southern politician dared speak out for their political or civil rights." Later, the civil rights revolution and the shift in the politics of American historical writing during the 1960s would render his assessment of Watson less defensible. For the moment, however, *Tom Watson* exemplified the essence of the new interwar historiographical initiatives: it spoke of the past in a tone richly inflected with present concerns. It was, Woodward conceded, "a book *for* the 1930s and *of* the 1930s, a book for hard times and hard scrabble, when rebellion was rife and the going was rough."[61]

A year after the publication of *Tom Watson*, another historical study of the South appeared that probed far more explicitly the impact of class relations on regional social and economic development. Roger Shugg's *Origins of Class Struggle in Louisiana* (1939), the book that emerged from his Princeton doctoral dissertation, was inspired on one level by the author's interest in Populism. "The agrarian crusade of the nineties," he observed, "appeared to be a class struggle without any roots except the current economic depression." Yet the book also owed much to Shugg's deep commitment to Marxism. Shugg suspected that such class tensions reached much further back into southern history and set his sights on finding "some continuity" by exploring white labor in a single locality during the antebellum period. He boldly stated his motives in the preface to the book, despite averring that he had "deliberately avoided treating" his subject from "a purely Marxian point of view because there was not sufficient evidence to justify it." Still, Shugg expressed his hope that his study of Louisiana might demonstrate "the value of examining local history in terms of classes." He did much to fulfill that promise in his impressive, deeply researched, and lucid historical analysis.

Shugg's ability to place his research on the South within a larger theoretical and historical perspective gave a power to his analysis that distinguished it sharply from more tepid and ambiguous meditations on southern labor history. Shugg took on, for instance, the category of "poor white" in an early chapter. This pejorative term, he noted, reduced whites to two categories in most of the scholarly literature—"mean whites" and "the deserving poor." As he explained the distinction:

> The former were described as incredibly ignorant and poverty-stricken, lazy, bibulous, filthy, promiscuous, violent, and "sunk into a depth of depravity." Their wretched condition was ascribed to their evil character, the product of degenerate ancestry which supposedly could be traced to the ne'er-do-well indentured servants, vagabonds, and criminals dumped on American shores in colonial times. Seldom has biological heredity been falsely invoked to explain social consequences so disastrous and so remote. The "deserving poor," on the other hand, were regarded as victims of environment, because if their poverty and ignorance were occasionally as woeful as among the much contemned "mean whites," at least it was not aggravated by similar vices.

Neither category, Shugg insisted, contained anything of worth for "the presumably impartial historian." Better to consider this class of Southerners "common people" or to insert a much-needed comma—"poor, white people"—to avoid loading the dice against indigent whites who were not slaveholders. Close examination of census records, Shugg reported, permitted a more nuanced understanding of the white population that revealed a diverse mix of laborers, artisans, yeoman farmers, "landless squatters, hunters, and fishermen," distributed unevenly in the commercial centers, rural areas, and the black belt of Louisiana.[62]

Everywhere in antebellum Louisiana, Shugg argued, "class distinctions were in the air: to accept them unconsciously was as natural as to breathe, because they were implicit in the economic and social order of the Old South." Like Buck, Shugg traced the absence of "overt class hostility" among whites to slavery and the plantation system. "Race prejudice," he noted, "filled the void of class hatred" by conferring upon impoverished whites an elevated status by virtue of skin color—and freedom. The planters' economic, political, and social dominance, and the absence of a "political party to serve the interests of the poor" did much to stave off "class struggle." Shugg carefully examined the culture of slaveholding to demonstrate how the planter aristocracy consolidated its "wealth and power" while managing "to vindicate the subordination of the common people." He likewise probed the "social conditions in the old regime" and concluded that "poor people in the country, contrary to a popular belief, did not enjoy good health to compensate for their poverty."[63]

Shugg reserved his harshest criticism for the economic oppression that accompanied slavery and the plantation economy. "The bulk of the population" in Louisiana did not benefit from "the prevailing agricultural regime," Shugg argued. Most white Louisianans did not own slaves, had difficulty acquiring them, found themselves barred from the region's best agricultural lands, and could not compete "on a large scale in the production of profitable staples such as cotton and sugar cane." Urban laborers, skilled and unskilled, likewise felt the burdens of the prevailing economic system. Despite growing struggles to organize in the immediate pre–Civil War period, Louisiana workingmen "made little progress toward organization." In addition to the divisions imposed by race, ethnicity, and nativity, they operated in a context deeply hostile to labor mobilization. "The South was hardly of a mind to bargain with workers of one race," Shugg dryly observed, "when it owned so many of another." Planters ran a minority government designed to protect their economic interests; they curtailed access to the franchise and the institutions of government to preserve their hegemony. A careful examination of suffrage restrictions and the dynamics of representation led to a single inescapable conclusion, Shugg asserted: "Louisiana was, truth to tell, a slave state policed by gentlemen; and the masses, having no real voice in the government, received from it no benefit." [64]

Shugg's examination of the social, political, and economic forces shaping antebellum Louisiana led him to cast the Civil War and Reconstruction in terms that accented the persistence of poverty and inequality in the postwar period. He construed Reconstruction as a tale of revolution and counterrevolution that began with the efforts of first white and then black labor "to rule the state and mold society in their own images" and that ended with "the final triumph of planters and merchants." Shugg rejected the notion that racial divisions were inevitable and wrote respectfully of the reform efforts undertaken to advance a "social revolution" during Reconstruction. But he wound up mournfully tracing the ways in which class solidarity once again fell victim to the machinations of elites in ways that equated class with race, encouraged hatred, and restored the abhorrent social, economic, and political inequalities of the old order.[65]

Responses to Shugg's book from historians were surprisingly warm given the reigning orthodoxies in the field of southern history. Paul Buck praised the project Shugg had undertaken: "Where others have talked of writing the history of the South in terms of the striving of its common folk, he has actually constructed a book around this central theme." Still, Buck expressed some discomfort with Shugg's insistence on class analysis. "At no point does his treatment become doctrinaire in interpretation," Buck observed in the *American Historical Review,* "but there are times when it does seem as though the valid insistence on class division had led to an oversimplification of a confused situation." Fred Shannon invoked Shugg's work in a scathing 1943 *American Historical Review* critique of Avery Craven's *Coming of the Civil War* and suggested that the senior southern historian ought to rethink his assertions that "the Negro could thrive under climactic and labor conditions that would kill white men" in light of Shugg's repudiation of such "hoary arguments."[66]

The two most critical views of Shugg's work emerged from opposite sides of the political and intellectual spectrum—and neatly captured the political polarities evident among historians in this period. The first came from Vanderbilt historian Frank Owsley, who was president of the Southern Historical Association when he reviewed Shugg's book in the *Journal of Southern History* in 1940. Owsley ridiculed Shugg's characterization of Louisiana's white majority as landless. "He seems to think of them all as proletarians," Owsley acidly commented. In fact, Owsley argued, a careful check of census manuscript records proved otherwise; most white Louisianans *did* own land, and the "very small fraction of the population who seem to have been genuine proletarians . . . seems to have been too unimportant in size to create a ripple upon the surface of an essentially property owning society." Owsley concluded his review with this comment: "One would certainly not say that Mr. Shugg has consciously made Procrustean use of his data in order that it might fit the Marxian bed; but one cannot avoid the feeling that the author—despite a book excellent in many respects—has permitted his Marxian assumption to make him less alert in discovering or using data that would not conform to the theory of the class struggle."

African American scholar Lawrence Reddick, by contrast, chided Shugg in the *Journal of Negro History* for not going further in his class-based interpretation. Reddick had earned a Ph.D. from the University of Chicago for a dissertation entitled "The Negro in the New

Orleans Press, 1850–1860," written—uneasily—under the supervision of Avery Craven. In the 1930s, as a young professor and emerging scholar of African American history, Reddick pressed for structural analysis of racial and economic inequality. Shugg's book, he complained, suffered from the lack of a theoretical discussion of class, a problem that was compounded when Shugg examined the plantation economy. Reddick explained: "Perhaps because of this theoretical mistiness, the author seems overly cautious and at times inconsistent in his description and interpretations. For example, the evidence presented in this book alone makes it clear that the ante-bellum South, especially in the late 'Forties and in the 'Fifties, presented a structure in which the small ruling class artfully controlled all other classes. Sometimes Dr. Shugg says so and then again he is not so certain." Nevertheless, Reddick considered Shugg's work an important corrective to the portrait of the South advanced by "sentimentalists and *I'll-take-my-standers.*" Indeed, he noted with approval that "a generation of more realistic scholars is rising up to describe the whole Southern society and to show the intense conflict which continually shook its foundation."[67]

By 1940 Reddick's perception that a new generation posed a fundamental challenge to the old orthodoxy was shared by many who took the measure of southern historiography. In an influential essay for the *American Historical Review* entitled "On Rewriting Reconstruction History," delivered first as a paper in 1939 at the Southern Historical Association, Howard K. Beale commented with approval on new trends. "It would seem that it is now time," Beale observed, "for a younger generation of Southern historians to cease lauding those who 'restored white supremacy' and instead to begin analyzing the restorationists' interests to see just what they stood *for* in opposing the Radicals." Among those Beale singled out for special praise were his student C. Vann Woodward, Paul Lewinson, Roger Shugg, James Allen, and W. E. B. Du Bois, despite his reservations about the Marxism of the latter two historians and his warning that class analysis not be "distorted" or overdone. (Beale described Shugg's point of view as "non-Marxian.")[68]

But the pendulum appeared to have swung a good deal too far for some other historians. Paul Buck delivered a paper at the Southern Historical Association in 1939 on changes in the tone of recent historical writing. He began by reflecting on a welcoming speech given by R. D. W. Connor when the American Historical Association met in Durham, North Carolina, in 1929. On that occasion, Buck recounted, Connor described the progress made in the South since Reconstruction in tones richly inflected with pride and optimism. "There have been no such articles written about the South since 1930," Buck soberly (and inaccurately) intoned. "We have had a decade where gloom has replaced optimism and apprehension self-confidence." Buck called for "a perspective that will take into account the various plus and minus factors in the equation." He couched his hope in the promise of new initiatives to modernize the South and stabilize southern agriculture.[69]

Other historians pinned their hopes for fuller understanding of the South on detailed archival research that would make possible a history of "the South's inarticulate masses," as Georgia College professor James Bonner wrote in 1944. Bonner, who had earned a Ph.D. degree from the University of North Carolina, urged historians to mine the manuscript records of the federal census to locate the "landless white" so elusive to scholars who lavished all their attention on "the small upper class, the prima donna group of ante-bellum Southern life." Here in the census schedules were "tens of thousands" of white Southerners who made up at least half of the population of the antebellum South. Bonner described the extraordinary possibilities presented to the historian by such seemingly mundane data: "Names on Schedules I, II, and IV of the seventh and eighth censuses, when alphabetized and collated into a single master file, result in a Domesday Book as rare as anything in Anglo-Saxon annals. While it is admitted that lives of people cannot be listed in columns and averaged, a master file such as this, to which all other available data are appended, will contain extensive and hitherto unused facts that can be made to yield an objective interpretation of the lives of the poor and illiterate." Using these three schedules, which listed "free inhabitants," "slave inhabitants," and "productions of agriculture," Bonner focused his own research on a single county in the lower Piedmont of Georgia to demonstrate how such data might illuminate social and economic dimensions of community life.[70]

What Bonner found in 1850s Hancock County, an area "somewhat representative of the old plantation cotton belt," was significant economic inequality despite the appearance of widespread prosperity, a vibrant local agrarian culture, and much commentary extolling the successes of prominent politicians and planters. "The actual situation," Bonner reported, "was something like that observed in the South from 1930 to 1940, when Federal subsidies brought a degree of prosperity to landowners in the cotton belt but forced tenants to become farm laborers or else encouraged them to seek urban employment." Indeed, Bonner compared the changes endured by local farmers forced off the land and wage earners to "the enclosure movement in England at the beginning of the century."[71]

The story Bonner told offered a detailed narrative of the declining fortunes of individual "landless farmers," as large-scale planters consolidated their land holdings and augmented their stores of slave labor. Tracing names found on the census of 1850 to schedules compiled by federal enumerators ten years later, Bonner found landless farmers who languished near the bottom of the economic order as tenants in 1850 only to wind up in the ranks of poorly paid industrial workers a decade later. His detailed compilation of statistical data, carefully constructed in tables, and his comparison of economic indices for over a thousand residents of Hancock County over a ten-year period resulted in an unusually sophisticated historical study.

In the end, his conclusions echoed those of Roger Shugg's: extensive class stratification among whites in an antebellum Southern community obscured by the veneer of racial solidarity. Bonner observed that "the presence of large numbers of black men in a society dominated by whites" provided a "floor" underneath even the most impoverished white Georgians, one "preserved through the legal sanction of a permanent, less privileged, servile class." From the "faded pages of the detailed census schedules" came the picture of an antebellum community whose economic divisions, Bonner concluded, ought to be easily recognizable to those living in modern American society.[72]

Little wonder, then, that the American Historical Association's reporter in surveying recent changes in historical writing would rather forlornly observe of the group's 1940 meeting that "as one reflects on the whole scene, ivory towers seem to be somewhat in disrepute." If southern history exemplified some of the most reactionary strains evident in the discipline, it likewise reflected radical challenges to a rigid historical orthodoxy. From the study of land and labor in white communities came fresh questions about the roots of class conflict and racial hierarchies—issues all too visible during the 1930s.[73]

*   *   *

The themes of class, culture, and community also surfaced in studies of northern labor during the 1930s. The initial work of scholars such as Caroline Ware and Norman Ware during the 1920s anticipated what became an explosion of interest in industrial workers during the Great Depression. Historians sensitive to the struggles of working-people sought to provide a context for contemporary social and economic dislocation. In placing workers and their lives at the center of historical discussion, they hoped to advance a reorientation of historical study that emphasized the importance of the "masses" to American society and culture. It was a theme perfectly matched to the historical moment. Mass unemployment, militant labor organization, a rising tide of political discontent, and the real threat of radical challenges to existing institutions made it difficult to discount the centrality of "ordinary" men and women to the life of the nation. Some historians saw in the history of working-class people an opportunity not only to enrich understanding of the past but also to uncover important truths about the essential character of the nation. For them, the story of the American past was deeply implicated in a narrative about the persistence of struggle, conflict, and inequality.

As always, the *Journal of Negro History* provided an important venue for new scholarship on the "inarticulate"—in this instance, black and white labor. In 1930, Carter Woodson wrote a lead essay for the *Journal* entitled "The Negro Washerwoman, a Vanishing Figure." Woodson noted the resentment many African Americans felt toward sentimental white portraits of the "Plantation Black Mammy." But he urged his race to consider "with veneration" women laundresses who performed backbreaking labor as domestic servants and in slavery before industrialization and mechanization brought the steam laundry. Woodson emphasized themes that historians of women would later underscore in detailing the gendered dimensions of slavery. He stressed the "double duty" of the woman slave, who worked all day only to "tax her body further" at day's end by devoting herself to chores within her own home and for her own family. And he highlighted the contributions free black women made by their labor to the survival of their families. An African American woman in the North, Woodson noted, was "often the sole wage earner of the family even when she had an able-bodied husband"—a fact he attributed to the difficulties black men faced in securing stable jobs and decent wages in the face of competition from white immigrant laborers.

The labor of black women permitted many families to improve their living standard, educate their children, and assist needy relatives and neighbors. For all these reasons, "women of this working class," Woodson insisted, formed the backbone of the black community.[74]

Woodson also coauthored with African American historian Lorenzo Greene a study entitled *The Negro Wage Earner* (1930), published by the Association for the Study of Negro Life and History. This book was actually written by Greene, who served as Woodson's assistant while completing his studies for a Ph.D. in history at Columbia University. Greene and Woodson's book was followed a year later by another on the black worker written by Sterling Spero, a white political scientist, and Abram Harris, an African American socialist economist trained at Columbia University. Both studies traced the patterns of African American work and the persistent discrimination endured on the job and at the hands of trade unions. Spero and Harris's book sharply criticized the American Federation of Labor's neglect of unskilled labor. As a reviewer for the *Journal of Negro History* explained, "It is not a working *class* organization but a craft oligarchy and seems to be as little interested in the plight of the unskilled worker as the employers themselves. . . . The authors illustrate again and again how this organization neglects and proscribes against the black toiler." Emmett Dorsey echoed Spero and Harris's criticism of black leaders who encouraged racial uplift through black capitalism. All ridiculed the notion that "we can accomplish what the whites of our class cannot accomplish which is to compete successfully with organized industry and business—by building up a separate economy."[75]

A subsequent history of African American banking by Abram Harris entitled *The Negro as Capitalist* (1936) took the point further as it characterized black business enterprise as striving on the part of "the Negro upper class to emulate" white "business ideals," "social values," and "economic habits." "It is, in brief," Harris argued, "a phase of the attempt to lay the economic foundation for a black bourgeois class"—an impossible task given that "Negro life has never afforded the economic basis for the development of a real black middle class." Harris, who combined a position teaching economics at Howard University with a range of political activities, advanced an unusually forceful and explicit class analysis of black labor. He lambasted black capitalists who lived "upon low-waged if not exploited labor." In reviewing Harris's study for the *Journal of Negro History* in 1937, economic historian Broadus Mitchell concluded that "the only hopeful" road to black economic advancement was through "a social reorganization looking to common ownership of the great means of production and productive effort applied for the sake of use rather than of profit." "Mass improvement" rather than "individual achievement" held the sole promise of ensuring real economic progress.[76]

During the Depression, the plight of impoverished workers also attracted the attention of historians interested in colonial America. The title of a 1931 study by Marcus Jernegan—*Laboring and Dependent Classes in Colonial America, 1607–1783: Studies of the Economic, Educational, and Social Significance of Slaves, Servants, Apprentices, and Poor Folk*—promised more than it delivered. Still, here was a notable effort to illuminate the lives of history's forgotten men and women. Jernegan emphasized the particular relevance of his subject to contemporary society, explaining that his book featured "the common and obscure people who made history by originating through their drab and stormy lives a number of problems that still remain major social problems in America today." In essays exploring religion among slaves, indentured servitude, public education, and poor relief, the historian attempted to uncover elements that shaped the lives of African American and white workingpeople in the New England and Virginia colonies. Jernegan, Norman Ware observed in the *American Economic Review,* "has left the beaten track of colonial history and with patience and insight has looked at certain aspects of life hitherto neglected." But, like Arthur Schlesinger, Sr., Ware regretted Jernegan's neglect of colonial artisans and journeymen, "for neither economists nor historians have gone back of the Revolution to study this class." Schlesinger criticized Jernegan for discussing only the insane who were poor as opposed to the broader social response to mental illness in the colonial period.[77]

Jernegan was not alone in his interest in those who occupied the bottom of the social and economic hierarchy in colonial America. Abbot Smith's 1934 *American Historical Review* essay "The Transportation of Convicts to the American Colonies in the Seventeenth Century" represented just a sample of Smith's extensive research on indentured servitude. His findings were impressive, fresh, and original; but they were also riddled with prejudice toward the men and women he studied. Smith claimed in 1935, for example, that "all the available evidence for the seventeenth century tends to show that average servants were at best irresponsible, lazy, and ungoverned, and at worst frankly criminal." He elaborated this point in subsequent work, including his 1947 monograph *Colonists in Bondage: White Servitude and Convict Labor in America, 1607–1776.*[78]

There was, however, something perversely refreshing in Smith's perspective on early American settlers, when measured against the pretensions that pervaded elite-focused studies of the colonial era. Determined to unveil the hoary myths enshrouding early British immigration to American shores, Smith composed an article for the *Journal of Economic History* provocatively entitled "Indentured Servants: New Light on Some of America's 'First' Families." In it Smith asserted, "The progenitor of many a proud American family found himself landed upon these shores not so much on account of his desire to seek freedom as because his person could be advantageously exchanged for a quantity of tobacco, lumber, or sassafras root." Oscar Handlin properly took Smith to task for his dehumanization of the poor and powerless. In a brilliant and fair-minded critique of Smith's *Colonists in Bondage,* Handlin found much to praise in his colleague's work, but he took on directly the author's crude prejudices. Noting that Smith "tends to regard the servants as a rather low lot," Handlin problematized Smith's portrait of the servants as "passive" forms of "cargo" moved about by more powerful forces and leaders. Handlin noted:

> This position, consistently maintained, involves serious difficulties. . . . People who are influenced by the absence or presence of opportunities are certainly not automata, and cannot properly be treated simply as cargo . . . the ultimate elements that made the decision between going and not going lay, in most cases, in the hearts and minds of the men and women who voluntarily signed on. The weakness in the conception of the servants' motivation extends into the discussion of their adaptation. Among these low people why were there so few runaways, why did so small a proportion ever have "occasion to come or to be brought before the bench of justice"? Above all, how account for their successful absorption and their useful role in American society?[79]

Other scholars digging in the archives wrote sympathetically of servants and slaves, including Lorenzo Greene, whose study *The Negro in Colonial New England, 1620–1776* provided a wealth of information about African American laborers. Although his book neglected slavery, Richard B. Morris, then a professor of history at City College in New York, exhaustively pursued the fate of free and bound labor in *Government and Labor in Early America* (1946). Morris's study won praise for detailing the burdens imposed on labor by politics, law, and business interests and because, as Marcus Jernegan put it, "it helps balance the content of our history which still emphasizes the events of political history, the activities of upper-class leaders, the evolution of political institutions, the conflicts of parties, and so forth." "This book," Jernegan observed approvingly, "treats of the people, their problems, and their exploitation by their masters." Some colonial historians expressed discomfort with the burgeoning monographic literature on class and labor. Charles MacLean Andrews warned of the dangers that accrued when subjects were studied apart from the context in which they occurred and thus given more weight "than its actual historical significance justifies." Among "such topics" were "the presence of a class conflict in colonial times, which in reality did not exist" and the struggle of workers to improve their conditions— something, Andrews asserted, that was "nowhere a conspicuous factor in colonial times."[80]

Yet the trend in labor history ran very much against the grain of Andrews's concerns during the Depression years. Innovative studies of local communities suggested that historians had much to gain from painstaking study of class, labor, and culture in microcosm. One of the most impressive monographs of this kind was Vera Shlakman's *Economic History of a Factory Town* (1934), which traced the impact of industrialization on Chicopee, Massachusetts. Shlakman scrutinized the process of class formation as industrial capitalism transformed Chicopee from a small New England agricultural town to a manufacturing center controlled by absentee merchant capitalists. In a stark version of the Yankee mill girl story, Shlakman recounted low wages, long hours, and oppressive conditions endured by women factory operatives. She questioned "the idea of the idyllic period in American labor history" that made of the 1830s a time when women workers enjoyed a "delightful" social and civic culture. "It is stretching the evidence too far," Shlakman maintained, "to make such activity a characteristic part of the factory life of the period." The rise of a "permanent factory population," the degradation of work, and the contraction of middle-class business and social activity proceeded apace during the late nineteenth century. Indeed, her analysis of the "decline of the middle class" made Shlakman's research an especially striking contribution to the literature on industrial development.[81]

A model of careful research in social and economic history, Shlakman's study offered a forceful analysis of class amid reams of statistical data and exhaustive research in company and town records. A talented economic and labor historian, Shlakman came under ferocious attack as a faculty member at Queens College in the late 1940s. She lost her position in 1952 for refusing to reveal to the McCarran Committee whether she belonged to the Communist Party. Still, during her time as a member of the faculty at Queens she influenced many students, including Herbert Gutman, who would one day earn renown as a pioneer in the "new" labor history of the 1960s and 1970s.[82]

Shlakman's detailed portrait of a factory town in western Massachusetts was followed in 1939 by another woman historian's ambitious study of a neighboring city. Constance Green, like Shlakman, saw her community study as "a case history of the industrial revolution in America." The focus in Green's case was on Holyoke, a farming community transformed by industrialization into a thriving mill town by the mid-nineteenth century. By analyzing virtually every dimension of the city's past, Green succeeded in producing a richly detailed study that integrated social, economic, political, and cultural history. Conflict between Catholics and Protestants, immigrants and native-born Americans, capital and labor comprised an important theme that gave coherence to Green's sweeping narrative. Her study likewise suggested how labor might be integrated into broad historical studies of urban and community development.[83]

Other historians of the 1930s found in labor history direct parallels to Depression-era America. One such scholar was Samuel Rezneck, a Polish-born immigrant who earned a Ph.D. from Harvard in 1926 and became a professor of history at Rensselaer Polytechnic Institute. In 1933, the *American Historical Review* published an article by Rezneck entitled "The Depression of 1819–1822, a Social History," which contained only an oblique reference to the nation's current economic catastrophe. "In this early precedent," Rezneck observed, "are illustrated all the major features of what has become a recurring phenomenon of American social and economic history." Yet echoes of the contemporary scene sounded throughout the narrative as Rezneck described widespread unemployment and poverty. He concluded that "in the wake of this early depression came an intensification of class consciousness, as between the rich and the poor, the creditors and the debtors, those who lived by honest labor and those who engaged in vicious speculation."[84]

Six years later, Almont Lindsey published an essay in the same journal that cast the great Pullman strike as a morality play with the paternalism of the corporation at the ethical core. The conflict pitted workers "grimly determined to improve their living standards which too often bred despair, suffering, and tragedy" against "the capitalists" who were "unscrupulous" and "uncompromising" in their treatment of their workers. Lindsay laid blame for the Pullman strike at the door of the Pullman Palace Company, though he conceded that in its rigidity, harsh labor practices, and paternalism, the business was "no different from any other corporation of this period."[85]

Yet historians of the 1930s also searched the past for heroic figures whose strength and courage amid hard times exemplified the potential power of workingpeople. Harry Carman offered a reappraisal of Knights of Labor leader Terence Powderly in 1941 that concluded the reformer was "a person of far greater stature than he has been credited with being." After quoting a passionate brief Powderly made for workingmen, Carman asked this question: "If this was the statement of a windbag, then what of Robert Owen, John Ruskin, Karl Marx, Theodore Parker, and those other nineteenth-century men and women who dared speak out against the evils of industrial capitalism?" Powderly owed much of his idealism, Carman suggested, to his tumultuous historical times, when industrial capitalism was not yet a "hardened" reality and "the mind of labor" contained a grander vision than "wage-consciousness."[86]

Historian Harvey Wish echoed many of these themes that same year in an *American Historical Review* essay that found in the person of Illinois reform governor John Peter Altgeld a hero worth rediscovering. Amid the Depression of 1893, Chicago's reform and labor leaders helped Altgeld enact a series of sweeping reform measures admirable for their substance and idealism. Anticipating future historians, Wish emphasized especially the remarkable circle of women reformers who spearheaded a series of social welfare reform initiatives and later "transferred" what they learned to Washington, where they became "pioneers of a greater Federal responsibility for dependent social groups—the embryo of contemporary legislation on social security." Thus in 1941 was scholarly recognition of women's role in welfare state building—a theme that would receive enormous attention decades later in the field of women's history.[87]

By 1939, many talented and energetic historians who had come of age during the interwar period believed the moment had come to redefine the scholarly enterprise of history. Repudiating, however politely, the "new" history that had so influenced them in their formative years, they found equal fault with rudderless social histories that accumulated fact without advancing coherent ideas and "facile generalization" that advanced bold interpretations devoid of evidence.[88]

Some argued that a new paradigm was needed, one that forged clearer connections between the discipline and the realities of contemporary history. The immediate crises confronting American society and the world at large in the 1930s mandated a new way of studying and explaining the course of history. As Caroline Ware put it in 1940, "both the course of events and the findings of the various social sciences made increasingly clear the inadequacy of all treatments of the past which dealt only with the articulate groups." She left no doubt that this redefinition of the past was a matter whose "urgency" devolved from present realities:

> No intellectual group can stand by while the society of which it is a part experiences drastic change, without being impelled to seek perspective on that change, an understanding of the basic forces at work, and the ability to distinguish between the superficial and the fundamental characteristics of the social order. Urban birth rates fall far below the level of replacement; mass unemployment; the erosion of land and men; the degradation of totalitarian war—these are the realities of today which provide the historian's milieu and inevitably shape the terms in which he will study the past.

The Depression, Ware and many of her contemporaries believed, rendered all but irrelevant the ideal of a disengaged, elite-centered history.[89]

Historians who shared this belief acted on their convictions as members of the program committee charged with planning the 1939 meeting of the American Historical Association. The committee included Ralph Gabriel, Merle Curti, and Ware herself; their hope was to encourage their colleagues to focus collectively on the compelling business at hand by organizing the sessions of the annual meeting around a single theme. They called the idea the "cultural approach to history"—a broad rubric that reflected the influence of cultural anthropology, the growing impact of the social science disciplines on history, and the conviction that politics and law alone could no longer provide a workable framework for historical inquiry. Indeed, scholars from outside the field of history were very much in evidence at the American Historical Association's 1939 meeting. An official report on the meeting stiffly concluded that for that reason "few of the papers presented are likely to be regarded as contributions to history."[90]

In fact, the papers covered an extraordinary range of topics and possibilities. They were loosely grouped around three categories— "the technique of cultural analysis and synthesis, the cultural role of ideas, and cultural conflict and nationality groups"—but in their range and imagination they easily defied that taxonomy. A volume of the best contributions, entitled *The Cultural Approach to History* and edited by Caroline Ware, appeared in 1940. It reflected much of the passion and imagination that had informed new trends in interwar historiography. Sprinkled among essays that ranged from Chinese to Balkan history were papers on population movement in the New South by Rupert Vance, an essay on the value of local history by Constance Green, Merle Curti's effort to examine the class dimensions of American intellectual life in the nineteenth century, and a range of other articles, including meditations on American folklore and documentary photography, all of which sought to give definition to "cultural history." No essay explicitly addressed African American history—an omission that reflected the Jim Crow realities that dominated the profession in the 1930s even amid the promised revolution in ideas.[91]

The round table on local history chaired by Constance Green at the 1939 meeting produced a telling consensus among the panelists, who included Hortense Powdermaker, Gerald Capers, and Vera Shlakman—all accomplished practitioners of the art of the community study. Focused analysis of a "locality having obvious geographic or cultural unity" might very well reorder the traditional priorities of history. The *American Historical Review* summarized the reaction of Gerald Capers, then a young instructor of history at Yale University, to such a possibility. "As Mr. Capers expressed it," the journal reported, "American history has been written from the top down, and only recently has the necessity of studying it from the bottom up been appreciated." A year later, Merle Curti used his powers as program chair to keep up the drumbeat. He selected for the 1940 meeting "four dominant themes: The Historical Profession; War and Society; The Common Man; and New Interpretations."

But instead the sound of war rumbling in the background dominated the 1940 meeting. Historian Robert Shuyler's paper "The Usefulness of Useless History" contained a particularly grim bit of foreshadowing. "'Background history,' interested in 'how we got this way,'" he observed, "serves the purposes of 'exponents of Progressive Education, champions of the New History, social scientists, journalists, the public generally'—to say nothing of totalitarian constructors of the 'new order.'" To link new departures in history to totalitarianism was to cast in dark ideological shadows the "cultural approach to history." In the end, the bold pronouncement of a new history in 1939 and 1940 once again appeared more ex post facto description than predictor of a turning point in historical writing.[92]

The Myth of Consensus History

Contemporary conservatism has a deadening effect on the historian's ability to take a conflict of ideas seriously. Either he disbelieves in the conflict itself (Americans having been pretty much of one mind), or he trivializes it into a set of psychological adjustments to institutional change. In either case, the current fog of complacency, flecked with anxiety, spreads backward over the American past. It is not likely in the near future that many critical scholars will emphasize the polarities that fascinated the great progressive historians, nor is it desirable that they should. . . . But we pay a cruel price in dispensing with their deeper values: an appreciation of the crusading spirit, a responsiveness to indignation, a sense of injustice.

—JOHN HIGHAM, "THE CULT OF THE 'AMERICAN CONSENSUS'" (1959)

In 1948, University of Pennsylvania historian Roy Nichols instructed readers of the *American Historical Review* to anticipate a sweeping "postwar reorientation of historical thinking." It was to be expected, Nichols explained, that "any great disturbance in the world of action or of intellect produces very noticeable effects upon the methods and controlling thought patterns of historians. It is probable that the recent war will prove no exception." Yet far from looking to the Allied victory and the United States' unparalleled position of strength in the postwar world as a triumphant starting point for a new history, Nichols dwelled on the uncertainties unleashed by the war. A sense of anxiety pervaded his prediction.[1]

Chief among Nichols's concerns were the escalating hostilities between the United States and the Soviet Union, two nations that had waged war as allies only to wind up divided by a bitter enmity. Conflict between these great powers, Nichols observed, escalated in the shadow of a new and utterly terrifying reality—the dawn of an era in which atomic energy had been harnessed to weapons of war. So fragile was the postwar world that even the United Nations, only recently created to secure the peace, appeared helpless in the face of rising world tensions. "All is confusion," Nichols wrote, "weighted heavily with dread."[2]

A little more than a decade later, John Higham confirmed Nichols's forecast of a reconfigured history in a provocative essay for *Commentary*. The 1940s, Higham wrote in 1959, had indeed brought about "a fundamental change of direction in the exploration of the American past." But gone was the apprehension so apparent in Nichols's piece. Instead, Higham's essay lamented the deadening confidence that had come to dominate postwar historical writing. The author regretted that a "consensus" of opinion now defined contemporary views of American history. So pervasive was its influence that the consensus amounted to a new orthodoxy every bit as empty and constraining as the one it had sought to replace. Turner, Beard, and the other Progressive historians, Higham argued, created a vision of American history steeped in class, sectional, and ideological conflict. Now those views had been repudiated. In their place, scholars were substituting a "placid, unexciting past."[3]

Higham traced the postwar historical consensus to several recent sweeping and powerful synthetic interpretations of American society. He named Daniel Boorstin's *The Genius of American Politics* (1953) and later *The Americans*, a multivolume work whose initial installment appeared in 1958, Louis Hartz's *The Liberal Tradition in America* (1955), David Potter's *People of Plenty* (1954), and to a lesser extent Richard Hofstadter's *Age of Reform* (1955) as important examples of "consensus history." Though each work differed in important respects, collectively they took the United States' apparent economic abundance, political stability, and domestic tranquility during the postwar years as a vantage point from which to examine the long course of the nation's history. Theirs was a search for the origins of America's essential liberal, democratic, and "homogenous" character.

They found their answers in what they viewed as the United States' unique historical trajectory. For Hartz, the absence both of a feudal past and the revolutionary struggles of Europe permitted a Lockean liberal strain to define America. With its valorizing of natural rights, private property, and popular government, this "liberal tradition" gave a distinctive cohesion to American society and enormous continuity to its history. Boorstin likewise stressed the absence in America

of the deep social and ideological conflict endemic to European societies. He emphasized peculiarly "American" talents and experiences
that provided over time extraordinary national and cultural unity.
Potter affirmed the existence of an American national character, for
him shaped and sustained by economic abundance. Hofstadter also
minimized the depth of social and economic conflict in the United
States by explaining away late-nineteenth and early-twentieth-century
crusades for social change as "archaic efforts to recapture the past."[4]

Taken together, such works represented, Higham charged, "a massive grading operation to smooth over America's social convulsions."
In place of conflict, postwar historians offered commonality. "Classes
have turned into myths, sections have lost their solidarity, ideologies
have vaporized into climates of opinion," Higham complained. "The
phrase '*the* American experience' has become an incantation." The
aridity of such an approach drained the past of life and meaning and
rendered the discipline incapable of addressing fundamental "moral
issues" embedded in American history. In calling for attention to "the
elements of spontaneity, effervescence, and violence in American history," Higham argued for a history that made room for instability and
conflict. Mindful of contemporary domestic anticommunist crusades,
Higham urged historians to explore moments that "have shaken our
society"—including "the Great Red Scares" of the twentieth century—and to do so with a reawakened consciousness of the moral
burdens of modern history.[5]

Higham's attack on "consensus history" had several ironic consequences the historian could not possibly have anticipated in 1959.
Most obviously, his gloomy prediction that an interest in the "great
polarities" that had divided Americans would not soon return proved
to be ill-timed, to say the least. For within a few short years of his essay's publication, the upheaval of the 1960s had shaken the political
and intellectual foundations of history, the discipline was yet again
"transformed" in the eyes of its practitioners, and a radical "new history" appeared. More consequentially, in challenging his colleagues
to shake off their complacency and in problematizing a mind-set he
considered poisonous to the field of history, Higham helped breathe
more life into the straw man of "consensus history."

Just as the work of consensus historians rested on a fallacious reading of the American past, so too did the paradigm of consensus history smooth away the "gradations" and subtleties of postwar histori-

ography. Higham's brilliant polemic became for later generations of historians not a challenge boldly laid down *in medias res* by a perceptive scholar of American history troubled by the direction of the discipline in the postwar years; rather, it came to serve as a fixed description of historical reality. The nuances of Higham's essay, the brave stance this scholar took, and the iconoclasm that made his remarks so fresh and intellectually bracing receded. And in their place came a simplistic summation of postwar historical writing that made of the late 1940s, the 1950s, and the early 1960s a stolid, unimaginative, and deeply conservative moment in the intellectual history of the discipline.[6]

The idea of consensus, to be sure, was alluring to many postwar historians, especially those seeking to "clobber," as one put it, the Progressive historians. During the late 1940s and throughout the 1950s, the ideological struggles of the Cold War, the dynamics of McCarthyism, and the liberal insistence on locating what Arthur Schlesinger, Jr., described as a "vital center" between extremism on the left and the right profoundly influenced the writing of American history. Many scholars did emphasize continuity and stability as the leitmotif of the American past, as their forebears had done. And certainly the ideological struggles of the postwar period gave such interpretations a distinct political—and presentist—cast. Furthermore, the economic interpretations of historical change favored by historians such as Charles Beard increasingly gave way to what Higham described as "psychological and ideological explanations," reflecting both the influence of the social sciences on the discipline of history and the "imperialism"—as Higham described it—"of the present." None of this was surprising given the political tensions, cultural mood, and intellectual trends of the postwar years.[7]

But the intellectual terrain of history in the two decades following World War II was more contested than the model of consensus allows. A spirited and forceful determination to highlight moments of conflict, to uncover struggles for social justice, and to detail the persistence of oppression and inequality remained alive. Some historians continued to focus on themes that had captivated imaginative scholars in the interwar years—political conflict, economic struggle, racial oppression, and the burdens borne by "ordinary" Americans. Race, class, and gender continued to inform the work of important historians. In fact, gender received growing emphasis during the postwar period. Countless books and articles during the 1940s and 1950s continued to strive to broaden the reach of history despite, and doubtless in some cases because of, the prevailing political scene. Indeed, to contrast consensus history with the work of such Progressive era figures as Turner and Beard was to ignore a more complex tradition in American historical writing that ran through the interwar years.

For dramatic effect, the contrast between Progressive history and consensus history well served critics of the postwar political and intellectual scene—then and now. But such a conceit narrows the intellectual trajectory of modern scholarship in American history. It obscures the ways in which a more critical, conflict-laden, and heterodox perspective on the American past persisted throughout the entire twentieth century, competing at times and always coexisting with more conservative views. To emphasize the dominance of consensus history is to render all the more inexplicable the apparently radical disjuncture between an "old" and a "new" history that appeared so dramatic amid the political upheaval of the 1960s. How did the discipline of history get to where it stood in the late 1960s? It has proven difficult to answer that question because historians themselves seem drawn to ahistorical narratives of their own history.

Indeed, Higham's affront to the idea of consensus—his call for historians to recover "the profoundest struggles and conflicts that the drama of history affords"—reflected some of the skepticism with which the purported new orthodoxy was greeted even in the 1950s. Consider two contemporaneous responses to the sweeping interpretations of American history advanced by political scientist Louis Hartz and sociologist Daniel Bell. A 1955 review of Hartz's *Liberal Tradition in America* published in the *William and Mary Quarterly* noted with bemusement the changing fashions of American history. "After World War I, United States intellectuals were writing that America was for the boobs and that civilized men could live only in Europe. Since World War II, however, a boom in Americana has claimed such uniqueness for America as to make Emerson's patriotic manifesto to scholars read like a bashful request." While generally praising Hartz's meditation on American history, this reviewer challenged Hartz's assertions that "Lockean America" had escaped social conflict in the absence of a "feudal legacy." A 1960 review of Bell's *The End of Ideology* likewise expressed doubts about such national chauvinism. Locating a blind spot in the author's conception of American society, the critic observed: "Bell appears to restrict the meaning of 'ideology' to the radicalisms of the left or right. . . . Nowhere is there any reference to an American democratic ideology." Such skepticism provides just a glimpse of the multiplicity of views among historians during the purported reign of consensus history. Far from evaporating from the scene, such varying perspectives on the American past furthered a lively conversation about the best way of making sense of the nation's history.[8]

It is perhaps not surprising that radicalism would become a focal point for competing visions of American history in the postwar period. Fears of communism framed the tensions of the Cold War. Virulent, harshly fought campaigns to root out political subversives spilled over into the sanctuary of American colleges and universities in the early postwar period. Academics responded to the anticommunist campaigns of the late 1940s and 1950s, and to the larger political tensions engendered by the Cold War, in various ways. Some ran for cover, hoping to escape or ignore the widening search for subversives. Others were forced to confront the dragnet. Some of those who cooperated with federal and state investigative committees reluctantly acceded to the climate of political repression; others advanced it. Still other historians openly challenged both the atmosphere and the specific tactics of McCarthyism.[9]

Whatever the reaction, a growing scholarly preoccupation with dissent in the American past reflected the contemporary political mood. Between 1945 and the early 1960s, an array of books and articles appeared examining the history of American socialism and communism. Biographical studies of significant radical figures proliferated, as did work that examined the intersection of race, ethnicity, and class in crusades for radical social change. The American Revolution came under reexamination as studies both repudiating and defending Beardian views appeared in the professional journals. Another topic of enormous interest to academic historians in the late 1940s and 1950s were the Alien and Sedition Acts—a preoccupation that only thinly disguised anxieties about current threats to civil liberties. As ever, Populism served as a medium through which historians explored deep conflict in the American past and debated competing views of rural agrarian struggles and the response to industrial capitalism in the late nineteenth century.

Postwar studies of radicalism defy easy categorization within the paradigm of a prevailing consensus history. And thus they serve as a useful example of the limits of the purported postwar orthodoxy. Certainly, some research explored American radicalism in an effort to prove that continuity, shared liberal values, and stability best defined the nation's history. But other work saw in America's many radical traditions a rich, complex, and often conflict-ridden struggle for power and uplift among disaffected Americans throughout United States history. In both cases, postwar historians were clearly struggling with ways of understanding better the political tensions of their own time. In doing so, they engaged in an intense and multifaceted conversation about American radicalism that not only mirrored many of the tensions and passions infusing political life throughout the Cold War period but that also demonstrated again the multiple strands that wove the texture of modern historiography.

The idea of American exceptionalism framed much of the debate over radicalism even before the rise of consensus history in the mid-1950s. Had there ever been an indigenous American radicalism separate from European traditions and ideals? This question bedeviled scholars interested in American radicalism. Chester McArthur Destler raised the issue in a late 1944 article entitled "Western Radicalism, 1865–1901" published in the *Mississippi Valley Historical Review,* and then in 1946 in a book of essays, *American Radicalism.* Destler cast his remarks for the *MVHR* in the context of a recent debate between Harvard University president James B. Conant and liberal essayist Max Lerner. Conant had expressed concern that the postwar period would be torn by fractious conflict between "reactionaries" seeking to overturn New Deal liberal reform and "European radicals" who would seek revolutionary change. He wondered who might serve as the new "American Radicals" and suggested that the transcendentalists provided a model of sane and responsible dissent. Conant's remarks inspired Lerner to suggest that the Harvard president look to Progressive and Populist reform traditions as more appropriate ideals for a reconfigured radicalism.

Destler suggested a third approach, derived from the tradition of "Western Radicalism." Stressing the reciprocal influence of eastern "urban-born" and western agrarian dissent, Destler argued for the existence of a powerful post–Civil War American radical tradition. Throughout the late nineteenth century, he observed, vigorous antimonopoly campaigns were waged in both East and West, among farmers and urban laborers. Labor associations and the ideas of urban working-class radicals inspired rural agrarians to pursue "collectivist" schemes designed to curb the power of corporate capitalists. Farmers crafted powerful arguments for regulatory government that in turn proved instructive to eastern reform interests. All this added up to a native radical strain in American thought that transcended the sharp sectional lines drawn by Turnerians. Destler lavished special attention on antimonopoly spokesman Henry Demarest Lloyd, single-taxer Henry George, and socialist Edward Bellamy as exemplars of this American heritage of dissidence.[10]

In the 1890s the Populists appeared with a coherent "system of radical thought" that was the legacy, Destler insisted, of "three decades of recurring unrest, agitation, and intercourse with radical and reform movements in the urban world." They voiced a commitment to certain forms of government regulation of business, and "to limited experiments with state socialism as a means of combating the great movement toward monopoly and economic concentration." Yet the crusade was not, Destler insisted, "socialistic either in purpose or spirit." The Populists sought mostly to strengthen capitalism, the historian claimed, and this sharply distinguished them from European Marxian socialists.[11]

Destler thus attempted to demonstrate simultaneously the existence of a genuinely radical late-nineteenth-century American reform tradition and its lack of connection to communism and socialism. On the one hand, he carefully explained the Populist reliance on the "labor-cost theory of value" and "antimonopolism"—twin creeds that provided the "ideological foundations of working-class movements in the United States." He emphasized the profoundly "radical character of Populist collectivism"—quoting approvingly a historian who claimed that in its time "Populist" was a more extreme "term of reproach than was 'Red' a generation later." But Destler was equally insistent that the ideas that inspired American radicalism had come from the "lower middle class," not a "job-conscious proletariat." In fact, the alliance between workers and farmers foundered when "indigenous radicalism" ran up against "an imported, proletarian Socialism" that "made its first great appeal to English-speaking wage earners in America in the depression ridden nineties."[12]

Destler's ambivalence toward radicalism led him to both regret and exalt the influence of the left on American reform politics. In 1896, opponents within the People's Party succeeded in marginalizing the coalition of "antimonopolist-Nationalist-labor-and-Socialist" forces. That outcome undermined "labor and left wing" support for Populism and doomed the movement. Still, Destler insisted that "the antimonopolist radicalism of the West survived as a vital force in American thought and politics." It could be traced through the Progressive years right down to the New Deal era and the gradual creation of "the democratic welfare state" and government regulation of monopoly capitalism. It was to men such as Robert LaFollette, George Norris, and Henry Wallace, Destler suggested, that President Conant should look for the legacy of American radicalism.[13]

In a 1947 review in the *American Historical Review*, Louis Hacker rebuked Destler's claims in *American Radicalism* that dissent in the United States bore little resemblance to European socialism. The distinction, Hacker insisted, was "too sharply drawn." As he put it: "America was no more isolated from the wind of European radical doctrine than it was from European thought generally; and just as Americans received Locke, Ricardo, and Spencer, they also received Owen, Fourier, Proudhon, Bakunin, and Marx. It is idle and unreal to claim that the first was American—and native to our culture—and the second European—and therefore alien." Nor could the range of radical sentiment in America be encompassed within "a single pattern." Radicalism in America moved along a spectrum "from right to left—there was the voluntarism of Samuel Gompers, gradualist Socialism, Lassalleanism, Marxian socialism, philosophical Anarchism, and Anarcho-Syndicalism." Indeed, Hacker insisted that by the early twentieth century "the Socialism of Debs and the Anarcho-Syndicalism of the I.W.W. spoke in an American tongue and struck responsive chords in the breasts of large numbers of native-born Americans." For Hacker, American radicalism reflected neither exclusively indigenous nor foreign origins, but was an amalgamation of both.[14]

Yet Hacker's efforts to construct his own synthesis of American political traditions ran into similarly harsh criticism in the next issue of the *American Historical Review*. Stanford professor Edgar Robinson found elements to praise in the source book for teaching American Civilization Hacker had prepared with Helene Zahler. But he rejected Hacker's singular explanation of American culture. "The title of this book is arresting," Robinson offered as an opening gambit. "It is not 'Shaping *an* American Tradition,' but '*The* Shaping of *the* American Tradition.'" The balance of Robinson's complaints are so evocative of contemporary criticism of American history texts they might have been written today rather than in 1947. Robinson decried Hacker's choice of subjects and documents, and his left-wing political bias. "One is certainly safe in concluding," Robinson noted, "that history is here being 'used' to present problems. The heavy emphasis upon revolt, upon minority rights, and upon the points of view of the rebel would seem to bear out this view." Noting that Hacker included 138 historical figures in his collection of documents, Robinson took umbrage at the cursory attention given to the central political figures in American political history. "The utterances of Lincoln are confined to his reply to Horace Greeley on saving the Union, and the Preliminary Emancipation Proclamation. There are no words of George Washington. The Declaration of Independence does not appear, nor does the Constitution of the United States." On the other hand, the "political manifestoes and such calls for action" of Ignatius Donnelly and Eugene Debs, while admittedly "valuable," were well represented.[15]

Such criticism did not dampen similar efforts to define a broader, and more radical, American political tradition. Two popular histories of this kind captured the attention of professional historians in the late 1940s. A 1946 collection of portraits of American reformers entitled *Critics and Crusaders: A Century of Protest* included reformers ranging from transcendentalist Margaret Fuller to socialist Daniel De Leon and anarchist Emma Goldman. The book won praise from a reviewer in the *American Historical Review* for its "perceptive biographical sketches" and "first-rate expositions such as the one summarizing Marx's doctrine of surplus value." Taken together, the portraits demonstrated "the immediacy and urgency of the long fight to preserve human freedom."[16]

A 1947 popular history entitled *Land of Liberty: Being an Informal History of the Common People and Their Heroes* by Fred Hamlin fared less well in the opinion of professional historians. The book offered a rather jaundiced people's history of the American nation, noting of early colonial America: "Never was a land, dedicated ostensibly to freedom, less free. Never were men, lured by the promise of freedom, more bitterly betrayed." The book made much of George

Washington's inauguration amid "the heart of Wall Street," assessed his administration as a "reign of dollars," and reserved praise for "the common people" as well as Thomas Jefferson, Walt Whitman, and Franklin Delano Roosevelt. An *American Historical Review* assessment of the book faintly praised the study as "interesting" but pointed out numerous errors of fact, including the assertion that after Woodrow Wilson's "great heart" had stopped beating, Attorney General A. Mitchell Palmer "began a vicious witch-hunt among immigrants, accompanied by murderous flouting of civil liberties." Lehigh University professor George Harmon dryly observed: "This was done under Wilson; his heart was still palpitating; and Palmer was his Attorney General."[17]

The 1950s brought more respected efforts to chart the course of a radical tradition. Harvey Goldberg's edited collection of essays entitled *American Radicals: Some Problems and Personalities* (1957) sought to reverse, one reviewer noted, the Turner thesis by examining "thinkers and doers who set themselves in opposition to the dream of an ever-expanding frontier." The book included explorations of figures as disparate as John Brown and Theodore Dreiser. From William Appleman Williams's sketch of Charles Beard to David Herreshoff's portrait of Daniel De Leon, the study documented "the richness and variety, the resources, the individuality, as well as the dilemmas of the radical past." A 1958 study by Donald R. McCoy, *Angry Men: Left-of-Center Politics in the New Deal Era,* portrayed with sympathy and compassion men such as A. J. Muste and Norman Thomas.[18]

This perspective likewise informed literary scholar Daniel Aaron's 1961 study, *Writers on the Left.* Sponsored by the liberal Fund for the Republic, which had itself been a target of McCarthyist attack in the 1950s, the book was part of a larger series exploring the impact of communism on American life. Aaron emphasized the social and economic context of the Great Depression in explaining the factors that drew gifted American intellectuals to the Communist Party in the 1930s. For this he was sharply criticized in the *Journal of Southern History.* The reviewer complained:

> What Mr. Aaron does not make sufficiently clear (though he is to be admired for not reviving old passions or beating the drum for a new witch hunt) . . . is the fact that what began in many ways as a revolt against stuffiness of certain bourgeois values . . . developed into a vital part of an undeclared war aimed at achieving by any and all means the overthrow of the American system of government. It is true, as Mr. Aaron states,

that the majority of intellectuals attracted to Communism never joined the party. But it is also true that there were many who did; rather more, I would suspect than Mr. Aaron believes. And Mr. Aaron says nothing at all about the hard core leftists working in what could have been a struggle, an actual war, for survival.

Such a response reflects the bitter tensions that continued to divide academics in their responses to the left and to anticommunism. Studies such as McCoy's and Aaron's, however, also gave evidence of the energy some scholars devoted to making historical sense of radicalism in ways that made intelligible left-wing political allegiances.[19]

That theme also informed a compelling 1957 study of World War I dissidents by H. C. Peterson and Gilbert Fite. *Opponents of War, 1917–1918* surveyed the range of groups within the United States who stood against the war and the political repression they experienced as a result of their convictions. The dissidents included socialists, the IWW, pacifists, and, as C. Vann Woodward observed in a passionate review of the book for the *American Historical Review,* "numerous minorities such as the Negroes, sundry labor and farmer organizations, and various aliens, who were victimized by the same oppression merely because they were vulnerable and unpopular with the oppressors." The furious attacks unleashed upon these dissidents, and even those who merely supported their right to free speech, figured centrally in Peterson and Fite's analysis. For Woodward, the book carried a clear and compelling message. His description of it in 1957 underscored his conviction that the story remained thoroughly relevant to contemporary Americans.

> This study makes it plain that the more revolting types of political oppression and brutality, commonly thought to be peculiar to the police state and associated with particular nations and particular political systems, were abundantly prevalent in the enlightened American democracy under a progressive and idealistic President. Political prisoners of the state, both men and women, were subjected to calculated starvation, inhuman tortures, and sadistic brutality. Books were burned, classrooms and churches invaded, homes ransacked and gutted, presses wrecked, courts intimidated, meetings broken up, and speakers beaten. Mobs with patriotic names took over communities and countryside, looting, burning, beating, and lynching. Freedom of speech was seriously defined by a judicial opinion handed down in that era as "criticism which is made friendly to the Government, friendly to the war, friendly to the policies of the Government." Thus defined, freedom of speech flourishes in all the police states.

Peterson and Fite drew explicit parallels between the history they explored and the contemporary political scene. They included a vigorous defense of freedom of speech in a final chapter and stressed, in a passage Woodward chose to quote, that "'present laws and actions . . . show a close relationship to the situation in World War I' and that 'this type of thinking is all too prevalent in mid-twentieth-century United States.'"[20]

The preoccupation with radicalism among some postwar historians resulted in biographical studies of important dissidents. These books often blended a tendency to look for the wellspring of radicalism in personal psychology and a wish to make some broad claims about the impact of historical context in shaping dissenting beliefs. Jonathan Grossman's 1945 biography of nineteenth-century trade union leader William Sylvis made note of Sylvis's contacts with Marx and the labor activist's often progressive ideological commitments. But the book also stressed Sylvis's pragmatism—a quality that made him a quintessential pioneer of the *American* labor movement. As Herbert Solow summarized it in the *American Historical Review,* "Sylvis had his eye primarily on the pie slab and Dr. Grossman's contribution is to show how he labored constantly to increase it."[21]

The appearance in 1949 of Ray Ginger's sympathetic biography of Eugene V. Debs, *The Bending Cross,* pursued a similar theme. Ginger reintroduced the socialist leader to the public as a thoughtful, humane, and tireless advocate of labor. Yet in portraying Debs as more an embodiment of the American Midwest than spokesman of European revolutionary socialism, Ginger stressed the native cast of Debs's radicalism. "The author rightly implies," a critic for the *American Historical Review* observed, "that Debs was a curious mixture of Karl Marx, John Brown, and James Whitcomb Riley." *The Journal of Negro History* saw in the Ginger portrait an affirmation of the African American struggle against racial inequality. "The work portrays at every turn Debs' deep and abiding sympathy for the oppressed of every class," William Brewer observed. "In regard to colored workers in the American labor market since the Civil War, Ginger shows that Debs was statesmanlike in opposing segregation which he insisted was divisive for all labor." Ginger's work made of Debs a figure whose radicalism transcended both the Socialist Party and his specific historical moment to speak across the ages of the need for economic justice and social equality.[22]

So influential was Ginger's portrait of Debs that a subsequent laudatory biography of Debs by H. Wayne Morgan published in 1962 prompted criticism of an allegedly pro-Debsian bias among historians. "Who else," a critic complained in the *Mississippi Valley Historical Review* in 1963, "has had such uniformly favorable treatment from biographer and historian?" The subtitle of a 1962 biography of Norman Thomas, "Respectable Radical," likewise aptly captured that author's effort to lionize the socialist leader as a figure who "bridged the worlds of liberalism and radicalism." By the early 1960s, biography thus served as an important vehicle for historical meditations on American radicalism. New studies appeared of Populist firebrand Ignatius Donnelly, Socialist Labor Party founder Daniel De Leon, and radical priest and IWW activist Thomas Hagerty. These portraits ranged from largely admiring (in the case of Donnelly) to harshly critical (De Leon) to poignant (Hagerty).[23]

Less palatable, judging from the reviews of historians, was Richard Drinnon's account of the life of anarchist Emma Goldman. Drinnon began his 1961 biography *Rebel in Paradise* by describing the affection he had acquired for his subject: "I may as well record here at the outset that I like her and trust her," he asserted. In emphasizing Goldman's criticism of Soviet communism and her libertarian commitments, Drinnon attempted to cast the anarchist's political philosophy in terms explicable to Americans. "Emma was simply an extreme federalist-democrat," Drinnon explained. She was, he argued, a figure who straddled the radical immigrant and native American radical traditions. Drinnon's portrait of Goldman earned some praise from a reviewer for the *Mississippi Valley Historical Review.* Robert K. Murray exclaimed: "Here is a superb story that will shock the staid, antagonize the close-minded, and surprise even the informed, since it reveals an Emma Goldman who was not a political lunatic but a remarkable woman of many facets—popularizer of the arts, defender of civil liberties, caustic critic of dictatorship, strong proponent of birth control, and, above all, a sensitive human being." But Murray sharply rejected Drinnon's attempt to ennoble Goldman's radicalism. "Despite Drinnon's attempt, anarchism of the type preached by Goldman cannot be compared with Jeffersonianism," he insisted. "She was *not* fighting the battle of 'liberty with responsibility' that we usually associate with the American liberal tradition."[24]

Indeed, Murray challenged Drinnon's depiction of Goldman as a figure ahead of her times who was victimized by a less than progressive nation:

> No amount of verbal washing will eradicate the fact that, even as a radical, Goldman was far removed from the basic trends and developments of the contemporary American scene. True, as Drinnon points out, the national reaction to Goldman indicated that Americans were not really ready for true dissent and that American society, despite its vaunted stability, could not yet sustain the onslaught of the likes of Emma Goldman. Still, as a careful assessment will indicate, Emma moved in that hostile environment as an interloper without any basic understanding. Her lack of contact with American reality meant that Emma Goldman was not only a rebel but also a stranger in Paradise.

Robert Bremner also expressed his distaste with Drinnon's enthusiasm for Goldman and her story. "The story of Miss Goldman's life necessitates the retelling of some particularly ugly episodes in American history," he noted in the *Journal of Southern History.* "The author relates these events with gusto and in a frankly partisan spirit." Too much of the narrative was "tedious, embarrassing, and occasionally ludicrous," he dismissively concluded. "Perhaps that is the way life is—especially Emma Goldman's." In trivializing Goldman and minimizing her historical significance, such reviews suggested that studies of women radicals had yet to find their audience. Still, Drinnon's efforts exemplified a determination among some scholars to integrate radicalism into the American tradition.[25]

Historians' efforts to probe the origins and character of American radicalism went well beyond collective studies of various dissidents. The debate on the true nature of American radical traditions was perhaps most forcefully revealed in the huge postwar literature on the history of American socialism. Among the earliest of these postwar studies were several focused on the German Forty-Eighters. Inspired by the centenary of the revolutions of 1848, these works explored German refugees who fled to the United States, bringing with them a political sensibility steeped in Marxism and an enduring commitment to radical beliefs.

The publication of Karl Obermann's enthusiastic 1947 biography of Joseph Weydemeyer proved to be an opening salvo in what would be a relentless battle to define American socialism. Weydemeyer's close association with Marx, his deep engagement in the German

Communist League, and his tireless commitment to the labor movement made him a compelling subject for historians eager to establish—or refute—the idea that European Marxism found fertile ground in nineteenth-century America. Obermann wrote from an explicitly Marxist perspective. He presented Weydemeyer as a "pioneer of American socialism" who successfully advanced radical workingmen's associations in New York, the antislavery cause, left-wing immigrant support for the election of Abraham Lincoln, and the emerging American labor movement. Economic historian Jonathan Grossman warned readers of the book's "Marxist flavor" but praised the study for casting new light "on the origin of the American labor movement; and . . . the influence of German immigrants on the development of American culture."[26]

That judgment was thoroughly rejected in Chester Destler's vitriolic review of Obermann's book in the *American Historical Review.* Destler's response demonstrated how an interest in American reform traditions and a furious anticommunism could be embodied in a single historian. "This is a communist tract for the times," Destler began his 1948 assessment. "It is the product of a continuing attempt by the publishers to identify communism with the American national tradition, a move that is identical with communist tactics in other countries where the example of Moscow is followed with abject fidelity." Destler was not wrong in associating Obermann's publisher, the International Publishers Company, with a series of left-wing studies. The press was closely affiliated with the American Communist Party and with New Century Publishers produced, it has been estimated, over 2 million pamphlets and books a year in the mid-1940s. (Books by Marxist historians such as Herbert Aptheker would very likely never have seen the light of day without such publishers.)[27]

Obermann's assertions that Marxism was "inextricably bound up with the anti-slavery cause, the homestead movement, antebellum labor organizations, and the Civil War" stuck in Destler's craw. But it was Obermann's enthusiasm for his subject that especially rankled his reviewer. As Destler explained: "Throughout the book Weydemeyer and his associates are described glowingly as 'democrats' and 'progressives' despite the fact that they sought to introduce conceptions of the class struggle, proletarianism, and revolutionary conspiracy into the world's greatest democracy." The book, Destler conceded, had value for "serious students of radicalism in America" for its revelations about the roots of American Marxism. But the historian flatly rejected the notion that that story could be interwoven with the narrative of indigenous radicalism. Rather, Obermann's study had value chiefly as an illustration of the nefarious propagandizing tactics employed by the Communist Party in contemporary America.[28]

Weydemeyer would again surface as a meaningful exemplar of American radicalism in 1962. The new academic journal *Labor History* reprinted in full, with an introduction by Hal Draper, Weydemeyer's 1852 essay "The Dictatorship of the Proletariat." The essay was first published in the *Turn-Zeitung,* a mid-nineteenth-century German immigrant socialist publication in New York. Draper argued that Weydemeyer's essay continued to be of historical interest for two reasons. First, "it may be something of a surprise to find out," he observed, that the term "dictatorship of the proletariat" was first coined "on our side of the Atlantic." And, Draper continued, the piece "was the first attempt at a summary of a Marxist view to an American audience and in an American publication." In this context Wedemeyer served to demonstrate the intersection of European and American labor movements and the radicalism of early American workingmen's associations.[29]

The same could be said of Carl Wittke's 1950 biography of Wilhelm Weitling, *The Utopian Communist,* and his 1952 collective portrait of the German Forty-Eighters, *Refugees of Revolution.* Both books fueled the debate over European socialism and American radicalism. Arthur Bestor praised Wittke's study of Weitling in the *American Historical Review* for demonstrating through the German revolutionary's life the importance of both the European and the American context in "the early history of socialism." The story Wittke told, Bestor concluded, "gives neither comfort to would-be American social revolutionists nor to superpatriots who believe the republic endangered by every foreign ism that is allowed a hearing on our shores." Bestor's own work on Owenite and Fourierist communitarian socialism, *Backwoods Utopias* (1950), balanced an appreciation for the importance of Owenite utopian experiments with an exploration of the factors that doomed them to extinction.[30]

Other historians, however, considered Wittke and Bestor naïve in their stress on the lasting contributions radicals had made to American society. "The case for Owenism as an important part of American interest in social experimentation," Alice Felt Tyler said of Bestor's study, "does not seem to me to have been proved." Tyler also reviewed Wittke's *Refugees of Revolution* for the *American Historical Review* and found it similarly wanting. The book emphasized the "cultural leaven" provided by the German Forty-Eighters, whose political ideals, cultural activities, and spirited civic engagement changed the German immigrant community as well as the host nation. But Tyler criticized Wittke for claiming "too much for his Germans in the way of cultural contributions. Even in the field of music, where their influence was most marked, there was much interest before they came and it would have grown had they gone elsewhere."[31]

Vera Shlakman, by contrast, used Wittke's perspective on the Forty-Eighters as a cudgel with which to beat Oscar Handlin's sweeping study of immigration to America, *The Uprooted* (1952). Her stinging review of both Wittke's and Handlin's books in the *Journal of Economic History* appeared only a few months after she had been dismissed from her job at Queens College in the fall of 1952 for taking the Fifth Amendment when questioned about her alleged membership in the Communist Party. Shlakman was acutely aware of the political relevance of historical research on nineteenth-century immigration. Wittke and Handlin's studies, she noted, "are timely in light of the interest aroused in American immigration policy by the passage of the McCarran-Walter Act"—legislation that permitted the attorney general to deport immigrants associated with communist organizations even if they were U.S. citizens. Shlakman found much to praise in Wittke's "stirring" account of the German Forty-Eighters, although she noted that *Refugees of Revolution* lavished too much attention on "the articulate intellectuals" given that "the rank and file" made up a greater proportion of "the revolutionary forces." Still, for all its weaknesses Wittke's account at least gave agency to the German immigrants.[32]

Shlakman missed this quality in *The Uprooted*, a narrative of the wrenching journey immigrants made to the United States and their heroic struggle to adapt to their new country. Widely admired by professional historians, the book was, Shlakman conceded, "written with passion and eloquence and sympathy." But Shlakman charged that Handlin had "slurred and distorted" the historical record by generalizing about 35 million European immigrants "of diverse origins and backgrounds" whom he described simply as "peasants." She appeared to be particularly rankled by Handlin's depiction of the immigrant's "passive and pathetic acceptance of his unhappy lot in Europe," his "suspicious dissociation from reform and radicalism during his American century," his "unyielding conservatism and docility." Such a portrait could not possibly account, she insisted, for Jewish garment workers who struggled to organize their industry, socialist cigar makers, militant Irish coal miners, migrant laborers who joined the IWW, and activist textile workers.[33]

Shlakman rejected out of hand Handlin's suggestion that innate conservatism among immigrants and suspicions of radicalism doomed class-based labor organization. The "calculated, divisive tactics of employers" and "exclusive policies of the A.F. of L.," she argued, provided more fruitful avenues for explaining the failure of mass mobilization of workers. Indeed, Shlakman rejected Handlin's work because it failed to provide a class analysis of the immigrant experience. As she explained:

> Much of what Mr. Handlin attributes to immigration is the story of the creation of a working class. It is not necessarily one of crossing the ocean to America, to be an alien in an alien land, but one of forcible ejection from the land to be transformed into wage laborer. The process is painful, and a continuing one. They also were uprooted who left the English fields to pour into Liverpool and Manchester, and later who were tractored off the Oklahoma farms (to borrow John Steinbeck's phrase) to flood Route 66 to the factory farms of California.

Far from embracing the consensus model, Shlakman invoked European history as an argument against American exceptionalism.[34]

Historical research on the American Socialist Party in the pre–World War I era crystallized these divergent perspectives among post–World War II historians. Much of the discussion swirled around the work of three young historians—Howard Quint, David Shannon, and Ira Kipnis—who made their reputations by undertaking new research on the Socialist Party. Howard Quint emphasized the distance between European Marxism and the socialist movement that took root in late-nineteenth-century America. Here was an argument for an indigenous radicalism that acknowledged the many faces of American socialism even as it judged the movement as part of a larger response to industrial capitalism. Quint argued forcefully that American socialism "owed more for its inspiration to Edward Bellamy's *Looking Backward* than it did to Karl Marx's *Das Capital.*" He set out to make his case by tracing the many streams that fed American socialism in its formative years.[35]

Quint introduced his argument in a 1949 essay for the *Mississippi Valley Historical Review* that revived socialist journalist Julius Wayland as a subject of historical interest while emphasizing the peculiarly American elements of Wayland's radicalism. Algie Martin Simons, a founding member of the Socialist Party and avid student of American Marxism, once described Wayland as "the greatest propagandist of Socialism that has ever lived." Quint didn't consider the assessment far-fetched. Wayland, who had been born in Indiana, managed to tap into Populist sentiment and labor unrest by means of weekly newspapers that "soft-pedaled involved discussions of socialist theory and concentrated on the more urgent issues of government assistance to farmers and unemployed factory workers." In so doing, Quint argued, Wayland "'Americanized' socialism." Quint's portrait treated Wayland with doses of irony so heavy they frequently lapsed into ridicule—a tone that likewise infused the historian's subsequent book-length study, *The Forging of American Socialism: Origins of the Modern Movement* (1953).[36]

Although the professional journals generally praised Quint's exhaustive research efforts and his objectivity, reactions to his book reflected some surprising qualities of the postwar historical discussion of American radicalism. The *American Historical Review* assigned the book to Harry W. Laidler, an outspoken socialist intellectual and activist. Laidler criticized Quint for not analyzing more fully the "European backgrounds of the American movement" and the ways in which specific Marxian philosophical principles had been adapted to the American scene. Seymour Bassett, himself a scholar of American socialism, trivialized Quint's book in the *Mississippi Valley Historical Review* because it lacked the power of more sweeping recent interpretations of American socialism. As "a treatise on the segments within any segment of American socialist history," Bassett wrote, the study could not hold a candle to Daniel Bell's "cleverly articulated narrative" on the origins of American Marxian socialism.[37]

Ira Kipnis's work, *The American Socialist Movement, 1897–1912* (1952), which appeared a year before Quint's study, provoked equally divisive responses. Kipnis analyzed political factionalism within the Socialist Party between left, center, and right elements but did so from a largely positive perspective on socialism's contribution to American politics. Historian David Shannon, who reviewed the book for the *Journal of Southern History*, rejected Kipnis's analytical categories while making note of his too evident biases. "The author's sympathies are obviously strongly with the party's Left," Shannon observed. "It would appear from this book that the Right had a monopoly on chicanery." Howard Quint likewise judged Kipnis's "sympathies" as being "glaringly with the 'impossibilists'." But in his review of the book for the *Mississippi Valley Historical Review*, Quint both accepted Kipnis's schema for the party and shared his disfavor of "the right wing's chauvinism, its authoritarian leadership, its hesitancy to support workingmen engaged in industrial conflicts, and its reactionary attitude toward immigration, women, and Negroes." Still, Quint reiterated his belief that "the syndicalism of the left made it completely unacceptable to the American populace."[38]

The *American Historical Review* offered Kipnis's book to Harry Laidler for review, with the result that the profession's most prestigious journal in 1953 weighed in against Kipnis for being too harsh in his criticism of the Socialist Party. As a Democratic Socialist himself, Laidler naturally took umbrage at Kipnis's criticism of the moderate wing of the party. As Laidler put it:

> He bitterly criticizes the party leadership for alleged lack of democracy, for their "opportunism," their "desire for power and office," their "chauvinism," etc. While the moderate socialists had their faults, few of the sweeping charges which Dr. Kipnis enumerates are substantiated by him in the main body of his text, nor can they be substantiated. In many cases . . . he gives to the reader an entirely false idea of the general attitude of the socialists toward trade union activities. The same is true of the socialists' attitude toward the rights of women, of Negroes, *et al.* Nor can one form any idea by reading this volume of the amount of ability, idealism, and dedication that went into the movement or of the real influence of the movement on social legislation, trade union development, and constructive social thinking during these days.

While it was true that Laidler diverged from Kipnis in the former's alliance with a more conservative form of socialism, the squabble in this case was over which wing of the Socialist Party deserved more admiration.[39]

David Shannon, whose examination of the Socialist Party carried the story from its birth in 1901 to its purported death in 1952, took a more detached and jaundiced view of the party than either Kipnis or

Laidler. His 1955 book *The Socialist Party of America: A History* laid much of the blame for the movement's failure on factionalism within the party. Although Shannon sought to "Americanize" the party by locating its heterogenous membership and ideas within the nation's political mainstream, he also concluded that "in a manner of speaking it was American history that defeated the socialists." Here again was the evocation of a distinctive American environment that proved hostile to theories of class conflict, third-party political movements, and broad philosophical commitments rather than practical programs. Such interpretations reflected the influence of the long-standing tradition of American exceptionalism. In this respect, the themes of consensus history informed a growing literature on American socialism that both acknowledged deep social, economic, and cultural conflict and dissidence while affirming the persistence of continuity, democratic values, and stability in the American national experience.[40]

The contradictions within this position were in full view in a two-volume compendium entitled *Socialism and American Life* that emerged from Princeton University in 1952. Prominent social scientists such as Daniel Bell, Sidney Hook, and Paul Sweezey contributed to the collection. A reviewer for the *Mississippi Valley Historical Review* quickly zeroed in on the inherent weaknesses in liberal historical analyses of radical movements. Stanford University scholar George Knoles observed: "The entire project indicates some paradoxical features of the development of socialism in America. Several authors suggest reasons why socialism has not been very successful in the United States (Hook and Sweezey, for example); yet the study seems written on the assumption that socialism has had an enormous influence on the development of the United States. This is a value judgment, of course, and admits of variable interpretation." Yet Knoles concluded his review by invoking the very same contradiction. He emphasized the existence of a genuine, and deeply indigenous, radical American tradition while taking pains to distinguish the home-grown variety from European socialism. "The tendency is all too strong in the reviewer's estimation to allege that liberal, progressive, and even some radical developments in American history are directly or indirectly the result of socialism," Knoles commented. "This tendency overlooks the strong, native, nonsocialist radicalism that has characterized American society since the colonial period."[41]

Studies of charismatic political activists and broad histories of the

Socialist Party represented two strong themes in the historical literature on American socialism in the postwar years. But monographic studies that attempted to probe into the popular sources of support for socialism also appeared in the 1950s. A 1954 essay by Grady McWhiney for the *Journal of Southern History* examined Louisianan votes for Eugene V. Debs in the 1912 presidential election, when the Socialist Party ticket ran ahead of the Republican slate headed by William Howard Taft. Although Woodrow Wilson carried Louisiana, McWhiney found it curious that "one of every fourteen Louisiana voters cast a ballot for a party supposedly dedicated to destroying the southern way of life . . . despite the fact that a native Southerner" was the Democratic nominee. McWhiney determined that the Socialists scored best in nearly the same hill parishes of Louisiana where support for the Populists had surged in the 1890s.[42]

Both movements tapped poorer white Protestants, according to McWhiney, though the Socialists enjoyed none of the support the Populists occasionally tapped among established planters in the region. But the Socialists succeeded in mobilizing unskilled lumber workers who had been deaf to the entreaties of the People's Party. "What success the Socialists had in Louisiana," McWhiney concluded, "resulted from the temporary alliance between the oppressed farmers and the lumber workers." The latter suffered from a "wretched existence" that included intolerable living conditions in lumber camps, low wages, long hours, and the strong-arm tactics of the timber companies. In analyzing the factors that ultimately led to the socialists' defeat and decline, McWhiney laid some blame at the feet of the Socialist Party, noting its internal factionalism and tensions with the IWW. However, more important to their defeat, in his view, was the relentless union busting of the lumber industry and "the combination of prosperity and witch-hunting brought about by World War I," which proved "devastating to radicalism in Louisiana." Once broken, the socialists never regained ground, though McWhiney suggested Huey Long's "Share Our Wealth" program might well be seen as a manifestation of socialism's legacy in the Louisiana of the 1930s.[43]

The efforts of the socialists to organize sharecroppers in Arkansas during the 1930s came under similar historical scrutiny in 1960. M. S. Venkataramani contributed a carefully researched essay to the *Mississippi Valley Historical Review* that credited Socialist Party chief Norman Thomas with raising public awareness of the inadequacy of New Deal agricultural policies for sharecroppers and tenants in the region. The efforts of Arkansas socialists to mobilize poor farmers through the Southern Tenant Farmers' Union unleashed harsh reprisals against the sharecroppers by local landowners, corporate interests, and apparently the local police. Eventually the Roosevelt administration took modest steps to address the inadequacy of relief measures for poor farmers. But neither the New Deal nor the efforts of Thomas, Venkataramani explained, succeeded in solving the problems of farm tenancy. Still, Venkataramani's was a respectful assessment of the impact of socialism on American politics in the 1930s.[44]

Postwar historians proved far more guarded in their judgments of the American Communist Party. Theodore Draper produced two important histories of the Communist Party under the sponsorship of the Fund for the Republic. *The Roots of American Communism* (1957) and *American Communism and Soviet Russia* (1960) won praise from historians for demonstrating the ways in which the emergence of communism in the United States owed something to a long tradition of radicalism in America but far more to the strict control exerted by the Soviet Union. The fact that Draper's publisher identified him as an ex-communist lent credibility to his account of the internal workings of the party. As Stow Persons explained in the *Mississippi Valley Historical Review:* "This fact has to be noted only because it should be said that no visible scars from that experience are evident. His rejection of Communism is complete, but it is the kind of dispassionate rejection to be found among thoughtful observers in all parts of the free world, and it does not show the marks of a personal crisis." Irving Howe and Lewis Coser's *The American Communist Party: A Critical History* (1957) likewise received a respectful review in the *American Historical Review* from then political scientist and lawyer Max M. Kampelman. But Kampelman chastised the authors for soft-pedaling the implications of even a brief flirtation with the party: "The authors minimize the indictment that the Communist party of the United States is an integral part of a strong international conspiracy designed to overthrow our government and is thus a clear and present threat to the democratic institutions of the United States. One can well grant the 'innocence' of many individual Communist party members and, at the same time, recognize that the sum total of the party mechanism, loyalties, affiliations, and membership makes up such a dangerous conspiracy." Indeed, the emerging literature on the history of American communism often depicted the party as a foreign import without any close connection or sensitivity to the nation's historical values or traditions. That theme, a reviewer for the *Journal of Southern History* stressed in a comment full of irony that appeared lost on its author, ought to prove "highly reassuring" to "all who are concerned about Communism as an internal menace."[45]

A preoccupation with race was also evident in new postwar historical research on American communism. Wilson Record's master's thesis for the University of North Carolina, published as *The Negro and the Communist Party* (1951), typified the prevailing argument. Record stressed that African Americans had rejected communism despite the party's exhaustive efforts to organize them. He attributed such resistance to the strong faith in liberal democratic values among African Americans, despite their suffering in American society, and to their suspicions of politically repressive regimes. Dictatorship, he observed, invoked the memory of slavery. Although African Americans had, Record observed, "played an important role in shaping the American radical tradition," they would not support an alien radicalism. Here again was the distinction between "native" and "imported" radical activism so central to postwar historiography.

Record's work received a warm reception, especially among African American leaders such as Walter White, chief of the National Association for the Advancement of Colored People. White faced the challenge of pursuing the fight against racism and discrimination in an era when outspoken criticism of American society invited suspicions of communist leanings. The *American Historical Review* assigned Record's book for review to White, who lauded the study as "definitive" proof that "the colored American has analyzed and rejected Communist appeals more accurately and promptly than any other segment of the population." Rayford Logan largely echoed this assessment, though he placed some blame on the party itself for undermining its appeal to African Americans through political bumbling and inconsistent rhetoric.[46]

Stanford University graduate student Vaughn Bornet questioned those assumptions in a 1952 essay for the *Journal of Negro History* entitled "Historical Scholarship, Communism, and the Negro." Bornet not only attacked Record for "serious defects" in his research, he also lambasted Walter White and others for writing approving reviews of Record's book. While endorsing the conclusion that "Communism has failed from the beginning to win the allegiance of nearly all Negro Americans," Bornet suggested that Record's research did little to illuminate the reasons for that failure. In making the point, Bornet posed a series of evocative questions for scholars:

> Did the Communist Party of America actually *fail* throughout the first three decades in its efforts to capture the allegiance of the Negro? Is there something special about the *doctrine* of Communism that makes its ideology a poor rallying point for the discontented? Is there something *unique* about the Negro or about the nature of his complaints against American conditions that has made the Communist solution to his problems seem impractical? Did white Communists always do the best they could with what they had? How many Negro leaders or organizations *lost faith* in political democracy and in the institution of private property in the era from 1920 to 1950? What were the motives of these people? Such questions deserve answers based on exhaustive research.

To illuminate African Americans' response to communism would require immersion, Bornet insisted, in both African American and Communist Party sources. Yet the absence of archival materials on leading American communists, African American party members, official party papers, and government records made it impossible to assess accurately the activities of American communists and their success with targeted groups. In expressing frustration at the inaccessibility of source material on the party, Bornet observed: "It appears that historians must await the pleasure of the Federal Bureau of Investigation before they can try to drain them of their fascinating story." Bornet also objected to Record's "sweeping" attacks on the Socialist Party, the AFL, and the CIO for failing to deal fairly and effectively with African Americans.[47]

Bornet went further in his comments on a sociological study entitled *Communism versus the Negro* that attacked the *Journal of Negro History* and its founder, Carter Woodson, for publishing the work of known Marxists such as Herbert Aptheker and for being communist influenced. Noting that one of Aptheker's published articles ended with the assertion "slavery was a horrid form of tyrannical rule," Bornet observed: "Abolitionists would have agreed, but many would have thought the wording too mild." Bornet's defense of Aptheker took pains to reject the latter's political sympathies; yet he strongly defended their intellectual value and their appearance in the *Journal of Negro History.* "It is hard to accuse Dr. Woodson of Communist 'sympathy' for including such articles in a magazine of Negro history," he concluded, "and a case could be made, by some, for blaming the editor if he had arbitrarily excluded them at that time."[48]

No one could possibly mistake Bornet as an advocate for left-wing political organizations or causes. He took pains to condemn communism and to distinguish himself from those who would minimize its threat to democracy. Yet the editor of the *Journal of Negro History* clearly felt some trepidation about publishing in 1952 even Bornet's cautious attacks on anticommunist crusaders who would "espouse that tenet of reactionary doctrine which looks on all change as necessarily evil." William Brewer, then acting editor of the *Journal,* stressed in a publisher's note introducing the article that the author possessed impeccable academic credentials and, as a World War II veteran and current Naval Reservist, a demonstrated record of patriotism. He added, in an effort to further distance himself from Bornet's remarks: "The comments he makes about the *Journal* and the Association for the Study of Negro Life and History are his own and do not necessarily represent the viewpoints of the Editorial Board or the Association. Dr. Bornet is not and has never been a member of the Association." This disclaimer was unusual, and was followed by another that appeared later in Bornet's article when the author was challenging criticism that the *Journal of Negro History* had received contributions from communist front organizations. When Bornet suggested that "it is barely possible that the *Journal* accepted a few small donations . . . in the 1930s without noticing the fact," Brewer placed an asterisk next to the paragraph. In a note, he vigorously disputed even the suggestion that the *Journal* had unwittingly received any such donations.[49]

No such disavowals were attached to publication of Vernell Olivier's "Pre-Marxist Russian Radicals and the American Civil War" in a 1953 issue of the *Journal of Negro History.* Olivier argued that pre-Marxist Russian socialists admired elements of the American Republic only to become disillusioned by the Civil War and Reconstruction, and that this disappointment prepared the ground for revolutionary Marxian socialism in Russia. He arrived at these conclusions by examining the writings of Aleksandr Herzen, Mikhail Bakunin, Nikolai Chernyshevskii, and Peter Lavrov for commentary on American slavery, the Civil War, and its outcome. Olivier's assertions that the American failure to live up to the nation's democratic promise had paved the way for Marxism carried a special resonance. During the postwar period, civil rights activists often invoked Cold War fears of communist expansionism to bolster their insistence on the need for the United States to address its racial problems. In this sense, Olivier's meditation on Russian radicalism, like so much of the postwar literature on radicalism, spoke to present political concerns.[50]

Certainly this was true of the tremendous postwar interest among historians in the late-eighteenth-century Alien and Sedition Acts. The 1950s and early 1960s saw the publication of several books that looked back to Revolutionary America for an earlier example of the nation's struggle to determine the parameters of freedom. John C. Miller's *Crisis in Freedom: The Alien and Sedition Acts* (1951) was an early case in point. Miller never made explicit reference, as one reviewer noted, to McCarthyism or even to the twentieth century in his study of eighteenth-century congressional measures to restrict the rights of aliens and curtail political dissent. Still, he cast his work as an exploration of a fundamental problem that lay at the heart of American democratic government. "Without doubt, liberty of speech and of the press lies at the heart of all liberty," Miller wrote. "In every society worthy to be called free there is an untrammeled play of public opinion; immunity from criticism is the privilege of no government officials; and the right of arguing about ideas is jealously guarded. . . . The issue, then and now, is the same: 'Whether the state can punish all words which have some tendency, however remote, to bring about acts in violation of law, or only words which directly incite to acts in violation of law.'" The language Miller used to describe the events of the late eighteenth century could not have failed to evoke powerful associations in readers of the mid-twentieth century. As Yale University law professor Fred Rodell observed: "He speaks of 'loyalty oaths' (then for aliens only), of 'witch-hunters,' 'subversive activities,' 'subversive ideas,' 'pinkish liberalism,' and 'fellow-travelers.' His accounts of the prosecuting zeal of federal judges ring a Medina-like bell—although most of the Sedition Act trials were high-handled by U.S. Supreme Court justices, on circuit, and there were apparently none with the guts of a Hugo Black or a William Douglas against the panicky partisan tide."[51]

Indeed, reviewers for the professional history journals largely endorsed Miller's implied analogy between late-eighteenth-century efforts at political repression and McCarthyism. Although Rodell found fault with Miller's pedestrian writing style, he asserted: "Professor Miller is right in seeing the basic issue as identical, then and now. Can Congress, in the name of national security, enact and have enforced a law or laws which impinge on and radically restrict the civil liberties of the people? Does or does not the First Amendment to the Constitution . . . mean what it says?" Indeed, the book was, in Rodell's view, "a parable for our times." All the more regrettable that it was so badly written, he lamented, for it "might have given pause to thousands upon thousands of ordinary folk—had his book been written in a manner to reach them." The *Mississippi Valley Historical Review* echoed these conclusions. "It is an ugly picture, this," University of Washington historian Max Savelle sadly concluded. "The picture of a nation persecuting its own citizens simply for dissenting from the views of, and for criticizing, the party in power. It is impossible to escape the dramatic parallel between the Sedition Act of 1798 and the Internal Security Act (the McCarran Act) of 1950 (and all the 'little McCarran Acts' passed in the states) and the circumstances that produced them." Less pessimistic about the book's potential audience than Rodell, Savelle hoped "that many American citizens may read it, and that there may take place that rarest of all historical events, a lesson learned from history!"[52]

That theme was implicit in the work of Cornell scholar James Morton Smith, who extended scholarly analysis of the Alien and Sedition Acts with his 1956 study *Freedom's Fetters: The Alien and Sedition Laws and American Civil Liberties.* Like Miller, Smith emphasized the reactionary nature of the legislation, portraying the system of laws and its administration as a serious threat to democratic government. His perspective on the tactics of the Federalists reflected Smith's belief that the eighteenth-century battle over First Amendment rights had considerable relevance. In a 1952 essay for the *William and Mary Quarterly,* he emphasized the continuing dangers of political repression: "Popular government rests on the right of the public to choose between opposing views. Since an informed public opinion is vital to republican government, freedom of expression is necessary for the formation of that opinion. If people cannot communicate their thoughts to one another without running the risk of prosecution, no other liberty can be secure because freedom of speech and of the press are essential to any meaning of liberty." Without any direct reference to McCarthyism, Smith thus invoked the significance of his research for contemporary America.[53]

Leonard Levy's *Legacy of Suppression* (1960) explicitly rejected any effort to pursue "presentism." Still, like others who examined the historical record, he turned to the past to take the measure of American fealty to freedom of expression. Levy stressed the attenuated nature of early American philosophical commitments to First Amendment rights. The glass of political liberty in America, Levy insisted, was placed on the table half empty, given the shared assumptions even among the revolutionary generation that some restraints on free speech and freedom of the press were necessary. Harold Hyman advanced a similar argument in his exploration of the long history of American loyalty tests, *To Try Men's Souls* (1959). However long or short they judged the tradition, however willing or hesitant to make reference to prevailing conditions, such studies reflected widespread concern about the dynamics of dissent and its repression in the 1950s.[54]

Postwar studies focusing on more recent efforts to suppress radicalism likewise reflected intense disquietude with political intolerance in the mid-twentieth century. Robert K. Murray's 1951 essay for the *Mississippi Valley Historical Review* examined the impact of post–World War I fears of communism on the dynamics of the Great Steel Strike of 1919. Anticommunist anxieties were so pervasive in American society after the war, Murray argued, that "no strike, no act of violence, no deviation from the norm failed to bring charges that the probable cause was domestic bolshevik activity." Such charges were greatly exaggerated, he maintained. Although "native radicals openly espoused the bolshevik philosophy and worked for internal revolution," Murray insisted that they were few in number and "there was no real reason to believe that the nation was in serious danger." That did not prevent the steel industry from ruthlessly exploiting latent fears of radicalism in its showdown with labor in 1919. When steelworkers struck to win their right to collective bargaining and more equitable working conditions, public opinion initially seemed on the side of the workingmen. The steel companies began a campaign of propaganda and systemic harassment to undermine that support by linking the strike to bolshevism.[55]

Murray emphasized that such labor anticommunism extracted a

high cost from all participants: "As soon as the word 'Red' was injected into any industrial dispute, the immediate issues were lost completely." Labor suffered from the public perception that unionism and campaigns for better wages and working conditions reflected the hidden hand of "sovietism." "The open shop principle rapidly became the 'American way,'" Murray observed, and the hostility to labor "fell heavily on the future fortunes of organized labor." Not until the CIO campaigns of the 1930s, he argued, would steel workers succeed in forcing the hand of "Big Steel" to recognize unionism. The public fear of radicalism also manifested itself in "a more subtle, but equally as deadly, fashion": it "underwrote the vigorous suppression of liberalism and plunged nonconformists into the full glare of public censure."[56]

Murray expanded these arguments in his book-length study of post–World War I antiradicalism, *Red Scare: A Study of National Hysteria, 1919–1920* (1955). As the title implied, Murray drew on the psychologizing then fashionable among postwar historians to cast the campaign as an example of a "national psychoneurosis." But the historian also reiterated his case that the internal menace of radicalism was greatly overstated, that capital deliberately fanned the flames of anticommunism to break the back of labor, and that the entire sorry episode left a bitter legacy for Americans. Further, Murray boldly defined his "approach to history" as "mainly moral," and he did nothing to conceal his abhorrence at the tone, injustices, and long-term outcome of the antiradical campaign.

Indeed, Murray's failure to exploit adequately the insights of psychology to explain the Red Scare provoked criticism from historian John Morton Blum. In a review of the book for the *Mississippi Valley Historical Review,* Blum acknowledged that Murray proved his case that "the 'Red Scare' was primarily a red herring dragged across the face of labor by proponents of the open shop; that newspapers by and large supplied not light nor learning but delusive inflammation that political leaders led not, instead reflecting and exploiting each shining hour of their country's shame; that the distemper penetrated, as such infections always had, judicial chambers." Blum regretted, however, that Murray had not gone beyond such "familiar" arguments to probe why Americans were "susceptible" to such hysteria. "About hysteria, after all," he observed, "psychology and social psychology in particular have had considerable to say. On this account, an approach to history that is 'mainly moral' becomes mainly thin." What he missed most in Murray's account was attention to the larger institutional, intellectual, and social context of the Red Scare. A much longer tradition of antiradicalism—one deeply bound up in the nativism, ethnic tensions, Populist "parochial suspicions," and anti-intellectualism of the preceding period—framed the events of the 1920s. As Blum explained his objection: "Dust jacket to the contrary, the 'Red Scare' is treated too much as an isolated episode, a reprehensible phenomenon, too little as the acute manifestation which it was of a complex, chronic American disease. This, Professor Murray wants desperately (as all readers of this journal also must) to cure; soon, perhaps, the moral necessity he feels will help to inspire the kind of comprehensive diagnosis—not yet available—from which therapy may proceed." These were themes Blum himself had explored in a 1950 essay entitled "Nativism, Anti-radicalism, and the Foreign Scare, 1917–1920." A reviewer of Murray's book for the *American Historical Review*, however, extracted a much clearer and more forceful message from Murray's analysis. "While the author is chary of drawing comparisons with the more complex present situation, he warns us of the dangers of an artificial nationalism," Selig Adler observed, "and argues that radicalism should be contained by removing the seedbeds of social decay from which it draws nourishment."[57]

Throughout the 1950s and early 1960s, historians continued to devote considerable energy to exploring the history of American antiradicalism. Studies such as John Higham's *Strangers in the Land* (1955), a brilliant exploration of the long history of nativism, made a case for continuity in American attitudes even as it emphasized the pervasiveness of conflict in responses to immigration. Other studies took a more episodic approach, examining less a tradition of antiradicalism than the discrete circumstances that gave rise to especially virulent attacks on dissent. Such was the case with Donald Johnson's book on the rise of the American Civil Liberties Union and the attacks on it—a study aptly entitled *The Challenge to American Freedoms* (1963). Still other scholars focused on the concerted attacks on specific individuals or political organizations. Sidney Fine's 1955 essay for the *American Historical Review*, "Anarchism and the Assassination of McKinley," stressed that "the American fear of anarchism was based on a lack of understanding as to the real nature of the anarchist doctrine," a division that was only deepened when an anarchist murdered the president in 1901. Philip Taft explored similar dynamics in his article "The Federal Trials of the IWW" in a 1962 *Labor History* article.[58]

In isolating the forces that encouraged antiradicalism, historian William Preston, Jr., emphasized the impact of war, social conflict, and economic depression on prevailing attitudes. But he stressed that the tactics pursued by the federal government and the judiciary in a climate receptive to antiradicalism sealed the fate of many aliens. In *Aliens and Dissenters* (1963), Preston used government documents to trace a powerful antidemocratic tradition in America advanced and maintained by federal policies and officials who conflated aliens with radicalism.[59]

That tradition was alive and well in the 1960s, Preston argued in a bold epilogue to *Aliens and Dissenters* that took on McCarthyism and continuing Cold War efforts to suppress radicalism. Recent acts of Congress such as the Alien Registration Act (1940), the Internal Security Act (1950), and the Immigration and Nationality Act (1952) "have made the radical-catching bills of the first two decades," Preston wrote, "seem simple and harmless." Nor had such tactics disappeared with the demise of Senator McCarthy: "In the security-conscious 1960s, the rights of a large portion of the population—aliens, naturalized citizens, and native born radicals—have been sacrificed to the safety of the state. These groups are becoming the real displaced persons of the cold war, less free and less protected than the rest of us. There has been a steady progression toward a federal policy based on fear rather than faith in people. Not only are we afraid of our own shadow, but we also would like to deport it." Theodore Saloutos strongly endorsed Preston's conclusion in the *American Historical Review*. He added, "the frightening thing is that the screening process employed in the surveillance of immigrant arrivals and radicals now has been extended to include thousands of Americans who are employed by agencies other than the federal government and defense industries. And this indirectly has affected many who are fearful of adopting dissenting positions, lest they be branded as subversives." Studies such as Preston's, and reaction to them, reflected profound concern and even frank doubt about the protection of freedom in the United States. They bear little resemblance to confident celebrations of democratic freedom, national unity, and stability that formed the interpretive heart of consensus history.[60]

Although Preston's was an unusually open attack on what he perceived as a persistent climate of political repression, some scholars turned their skills to the subject of McCarthyism itself in an effort to historicize recent developments. Such efforts diverged sharply from the then popular approach of "psychologizing" McCarthyism. Scholars such as Daniel Bell and Richard Hofstadter emphasized the "status anxieties" embodied in McCarthyism. To see the anticommunist crusade as the latest manifestation of American anti-intellectualism and hostility to elites—a strain Hofstadter traced to Populism—minimized the role of elites in the campaign. John Caughey's *In Clear and Present Danger* (1958) took a different tack. It was perhaps the boldest intellectual effort on the part of a historian to confront the tactics of anticommunists.

Caughey came by his concerns honestly. He had been among a group of academics dismissed by the University of California in the early 1950s for refusing to sign a loyalty oath. His book was less historical analysis than a polemic that spared no aspect of McCarthyism. As a critic for the *American Historical Review* described the book: "the reign of the inquisitors, the drift toward a police state, the descent into McCarthyism, the decline and fall of the Fifth Amendment, the shackling of the mind—these are the headings under which the Caughey documentation is presented." Carl Wittke honored Caughey's courage and endorsed his apprehensions in a laudatory 1958 review for the *Mississippi Valley Historical Review*. He concluded: "This is a good book, and a very depressing one for all who believe that love of freedom and liberty made America unique, and that honest dissent hitherto has been a good safety valve and a stimulant to progress. . . . Professor Caughey recalls many incidents which already have become dimmed in the public memory. He sounds the call to arms for a patriotic defense of civil liberties—a cause that is as important today as war upon treason within and preparedness against attacks from without." The same tone characterized a pamphlet entitled "Academic Freedom in a Time of Crisis," which Vera Shlakman prepared with other members of the New York Teachers Union in the early days of her struggle at Queens College. Written in the midst of a heated political battle, the broadside issued this warning: "The dragnet is wide enough, the bills and laws are worded loosely enough to catch anyone whose life is not so narrow that he has never been stirred to speech or action by great events." However effective they may have been in addressing immediate threats to academic independence, such comments indicate that dissidence of various sorts survived the postwar reconfiguration of American historiography.[61]

If the model of consensus history did little to account for the complexities of historical work on American radicalism, so too did it fail to describe studies on a whole range of subjects that challenged continuity, shared values, and an absence of conflict as the primary themes in American historical development. Research on race, slavery, Native American history, labor, and women's history continued apace between 1945 and 1965. And much of this work gave evidence of diversity rather than allegiance to a rigid orthodoxy; it exemplified less a reign of conservatism than a posture of continued political engagement.

Radical historians are of course the most compelling example of the dissent from consensus. Historians such as Herbert Aptheker and Philip Foner, while acknowledged as exceptions to general trends, have been largely sidelined in discussions of American historiographical traditions. The basic historiographical irrelevance (to put it crudely) of radical historians has been assumed in part because such scholars dissented from dominant lines and styles of interpretation. Yet the marginalizing of such figures demonstrates the tautological character of the American historiographical tradition: they lack importance to historiography because they have not been considered important figures.

It cannot be persuasively argued that radical historians have been largely set aside within the historiographical narrative because their work was excessively ideological. Prevailing paradigms of historical writing posit rigid ideological positions to all manner of historians upon whom they have lavished attention. Nor can the inattention to Marxist historiography be justified because the work of radicals was "wrong." For who defends Beard's and Turner's sweeping interpretations anymore, despite the reams of paper expended on them? Indeed, the reification of a few "seminal" figures—such as Beard or Turner—continues despite the widespread repudiation of their work by subsequent generations of historians.[62]

The notion that figures outside the interpretive mainstream merit little attention because they lacked influence on major historical trends fulfills its own prophesy—and it has done so repeatedly. Within the narrative of American historiography, intellectual influence assumed and asserted has augmented itself, while inattention has ensured the continued obscurity of countertraditions. However alone they may have been in their convictions, Marxist historians were not ignored intellectually in their own time, even if they paid a high professional price for their political and intellectual convictions. To be sure, they may have felt alone and isolated from the historical profession. But their work even then belonged to the record of American historical writing, whether or not commentators on historiography have subsequently deemed their scholarship worthy of explication. Furthermore, if one judges the trajectory of historical writing over more than a century, one might well argue that not a few trends in contemporary historical writing moved in the direction of the radical historians. Ironically, the modern preoccupations with class, race, culture, and to a lesser extent gender can be easily detected among the work of scholars who are often judged as lacking staying power or influence.

Aptheker and Foner serve as excellent cases in point. Both scholars were rediscovered by New Left historians in the 1960s as heroic predecessors in the struggle to advance a more politically engaged and inclusive history. Yet throughout their careers, they remained vigorous proponents of a radical history that cut across the political boundaries imposed by Old Left/New Left, old history/new history, conflict/consensus dichotomies. Even as a graduate student at Columbia University in the late 1930s, Aptheker energetically took on the task of challenging verities in leading historical studies of slavery. He wrote his master's thesis on Nat Turner's rebellion in an effort to challenge Ulrich B. Phillips. "At the time," Aptheker later recalled, "it was the only major slave revolt known. And it was opposite of the stereotype, and I knew that Ulrich B. Phillips' portrayal of slaves as docile and all that was more than just false, it was vicious and racist." While pursuing his research in Washington at the Library of Congress, Aptheker made the acquaintance of Carter Woodson. So began a long association that ultimately gave Aptheker, in the *Journal of Negro History,* an important venue for his work.[63]

Aptheker expanded his work on Turner in his dissertation on slave revolts prepared at Columbia. Published in 1943 by Columbia University Press, *American Negro Slave Revolts* exhaustively mined primary sources to compile a record of some 250 insurrections among groups of slaves numbering ten or more. Resistance among slaves, Aptheker insisted, was not only common, it fed a constant undercurrent of anxiety among slaveowners that made antebellum Southern society a cauldron of conflict and unrest. Not surprisingly, that interpretation met with harsh rejection from leading conservative white southern historians. Avery Craven dismissed Aptheker's findings in the *Journal of Economic History* as "neither new nor, if properly interpreted, important. What is new is that commonly accepted facts are magnified and distorted to support sweeping generalizations." Rebelliousness among slaves and cruelty among masters, Craven added, were "but one part of the picture and often a rather small part of the whole." In a familiar 1940s era verdict on Aptheker's work, intended as an insult, Craven likened Aptheker's views of slavery to those of the abolitionists.[64]

But it was J. G. de Roulhac Hamilton's 1944 review of Aptheker's thesis in the *American Historical Review* that reflected the full weight and persistence of reactionary defenses of slavery among historians. Hamilton charged Aptheker with swallowing "whole every rumor that found its way into print or manuscript in the jittery South." While conceding that cruelty existed among slaveholders just as it did "wherever sadistic men and women" existed, Hamilton insisted that "the whole body of authentic sources proves fairly conclusively that cruelty was the exception rather than the rule." He further suggested that African Americans who endured slavery came out of the experience in a condition that compared favorably with blacks in Africa "today." Similarly racist views surfaced in an *AHR* review of Aptheker's 1938 study *The Negro in the Civil War*. "This little volume would make an excellent Emancipation Day oration before an audience composed of Negroes, Marxists, and descendants of William Lloyd Garrison," B. I. Wiley asserted. Rejecting Aptheker's observation that some African Americans assisted northern soldiers and that others fought bravely in the Union Army, Wiley concluded that a more accurate interpretation would show "the average slave waiting opportunistically for Northern armies to bring freedom close enough for him to grasp it."[65]

But other scholars found much to praise in Aptheker's pioneering work. Lewis McMillan described *American Negro Slave Revolts* in the *Mississippi Valley Historical Review* as "a narrative of two thrilling though tragic centuries" grounded in "painstaking" research. W. M. Brewer likewise praised the study in the *Journal of Negro History*. Aptheker had reached, Brewer asserted,

> the highest levels of historiography through judicial handling of sources and materials which have been by-passed or ignored by writers who have consistently tried to portray slavery as a benevolent society in which slaves were kindly treated and generally contented. The author cites incontrovertible evidence which proves the opposite. . . . The values of this painstaking investigation in neglected cultural and social history are significant in that they suggest further studies and blast the accepted historical traditions concerning slavery and the true role of slaves in that society. Here is a new and penetrating interpretation of disregarded historical evidence of the rarest quality which is the high function of scientific history.

In an unusually blunt ad hominem complaint to the *American Historical Review*—then a rare event in the genteel community of historians—Vassar professor Kenneth Porter sternly censured J. G. de Roulhac Hamilton for his treatment of Aptheker. Porter wrote in a published letter to the editor:

> The reviewer . . . has not treated the volume with seriousness; he has merely attempted a brisk brush-off. The review really terminated with, and is summed up in, the first sentence in the third paragraph: "In my judgment he fails completely to prove his thesis." The page which follows is devoted to misrepresentation of Dr. Aptheker's methods, defense of slavery, and a sweeping charge of unspecified errors and defects, the whole riddled with contradictions and unsupported by specific evidence or examples.

Porter ended his vigorous defense of Aptheker by stressing that "I have never met nor corresponded with Dr. Aptheker; I am not even acquainted with anyone who knows him. I believe that he is now in one of the armed services. He is at any rate a serious student who deserves better treatment from a scholarly journal than a review which is merely a resentful reaction to a distasteful theory."[66]

It is unlikely that Porter was unaware of Aptheker's Marxism, for the author had published widely in left-wing journals while earning his credentials as a professional historian. Nor did Aptheker make any secret of his political beliefs—on the contrary. Even as an Army captain serving in the artillery during the Second World War,

Aptheker later recollected, "I was known as a Communist; I wrote for the *New Masses* while I was in the service." Aptheker joined the Communist Party in 1939. There is no question that his outspoken Marxist convictions, work for the party, and radical political activism prevented him from acquiring an academic appointment at a major university—a fact that became apparent early on in his career as a historian. After the war, Aptheker remembered, "I tried getting a job at Columbia, but one of my favorite professors there, taught ancient history, was happy to see me but he said to me, 'Aptheker, Columbia would never hire a man with your views.'" Aptheker lectured widely, wrote countless books and articles on African American history throughout the postwar period, published and was reviewed in professional historical journals. But until he was appointed to the faculty at Bryn Mawr College in 1969, he had held only part-time teaching positions, including one at a Bronx community college.[67]

Philip Foner's career followed a trajectory that reflected many of the same struggles endured by Aptheker. The son of Russian immigrants who grew up on the Lower East Side of Manhattan, Foner graduated from City College in 1932. Along with his brother Jack, he earned a Ph.D. in history from Columbia University under the direction of Allan Nevins. Both brothers went off to teach at City College. Philip Foner produced an excellent early book entitled *Business and Slavery: The New York Merchants and the Irrepressible Conflict* (1941), which explored the willingness of many northern merchants to overcome their instinctual opposition to slavery in the service of their economic interests. The book received warm reviews—particularly from southern historians, who were easily persuaded by an interpretation that stressed the selfish economic motives of northern businessmen. This was not Beardian history. Foner did not reduce the New York merchants to their material investments; he emphasized the shifting character of their political perspectives and the impact of rapidly changing events on their behavior. Indeed, Arthur Cole observed in the *Mississippi Valley Historical Review* that Foner "corrects in his particular field the over-simplified economic interpretation of the causes of the Civil War." Avery Craven's *American Historical Review* assessment pronounced *Business and Slavery* "an excellent study. The research is thorough and well balanced." It seemed an auspicious start to Foner's academic career.[68]

The historian's fortunes soon changed, however, amid the anticommunist investigations of the war and postwar period. Although Foner had secured an academic appointment at City College, he was ousted from the faculty in 1941 amid the Rapp-Coudert hearings probing Communism in the New York school system. His brother Jack also lost his position in City's history department as a result of the investigation. This was the end of Philip Foner's regular employment as an academic historian on a university faculty for over twenty years. Yet, like Aptheker, Foner wrote many books and articles contributing to his chosen field. Among his early efforts was a two-volume anthology of Thomas Paine's writings published in 1945. The collection earned praise in the *American Historical Review* as "a really monumental contribution . . . of first-hand materials, excellently edited." In subsequent years, Foner produced several other documentary histories, including a 1952 three-volume edition of Frederick Douglass's writings that Kenneth Stampp commended in the *American Historical Review* as "a major contribution to nineteenth-century political and social history."[69]

Foner's *History of the Labor Movement in the United States, from Colonial Times to the Founding of the American Federation of Labor* (1947) received a more mixed reception from professional historians who objected to his Marxian interpretation. In challenging the emphasis of John Commons and his disciples on the pragmatic "job conscious unionism" of American workers, Foner stressed that history demonstrated the existence of class consciousness among American workers. His was a far more idealistic and reform-minded labor movement than other historians would have it. Foner also emphasized race and gender as critical variables in his discussion of labor. But he failed to persuade historians who objected to his ideological orientation, his interpretation, and his passionate engagement in his subject. "Labor is invariably the hero who is never even muddle-headed—just put upon by capital," Clarence Long objected in a 1949 issue of the *American Historical Review*. "I do not dispute his thesis that the working class made a great contribution to the growth of our social ideals. I have become convinced, moreover, that J. P. Morgan added more spans to a bridge to socialism than Norman Thomas could in ten lifetimes. But I do get bored with such a paragon of virtue. Labor just couldn't be this good; or capital this bad." The *Journal of Negro History* leveled the same criticism in a review of Foner's second volume of his *History of the Labor Movement in the United*

States (1955). "Marx, the dead saint, and Engels, the living disciple," the reviewer complained, "parade through the pages of this book through their dicta." Whatever the merits of these criticisms, Foner's work advanced a vision of American history that placed ordinary Americans at the very center of the narrative. In so doing, he anticipated many themes that New Left historians would pursue in the 1960s, including those who would find fault with his historical analysis.[70]

Left-wing historians such as William Appleman Williams, who managed to remain in the academy, provided an important bridge to a new cohort of graduate students. Williams's work on American diplomatic history, most notably *The Tragedy of American Diplomacy* (1959), recast celebratory tales of American expansionism into a critical analysis that traced the growth of an imperialism driven by corporate capitalism. In 1961 Williams published a sweeping reinterpretation of American national development, *The Contours of American History*, which viewed history through the lens of historical epochs defined by mercantilism, laissez-faire, and industrial capitalism. Such ideas invigorated Williams's graduate students at the University of Wisconsin, who in 1959 founded a new journal devoted to radical historical analysis. Among the contributors to and editors of *Studies on the Left* were Staughton Lynd, James Weinstein, Eugene Genovese, Aileen Kraditor, Joan Wallach (Scott), Gabriel Kolko, and an array of other scholars whose work directly challenged conservative and liberal historical models. By the late 1950s, Weinstein, Genovese, Kolko, Lynd, Herbert Gutman, Kraditor, David Montgomery, and many other talented scholars were all deeply engaged in research that would soon powerfully shape yet another "new history"—one whose course would be charted in part by the political events of the 1960s and that would involve a profound rejection of the consensus model.[71]

Other fields of inquiry within the discipline of history in the postwar period neither affirmed the ideal of consensus nor advanced a radical counternarrative. Yet their existence raises questions about the adequacy of prevailing ways of understanding postwar historical writing. Women's history serves as a particularly evocative example. Much research in this field continued to be carried out by "amateur" historians—those who were not professionally trained in a graduate program. The persistence of gender discrimination within the historical profession makes that fact unsurprising. Still, research by amateurs on American women captured the attention of academic historians, who devoted space in professional journals to description and assessment of such studies. Furthermore, professional historians also pursued important new scholarly work in women's history in the postwar period in their explorations of the lives of ordinary women, reformers, political and economic inequality, race relations, the family, slavery, and feminism. These topics would prove to be of enduring interest to contemporary historians.

Biography continued to be a popular form of examining women's experience, as it had been for centuries. Many of these works focused on women whose historical significance was derived from their association with important male figures. A new study of Abigail Adams and a collection of her letters appeared in the late 1940s. The early 1950s brought a popular collective biography of the three Peabody sisters—one the wife of Nathaniel Hawthorne, the other Mrs. Horace Mann, and the third a "spinster" and "public pest for good causes."[72]

The women surrounding Abraham Lincoln remained a subject of lively attention. Ruth Randall, the wife of Lincoln historian James Randall, produced a biography of Mary Todd Lincoln that sought to correct the widely accepted image of the president's wife as a mentally ill shrew who tormented her husband. Writing with sympathy and respect for Mrs. Lincoln, Randall acknowledged the emotional instability apparent in her subject's later years while attempting to draw a fuller portrait of Mary Lincoln's character and her relationship to the president. The book was widely reviewed in professional history journals in part no doubt because of James Randall's standing, but male reviewers found it difficult to swallow Mrs. Randall's revisionism. A warm response to the study in the *American Historical Review* praised Randall's book on Mary Lincoln as "magnificent," "carefully documented," a scholarly study that "exploded" the old myths and portrayed "the real Mary Lincoln." But the reviewer could not quite let go of the old approach to Mary Lincoln. He concluded, "However, as this reviewer lays this book aside, a recurring thought again comes to mind. Would Abraham Lincoln's life have been easier had he had a wife not handicapped by the shortcomings of Mary Lincoln?"[73]

Avery Craven found much to praise in the study. "Mrs. Randall," he noted, "has certainly made the best case possible for Mary Lincoln and her marriage." But this prominent southern historian was not persuaded by the revisionism, and he particularly rejected Ruth Randall's compassion for Mrs. Lincoln. Given his prominence as a scholar, Craven seemed unusually willing to suspend the historian's posture of detachment and distance in assessing the life of Mrs. Lincoln. Indeed, his response to her biography seemed less that of a scholar than a would-be suitor sizing up an available woman, as the following passage makes plain.

> Mrs. Randall . . . proceeds to create from sounder materials the "true" picture of Mary Lincoln and her marriage. And what are the essential features of that picture and what final conclusions must the objective reader draw? In the first place it is perfectly clear from Mrs. Randall's own statements that Mary Lincoln was not the kind of a woman that most men would want for a wife. She had an uncontrollable temper and a bitter tongue. She was ever emotionally immature, impulsive, and imprudent. She was susceptible to insincere flattery, intensely vain and highly nervous, inordinately ambitious, and unreasonably jealous of anyone who even remotely crossed her path. She was extravagant in her tastes and admittedly a little insane in matters of finance. She meddled secretly in her husband's affairs and sometimes embarrassed him by making promises of public favors which he could not possibly grant. She spoiled her children. . . . She had a tendency to view things personally. . . . For all these shortcomings Mrs. Randall offers the excuse of "feminine sick headaches" and what the modern psychologist views as irresponsibility in certain fields of action.

A review in the *Journal of Southern History* expressed doubts in similar terms.[74]

Nineteenth-century female abolitionists and reformers attracted the attention of amateur and professional historians alike who recognized the compelling role women had played in antebellum moral crusades. Lillian O'Connor's intriguing *Pioneer Women Orators: Rhetoric in the Ante-Bellum Reform Movement* (1954) studied the oratory of twenty-seven women who lectured about abolition, temperance, and women's rights, including Frances Wright, Elizabeth Cady Stanton, Ernestine Rose, and Amelia Bloomer. Temperance leader Frances Willard was the focus of Mary Earhart's 1944 biography. Columbia University historian John Krout largely praised the latter work but regretted it did not offer a more "careful analysis of the campaigns for temperance and for woman suffrage in the generation before Miss Willard became an active participant." Such an approach would have better illuminated an important theme Krout missed in Earhart's book: the larger "social significance" of the Women Christian Temperance Union "not only for women but for the entire nation."[75]

Two biographies of nineteenth-century Quaker activist Anna Elizabeth Dickinson appeared, one a scholarly study. Both traced the career of this young abolitionist over whom, a reviewer noted, "curiously enough, political historians seem to have drawn a veil." Dickinson played a fascinating role in national party politics as a compelling orator for abolitionism and later the Radical Republicans. A popular study of Laura Haviland traced the involvement of this Quaker woman with the underground railway. A reviewer for the *Journal of Negro History* regretted its many deficiencies as scholarship, for "the purpose is a wholly admirable one. The story of Laura Haviland needs to be told; hers is too valuable a life to be forgotten." A biography of Lydia Maria Child likewise disappointed historian Louis Filler. He had hoped for a more scholarly treatment of a woman who deserved attention, he argued in the *Journal of American History,* as "a groundbreaker in several fields and as a personality."[76]

Biographies of Harriet Beecher Stowe proliferated in the postwar years, though all met with searching criticism from historians. Edward Wagenknecht's *Harriet Beecher Stowe* drew on records at Radcliffe College's Women's Archives (now the Schlesinger Library) in constructing a psychological study. The *Journal of American History* judged that an improvement on previous efforts to tell Stowe's life story. The *Journal of Negro History* found two popular studies of Stowe written for young readers worthy of review but of limited intellectual value. Johanna Johnston's study of Stowe, *Runaway to Heaven,* reflected profound ignorance of African American history, one reviewer argued. Johnston's reference to "contented Negroes" and "a rare and unlikely slave uprising" offended Edna Jackson, who suggested that if the book was assigned to young readers "the wise teacher will indicate that the Negro slaves were not content and that slave uprisings and rebellions occurred from the inception of slavery."[77]

Another study of Stowe's many achievements, written for children and promoted by its publisher as "a career story," met with a similar reception. A reviewer for the *Journal of Negro History* found the book a dubious model for impressionable young women. Despite the author's "profound sympathy for the enslaved and oppressed people of the period her book portrays," the author's "choice of words" gave the reviewer an "unexpected mental jolt when he meets, three times, in the space of twenty-six consecutive lines, the old stereotypes which have a way of creeping into so many of the works of well-intentioned authors of the 'majority group' in America." He referred here to the author's use of "pickaninnies" to describe young African American children. "Repetition of this sort, even though it appears only once in the entire book, becomes questionable—to one reader at least," the reviewer observed, "and can be labelled simply as being in bad taste, if one is to be *kind* as a reviewer."[78]

Much more satisfying were early biographical studies focusing on African American women. Lawyer and feminist Pauli Murray told the story of her own family in *Proud Shoes: The Story of an American Family* (1956). A reviewer for the *Journal of Negro History* asked: "Where does a sensitive Negro woman, reared in a world in which skin color is the greatest single fact of daily existence, seek refuge as she is buffeted by the winds of racial prejudice?" The answer, Murray demonstrated, could be found in "the story of . . . her maternal grandparents." A 1957 biography of Mary McLeod Bethune traced the life of an African American leader who was said to have remarked of herself, "I believe, first of all, in God, and next of all, in Mary McLeod Bethune." The book offered not only a compelling and sympathetic portrait of this extraordinary woman, the *Journal of Negro History* observed, but "the backdrop of the political and social ferment of the Negro's long struggle for full citizenship." The use of women's life histories for inspiration likely informed Sadie Daniel St. Clair's 1949 essay for the *Journal of Negro History* detailing the activities of Myrtilla Miner. The founder of a teaching preparatory school for black women that became known as Miner Teachers College, Miner was, St. Clair argued, the counterpart to more widely heralded late-nineteenth-century founders of colleges for elite white women.[79]

New studies of female religious figures likewise captured the attention of historians. Emery Battis's *Saints and Sectaries* examined the life of Anne Hutchinson and her involvement in the Antinomian controversy. Battis drew on the social sciences to explore the psychological facets of Hutchinson's iconoclasm and included an appendix entitled "A Diagnosis of Mrs. Hutchinson's Behavior in Terms of Menopausal Symptoms." A reviewer for the *American Historical Review* appeared to have no problem with such an analysis. But a biography of spiritualist Margaret Fox earned sharp criticism from Sydney Ahlstrom in the *Journal of American History* for failing "to provide precisely the kind of explanations that historians are most capable of giving, neither making spiritualism an intelligible aspect of American life nor clarifying the distinguishing marks of the movement which at least seems to stem from Margaret Fox and the Hydesville rappings of 1848." Neither review objected to the absence of what contemporary historians would call "gender analysis," nor did either book reflect much interest in their protagonists as women.[80]

The same could be said of some, but by no means all, new work on women social activists. The early 1960s brought renewed interest in Mother Jones, Florence Kelly, Molly Dewson, Jane Addams, the Women's Trade Union League, and the larger circle of women Progressive reformers. Allen Davis's 1964 essay for the *American Historical Review* entitled "The Social Workers and the Progressive Party" documented the extraordinary collection of women activists who helped shape the 1912 campaign, but it offered little in the way of gender analysis. His 1964 article for *Labor History,* however, insisted that historians had wrongly trivialized the Women's Trade Union League, which "deserves more attention . . . since it played an important part in the long struggle to aid working women."[81]

James T. Patterson advanced a similar argument in a 1964 *Labor History* study, "Mary Dewson and the American Minimum Wage Movement." Women in the Progressive movement conjured up images, he said, of a "respectable, overly-protected, and over-clothed maiden whose vacuity was disturbed, if at all, by a handful of spinsters holding strident rallies for women's suffrage." That portrait grossly distorted women's real importance to the reform campaigns of the Roosevelt era. Patterson explained:

> These impressions have helped to obscure the significant role played by a somewhat different cast of women reformers in the related and contemporary quest for social justice. Viewing the ballot as part of a much broader program to endow women with equal economic and educational opportunity, they pressed their objectives long after progressivism and women's suffrage agitation became aspects of a bygone age. To recapture the motivations of these women reformers will therefore help to reveal the broad character of the women's movement and its relation to social reform from progressivism through the New Deal.

Dorothy Blumberg contributed to that effort in an essay for *Labor History* that explored Florence Kelley's unpublished correspondence with Friedrich Engels. Her subsequent biography of Kelley provided readers with their first full exposure to the life of this remarkable Progressive era reformer.[82]

Throughout the postwar period, much attention focused on women during the Civil War era. In 1950 the *Journal of Southern History* published a letter Mrs. Jefferson Davis had written in 1866 while her husband was imprisoned at Fort Monroe, Virginia. While the appearance of such a document was not unusual, given the recognized historical significance of her husband, it provided an unusual perspective on Davis's fate and the humiliation experienced by the defeated Confederate hierarchy. Numerous diaries of southern women published in the postwar years fleshed out that portrait. A new edition of Mary Boykin Chesnut's *Diary from Dixie,* first printed in 1905, was issued in 1949 to the praise of reviewers, who found historical significance in its "faithful portrayal of a society at war" by "an intelligent woman." *Brokenburn: The Journal of Kate Stone, 1861–1868* (1955) revealed "the rapidly vanishing way of life on a large cotton plantation" through the eyes of a "well-educated, intelligent, observant young woman of twenty." Among the flurry of books published during the Civil War centennial were several edited diaries of Confederate women, including Phoebe Yates Pember's *A Southern Woman's Story: Life in Confederate Richmond* (1959), Kate Cumming's *Kate: The Journal of a Confederate Nurse* (1959), and Patience Pennington's *A Woman Rice Planter* (1961).[83]

Two of the most celebrated diaries of the period revealed not only divergent aspects of women's experience in the Old South, but the continued struggle to come to terms with slavery among contemporary historians. Reaction to John Scott's new edition of Fanny Kemble's *Journal of a Residence on a Georgian Plantation in 1838–1839* (1961) illuminates the tensions. A reviewer for the *Journal of Southern History* conceded that "some of its descriptions of the business aspects of plantation operations are trustworthy, and some of its portrayals of social life and slave management are dependable" but warned that the *"Journal* should be read with extreme care." It contained a "plethora" of "moralizing sections" detailing Kemble's antislavery convictions. "If one read only Miss Kemble's account," the reviewer concluded, "he would have a distorted view of slavery in the Old South." The *Journal of Negro History,* however, praised the publication of Kemble's work as a "literary event." The power of the di-

ary came precisely from Kemble's extraordinary insight into plantation life and "the plight of female slaves." As the reviewer explained:
"It is her record of the slave system on a large plantation which makes
this an inestimable contribution to American social history. Careful attention is given to the incredibly filthy surroundings of slaves;
the inadequate provisions for health; the 'low diet' of bondsmen; the
frequent, brutal floggings of blacks—even pregnant field hands; the
alarming rate of infant mortality among Negroes; the evil effects of il-
legitimacy and absenteeism; the dilemmas of slave baptism and Christian instruction." When the authenticity of the diary was challenged
by southern historians, Scott mounted a vigorous defense, including a
detailed rebuttal in the *Journal of Negro History.*[84]

Ray Billington's 1953 publication of Charlotte Forten's journal
likewise sparked a divergence of opinion among historians. *The Journal of Negro History* lauded the book as a brilliant contribution in revealing the life and sensibilities of a free black woman who devoted
herself to abolition and to teaching newly emancipated slaves in the
Sea Islands. Indeed, the reviewer stressed that Forten's *Journal* carried
a special message for Americans at the middle of the twentieth century. Charles Thomas observed: "The publication of the *Journal* this
year was indeed timely. Today when investigations, reminiscent of in-
quisitions, have forced many liberals underground and have made
others afraid to speak out against the cleavage between Americans'
profession and implementation of democratic principles, it is reassuring to read the impressions of a fearless woman who, almost a century
ago, made the effects of racial prejudice terrifyingly clear." But a reviewer for the *Mississippi Valley Historical Review* offered a more
tepid endorsement. Billington's introduction, Louisiana State University historian Edwin Adams Davis complained, was "unduly sympathetic—almost reverent. There is little doubt that some readers of the
Journal will reach the conclusion that the diarist, after all, was hyper-
sensitive—almost to the point of being psychotic." The *Journal's* major historiographical value stemmed from its depiction of "the intense
emotional feeling of the free Negro members of the antislavery-aboli-
tionist group in the North during the late antebellum and Civil War
periods." Elsie Lewis, in the *Journal of Southern History,* praised the
Journal as a "notable addition . . . to the history of the nation" that
was valuable in showing "an educated, wealthy, prominent free Negro family in America." Lewis observed that "Professor Billington

seems to conceive the importance of the *Journal* . . . to be essentially its revelation of the effects of racial prejudice on an individual." She suggested that it might be viewed equally for what it revealed about Forten's "maturity of development" and "achievements."[85]

The sexual dynamics of slavery came under scrutiny in Pearl Graham's prescient 1961 essay for the *Journal of Negro History* entitled "Thomas Jefferson and Sally Hemings." A close analysis of papers, Graham asserted, "are consistent with the supposition that he was the father of all Sally Hemings' children." Graham carefully perused archival records and conducted interviews with descendants of the Hemings family. The female relatives not only provided important details from the family's history, Graham wrote; their "descent from Jefferson is further substantiated by the Mendelian Law of Heredity." Daguerreotypes provided by the family suggested a strong resemblance to the president. The lessons of this episode stretched far beyond individual hypocrisy and misdeeds, Graham asserted. The miscegenation it revealed was hardly unusual on plantations, and Jefferson's hypocrisy was self-evident. But "translated into terms of today's racial problems," Graham concluded, the implications were more troubling.

> Jefferson would sanction South African apartheid, as well as Negro hegemony in central Africa, and the expulsion of whites from that territory. The present policies of the NAACP he would regard as the partial fulfillment of his prophecy of "convulsions which will never end but in the extermination of one or the other race," and, reluctantly no doubt, he would decree that the blacks must be the race to be exterminated. How far he might be willing to go in carrying out these principles is problematic. . . . In theory, he was not so far from Hitler, with his concept of a Master Race. But few men are ever wholly consistent in their attitudes and actions with regard to race relationships, and Jefferson—unlike Hitler—was not one of those few. He preached against miscegenation . . . but practiced it. He preached the urgent necessity of removing all freed blacks from white-occupied lands . . . but besought Virginia to permit his own emancipated sons to remain in that state.

This extraordinary meditation on Jefferson and Heming's relationship ultimately affirmed that Jefferson ought to be forgiven "for the evil that he did" in view of his "great service" to his country.[86]

Postwar historians likewise turned their attention to the convergence of abolitionism and feminism. Marxist historian Morris U. Schappes offered Ernestine Rose's "Address on the Anniversary of

West Indian Emancipation" to the *Journal of Negro History* for publication in 1949. Rose, Schappes explained in his introduction, was an immigrant Jewish women's rights activist, atheist, and utopian socialist as well as an abolitionist. In her 1853 remarks, Rose offered the following: "But permit me to say that the slaves of the South are not the only people that are in bondage. All women are excluded from the enjoyment of that liberty which your Declaration of Independence asserts to be the inalienable right of all . . . I go for the recognition of human rights, without distinction of sect, party, sex, or color." In 1952, Frederick Tolles published *Slavery and "the Woman Question,"* an edition of the diary entries Lucretia Mott wrote while attending the 1840 World Anti-Slavery Convention. A reviewer for the *Journal of Negro History* noted that the edition, "when read with contemporary accounts of the women's movement and of abolition . . . provides first hand confirmation of their presentation." Gerda Lerner's penetrating essay "The Grimké Sisters and the Struggle against Race Prejudice" in a 1963 issue of the *Journal of Negro History* stressed the courageous, though too rare, stand these southern white women had taken against racial oppression. Lerner also traced the convergence of feminism and abolitionism through the lives of the Grimkés in a book-length study of the abolitionist sisters.[87]

Such work anticipated in powerful ways the renewed interest in women's history that would soon become a distinct and vibrant subdiscipline in the latter 1960s. Eleanor Flexner's exceptional *Century of Struggle* (1959) marked a moment of real significance in burgeoning work on the women's rights movement. Flexner, who came to her study of feminism from a deep immersion in left-wing political activities, including a close association with the American Communist Party, crafted an extraordinarily penetrating study that was less a history of suffrage than an attempt to synthesize women's broader historical experience in America. The book emphasized race and class throughout its analysis of women's history. Such an approach was widely praised by historians, including Gertrude Rivers of Howard University, who made note in the *Journal of Negro History* of Flexner's unusual attention to "the Negro woman with her double handicap" and to the African American women who struggled for women's rights and racial equality.[88]

Flexner's book paved the way for a new approach to women's history that was rich, analytical, and archivally based, and that moved beyond a preoccupation with individual heroic figures. Aileen Kraditor brought these qualities to her brilliant book, *The Ideas of the Woman Suffrage Movement* (1965). The study probed the ideological underpinnings of feminism and of the movement's opponents in the late nineteenth and early twentieth century. Anne Firor Scott undertook the difficult task of assessing the impact of women's suffrage in an imaginative 1964 essay for the *Journal of Southern History* entitled "After Suffrage: Southern Women in the Twenties." Her essay challenged arguments that the Progressive era marked the end of reform. Indeed, Scott noted the growing conviction among many activists that state responsibility for social welfare required expansion. "To the growth of this idea and its application in law, Southern women made a considerable contribution," the historian noted in a comment that anticipated in striking ways future research on women and welfare state building. But the southern example also revealed, Scott stressed, that "in spite of the impressive record of accomplishment, the high expectations of the women who had led the suffrage movement did not come to pass." The legacy of women's suffrage left "troublesome questions still unanswered" for historians—ones to which, Scott concluded, "historians of women must now begin to turn their attention." Soon, of course, they would do so, as a new generation of women historians began the process of reexamining history.[89]

The repudiation of consensus history that became a central preoccupation among young historians during the 1960s took the intellectual dominance of consensus as a starting point. But in doing so, competing historiographical perspectives on the American past were lost, as the influential conservative tradition was spread backward over the entire postwar period. Thus was John Higham's prophecy of the "cult of consensus" fulfilled. The grand sweep of bold, synthetic interpretations that emphasized the liberal foundations of the American historical experience gave consensus history tremendous intellectual power in its own time and for decades beyond. Still, amid the celebration of freedom, some interpreters of American history were determined to ensure that conflict, inequality, political repression, and dissidence remained critical themes in the history of the nation. Those subjects would prove remarkably resilient as American historical writing evolved in the late twentieth century.

Epilogue

Their present was no longer ours.

—RICHARD HOFSTADTER, *THE PROGRESSIVE HISTORIANS* (1970)

In the early 1960s, several American historians began to note in scholarly journals that their discipline seemed to be changing. History appeared to be breaking through the chrysalis of the past and emerging in a dazzling new form. Two trends apparently were instrumental in this metamorphosis. One was the explosion of exciting new work in social history, much of it making use of quantitative methods and ideas borrowed from the social sciences. Economic historians were revisiting perennial problems in the American past with inventive empirical tools that promised to revolutionize understanding of subjects such as slavery, industrial development, and the conditions of work. Political historians, drawing on early work by Richard McCormick and Lee Benson, were exploring the impact of ethnic and cultural pluralism on the distribution of power and on political behavior. Social historians, inspired in no small part by Stephan Thernstrom's findings, were pursuing mobility studies that charted the life fortunes of Americans in a range of settings. Community studies likewise were making imaginative use of demography, family reconstitution, and a range of other approaches to explore distant lives and places. Labor historians, stimulated by Herbert Gutman's early work and by the work of British scholars such as E. P. Thompson, were uncovering the experience of working-class Americans. Indeed, underpinning much of the new research was a desire to recover how "ordinary" Americans had experienced—and made—the nation's history.

The second trend often, but not always, dovetailed with the first, much to the discomfort of some observers. It imbued fresh approaches to historical study with political passions borne of the 1960s. In places such as the University of Wisconsin, the tide had begun to turn well before the 1960s. Herbert Gutman, Warren Susman, William Preston, and Harvey Goldberg, among other graduate students, credited professors such as Merle Curti, Howard K. Beale, and Merrill Jensen with encouraging their efforts to advance a more searching and critical history. Left-leaning professors William Appleman Williams and Fred Harrington likewise supported young scholars intent on challenging liberal views of American history forged in the Cold War era. Amid the idealism of the Kennedy years, the hopeful days of the civil rights movement, and the early stirrings of the New Left, the iconoclasm spread as a rising generation of scholars began to bring a radical skepticism to the apparently self-satisfied and complacent views of the American past that John Higham had labeled "consensus" history. By the mid-1960s, smoldering doubts erupted into outright rejection of "traditional" and liberal history as the war in Vietnam, racial tensions, campus unrest, and emerging liberation movements transformed the American political landscape. History, like so many other elements of American society, was buffeted by a turmoil that seemed inescapable.[1]

Yet despite the energy and bravado that accompanied the new initiatives in historical research, it took some time before these developments coalesced into an explicit paradigm that would be designated as a "new history." Until well into the 1960s, most essays in the professional journals were invoking Progressive historians when they made reference to the "new history." John Hope Franklin was among the first to demarcate a modern "new history" from the Progressive vintage when he wrote an essay for the *Journal of Negro History* in 1957 entitled "The New Negro History." Invoking the mighty contemporary struggle for black "equality and freedom," Franklin joined current research in African American history to the prevailing social and political context. "The new Negro history, then," Franklin wrote, "is the literary and intellectual movement that seeks to achieve the same justice in history that is sought in other spheres."[2]

Franklin evinced a profound historiographical consciousness as he sought to characterize the "new Negro history." He located in the antebellum period the first powerful protests against narratives of the American past that "distorted" or robbed African Americans of their place in history. He described George W. Williams's 1883 study as "the first serious history of the Negro in the United States." And to Carter Woodson and his colleagues at the Association for the Study of Negro Life and History Franklin credited decades of scholarly effort devoted to "exploding the myths." As he described their efforts:

> This was, perhaps, the most far-reaching and ambitious effort to rewrite history that has ever been attempted in this country. But it was more than an attempt to rewrite history. It was a remarkable attempt to rehabilitate a whole people—to explode racial myths, to establish a secure and respectable place for the Negro in the evolution of the American social order, to develop self-respect and self-esteem among those who had been subjected to the greatest indignities known in the Western world. Finally, it was a valiant attempt to force America to keep faith with herself, to remind her that truth is more praiseworthy than power, and that justice and equality . . . should apply to all its citizens and *even* to the writing of history.

In 1957, Franklin asserted that the "new Negro history" was a product of "the last two decades" of scholarly work—parameters that acknowledged the historiographical achievements of scholars of the Depression and the World War II era. Yet even in his effusive praise for Woodson, Franklin stressed the ways in which dramatic social and political changes in recent years accelerated the ascent of "the new Negro history." In this, Franklin both recognized and applauded the convergence of politics and history as foundation stones for new scholarly initiatives.[3]

Franklin's use of the phrase "new history" attracted some attention from other historians, but during the early 1960s only scattered references to contemporary scholarship evoked the adjective. A report of the 1960 meeting of the Mississippi Valley Historical Association described a panel organized by the "the new labor history group." One year later, a review in the *Journal of Southern History* praised an essay by James Rawley that laid out an agenda for the future of political history—"a 'New Political History' we might call it." But a 1966 review in the *Journal of American History* noted "approaches developed in the most recent historical writing—what could almost be called the 'new' history" and pointed to the work of Oscar Handlin, Richard Hofstadter, David Potter, and C. Vann Woodward.[4]

A year later, University of Kansas historian Donald McCoy explicitly severed the Progressive "new history" from what was currently taking place in the historical profession. "The New History proclaimed by James Harvey Robinson in 1912," McCoy asserted in a 1967 essay for the *Journal of American History,* "was neither new nor exactly history." He went on to explain that "the really new history in America—that which has become increasingly interested in discovering the totality of human life and its environments—has been developing not by plan or proclamation but by private experiments and public interest." Historians who were vigorously engaged in fresh research efforts, and perhaps especially those who shared with likeminded colleagues radical political convictions, understood that they were advancing a new kind of historical scholarship.[5]

Still, paradigmatic statements giving shape to the idea of another "new history" borne of the 1960s emerged only slowly, as close examination of professional historical journals reveals. Between 1959 and 1970, the phrase "the new social history" appeared in the major scholarly journals only five times in reference to recent work in American history. (It was attached even less often to studies in the European field.) The 1970s brought far more frequent characterization of contemporary historical scholarship in such terms. Over one hundred essays and reviews made use of the idea between 1971 and 1980 to describe innovative trends in American history. Fifteen years later, the "new social history" had clearly arrived. The phrase was used on over four hundred separate occasions in the discipline's leading journals from 1981 to 1995 to portray recent trends in the writing of history.[6]

Ironically, an attack on the New Left appears to have helped crystallize the idea that the "new history" had arisen from the political maelstrom of the 1960s. Written in 1965, but published two years later, New York University professor Irwin Unger's essay for the *American Historical Review* advanced through criticism the framing of a modern "new history" paradigm. Unger previewed his complaints in an April 1967 panel, chaired by Merle Curti, entitled "American History and the New Left," which was held during the annual meeting of the Organization of American Historians. Over eight hundred historians gathered to hear the discussion, in which Unger accused New Left historians of "present-mindedness" and "distortion of facts" in their effort to mine the past for historical precedents to guide "contemporary radicals."[7]

Unger's *American Historical Review* essay, published shortly after the professional meeting, expanded his earlier commentary with a flurry of punches aimed at what the historian viewed as lamentable historiographical tendencies among the younger generation. Unger explicitly joined the emergence of "the new political Left in America," which he saw as evident "almost everywhere throughout the country," to looming changes in historical study. Just as members of the New Left were seeking to transform society through peace marches, protests, and rent strikes, so they were making their influence felt in academic disciplines. "They are now beginning to create a new, radical history, particularly a new, radical American history," Unger warned.

In making his case, Unger recast American historiography in ways that would place contemporary developments in a very harsh light. Until the 1940s, he claimed, in a loose summation of John Higham's argument, the dominant theme in historical study was "class conflict." Any competing interpretations—such as Turner's frontier thesis—"by the 1930's had been thoroughly demolished, it seemed, by the combined attack of Marxists and 'progressives.'" Here was the long shadow of Charles Beard, cast over the entire record of American historical writing for the first half of the twentieth century—a vision that flattened the rich and varied architecture of modern historical writing. Only with the arrival of the consensus "new history" in the post–World War II period, according to Unger, were historians able to "escape the Beardian matrix which imprisoned American history in the first four decades of this century." Now came "the young radicals" who, though paying obeisance to Beard as "the Moses of the New Left," answered to no "masters." However much they claimed to admire Beard, "the homage is ceremonial." For the New Left's true devotion was to a burning conviction of "America's total depravity." Though Unger praised some young scholars, such as Stephan Thernstrom and Walter LaFeber, for their impressive research findings and insisted that "the young radicals" deserved the attention and respect of the historical profession, he drew a line in the sand that separated current developments from the discipline's past.[8]

In fact, Unger expressed puzzlement at the failure of New Left historians to follow the lead of their predecessors. Noting that "in the 1930's and 1940's, radical historians wrote passionate, engaged studies of the labor movement," he observed that "radical intellectuals no longer regard the laboring man in the same approving way." He acknowledged, too, the work of Old Left historians such as James Allen and W. E. B. Du Bois and contrasted their respect for "scientific history" with their successors' "contempt" for "pure" historical study. For all the excessiveness of Unger's polemic, he detected a disjuncture between the history of the Old Left and that of New Left historians.[9]

In a fierce response published in the February 1968 issue of the *American Historical Review,* Eugene Genovese damned Unger with faint praise by forthrightly acknowledging what the historian viewed as the intellectual errors of the New Left. Genovese wrote of Unger's analysis:

> I agree with him that a radical politics does not require repudiation of the consensus view of American history; that such a view must be examined empirically and without bias; and that present-mindedness mars much of the new Left-wing historiography, just as it marred much of the old. I see no principled objection to the consensus view in its more sophisticated versions, although if the bloody years 1861–1865 formed part of that consensus, we need a new vocabulary. In general, no Marxist ought to be embarrassed if the consensus view withstands the attacks of its critics: We should then have before us the particular history of the process by which the American bourgeoisie established its hegemony. We would not thereby be required to join the celebration.

However, Genovese rejected Unger's effort to place the New Left in opposition to the Old Left. Unger made "too sharp a distinction between the Old and New Left," Genovese insisted, for both groups "have had a tendency to exaggerate confrontation and have, accordingly, failed to see the processes by which ruling classes may avoid such confrontation." Indeed, he insisted that tendencies toward presentism and economic determinism, "contrary to Professor Unger's implications, have plagued the historiography of the Left as a whole (and not only the Left!) for a century."[10]

But Genovese's long view of leftist historiography would soon be obscured by a growing tendency to elaborate and reconfigure historiography in ways that stressed the distinctiveness of contemporary imperatives. Criticism of a left-leaning "new history" only served to deepen the cleavages as opponents and advocates reinvoked consensus history as the embodiment of traditional historical analysis. Such a comparison provided a stark contrast with recent trends, even if its use, at times, took on the appearance of a straw man. A series of essays published in 1967 by Random House under the editorship of Barton Bernstein entitled *Towards a New Past: Dissenting Essays in American History* marked a turning point of sorts in the struggle to define a new historiographical tradition. The book included essays by Jesse Lemisch, Eugene Genovese, Michael Lebowitz, James McPherson, Stephan Thernstrom, Christopher Lasch, Staughton Lynd, Lloyd Gardner, Robert Freeman Smith, Marilyn Blatt Young, and Bernstein himself, with contributions ranging from "The American Revolution Seen from the Bottom Up" (Lemisch) to "The Cultural Cold War" (Lasch). Bernstein's introduction attempted to set these diverse and compelling studies against older historiographical traditions.

In what would soon be a familiar reworking of American historical writing, Bernstein looked back approvingly on the ideals of the Progressive historians. "For Turner and Beard, for Carl L. Becker and Schlesinger, for the progressive historians in general," Bernstein observed, "history was more than past politics and military battles." Particularly noteworthy were the Progressive historians' efforts to pursue studies "relevant to the present" that might serve the cause of "liberal, democratic reform" initiatives.[11]

Bernstein's brief outline of historiography essentially offered a drama composed of three acts. Progressive history was the first; Bernstein outlined it by focusing on the work of Vernon Parrington and Charles Beard as exemplary of the Progressive preoccupation with "upheaval and 'revolutions,' upon conflict between rival ideologies." But such a "synthesis" had its limitations, Bernstein observed, "and it failed to deal adequately with racism, slavery, and imperialism." Beard's writing on foreign policy during the 1930s "would later guide and inspire a prominent school of younger 'left' historians (the so-called Wisconsin School associated with Professors Fred Harvey Harrington and William Appleman Williams)." But that influence could not save Progressive history from "monographic attack before Pearl Harbor, and . . . the sustained assaults of the postwar years."[12]

Bernstein drew heavily on John Higham's critique of consensus history in describing the second stage in modern American historiography—one dominated by "a new and more conservative view of the American past." The historians of the 1950s, Bernstein explained, rejected the Progressive focus on conflict in favor of themes of "continuity" and "the accomplishments of democratic capitalism." Furthermore, although such a stance was deeply intertwined with the prevailing political mood of post–World War II America, historians valorized objectivity and largely rejected the notion that historical research bore any relevance to "the need or possibility for change" in contemporary society. This despite the fact, Bernstein pointed out, that "their history often reflected the needs and values of the fifties."[13]

Bernstein concluded his succinct overview of modern historical writing by sketching out a third act, which began "during the early sixties" and that was leading inexorably to a "break down" of "the conservative consensus." The new revisionist history clearly belonged to political currents running fast in contemporary America. As he described the impetus: "For many, the rediscovery of poverty and racism, the commitment to civil rights for Negroes, the criticism of intervention in Cuba and Vietnam, shattered many of the assumptions of the fifties and compelled intellectuals to re-examine the American past. From historians, and particularly from younger historians, there began to emerge a vigorous criticism of the historical consensus." Yet Bernstein acknowledged that it was no simple matter to trace the origins of the 1960s zeitgeist. "Some, like Professors Eugene Genovese, Jesse Lemisch, and Michael Lebowitz, were traveling along this path without the spur of events," Bernstein observed. While others might have found their way "independently" to "new perspectives on the past,'" still others "who acknowledge the impact of events upon their developments are unsure of the precise influence." Bernstein's thoughtful reflections did not identify any particular historians other than the distant Progressives as decisive models or forerunners.[14]

It was not easy, Bernstein acknowledged, to capture what unified the work of the contributors to the present volume. Although "in discussing this still small but apparently growing movement within the past few years, the historical profession has come to speak of a 'New Left,'" Bernstein admitted that the phrase lacked precision. "The term does denote a group of various 'left' views—whether they be Marxist, neo-Beardian, radical, or left-liberal." In the end, what seemed to best distinguish the fresh, dissenting voices in the profession was their "exciting" and innovative research and their break "with the earlier consensus."

Contributors to the volume offered varying points of departure as they introduced their findings. Jesse Lemisch explicitly rejected the emphasis on elite-centered and consensus-driven models of early colonial America. "Our earliest history has been seen as a period of consensus and classlessness, in part because our historians have chosen to see it that way," he complained. Stressing the need to recover the voices of "the inarticulate," Lemisch concluded that "all of our history needs re-examination from this perspective. The history of the powerless, the inarticulate, the poor has not yet begun to be written because they have been treated no more fairly by historians than they have been treated by their contemporaries." Eugene Genovese invoked a more expansive historiographical vision in his sharply critical piece, "Marxian Interpretations of the Slave South"; he emphasized the origins and inadequacy of 1930s radical perspectives.[15]

In an assessment of *Towards a New Past* written for the *American Historical Review,* Aileen Kraditor echoed Genovese's criticisms by noting that some essays in the volume provided a "refreshing" antidote to "the simplistic, unimaginative, and dogmatic uniformity with which most earlier—and a few modern— antiestablishment historians read the historical record and guaranteed its opacity." She found fault with Jesse Lemisch's rendition of the American Revolution, however, and her criticism provoked a quick letter of outrage from the radical colonial historian.

The exchange between the two that followed revealed that internecine struggles over interpretation, ideology, evidence, and historical standards among radical historians were under way. Kraditor praised Genovese's perceptive analysis while upbraiding Lemisch for, among other perceived inadequacies, his ahistoricism. As Kraditor expressed it in her letter to the editor:

> It is ironic that the epigram that those who will not learn from history are condemned to repeat it applies to historians too; New Left historians, rail as their activist comrades may against the "Old Left," repeat the errors of Leftist historians of the 1930's and 1940's. I refer particularly to two errors: The first, the antihistorical attitude mentioned in the previous paragraphs, I dealt with in my review and need not discuss here. The second is the economic-determinist assumption that objectively antagonistic interests necessarily generate widespread antiruling class ideas in every period.

Standing at a very different vantage point, David Donald likewise unhappily heard many echoes of the Old Left in the essays—and said so in a very critical review of *Towards a New Past* published simultaneously with Kraditor's in the *American Historical Review* (an apparent attempt by the journal's editors to provide equal time to radicals and their critics). "Here, then, are the voices of the New Left," Donald concluded, "mostly neither new nor left."[16]

Amid the intense political turmoil of the late 1960s and early 1970s

and the enormously heated rhetoric that defined the mood of the period, accusations of presentism and ahistoricism flew fast and furious
among historians of various ideological persuasions. James Hutson,
for example, rejected Jesse Lemisch's analysis of working-class agitation in Revolutionary America in a 1971 essay for the *William and
Mary Quarterly* and, in doing so, accused contemporary radical historians of being "'plagued' by 'an almost deliberate presentism.'" But
Hutson's "innuendo and exaggerated language," Lemisch retorted,
reflected "Hutson's own brand of presentism." "Hutson's reading,"
Lemisch observed, "indicates that somebody sold him a seat from
which he can see only the left fielder, and not too well at that." Both
historians, however, shared a common point of reference: a historiographical vision that reified consensus history as the guiding star of
modern historical analysis. Given the early dominance of Beard's
fresh interpretation of Revolutionary America and the harsh criticisms it came under during the early postwar era, such a preoccupation among early American historians is perhaps understandable.[17]

At the same time, there was no shortage of models for historians
searching for the roots of the present "new history" had they been
inclined to invoke an alternative historiographical tradition. Many
younger scholars, of course, examined with profit, interest, and deep
admiration the work of earlier social historians. But it was in the nature of the task that the framing of a "new history" paradigm discouraged lingering in the past. This was especially true when the extraordinary drama of the present so deeply invigorated historical inquiry
and when the ideological weight of consensus history provided such
an apt and tempting contrast to current passions. The new history's
most outspoken conservative opponents ironically shared this perspective.

Before long the modern "new history" paradigm stripped away
many of the complexities that had come to define a rich historiographical tradition built up over a century of professional American
historical writing. Through many repeated iterations, it became the
conventional wisdom—not only for the new historians but for their
critics, who rejected what they considered an ill-conceived preoccupation with conflict, poverty, racism, sexism, and inequality. Other than
the remote Progressive historians, who were invoked to encapsulate
the mood of historical writing prior to the era of consensus historians,
the many variegated strands of writing about the American past were
lost to the discipline.[18]

Indeed, as the political rhetoric cooled in the increasingly conservative climate of the 1970s, the "new history" paradigm only gained in force, even as some observers constructed a larger historical understanding of its origins. Many commentators of the 1970s often located the roots of the "new social history" in European progenitors. The work of the Annalistes, of British radical historians such as E. P. Thompson, and historical demographers such as Peter Laslett was often invoked as the inspiration for the new social historians, and properly so. But this rendition had the advantage of avoiding unpleasant evocations of what many apparently considered a decidedly less romantic or heroic set of traditions (some left, some liberal, some without any easily captured political overtones) in American historical writing. It also, ironically, upheld a kind of reverse American intellectual exceptionalism that gave historical research of the 1960s no home-grown tradition. Even Progressive history was increasingly set aside as a forerunner of modern trends. As Lawrence Veysey wrote in a 1979 essay entitled "The 'New' Social History in the Context of American Historical Writing":

> The "new" social history, greatly influenced by the French *Annales* school, has turned out to be very diverse. . . . Sometimes its novelty and distinctiveness have been questioned by its critics, who point out that much the same version of history had been put forth by such American figures as James Harvey Robinson, under the very label of the "new history," in the early years of this century. Yet that affinity was more rhetorical than real for the social historians of the 1960s, like the social activists, had for the first time glimpsed the true "bottom" layer of the society in a sustained way, and their standards of evidence and argument genuinely broke deeper ground.

Contrasting the work of Sam Bass Warner with Carl and Jessica Bridenbaugh on eighteenth-century Philadelphia, and that of Stephan Thernstrom with Oscar Handlin, Veysey stressed that Warner's and Thernstrom's research was far more sophisticated. Whatever their relative merits, the connections between earlier social history and its latest incarnation rarely received much sustained attention. (Thernstrom, it should be noted, was Handlin's student.)[19]

The extraordinary achievements of contemporary social history, its distinctive and powerful contributions to historical knowledge, the larger thrust of historical inquiry in the modern era—all deserve the full acknowledgment they have received in contemporary accounts of American historiography. The volume of work alone, the collective consciousness among contemporary "new historians" that they were advancing innovative forms of historical understanding, the proliferation of distinctly defined subdisciplines such as women's history with a self-identified corps of highly skilled practitioners, the rapid transformation of textbooks, college curricula, history departments, professional organizations, and the place made within all these settings for fresh approaches to American history—all differ markedly from early-twentieth-century initiatives. Yet the tendency to lift such achievements from the matrix of history itself remains a striking feature of American historiography. It is entirely fitting that contemporary scholarship be sharply distinguished from previous intellectual traditions. But over time—and increasingly, so it seems—the stress on discontinuity has tended toward erasure of the past.

It is tempting to trace this tendency to elements specific to the 1960s and 1970s—to the split between the Old and New Left and between radical and conservative historians on college campuses riven with dissent and conflict, to the intransigence of conservatives as well as the passions of some New Left historians, to the rise of a new and large generation of historians. But to do so would be to ignore more fundamental determinants of historical memory that have long shaped the ways in which historians themselves have thought about their discipline.

In their work and in their sense of themselves, historians must struggle with a difficult undertaking: how to remember faithfully and yet continually recreate the past. That other scholars have preceded them in this endeavor greatly complicates their task. For although historical knowledge often advances by building upon the research of scholarly predecessors, it cannot expand by simply endorsing or amplifying previous research. Rather, understanding of the past progresses as historians reconsider, integrate, challenge, set aside, and even sometimes raze to the ground the work of other practitioners. Making the past new requires a breadth of imagination and deftness of tone and sensibility that remain among the most formidable challenges imposed by an unforgiving discipline.[20]

For over a century, American historians have struggled continually to reinvent history. In so doing, they have acclaimed and derided, emulated and dismissed previous scholarship. Whatever their posture, the newness of the past has remained a powerful imperative to every generation of historians in the modern era. Buffeted by the vast social, political, economic, and cultural changes of the twentieth century, historians have written from experience both imagined and lived. It is perhaps an inescapable paradox that much attention to the past has been inspired by a sense of immediacy.

Richard Hofstadter captured this tension well when he examined the Progressive historians amid a climate of intellectual and political upheaval in the late 1960s. Reflecting on the generation of historians to which he belonged, those born after World War I, Hofstadter described their deep discomfort with Progressive history. "Progressive history had been written to meet several needs that are no longer felt in the same way," he observed, "and it began to seem, to members of my generation, somewhat too insular and too nostalgic." It was, Hofstadter stressed, the times in which post–World War I historians lived—scarred as they were by the Great Depression and World War II—that turned them away from their predecessors.

> We found ourselves living in a more complex and terrifying world, and when we set about criticizing the Progressive historians I believe it was with a keener sense of the difficulties of life and of the problem of rendering it in intelligible historical terms. Even those of their guiding ideas that still seemed to be valid now seemed marginal rather than central; and many of their interpretative ideas rested on some kind of identification of the past and present that we could easily see through, not because we were cleverer but because *their* present was no longer ours. Gradually they ceased to be the leading interpreters of our past and became simply a part of it.

And yet the wave Hofstadter felt his generation riding would soon itself break against a wall of resistance from younger historians who would reject a post–World War II present-mindedness. For scholars coming of professional age in the 1960s could say, with equal veracity, as they considered the work of their elders: "their present was no longer ours."[21]

Hofstadter detected a "parricidal" quality to the unrelenting tide of historical revisionism. He spoke of the "perennial battle we wage with our elders, particularly with our adopted intellectual fathers." And he recognized the intellectual and professional incentives that encouraged historians to recess the significance of their predecessors' scholarship. "If we are to have any new thoughts," he explained, "if we are to have an intellectual identity of our own, we must make the effort to distinguish ourselves from those who preceded us, and perhaps pre-eminently from those to whom we once had the greatest indebtedness. Even if our quarrels are only marginal and minor . . . we must make the most of them." But the tendency to accentuate those differences have come with some costs.[22]

Historians have paid a price in granting critical inroads to opponents of the "new history" who have been all too quick to endorse the view that contemporary interest in race, gender, class, ethnicity, and a host of similar concerns are indeed a legacy of the 1960s. What champions of a more heterodox American history celebrate, their adversaries firmly reject as misguided efforts to "politicize" narratives of the national experience. Honest differences properly divide views of what best constitutes the writing and teaching of American history. But neither advocates nor antagonists of the "new history" advance their case by resorting to presentism when they root modern historical imperatives shallowly in the soil of the 1960s. For that moment has now come and gone, and its contested history has produced no consensus of opinion. Rather, it remains a touchstone of tensions that continue to haunt the American national experience.

History is impoverished when the broad trajectory of the discipline is needlessly foreshortened and truncated. Historians who devoted a lifetime to chronicling the lives of the inarticulate have long mattered deeply to the field of American history. This rich heritage provides a powerful and stirring affirmation of many trends in contemporary history. To overlook the place of such scholars not only deprives younger historians of a powerful example, it leaves a distorted and brittle sense of the history of the discipline.

There is, finally, a moral accounting that ought to weigh heavily on professional memory. Women and African American historians, those who lost their jobs and then their reputations to obscurity, surely deserve a place in the narrative of American history. Not only were these scholars important figures in their own right; they shared with their successors many profound political and intellectual affinities. Stretching across the country, decade after decade, in times of war and through seasons of peace, in years of struggle and through decades of complacency, many generations of scholars have cared about the ways in which average Americans—workingpeople, the poor, the inarticulate, ethnic and religious minorities, dissenters—experienced and shaped history. The early achievements of historians who hacked a path through hardened versions of what mattered in the American past demonstrate that an engaged history has been the hallmark of the twentieth century.

Notes
Index

Notes

Prologue

1. On the new history see especially Eric Foner, ed., *The New American History* (Philadelphia: Temple University Press, 1990); Joyce Appleby, Lynn Hunt, and Margaret Jacob, *Telling the Truth about History* (New York: W. W. Norton, 1994); Peter Novick, *That Noble Dream: The "Objectivity Question" and the American Historical Profession* (Cambridge, U.K.: Cambridge University Press, 1988); John Higham, *History: Professional Scholarship in America* (Baltimore: Johns Hopkins University Press, 1989); Michael Kammen, ed., *The Past before Us* (Ithaca: Cornell University Press, 1980); Peter Burke, ed., *New Perspectives on Historical Writing* (University Park: Pennsylvania State University Press, 1991); Paul Buhle, *History and the New Left* (Philadelphia: Temple University Press, 1990); Lawrence C. Levine, "The Unpredictable Past: Reflections on Recent American Historiography," *American Historical Review* 94, 3 (June 1989); John Higham and Paul Conkin, *New Directions in American Intellectual History* (Baltimore: Johns Hopkins University Press, 1979). Recent work that attends to the longer tradition of American historical writing, while still emphasizing the transforming impact of contemporary scholarship, are R. David Edmunds, "Native Americans, New Voices: American Indian History, 1895–1995," *American Historical Review* 100, 3 (June 1995); Earl Lewis, "To Turn as on a Pivot: Writing African Americans into a History of Overlapping Diasporas," *American Historical Review* 100, 3 (June 1995); Mark Leff, "Revisioning U.S. Political History," *American Historical Review* 100, 3 (June 1995); Lawrence Levine, *The Opening of the American Mind: Canons, Culture, and History* (Boston: Beacon Press, 1996); and Gary B. Nash, Charlotte Crabtree, and Ross E. Dunn, *History on Trial: Culture Wars and the Teaching of the Past* (New

York: Knopf, 1997). American historians were also influenced by intellectual trends in European history, as Dorothy Ross underscores especially in "Grand Narrative in American Historical Writing: From Romance to Uncertainty," *American Historical Review* 100, 3 (June 1995). Among the most influential European works were E. P. Thompson, *The Making of the English Working Class* (New York: Vintage, 1966) and Peter Laslett, *The World We Have Lost* (New York: Scribner, 1965). The work of the Annales school also served as an inspiration for the new social history and received a good deal of attention in the United States in the 1970s. On the Annalistes see especially Traian Stroianovich, *French Historical Method: The Annales Paradigm* (Ithaca: Cornell University Press, 1976); Peter Burke, *The French Historical Revolution* (Stanford: Stanford University Press, 1990); and Carole Fink, *Marc Bloch* (Cambridge, U.K.: Cambridge University Press, 1989). For a superb account of the wide and deep roots of African American historiography, one that successfully challenges presentist paradigms, see Wilson Jeremiah Moses, *Afrotopia: The Roots of African American Popular History* (Cambridge, U.K.: Cambridge University Press, 1998).

2. See, for example, Irwin Unger, "The 'New Left' and American History: Some Recent Trends in United States Historiography," *American Historical Review* 72, 3 (April 1967); Theodore S. Hamerow, *Reflections on History and Historians* (Madison: University of Wisconsin Press, 1987); Gertrude Himmelfarb, *The New History and the Old* (Cambridge: Harvard University Press, 1987). Himmelfarb notes that the "new history" of recent years is not so new and ties its agenda to developments at the turn of the century and even earlier. Himmelfarb, *The New History and the Old*, pp. 1–7 and Chapter 1 passim. Her critique, focused largely on European history, stresses the abandonment of political history and the dominance of social history in the profession today.

3. David Brody, "The Old Labor History and the New: In Search of the American Working Class," *Labor History* 20 (Winter 1979); Thomas A. Kruegar, "American Labor Historiography, Old and New: A Review Essay," *Journal of Social History* 4 (Spring 1971); Alice Kessler-Harris, "Social History," in Foner, ed., *The New American History;* Higham, *History,* pp. 247–251; Allan G. Bogue, "United States: The 'New' Political History," in Robert P. Swierenga, ed., *Quantification in American History: Theory and Research* (New York: Atheneum, 1970); and Herbert G. Gutman and Donald H. Bell, *The New England Working Class and the New Labor History* (Urbana: University of Illinois Press, 1987). In this last collection, Gutman emphasizes that the model of an "old" and "new" labor history was overdetermined and neglected important work done between 1930 and 1950 by several important women labor historians especially. David Montgomery also thoughtfully reviews a longer tradition in labor history in "The Conventional Wisdom," *Labor History* 13, 1 (Winter 1972). Bogue also notes that Frederick Jackson Turner and Orin G. Libby endorsed some form of quantitative methods in

the Progressive era: Bogue, "United States: The 'New' Political History," p. 37.

4. Appleby, Hunt, and Jacob, *Telling the Truth about History,* p. 154. See also ibid., Chapter 4 passim; Ross, "Grand Narrative," on post–World War II historiography especially, John Higham, "Beyond Consensus: the Historian as Moral Critic," *American Historical Review* 67, 3 (April 1962); Richard H. Pells, *The Liberal Mind in a Conservative Age: American Intellectuals in the 1940s and 1950s* (New York: Harper and Row, 1985); Novick, *That Noble Dream;* John Higham, "Introduction," in Higham and Conkin, *New Directions in American Intellectual History;* John Higham, "The Cult of 'American Consensus,'" *Commentary* 27 (February 1959).

5. In the 1960s and early 1970s, it was possible to identify *two* new histories, Robert Berkhofer insisted. One was the province of New Left historians, the other of historians who embraced new methodological advances such as cliometrics but who did not share the political sympathies of radical historians. Robert Berkhofer, "The Two New Histories: Competing Paradigms for Interpreting the American Past," *OAH Newsletter* 11 (May 1983). And some historians challenged from the left the narrowing of social history to the point where an understanding of its larger political significance all but disappeared. See Elizabeth Fox-Genovese and Eugene Genovese, "The Political Crisis of Social History: A Marxian Perspective," *Journal of Social History* 10 (Winter 1976); Eugene Genovese and Elizabeth Fox-Genovese, *The Fruits of Merchant Capital* (Oxford: Oxford University Press, 1983); Tony Judt, "A Clown in Regal Purple: Social History and the Historians," *History Workshop* 7 (Spring 1979). A changed political environment did much to soften these distinctions in the 1980s. On quantitative history see, for example, Robert Berkhofer, *A Behavioral Approach to Historical Analysis* (New York: Free Press, 1969); the essays in Swiergenda, *Quantification in American History;* Don Karl Rowney and James Q. Graham, Jr., eds., *Quantitative History* (Homewood, Ill.: Dorsey Press, 1969); Edward Shorter, *The Historian and the Computer* (Englewood Cliffs, N.J.: Prentice-Hall, 1971). Among the most important studies done in the 1960s and 1970s that exemplified the use of quantitative methods were Robert Fogel and Stanley Engerman's highly controversial study of American slavery, *Time on the Cross* (Boston: Little, Brown, 1974); Lee Benson, *The Concept of Jacksonian Democracy* (Princeton: Princeton University Press, 1961); Stephan Thernstrom, *Poverty and Progress: Social Mobility in a Nineteenth Century City* (Cambridge: Harvard University Press, 1964); Philip Greven, *Four Generations* (Ithaca: Cornell University Press, 1970); Kenneth Lockridge, *A New England Town* (New York: W. W. Norton, 1970); John Demos, "Notes on Life in Plymouth Colony," *William and Mary Quarterly* 22, 2 (April 1965) and Demos, *A Little Commonwealth* (New York: Oxford University Press, 1970).

6. Foner, "Introduction," in *The New American History,* pp. vii–ix; Appleby,

Hunt, and Jacob, *Telling the Truth about History*, Chapter 4 esp.; Burke, "Overture: The New History, Its Past and Its Future," in *New Perspectives on Historical Writing*; Higham, *History*, pp. 241–243, 247–252; Levine, "The Unpredictable Past," pp. 671–677; Lynn D. Hunt, *The New Cultural History* (Berkeley: University of California Press, 1989); Higham and Conkin, *New Directions in American Intellectual History*.

7. James Harvey Robinson, *The New History* (New York: Macmillan, 1912); Novick, *That Noble Dream*, pp. 235–236, 240–241; Alan Dawley, *Struggle for Justice: Social Responsibility and the Liberal State* (Cambridge: Harvard University Press, 1991), pp. 6–10; Dorothy Ross, *The Origins of American Social Science* (Cambridge, U.K.: Cambridge University Press, 1991), pp. 339–347; Appleby, Hunt, and Jacob, *Telling the Truth about History*, Chapter 4; Higham, *History*, p. 244; Buhle, *History and the New Left*, pp. 18–20; Warren I. Susman, *Culture as History* (New York: Pantheon, 1984), Chapters 1 and 2, p. 101. Buhle takes a wider view of the roots of the new history than many scholars, emphasizing the growth of radicalism at the University of Wisconsin in the 1950s.

8. Appleby, Hunt, and Jacob, *Telling the Truth about History*, p. 148; Foner, ed., *The New American History*, p. vii.

9. There is a large literature, particularly among European historians, on the topic of historical memory, much of it inspired by World War II, the Nazi Occupation, the Holocaust, and the human and psychological devastation that ensued. See especially Charles Maier, *The Unmasterable Past* (Cambridge: Harvard University Press, 1988); Henry Rousso, *The Vichy Syndrome: History and Memory in France since 1944* (Cambridge: Harvard University Press, 1991); Lucy Dawidowicz, *The Holocaust and the Historians* (Cambridge: Harvard University Press, 1981); Tom Segev, *The Seventh Million: The Israelis and the Holocaust* (New York: Hill and Wang, 1993); Tony Judt, *Past Imperfect: French Intellectuals, 1944–1956* (Berkeley: University of California Press, 1992); Dominick LaCapra, *Representing the Holocaust* (Ithaca: Cornell University Press, 1994). Among the many interesting recent studies dealing with memory, history, and national identity are Anthony Molho and Gordon S. Wood, eds., *Imagined Histories: American Historians Interpret the Past* (Princeton: Princeton University Press, 1998); Michael Kammen, *Mystic Cords of Memory: The Transformation of American Culture* (New York: Vintage, 1993); Michael Shudson, *Watergate in American Memory* (New York: Basic, 1992); and Robert Gildea, *The Past in French History* (New Haven: Yale University Press, 1994). Anne Firor Scott's *Unheard Voices: The First Historians of Southern Women* (Charlottesville: University of Virginia Press, 1993) is an important historiographical corrective that restores to memory the work of several imaginative women historians of the South. Dorothy Ross and Peter Novick have both emphasized the impact of the changing composition of the historical profession on the character of contemporary historical writing: see Ross, "Grand Narrative," p. 663; and Novick, *That Noble Dream*, Chapters 12 and 14. On the role of women

scholars in the earlier twentieth century see Jacqueline Goggin, "Challenging Sexual Discrimination in the Historical Profession: Women Historians and the American Historical Association, 1890–1940," *American Historical Review* 97, 3 (June 1992). For women who were not professionally trained as historians see Ellen DuBois, "Making Women's History: Activist Historians of Women's Rights," in Leon Fink, ed., *Intellectuals and Public Life* (Ithaca: Cornell University Press, 1995); Nancy Cott, *A Woman Making History* (New Haven: Yale University Press, 1991); Bonnie G. Smith, "The Contribution of Women to Modern Historiography in Great Britain, France, and the United States, 1750–1940," *American Historical Review* 89, 3 (June 1984); and Bonnie Smith, *The Gender of History: Men, Women, and Historical Practice* (Cambridge: Harvard University Press, 1998). For an excellent and very imaginative series of essays on African Americans and historical memory see Genevieve Fabre and Robert O'Meally, *History and Memory in African-American Culture* (New York: Oxford University Press, 1994).

10. On the Progressive historians see, among many other works, Richard Hofstadter's classic *The Progressive Historians* (New York: Vintage, 1970); Ernst A. Breisach, *American Progressive History* (Chicago: University of Chicago Press, 1993); Ross, *The Origins of American Social Science;* Novick, *That Noble Dream;* Higham, *History;* Ray A. Billington, *Frederick Jackson Turner* (New York: Oxford University Press, 1973); Ellen Nore, *Charles A. Beard* (Carbondale: Southern Illinois University Press, 1983); Cushing Strout, *The Pragmatic Revolt in American History* (New Haven: Yale University Press, 1958); Morton White, *The Revolt against Formalism* (New York: Viking Press, 1949); Nancy Cott, ed., *A Woman Making History* (New Haven: Yale University Press, 1991); Robert A. Skotheim, *American Intellectual Histories and Historians* (Princeton: Princeton University Press, 1966); Burleigh Wilkins, *Carl Becker* (Cambridge: MIT Press, 1961); J. H. Hexter, "Carl Becker and Historical Relativism," in *On Historians* (Cambridge: Harvard University Press, 1979); John Mack Faragher, *Rereading Frederick Jackson Turner* (New York: Henry Holt, 1994); and David Noble, *Historians against History* (Minneapolis: University of Minnesota Press, 1965).

11. Despite their omission from many general accounts of American historiography, African American scholars have been the focus of several excellent focused studies in recent years. See Jacqueline Goggin, *Carter G. Woodson: A Life in Black History* (Baton Rouge: Louisiana State University Press, 1993); David Levering Lewis, *W. E. B. Du Bois, 1869–1919* (New York: Henry Holt, 1993); August Meier and Elliott Rudwick, *Black History and the Historical Profession, 1915–1980* (Urbana: University of Illinois Press, 1986); Kenneth Robert Janken, *Rayford Logan and the Dilemma of the African-American Intellectual* (Amherst: University of Massachusetts Press, 1993); Lewis, "To Turn as on a Pivot"; and Francille R. Wilson, "The Segregated Scholars: Black Labor Historians, 1895–1950," Ph.D. diss., University of Pennsylvania, 1988. On W. E.B. Du Bois and the problem of historical mem-

ory see David Blight's superb essay "W. E. B. Du Bois and the Struggle for American Historical Memory," in Fabre and O'Meally, *History and Memory in African-American Culture.*

12. Novick, *That Noble Dream,* p. 178.

13. Both Novick and Higham emphasize the prevalence of relativist perspectives; see Novick, *That Noble Dream;* and Higham, *History.*

14. Warren Susman was one of the few historians to call attention to the historiographical significance of the cultural approach to history; see his *Culture as History,* p. 101. Higham briefly discusses the 1939 American Historical Association meetings in *History,* pp. 119–120.

15. On consensus history see Novick, *That Noble Dream,* pp. 333–360; Higham, *History,* Chapter 6; Higham and Conkin, eds., *New Directions in American Intellectual History.* Young historians of the 1960s were hardly alone in treating consensus history as a fixed reality. Irwin Unger not only embraced but celebrated consensus as the defining element of postwar historiography—a model he described as "the new postwar history." He attacked New Left historians for rejecting its value in favor of their "exaggerated present-mindedness." See Irwin Unger, "The 'New Left' and American History: Some Recent Trends in United States Historiography," *American Historical Review* 72, 4 (July 1967): 1239–1244, 1257.

1. Industrial Society and the Imperatives of Modern History

1. Edward Eggleston, "The New History," Annual Report of the American Historical Association, 1900, vol. 1 (Washington, D.C.: Government Printing Office, 1901), p. 47. On the American Historical Association see David D. Van Tassel, "From Learned Society to Professional Organization: The American Historical Association, 1884–1900," *American Historical Review* 89, 4 (October 1984); Thomas Haskell, *The Emergence of Professional Social Science* (Urbana: University of Illinois Press, 1977); John Higham, *History: Professional Scholarship in America* (Baltimore: Johns Hopkins University Press, 1989); Peter Novick, *That Noble Dream: The "Objectivity Question" and the American Historical Profession* (Cambridge, U.K.: Cambridge University Press, 1988).

2. Higham, *History,* Chapter 1; Novick, *That Noble Dream,* Chapter 2; Dorothy Ross, *The Origins of American Social Science* (Cambridge, U.K.: Cambridge University Press, 1991), Part II, passim and Chapters 5 and 8; Haskell, *Emergence of Professional Social Science;* Mary O. Furner, *Advocacy and Objectivity: A Crisis in the Professionalization of American Social Science, 1865–1905* (Lexington: University of Kentucky Press, 1975).

3. Higham, *History,* pp. 150–170; Ross, *Origins of American Social Science,* pp. 265–266; Woodrow Wilson, *Division and Reunion, 1829–1889* (New York: Longmans, Green, and Co., 1893); John Bach McMaster, *History of*

the People of the United States: From the Revolution to the Civil War (New York: D. Appleton and Co., 1883–1913); James Ford Rhodes, *History of the United States from the Compromise of 1850* (New York: Harper and Bros., 1892); William A. Dunning, *Essays on the Civil War and Reconstruction and Related Topics* (New York: Macmillan, 1897); John David Smith, *An Old Creed for the New South: Proslavery Ideology and Historiography, 1865–1918* (Westport, Conn.: Greenwood Press, 1985).

4. Richard Hofstadter makes much of the impact of the historical context on the preoccupations of the Progressive historians; see Hofstadter, *The Progressive Historians* (New York: Vintage, 1970), especially Part I.

5. *Dictionary of American Biography*, s.v. "Sloane, William Milligan," p. 214; Lillian Handlin, *George Bancroft: The Intellectual as Democrat* (New York: Harper and Row, 1984); David Levin, *History as Romantic Art* (Stanford: Stanford University Press, 1959); Watt Stewart, "George Bancroft," in William T. Hutchinson, ed., *The Marcus W. Jernegan Essays in American Historiography* (Chicago: University of Chicago Press, 1937); Dorothy Ross, "Historical Consciousness in Nineteenth-Century America," *American Historical Review* 89, 4 (October 1984); Dorothy Ross, "Grand Narrative in American Historical Writing: From Romance to Uncertainty," *American Historical Review* 100, 3 (June 1995). Nineteenth-century patrician historians such as Bancroft, influenced in part by the legacies of the American Revolution and Jacksonian democracy, had also made reference to the centrality of the "people" to the heroic march of American history. But most did not write social histories that accounted for the experience of ordinary Americans. See Robert Allen Skotheim, *American Intellectual Histories and Historians* (Princeton: Princeton University Press, 1966), Chapter 1.

6. William M. Sloane, "History and Democracy," *American Historical Review* 1, 1 (October 1895): 6, 4; *Dictionary of American Biography*, s.v. "Sloane, William Milligan," p. 214; Ross, "Grand Narrative," pp. 651–656.

7. Sloane, "History and Democracy," pp. 6, 5.

8. Ibid., pp. 8–10.

9. Ibid., pp. 11–12.

10. Ibid., pp. 14–15.

11. Ibid., pp. 16–17.

12. Morey Rothberg, "Introduction," in Morey Rothberg and Jacqueline Goggin, eds., *John Franklin Jameson and the Development of Humanistic Scholarship in America*, vol. 1 (Athens: University of Georgia Press, 1993), pp. xxix–xxx and passim; Ross, *Origins of American Social Science*, pp. 266–270; John Franklin Jameson, "An Introduction to the Study of the Constitutional and Political History of the States," in Rothberg and Goggin, eds., *John Franklin Jameson*, p. 24. For Jameson's later support of efforts to advance African American history see August Meier and Elliott Rudwick, "J. Franklin Jameson, Carter G. Woodson, and the Foundations of Black Historiography," *American Historical Review* 89, 4 (October 1984).

13. Rothberg, "Introduction," pp. xxviii–xxix; Rothberg and Goggin, eds., *John Franklin Jameson,* pp. 3–4.
14. John Franklin Jameson, "The Disturbances in Barbados in 1876," in Rothberg and Goggin, eds., *John Franklin Jameson,* pp. 8–9.
15. Jameson, "The Disturbances in Barbados," pp. 10, 8–10.
16. Ibid., p. 10.
17. Ibid., p. 11.
18. Ibid.
19. Ibid., pp. 11–12.
20. Rothberg and Goggin, eds., *John Franklin Jameson,* p. 4; Jameson, "The Disturbances in Barbados," p. 5.
21. Jameson, "An Introduction to the Study of the Constitutional and Political History of the States," in Rothberg and Goggin, eds., *John Franklin Jameson,* p. 16.
22. Jameson, "An Introduction to the Study," p. 18.
23. Ibid., pp. 18–19, 17.
24. Ibid., p. 19.
25. Ibid., pp. 24–26.
26. Ibid., p. 19.
27. John Franklin Jameson, "Lectures on the Constitutional and Political History of the South," in Rothberg and Goggin, eds., *John Franklin Jameson,* p. 165 and passim.
28. Jameson, "Lectures on the Constitutional and Political History," pp. 156–157; Rothberg, "Introduction," pp. xxxii–xxxiii; Rothberg and Goggin, eds., *John Franklin Jameson,* pp. 203–204; Ross, *Origins of American Social Science,* pp. 267–268; John Franklin Jameson, "The Revolution as a Social Movement: Lectures on Slavery and the West," in Rothberg and Goggin, eds., *John Franklin Jameson,* p. 205.
29. Jameson, "The Revolution and Slavery," in Rothberg and Goggin, eds., pp. 219, 212, 208, 206–208.
30. Ibid., pp. 214–219; Pauline Maier, "The Transforming Impact of Independence, Reaffirmed: 1776 and the Definition of American Social Structure," in James A. Henretta, Michael Kammen, and Stanley N. Katz, eds., *The Transformation of Early American History: Society, Authority, and Ideology* (New York: Knopf, 1991), pp. 194–195 and passim; Bernard Bailyn, *The Ideological Origins of the American Revolution* (Cambridge: Harvard University Press, 1967), pp. 235–246; Bernard Bailyn, *Faces of Revolution* (New York: Vintage, 1992), Chapter 8.
31. Jameson quoted in Ross, *Origins of American Social Science,* pp. 257–268; Rothberg, "Introduction," pp. xxix, xxviii–xxx; Morey D. Rothberg, "'To Set a Standard of Workmanship and Compel Men to Conform to It': John Franklin Jameson as Editor of the American Historical Review," *American Historical Review* 89, 4 (October 1984): 958–959.
32. Jameson, "Lectures on Constitutional and Political History," pp. 160–161.

33. J. Franklin Jameson, *The History of Historical Writing in America* (New York: Greenwood Press, 1891), pp. 138–145.

34. Ross, "Historical Consciousness in Nineteenth-Century America," pp. 916–917; John L. Thomas, *Alternative America: Henry George, Edward Bellamy, Henry Demarest Lloyd, and the Adversary Tradition* (Cambridge: Harvard University Press, 1983); Lawrence Goodwyn, *The Populist Moment* (New York: Oxford University Press, 1978); Sidney Fine, *Laissez-Faire and the General Welfare State* (Ann Arbor: University of Michigan Press, 1967); Paul Avrich, *The Haymarket Tragedy* (Princeton: Princeton University Press, 1984); Paul Avrich, *Anarchist Portraits* (Princeton: Princeton University Press, 1988).

35. *Dictionary of American Biography,* s.v. "McMaster, John Bach," pp. 140–41; John B. McMaster, *A History of the People of the United States,* vols. 1–8 (New York: D. Appleton & Co., 1883–1913); McMaster quoted in Skotheim, *American Intellectual Histories,* pp. 18–19; Ross, "Historical Consciousness," pp. 918–919; Higham, *History,* pp. 150–157; William T. Hutchinson, "John Bach McMaster," in Hutchinson, ed., *Marcus W. Jernegan Essays,* pp. 122–125, 131, and passim.

36. McMaster quoted in Hutchinson, "John Bach McMaster," p. 139; see also pp. 133–139. Smith, *An Old Creed for the New South,* p. 112.

37. Hutchinson, "John Bach McMaster," p. 128.

38. Ibid., pp. 132, 139.

39. Jameson, "An Introduction to the Study," p. 18; Charles Levermore, "Review of John Bach McMaster, *A History of the People of the United States,*" *American Historical Review* 1, 1 (October 1895): 171.

40. Alice Morse Earle, *Colonial Dames and Good Wives* (Boston: Houghton Mifflin, 1895); Nina Baym, *American Women Writers and the Work of History* (New Brunswick, N.J.: Rutgers University Press, 1995); Bonnie Smith, "The Contributions of Women to Modern Historiography," *American Historical Review* 89, 3 (June 1984): 720 and passim; *Notable American Women 1607–1950,* s.v. "Earle, Alice Morse," pp. 541–542; Bonnie G. Smith, *The Gender of History* (Cambridge: Harvard University Press, 1998), pp. 157, 163.

41. Alice Morse Earle, *Child Life in Colonial Days* (New York: Macmillan, 1899), pp. vii–xi.

42. Sloane, "History and Democracy," p. 22. See volumes 1–5 of the *American Historical Review* for the minor reviews of books by women.

43. Edward G. Porter, "Review of *Home Life in Colonial Days,*" *American Historical Review* 4, 3 (April 1899): 545; William B. Weeden, "Review of *Child Life in Colonial Days,*" *American Historical Review* 5, 4 (July 1900): 766.

44. Among the few historians who have emphasized Eggleston's singular contributions to American history are Bernard Bailyn, *Education in the Forming of American Society* (New York: W. W. Norton, 1972), pp. 5–6, 74–75; Arthur Schlesinger, Sr., "Introduction," in Edward Eggleston, *The Transit of*

Civilization: From England to America in the Seventeenth Century (Boston: Beacon Press, 1959); Skotheim, *American Intellectual Histories;* Charles Hirschfield, "Edward Eggleston: Pioneer in Social History," in Eric F. Goldman, ed., *Historiography and Urbanization: Essays in Honor of W. Stull Holt* (Baltimore: Johns Hopkins University Press, 1941). Higham notes in a footnote that Eggleston's contributions to the study of American history were "unique." Higham, *History,* p. 155, n. 7.

45. Edward Eggleston and Lillie Eggleston Seelye, *Tecumseh and the Shawnee Prophet* (New York: Dodd, Mead and Co., 1878), pp. 13–14, 326–327, 23; Hirschfeld, "Edward Eggleston." For white views of Native American life in the nineteenth century see especially Robert F. Berkhofer, Jr., *White Man's Indian: Images of the American Indian from Columbus to the Present* (N.Y.: Vintage, 1978); Roy Harvey Pearce, *Savagism and Civilization: A Study of the Indian and the American Mind* (Baltimore: Johns Hopkins University Press, 1967).

46. Eggleston quoted in Schlesinger, "Introduction," p. x; remarks on Macaulay in Eggleston, "The New History," pp. 44–45; Hirschfeld, "Edward Eggleston," pp. 198–200, 209–210; Skotheim, *American Intellectual Histories,* pp. 48–53; Edward Eggleston, *The Beginners of a Nation: A History of the Source and Rise of the Earliest English Settlements in America with Special Reference to the Life and Character of the People* (New York: D. Appleton and Co., 1900); William Randel, *Edward Eggleston* (New York: Twayne, 1963), Chapters 1–4, pp. 124–127; Schlesinger, "Introduction," pp. vii–xi.

47. Eggleston quoted in Hirschfeld, "Edward Eggleston," pp. 191–192; Eggleston, *The Beginners of a Nation,* pp. ix–x.

48. Eggleston, *The Beginners of a Nation,* p. viii.

49. Ibid., pp. vii–viii.

50. Ibid., pp. 3, 20.

51. Ibid., p. 64, n. 4; p. 92.

52. Ibid., pp. 26, 29, 57, 59.

53. Ibid., pp. 300, 266–267, 329–333.

54. Ibid., pp. 340–342.

55. Herbert L. Osgood, "Review of *The Beginners of a Nation,*" *American Historical Review* 2, 3 (April 1897): 529–530.

56. Osgood, "Review," p. 530; popular reviews quoted in Randel, *Edward Eggleston,* pp. 139–141.

57. Eggleston, *The Transit of Civilization,* preface, n.p., and Chapter 1.

58. Ibid., pp. 296–297, 302–303.

59. Ibid., pp. 302–304, 305–307.

60. Barrett Wendell, "Review of *The Transit of Civilization,*" *American Historical Review* 6, 4 (July 1901): 804–805; Andrews quoted in Randel, *Edward Eggleston,* p. 143.

61. Randel, *Edward Eggleston,* p. 143; Eggleston, "The New History," p. 37. The phrase "the new history" had been used by University of Michigan

professor Earle Dow in an 1898 essay discussing the controversy over Lamprecht's "Deutsche Geschichte." See Earle Dow, "Features of the New History: Apropos of Lamphrecht's 'Deutsche Geshichte,'" *American Historical Review* 3, 3 (April 1898); Ernest A. Breisach, *American Progressive History* (Chicago: University of Chicago Press, 1993), pp. 29–30. On the Lamprecht controversy see Georg Iggers, *German Conception of History* (Middletown, Conn.: Wesleyan University Press, 1968); Fritz Ringer, *Decline of the German Mandarins* (Hanover, N.H.: University Press of New England, 1990).

62. Randel, *Edward Eggleston,* p. 143; Eggleston, "The New History," pp. 47, 39, 40.

63. Eggleston, "The New History," p. 47.

64. David Levering Lewis, *W. E. B. Du Bois: The Biography of a Race, 1869–1919* (New York: Henry Holt, 1993), pp. 18–32 and Chapter 2.

65. Ibid., Chapter 5.

66. Du Bois quoted in ibid., p. 101, and David Blight, "W. E. B. Du Bois and the Struggle for Americn Historical Memory," in Genevieve Fabre and Robert O'Meally, eds., *History and Memory in African-American Culture* (New York: Oxford University Press, 1994), pp. 47–48; W. E. B. Du Bois, "Jefferson Davis as a Representative of Civilization," in Nathan Huggins, ed., *W. E. B. Du Bois: Writings* (New York: Library of America, 1986).

67. Lewis, *W. E. B. Du Bois,* p. 102 and Chapter 5 passim.

68. Ibid., pp. 143–145 and Chapter 6 passim.

69. W. E. Burghardt Du Bois, *The Suppression of the African Slave Trade to the United States of America, 1638–1870* (New York: Russell & Russell, 1965), p. v.

70. Ibid., p. v; Lewis, *W. E. B. Du Bois,* pp. 155–161.

71. Du Bois, *Suppression of the African Slave-Trade,* pp. 198, 151–152, 327–329.

72. Ibid., pp. 197–198. See Blight's essay "W. E. B. Du Bois" for a brilliant analysis of Du Bois and historical memory.

73. Du Bois, *Suppression of the African Slave-Trade,* pp. 198–199.

74. "Review of *The Suppression of the African Slave-Trade,*" *American Historical Review,* 2, 3 (April 1897): 557, 559.

75. For some thoughtful recent discussions see Breisach, *American Progressive History;* John Mack Faragher, *Rereading Frederick Jackson Turner* (New York: Henry Holt, 1994); and Richard White and Patricia Nelson Limerick, *The Frontier in American Culture* (Berkeley: University of California Press, 1994).

76. Frederick Jackson Turner, "The Significance of History," in Faragher, *Rereading Frederick Jackson Turner,* pp. 12–13.

77. Turner, "The Significance of History," pp. 13, 15.

78. Ibid., pp. 18–19.

79. Ibid., pp. 19–20; Frederick Jackson Turner to Carl Willian Blegen, 16 March

1923, Frederick Jackson Turner Papers, Box 32, The Huntington Library, San Marino, California.

2. Advancing a Progressive New History

1. James Harvey Robinson, *The New History* (New York: Macmillan, 1912), pp. 24–25; Richard Hofstadter, *The Progressive Historians* (New York: Vintage, 1970); Ernst Breisach, *American Progressive History* (Chicago: University of Chicago Press, 1993); Dorothy Ross, *Origins of American Social Science* (Cambridge, U.K.: Cambridge University Press, 1991); John Higham, *History: Professional Scholarship in America* (Baltimore: Johns Hopkins University Press, 1989); Cushing Strout, *The Pragmatic Revolt in American History: Carl Becker and Charles Beard* (New Haven: Yale University Press, 1958); Peter Novick, *That Noble Dream: The "Objectivity Question" and the American Historical Profession* (New York: Cambridge University Press, 1988); Robert Skotheim, *American Intellectual Histories and Historians* (Princeton: Princeton University Press, 1966); Ellen Nore, *Charles Beard: An Intellectual Biography* (Carbondale: Southern Illinois University Press, 1983); Ray A. Billington, *Frederick Jackson Turner: Historian, Scholar, Teacher* (New York: Oxford University Press, 1973); Gerald D. Nash, *Creating the West: Historical Interpretations, 1890–1990* (Albuquerque: University of New Mexico Press, 1991).
2. On the goals of the emerging discipline of history, see especially Ross, *Origins of American Social Science*, esp. Chapter 8; Breisach, *American Progressive History*; Higham, *History*.
3. On Robinson and the new history paradigm see Skotheim, *American Intellectual Histories*, pp. 66–86; Breisach, *American Progressive History*; Luther Hendricks, *James Harvey Robinson: Teacher of History* (New York: King's Crown Press, 1946); Novick, *That Noble Dream*, Chapter 4; Higham, *History*, pp. 110–116; David Gross, "The 'New History': A note of Reappraisal," *History and Theory* 13, 1 (February 1974): 53–58.
4. On Beard, see especially Nore, *Charles Beard;* Hofstadter, *The Progressive Historians;* Breisach, *American Progressive History;* Howard K. Beale, *Charles Beard: An Appraisal* (Lexington: University of Kentucky Press, 1954); David W. Marcell, *Progress and Pragmatism: James, Dewey, Beard, and the American Idea of Progress* (Westport, Conn.: Greenwood Press, 1974); Ian Tyrell, *The Absent Marx: Class Analysis and Liberal History in Twentieth Century America* (Westport, Conn.: Greenwood Press, 1986); Ross, *Origins of American Social Science;* Higham, *History;* and Novick, *That Noble Dream.*
5. Nore details Seligman's lasting influence on Beard. "In his own numerous later writings Beard never really ventured beyond his teacher's conception." Nore, *Charles Beard*, p. 31.
6. Charles Hull, "Review of Edwin R. A. Seligman, *Essays on Taxation,*"

American Historical Review 1, 3 (April 1896): 565. On Seligman and the Gilded Age economists see especially Ross, *Origins of Social Science,* Chapters 4 and 6; and Leon Fink, "'Intellectuals' versus 'Workers': Academic Requirements and the Creation of Labor History," *American Historical Review* 96, 2 (April 1991): 402–403.

7. Edwin R. A. Seligman, *The Economic Interpretation of History* (New York: Columbia University Press, 1902), pp. 56, 106–109, 130–132; Ross, *Origins of American Social Science,* pp. 188–189; Hofstadter, *The Progressive Historians,* pp. 197–200.

8. Seligman, *Economic Interpretation of History,* pp. 1–2. Seligman lamented the fact that more social histories had not until very recently attended to the economic "aspect of the transitions which they describe." Ibid., p. 75.

9. Ibid., pp. 3, 67, 155–158.

10. Ibid., pp. 163–164, 86, 165.

11. Ibid., pp. 7, 19.

12. "The Meeting of the American Historical Association at Philadelphia," *American Historical Review* 8, 3 (April 1903): 412; C. W. Alvord, "Review of Edwin R. A. Seligman, *The Economic Interpretation of History,*" *American Historical Review* 8, 3 (April 1903): 519.

13. "The Meeting of the American Historical Association at Chicago," *American Historical Review* 10, 3 (April 1905): 504–506; "Notes and News," *American Historical Review* 9, 2 (January 1904): 416.

14. On marginalism see especially Ross, *Origins of American Social Science,* Chapter 6. Edith Abbott, *Women in Industry: A Study of American Economic History* (New York: D. Appleton and Co., 1910); Edith Abbott, *The Wages of Unskilled Labor in the United States, 1850–1900* (Chicago: University of Chicago Press, 1905); Edith Abbott, "Harriet Martineau and the Employment of Women in 1836," *Journal of Political Economy* 14, 10 (December 1906); Sarah Scovill Whittelsey, "Massachusetts Labor Legislation," *Annals of the American Academy of Political and Social Science,* Supplement, 17 (January 1901). On late-nineteenth and early-twentieth-century research on labor history see David Montgomery, "The Conventional Wisdom," *Labor History* 13, 1 (Winter 1972).

15. John R. Commons, *American Shoemakers, 1648–1895* (Cambridge: Harvard University Press, 1909); John R. Commons, *Horace Greeley and the Working Class Origins of the Republican Party* (New York: Ginn and Co., 1909); John R. Commons, Ulrich B. Phillips, Eugene A. Gilmore, Helen L. Sumner, and John B. Andrews, eds., *A Documentary History of American Industrial Society* (Cleveland: A. H. Clark Co., 1910–1911); John R. Commons et al., eds., *History of Labor in the United States* (New York: Macmillan, 1918). For one of the most penetrating critiques of Commons see Alan Dawley, *Class and Community: The Industrial Revolution in Lynn* (Cambridge: Harvard University Press, 1976), esp. pp. 144–145. Leon Fink has done a masterful job of rethinking Commons's place in American labor

history. See, for example, "'Intellectuals' versus 'Workers'"; Leon Fink, Stephen T. Leonard, Donald M. Reid, eds., *Intellectuals and Public Life: Radicalism and Reform* (Ithaca: Cornell University Press, 1990); Leon Fink, *Progressive Intellectuals and the Dilemmas of Democratic Commitment* (Cambridge: Harvard University Press, 1997).

16. James Ford Rhodes, "The Molly Maguires in the Anthracite Region of Pennsylvania," *American Historical Review* 15, 3 (April 1910): 561.

17. Martin Bulmer, Kevin Bales, and Kathryn Kish Sklar, eds., *The Social Survey in Historical Perspective 1880–1940* (Cambridge, U.K.: Cambridge University Press, 1991); Mary O. Furner and Barry Supple, *The State and Economic Knowledge* (Cambridge, U.K.: Cambridge University Press, 1990); Michael J. Lacey and Mary O. Furner, *The State and Social Investigation in England and America* (Cambridge, U.K.: Cambridge University Press, 1993).

18. Ross, *Origins of Social Science*, pp. 202–203; Fink, "'Intellectuals' versus 'Workers'"; Fink, *Progressive Intellectuals*.

19. Frederick Jackson Turner, *The Rise of the New West, 1819–1829* (New York: Harper and Bros., 1906).

20. "Notes and News: America," *American Historical Review* 6, 1 (October 1902): 197; Albert Bushnell Hart, "Editor's Introduction to the Series," in Edward Cheyney, *European Background of American History, 1300–1600,* American Nation Series, vol. 1 (New York: Harper and Brothers, 1904), pp. xv–xvii. The later volumes of Edward Channing's multivolume *History of the United States* (1905–1925) also reflect a concerted effort on the part of that Brahmin historian to explore social and economic dimensions of American history.

21. Billington, *Frederick Jackson Turner,* p. 220; Wilbur R. Jacobs, *The Historical World of Frederick Jackson Turner* (New Haven: Yale University Press, 1968), pp. 184–185.

22. Frederick Jackson Turner, "The Colonization of the West, 1820–1830," *American Historical Review* 11, 2 (January 1906): 325; Frederick Jackson Turner, "The South, 1820–1830," *American Historical Review* 11, 3 (April 1906): 560, 573.

23. See, for example, Patricia Nelson Limerick, "Turnerians All: The Dream of a Helpful History in an Intelligible World," *American Historical Review* 100, 3 (June 1995); Patricia Nelson Limerick, Clyde A. Milner II, and Charles E. Rankin, eds., *Trails: Toward a New Western History* (Lawrence: University Press of Kansas, 1991); Nash, *Creating the West;* William Cronon, George Miles, and Jay Gitlin, eds., *Under an Open Sky: Rethinking America's Western Past* (New York: W. W. Norton, 1992); Richard White, "Frederick Jackson Turner and Buffalo Bill," in James Grossman, ed., *The Frontier in American Culture: Essays by Richard White and Patricia Nelson Limerick* (Berkeley: University of California Press, 1994). John Mack Faragher has raised pointed questions about the "old" and "new" Western history para-

digm; see "Afterword" in John Mack Faragher, *Rereading Frederick Jackson Turner* (New York: Henry Holt and Co., 1994). See also Donald Worster, *Under Western Skies: Nature and History in the American West* (New York: Oxford University Press, 1992).

24. On Phillips see especially Merton L. Dillon, *Ulrich Bonnell Phillips: Historian of the Old South* (Baton Rouge: Louisiana State University Press, 1985); John David Smith and John C. Inscoe, *Ulrich Bonnell Phillips: A Southern Historian and His Critics* (New York: Greenwood Press, 1990); John David Smith, *An Old Creed for the New South: Proslavery Ideology and Historiography, 1865–1918* (New York: Greenwood, 1985); August Meier and Elliott Rudwick, *Black History and the Historical Profession* (Urbana: University of Illinois Press, 1986).

25. Ulrich B. Phillips, "The Origin and Growth of the Southern Black Belts," *American Historical Review* 11, 4 (July 1906).

26. Ibid., p. 798.

27. Ulrich B. Phillips, *American Negro Slavery: A Survey of the Supply, Employment, and Control of Negro Labor, as Determined by the Plantation Regime* (New York: D. Appleton, 1918); Phillips quoted in Eugene Genovese, "Ulrich Bonnell Phillips as an Economic Historian," in Smith and Inscoe, *Ulrich Bonnell Phillips*, p. 204. Phillips's classic study of the culture of plantation slavery did not appear until the 1920s: Ulrich B. Phillips, *Life and Labor in the Old South* (Boston: Little, Brown, 1929).

28. Phillips, "Origin and Growth of the Southern Black Belts," p. 805. On the racism of Phillips, see W. E. B. Du Bois, "Review of *American Negro Slavery*," *American Political Science Review* 12, 4 (November 1918): 722. For other examples of economic histories of plantation slavery that depicted the planters as benign or victimized see Alfred Holt Stone, "Some Problems of Southern Economic History," *American Historical Review* 13, 4 (July 1908); and Alfred Holt Stone, "The Cotton Factorage System of the Southern States," *American Historical Review* 20, 3 (1915).

29. George Burton Adams, "History and the Philosophy of History," *American Historical Review* 14, 2 (January 1909): 224.

30. Ibid., pp. 224, 226.

31. Ibid., pp. 226, 221, n. 1.

32. Ibid., pp. 226, 228, 229–230.

33. Ibid., pp. 228–230, 235–236.

34. Frederick Jackson Turner, "Social Forces in American History," *American Historical Review* 16, 2 (January 1911): 217.

35. Ibid., p. 225.

36. Ibid., pp. 221–224.

37. Ibid., pp. 226–227, 230.

38. Ibid., pp. 231–233.

39. Nore, *Charles Beard*, Chapters 1–4.

40. Beard and Robinson quoted in Skotheim, *American Intellectual Histories,* pp. 89–90; Nore, *Charles Beard,* Chapter 3.
41. Nore, *Charles Beard,* especially Chapters 3 and 4; Hofstadter, *The Progressive Historians,* pp. 197–200.
42. Beard quoted in Nore, *Charles Beard,* pp. 56–57. Charles Beard, *An Economic Interpretation of the Constitution of the United States* (New York: Macmillan, 1913).
43. Beard, *An Economic Interpretation of the Constitution;* Nore, *Charles Beard,* pp. 56–59; Breisach, *American Progressive History,* Chapter 9; Ross, *Origins of Social Science,* pp. 343–344.
44. *Dictionary of American Biography,* s.v. "Libby, Orin Grant," pp. 429–430; Hofstadter, *The Progressive Historians,* p. 191; Turner quoted in Billington, *Frederick Jackson Turner,* p. 126; Nore, *Charles Beard,* pp. 64–65.
45. Quoted in Hofstadter, *The Progressive Historians,* pp. 212–213.
46. Andrew C. McLaughlin, "American History and American Democracy," *American Historical Review* 20, 2 (January 1915): 260.
47. Charles Beard, *Economic Origins of Jeffersonian Democracy* (New York: Macmillan, 1915), frontispiece, p. vii.
48. Ibid., p. 467.
49. Guy S. Callender, "The Position of American Economic History," *American Historical Review* 19, 1 (October 1913): 80; Victor S. Clark, "The Influence of Manufactures upon Political Sentiment in the United States from 1820–1860," *American Historical Review* 22, 1 (October 1916): 58.
50. Charles Beard, *Contemporary American History, 1877–1913* (New York: Macmillan, 1920), pp. 14, 22, 26.
51. Ibid., p. vi.
52. *Dictionary of American Biography,* s.v. "Semple, Ellen Churchill," p. 583; *Notable American Women,* s.v. "Semple, Ellen Churchill," p. 260.
53. Breisach, *American Progressive History,* pp. 23–24, 82.
54. *Notable American Women,* "Semple," pp. 260–261.
55. Ellen Churchill Semple, *American History and Its Geographic Conditions* (Boston: Houghton Mifflin, 1903), title page, p. 280.
56. Ibid., pp. 280, 283, 285.
57. Ibid., pp. 77, 82.
58. Ibid., pp. 80–81.
59. Ibid., p. 335.
60. Ibid., pp. 1, 428.
61. Albert Bushnell Hart, "Review of Albert Perry Brigham, *Geographic Influences in American History,* and Ellen Churchill Semple, *American History and Its Geographic Conditions,*" *American Historical Review* 9, 3 (April 1904): 571–572. For a later example of the environmental approach to history see Ellsworth Huntington, "Changes of Climate and History," *American Historical Review* 18, 2 (January 1913).

62. Alfred H. Lloyd, "History and Materialism," *American Historical Review* 10, 4 (July 1905): 727.
63. "The Meeting of the American Historical Association at Madison," *American Historical Review* 13, 3 (April 1908): 435–437.
64. See "Meeting of the American Historical Association at Madison," pp. 435–458; various early volumes of the *Mississippi Valley Historical Review,* esp. 1, 2 (September 1914); 3, 2 (September 1916); and 4, 2 (September 1917).
65. "Review of Albert Bushnell Hart, *American History Told by Contemporaries,*" *American Historical Review* 6, 3 (April 1901): 591–592. Jameson's authorship is revealed in Morey Rothberg and Jacqueline Goggin, eds., *John Franklin Jameson and the Development of Humanistic Scholarship in America* (Athens: University of Georgia Press, 1993), p. 362.
66. Frederic Paxson, "The Cow Country," *American Historical Review* 22, 1 (October 1916): 69; Billington, *Frederick Jackson Turner,* p. 306.
67. Paxson, "Cow Country," pp. 79, 81–82. See also the description of a 1907 paper by Paxson in "The Meeting of the American Historical Association at Madison," *American Historical Review* 13, 3 (April 1908): 451.
68. Alexander Brown, "Review of Philip Alexander Bruce, *Economic History of Virginia in the Seventeenth Century,*" *American Historical Review* 1, 3 (April 1896): 539; Smith, *An Old Creed for the New South,* pp. 173–177.
69. See, for example, the notice of Frederick Starr's activities in "Notes and News," *American Historical Review* 5, 2 (December 1899): 421.
70. "The Meeting of the American Historical Association at Providence," *American Historical Review* 12, 3 (April 1907): 503; *Notable American Women,* s.v. "Abel, Annie Heloise," pp. 4–6.
71. "Meeting of the American Historical Association at Madison," *American Historical Review* 13, 3 (April 1908): 452–453; Annie Heloise Abel, "The Indians in the Civil War," *American Historical Review* 15, 2 (January 1910).
72. Abel, "The Indians in the Civil War," p. 296.
73. "Meeting of the American Historical Association at Madison," pp. 452–453; Abel, "Indians in the Civil War." For examples of other articles addressing Native American history see Max Farrand, "The Indian Boundary Line," *American Historical Review* 10, 4 (July 1905); Charles C. Smith, "Review of *Pioneers of New France in New England* by James Phinney Baxter," *American Historical Review* 1, 3 (April 1896); Herbert E. Bolton, "The Mission as a Frontier Institution in the Spanish-American Colonies," *American Historical Review* 23, 1 (October 1917); "The Meeting of the American Historical Association at Washington," *American Historical Review* 21, 3 (April 1916). For a discussion of Native American historiography see R. David Edmunds, "Native Americans, New Voices: American Indian History, 1895–1995," *American Historical Review* 100, 3 (June 1995). Abel is not mentioned in Edmunds's article.
74. Adna Ferrin Weber, *The Growth of Cities in the Nineteenth Century: A*

Study in Statistics (New York: Macmillan, 1899); "Biographical Note" in Adna Ferrin Weber, *The Growth of Cities in the Nineteenth Century* (Ithaca: Cornell University Press, 1963), pp. x–xi; Walter F. Willcox, "Review of Adna Weber, *The Growth of Cities in the Nineteenth Century,*" *American Historical Review* 5, 2 (December 1899): 350–351.

75. Albert Bushnell Hart, "Imagination in History," *American Historical Review* 15, 2 (January 1910): 238–239, 245.

76. Theodore Roosevelt, "History as Literature," *American Historical Review* 18, 3 (April 1913): 477, 479.

77. Ibid., p. 485.

78. John Bach McMaster, "Old Standards of Public Morals," *American Historical Review* 11, 3 (April 1906): 515–516; "The Meeting of the American Historical Association at Washington and Richmond," *American Historical Review* 14, 3 (April 1909): 431–433, 444.

79. On Becker see especially Skotheim, *American Intellectual Histories;* Burleigh Wilkins, *Carl Becker: A Biographical Study in American Intellectual History* (Cambridge: Harvard University Press, 1961); Novick, *That Noble Dream;* Breisach, *American Progressive History;* Robert E. Brown, *Carl Becker on History and the American Revolution* (East Lansing, Mich.: Spartan Press, 1970).

80. Carl Becker, "The Growth of Revolutionary Parties and Methods in New York Province: 1765–1774," *American Historical Review* 7, 1 (October 1901): 56; Higham, *History,* p. 180; "The Meeting of the American Historical Association at Cincinnati," *American Historical Review* 22, 3 (April 1917): 526–527; Arthur Schlesinger, *The Colonial Merchants and the American Revolution, 1763–1776* (New York: Columbia University Press, 1918); Tyrell, *Absent Marx,* p. 21.

81. "The Meeting of the American Historical Association at New York," *American Historical Review* 15, 3 (April 1910): 486–487; Kendric Charles Babcock, "The Scandanavian Element in American Population," *American Historical Review* 16, 2 (January 1911): 300.

82. See, for example, "Notes and News," *American Historical Review* 9, 4 (July 1904): 866, 880; "Notes and News," *American Historical Review* 9, 2 (January 1904): 430–431; "Notes and News," *American Historical Review* 8, 4 (July 1903): 822.

83. "Minor Notices," *American Historical Review* 5, 3 (April 1900): 620; "The Meeting of the American Historical Association at Washington," *American Historical Review* 21, 3 (April 1916): 457.

84. Carl Russell Fish, "Social Relief in the Northwest during the Civil War," *American Historical Review* 22, 2 (January 1917): 324; *Dictionary of American Biography,* s.v. "Fish, Carl Russell," pp. 297–298.

85. Alfred Holt Stone, "Some Problems of Southern Economic History," *American Historical Review* 13, 4 (July 1908).

86. Du Bois, "Review of *American Negro Slavery,*" pp. 725, 723; Smith and Inscoe, *Ulrich Bonnell Phillips,* pp. 83–84. On the wider tradition of African American historiography see Wilson Jeremiah Moses, *Afrotopia: The Roots of African American Popular History* (Cambridge, U.K.: Cambridge University Press, 1998).

87. David Levering Lewis, *W. E. B. Du Bois: Biography of a Race 1868–1919* (New York: Henry Holt, 1993), pp. 383–385.

88. "The Meeting of the American Historical Association at New York," *American Historical Review* 15, 3 (April 1910): 489; W. E. B. Du Bois, "Reconstruction and Its Benefits," *American Historical Review* 15, 4 (July 1910): 799.

89. "Meeting at New York," p. 489; W. E. B. Du Bois, "Reconstruction and Its Benefits"; Lewis, *W. E. B. Du Bois,* p. 383; Meier and Rudwick, *Black History and the Historical Profession,* especially Chapter 1.

90. Wilbur Siebert, "Light on the Underground Railroad," *American Historical Review* 1, 3 (April 1896); Marcus Jernegan, "Slavery and Conversion in the American Colonies," *American Historical Review* 21, 3 (April 1916): 516–517. See also Wilbur Siebert, *Underground Railroad from Slavery to Freedom* (New York: Macmillan, 1898); Larry Gara's discussion of Siebert in *Liberty Line: The Legend of the Underground Railroad* (Lexington: University Press of Kentucky, 1996); and Smith's discussion of work done at Johns Hopkins on slavery at the turn of the twentieth century in *An Old Creed for the New South,* Chapter 5, especially the discussion of Harrison Trexler, pp. 151–153.

91. Jernegan, "Slavery and Conversion," pp. 516–519. For a recent discussion of African American historiography see Earl Lewis, "To Turn as on a Pivot: Writing African Americans into a History of Overlapping Diasporas," *American Historical Review* 100, 3 (June 1995).

92. Meier and Rudwick, *Black History and the Historical Profession,* pp. 6–7; Lewis, "To Turn as on a Pivot."

93. The single best source on Woodson is Jacqueline Goggin's superb biography, *Carter G. Woodson: A Life in Black History* (Baton Rouge: Louisiana State University Press, 1993). For his early life see Chapters 1 and 2.

94. Quoted in ibid., pp. 21, 26; see also Chapter 1.

95. Jacqueline Goggin, "Countering White Racist Scholarship: Carter G. Woodson and the *Journal of Negro History,*" *Journal of Negro History* 68, 4 (Fall 1983); Goggin, *Carter G. Woodson,* pp. 35–36.

96. Goggin, "Countering White Racist Scholarship," pp. 361–365.

97. George Wells Parker, "The African Origin of the Grecian Civilization," *Journal of Negro History* 2, 3 (July 1917): 334, 336, 343–344. For an illuminating discussion of Parker and the larger context of African American history, see Wilson Jeremiah Moses, *Afrotopia: The Roots of African American Popular History* (Cambridge, U.K.: Cambridge University Press, 1998).

3. Native Americans and the Moral Compass of History

1. Peter Novick, *That Noble Dream: The "Objectivity Question" and the American Historical Profession* (Cambridge, U.K.: Cambridge University Press, 1988), pp. 178–179; Ian Tyrrell, *The Absent Marx: Class Analysis and Liberal History in Twentieth Century America* (Westport, Conn.: Greenwood Press, 1986), pp. 21–22, Chapters 1 and 2.

2. See the overview of historiography, for example, in Wilcomb E. Washburn and Bruce Trigger, "Native Peoples in Euro-American Historiography," in Bruce G. Trigger and Wilcomb E. Washburn, eds., *Cambridge History of the Native Peoples of the Americas,* vol. 1, part 1 (Cambridge, U.K.: Cambridge University Press, 1996), pp. 61–124; Reginald Horsman, "Well-Trodden Paths and Fresh Byways: Recent Writing on Native American History," *Reviews in American History* 10, 4 (December 1982); Daniel K. Richter, "Whose Indian History?" *William and Mary Quarterly,* 3rd Series, 50, 2 (April 1993): 379–380, 390–393; Wayne Bodle, "Themes and Directions in Middle Colonies Historiography, 1980–1994," *William and Mary Quarterly* 51, 3 (July 1994): 384–385; Gary B. Nash, "The Image of the Indian in the Southern Colonial Mind," *William and Mary Quarterly,* 3rd Series, 29, 2 (April 1972); James Axtell, "The Ethnohistory of Early America: A Review Essay," *William and Mary Quarterly,* 3rd Series, 35, 1 (January 1978); James H. Merrell, "Some Thoughts on Colonial Historians and American Indians," *William and Mary Quarterly,* 3rd Series, 46, 1 (January 1989); R. David Edmunds, "Native Americans, New Voices: American Indian History, 1895–1995," *American Historical Review* 100, 3 (June 1995); William T. Hagan, "The New Indian History," in Donald L. Fixico, ed., *Rethinking American Indian History* (Albuquerque: University of New Mexico Press, 1979); Donald L. Fixico, "Methodologies in Reconstructing Native American History," in Fixico, ed., *Rethinking American Indian History;* James Riding In, "Scholars and Twentieth Century Indians: Reassessing the Recent Past," in Colin G. Calloway, ed., *New Directions in American Indian History* (Norman: University of Oklahoma Press, 1987); Devon A. Mihesuah, ed., *Natives and Academics: Researching and Writing about American Indians* (Lincoln: University of Nebraska Press, 1998); Kerwin Lee Klein, *Frontiers of Historical Imagination* (Berkeley: University of California Press, 1997); Robert Berkhofer, Jr., *The White Man's Indian* (New York: Vintage, 1978); and Robert Carriker, "The American Indian from the Civil War to the Present," in Michael P. Malone, ed., *Historians and the American West* (Lincoln: University of Nebraska Press, 1983). There is likewise a very large literature on white images of Native Americans, including Berkhofer, *The White Man's Indian;* Susan Scheckel, *The Insistence of the Indian* (Princeton: Princeton University Press, 1998); and Philip J. Deloria, *Playing Indian* (New Haven: Yale University Press, 1998).

3. "The Fourteenth Annual Meeting of the Mississippi Valley Historical Associ-

ation," *Mississippi Valley Historical Review* 8, 1–2 (June–September 1921): 6. The scholar from Ohio State University was George A. Wood.

4. William Christie MacLeod, *The Origin of the State Reconsidered in the Light of the Data of Aboriginal North America* (Philadelphia: Westbrook Publishing Co., 1924); William Christie MacLeod, *The American Indian Frontier* (New York: Knopf, 1928), pp. vii–ix. For another reading of MacLeod, see Klein, *Frontiers of Historical Imagination,* pp. 145–148.

5. MacLeod, *The American Indian Frontier,* pp. 528–532.

6. Ibid., pp. 375–378.

7. A. J. Morrison, "The Virginia Indian Trade to 1673," *William and Mary Quarterly Historical Magazine,* 2nd Series, 1, 4 (October 1921): 219–220; William Montgomery Sweeny, "Some References to Indians in Colonial Virginia," *William and Mary Quarterly Historical Magazine,* 2nd Series, 16, 4 (October 1936). See also John P. Corry, *Indian Affairs in Georgia, 1732–1756* (Philadelphia: George S. Ferguson Co., 1936).

8. D. Huger Bacot, "The South Carolina Up Country at the End of the Eighteenth Century," *American Historical Review,* 28, 4 (July 1923): 684–689. For a superb study of regionalism and intellectual life in the interwar period see Robert L. Dorman, *Revolt of the Provinces: The Regionalist Movement in America, 1920–1945* (Chapel Hill: University of North Carolina Press, 1993).

9. David K. Bjork, "Documents Regarding Indian Affairs in the Lower Mississippi Valley, 1771–1772," *Mississippi Valley Historical Review* 13, 1 (December 1926): 398.

10. *Contemporary Authors,* s.v. "Crane, Verner Winslow," 113:105; Verner W. Crane, *The Southern Frontier, 1670–1732* (Durham, N.C.: Duke University Press, 1929); R. S. Cotterill, "Review of *The Southern Frontier,*" *Mississippi Valley Historical Review* 16, 1 (June 1929): 104; A. P. Whitaker, "Review of *The Southern Frontier,*" *American Historical Review* 34, 4 (July 1929); Frederick E. Hoxie and Harvey Markowitz, *Native Americans: An Annotated Bibliography* (Pasadena, Calif.: Salem Press, 1991).

11. "Twenty-Second Annual Meeting of the Mississippi Valley Historical Association," *Mississippi Valley Historical Review* 16, 2 (September 1929); Philip M. Hamer, "John Stuart's Indian Policy during the Early Months of the American Revolution," *Mississippi Valley Historical Review* 17, 3 (December 1930). See also Helen Louise Shaw's 1929 paper on Stuart's administration of the Southern Indian Department, "North Carolina Meeting of the American Historical Association," *American Historical Review* 35, 3 (April 1930); Philip Hamer, "Review of *British Administration of the Southern Indians, 1756–1783,*" *Mississippi Valley Historical Review* 18, 3 (December 1931); John Richard Alden, *John Stuart and the Southern Colonial Frontier: A Study of Indian Relations, War, Trade, and Land Problems in the Southern Wilderness, 1754–1775* (Ann Arbor: University of Michigan Press, 1944); *Contemporary Authors,* s.v., "Alden, John Richard," 11:18–19. Louis Knott

Koontz, "Review of *John Stuart and the Colonial Frontier,*" *William and Mary Quarterly,* 3rd Series, 1, 4 (October 1944): 409; Clarence E. Carter, "Review of *John Stuart and the Southern Colonial Frontier,*" *American Historical Review* 50, 3 (April 1945): 546; W. Neil Franklin, "Review of *John Stuart and the Southern Colonial Frontier,*" *Journal of Southern History* 10, 4 (November 1944): 491–492; Theodore C. Peace, "Review of *John Stuart and the Southern Colonial Frontier,*" *Mississippi Valley Historical Review* 31, 3 (December 1944): 452–453; Lawrence Henry Gipson, "Review of *John Stuart and the Southern Colonial Frontier,*" *Journal of Modern History* 17, 1 (March 1945): 54–55.

12. Charles H. Ambler, "Review of the *American Indian as Participant in the Civil War,*" *Mississippi Valley Historical Review* 6, 4 (March 1920): 578–579.

13. August Meier and Elliott Rudwick, *Black History and the Historical Profession, 1915–1980* (Urbana: University of Illinois Press, 1986), pp. 95–96; Frank J. Klingberg, "The Indian Frontier in South Carolina as Seen by the S.P.G. Missionary," *Journal of Southern History* 5, 4 (November 1939): 483–485, 499–500. A 1936 essay in the *Journal of Negro History* celebrated the accomplishments of two African American missionaries who had sought to convert Native Americans to Protestantism while implying that the previous efforts of Roman Catholic missionaries left the Indians in a "drunken," "debauched," and "worthless" condition. Arthur A. Schomburg, "Two Negro Missionaries to the American Indians, John Marrant and John Stewart," *Journal of Negro History* 21, 4 (October 1936): 402. For other examples of work on Indian missionaries during the interwar period, including the work of two women historians, see the reference to Grace Nute's paper "Government Policy with Respect to Missions among the Indians," in the American Historical Association's *Annual Report for the Year 1931* (Washington, D.C.: Government Printing Office, 1932), p. 35; Martha Edwards, "A Problem of Church and State in the 1870s," *Mississippi Valley Historical Review* 11, 1 (June 1924); Frank J. Klingberg, ed., *The Carolina Chronicle of Dr. Francis Le Jau, 1706–1717,* University of California Publications in History, 53 (Berkeley: University of California Press, 1956); Edgar Pennington, "Reverend Francis Le Jau's Work among Indians and Negro Slaves," *Journal of Southern History* 1, 4 (November 1935). For a sample of scholarly work on the fur trade concerned with traders' intersection with Native Americans see Grace Lee Nute, "The Papers of the American Fur Company," *American Historical Review* 32, 3 (April 1927).

14. James W. Patton, "The Fifth Annual Meeting of the Southern Historical Association," *Journal of Southern History,* 6, 1 (February 1940): 76–77. See also "Review of the *Thirty-Third Annual Report of the Bureau of American Ethnology,*" *Mississippi Valley Historical Review,* 7, 2 (September 1920): 177–179; "Review of *Seneca Myths and Folk Tales,*" *American Historical Review,* 30, 2 (January 1925): 435; and Richard H. Shryock, "Cultural Fac-

tors in the History of the South," *Journal of Southern History,* 5, 3 (August 1939): 333–346.

15. Maurice A. Mook, "Virginia Ethnology from an Early Relation," *William and Mary Quarterly Historical Magazine,* 2nd Series, 23, 2 (April 1943): 103, 101–103, 111, 121; Maurice A. Mook, "The Anthropological Position of the Indian Tribes of Tidewater Virginia," *William and Mary Quarterly Historical Magazine,* 2nd Series, 23, 1 (January 1943). In this latter essay, Mook challenges the scholarly division of southeastern and northern Algonkian tribes as being derived from political "rather than cultural data" (p. 29). See also Maurice A. Mook, *The Algonkian Ethnohistory of the Carolina Sound* (Philadelphia, 1944), reprint from the *Journal of the Washington Academy of Sciences* 34, 6 and 7 (June 15 and July 15, 1944).

16. Chapman J. Milling, *Red Carolinians* (Chapel Hill: University of North Carolina Press, 1940), pp. xi–xiii.

17. Ibid., pp. 3–6.

18. Ibid., p. 3; R. S. Cotterill, *The Old South: The Geographic, Economic, Social, Political, and Cultural Expansion, Institutions, and Nationalism of the Ante-bellum South* (Glendale, Calif.: Arthur H. Clark Co., 1936), p. 11; Angie Debo, "Review of *Red Carolinians,*" *American Historical Review* 46, 4 (July 1941): 920.

19. Carter Woodson, "The Relations of Negroes and Indians in Massachusetts," *Journal of Negro History* 5, 1 (January 1920): 45–57.

20. Meier and Rudwick, *Black History and the Historical Profession,* pp. 106–107; *Contemporary Authors,* 1969, s.v. "Porter, Kenneth Wiggins," p. 907; *Contemporary Authors,* New Revisions Series, s.v. "Porter, Kenneth Wiggins," 2: 530–531; Kenneth Porter, *Black Seminoles: History of a Freedom Seeking People* (Gainesville: University Press of Florida, 1996 [reprint]); Kenneth Porter, *Christ in the Breadline* (North Montpelier, Vt.: Driftwind Press, 1932); Kenneth Porter, *The Negro on the American Frontier* (New York: Arno Press, 1971 [reprint]); Kenneth Porter, *Relations between Negroes and Indians within the Present Limits of the United States* (New York: Associated Publishers, 1933); Kenneth Porter, *John Jacob Astor: Business Man,* 2 vols. (Cambridge: Harvard University Press, 1931); Kenneth Porter, *The Jacksons and the Lees: Two Generations of Massachusetts Merchants* (Cambridge: Harvard University Press, 1937).

21. Kenneth Porter, "Relations between Negroes and Indians within the Present Limits of the United States," *Journal of Negro History* 17, 3 (July 1932): 287–288; Kenneth Porter, "Notes Supplementary to 'Relations between Negroes and Indians,'" *Journal of Negro History* 18, 3 (July 1933): 286.

22. Porter, "Notes Supplementary to 'Relations between Negroes and Indians,'" pp. 319–321. See also Wilton Marion Krogman, "The Racial Composition of the Seminole Indians of Florida and Oklahoma," *Journal of Negro History* 19, 4 (October 1934): 412–430, and G. David Houston's effort to convey the pro-Indian concerns of African American Mississippi senator B. K.

Bruce during Reconstruction in "A Negro Senator," *Journal of Negro History* 7, 1 (January 1922): 252. At the 1940 meeting of the American Historical Association, Rayford Logan noted the ways in which Indians and African Americans were united in their joint victimization by the American Colonization Society. Jesse Dunsmore Clarkson, "Escape to the Present," *American Historical Review* 46, 3 (April 1941): 546.

23. "Review of *The Historic Trail of the American Indians,*" *Journal of Negro History* 19, 4 (October 1934): 442–443.

24. Milling, *Red Carolinians,* pp. 364–365; Porter, "Relations between Negroes and Indians," p. 288, n. 2.

25. *Contemporary Authors,* s.v. "Gates, Paul Wallace," 2: 242; Paul Wallace Gates, "The Homestead Law in an Incongruous Land System," *American Historical Review* 41, 4 (July 1936): 652–655, 672–681; Harry N. Scheiber, "The Economic Historian as Realist and as Keeper of Democratic Ideals: Paul Wallace Gates's Studies of American Land Policy," *Journal of Economic History* 40, 3 (September 1980): 588. For Gates's political affiliations and break with Turner, see Novick, *That Noble Dream,* pp. 322–323, and John Higham, *History: Professional Scholarship in the United States* (Baltimore: Johns Hopkins University Press, 1989), p. 202. For an equally devastating critique of the Homestead Act, which concludes that the law benefited "only monopolists and persons of fairly ample means" while doing virtually nothing for urban workers, see Fred Shannon, "The Homestead Act and the Labor Surplus," *American Historical Review* 41, 4 (July 1936): 644–651.

26. Paul Wallace Gates, "Review of *A Continent Lost—A Civilization Won: Indian Land Tenure in America,*" *American Historical Review* 43, 3 (April 1938): 636; Scheiber, "The Economic Historian as Realist," pp. 587–589. Gates went on to do important work on Indian land cessions and their legacies; see especially Paul Gates, *Fifty Million Acres* (Ithaca: Cornell University Press, 1954), and Paul Gates, ed., *The Rape of Indian Lands* (New York: Arno Press, 1979). For more on the land question, see, for example, Roy M. Robbins, *Our Landed Heritage, 1776–1936* (Princeton: Princeton University Press, 1942); Louis Pelzer, "Review of *Our Landed Heritage,*" *American Historical Review* 48, 2 (January 1943); Paul W. Gates, "Review of *Our Landed Heritage,*" *Mississippi Valley Historical Review* 28, 4 (March 1942); Henry W. Tatter, "Review of *Our Landed Heritage,*" *Journal of Southern History* 8, 3 (August 1942).

27. Randolph C. Downes, "Review of *A Continent Lost—A Civilization Won,*" *Mississippi Valley Historical Review* 24, 2 (September 1937): 252; *Contemporary Authors,* s.v. "Downes, Randolph Chandler," pp. 152–153.

28. Randolph G. Downes, "Creek-American Relations, 1790–1795," *Journal of Southern History* 8, 3 (August 1942): 350–353, 358. See also Wesley Frank Craven, "Indian Policy in Early Virginia," *William and Mary Quarterly,* 3rd Series, 1, 1 (January 1944).

29. R. S. Cotterill, "Federal Indian Management in the South, 1789–1825," *Mis-*

sissippi Valley Historical Review 20, 3 (December 1933): 333. See also Robert S. Cotterill, "The Virginia-Chickasaw Treaty of 1783," *Journal of Southern History* 8, 4 (November 1942): 483–496.

30. Cotterill, "Federal Indian Management," pp. 351, 346–347, 350–351; R. S. Cotterill, "Review of *Uncle Sam's Stepchildren*," *Journal of Southern History* 8, 3 (August 1942): 431–432; Cotterill, *The Old South*, pp. 267–269, 171–172, and chapters entitled "Secession" and "The Struggle for Independence." See also R. S. Cotterill, "The Virginia-Chickasaw Treaty of 1783," *Journal of Southern History* 8, 4 (November 1942). In 1954, Cotterill published a monograph on the southern Indians entitled *The Southern Indians: The Story of the Civilized Tribes before Removal* (Norman: University of Oklahoma Press, 1954).

31. J. P. Dunn, "Review of *When Buffalo Ran*," *Mississippi Valley Historical Review* 7, 4 (March 1921): 409; Kendric Babcock, "Review of *A History of Minnesota*," *American Historical Review* 30, 3 (April 1925): 624; Don Russell, "Review of *The Bannock Indian War of 1878*," *Journal of the American Military History Foundation* 2, 3 (Autumn 1938): 167. For a historian's explicit meditation on contemporary federal Indian policy see Randolph C. Downes, "A Crusade for Indian Reform, 1922–1934," *Mississippi Valley Historical Review*, 32, 3 (December 1945). For a contrary, and far more positive, assessment of federal policy toward Native Americans written during this period see George Dewey Harmon, *Sixty Years of Indian Affairs* (Chapel Hill: University of North Carolina Press, 1941). On the Dawes Act and the history of federal policy, see Frederick E. Hoxie, *A Final Promise: The Campaign to Assimilate the Indians, 1880–1920* (Lincoln: University of Nebraska Press, 1984); Francis P. Prucha, *The Great Father: The United States Government and the American Indians*, 2 vols. (Lincoln: University of Nebraska Press, 1984); Frederick E. Hoxie, "The Curious Story of Reformers and the American Indian," and Alvin M. Josephy, Jr., "Modern America and the Indian," both in Frederick E. Hoxie, ed., *Indians in American History* (Arlington Heights, Ill.: Harlan Davidson, 1988); Sandra L. Cadwalader and Vine Deloria, Jr., *The Aggression of Civilization: Federal Indian Policy since the 1880s* (Philadelphia: Temple University Press, 1984); Vine Deloria, Jr., *American Indian Policy in the Twentieth Century* (Norman: University of Oklahoma Press, 1985); Wilcomb Washburn, *Assault on Indian Tribalism* (Philadelphia: Lippincott, 1975); Leonard A. Carlson, *Indians, Bureaucrats, and Land: The Dawes Act and the Decline of Indian Farming* (Westport, Conn.: Greenwood Press, 1981); Paul Stuart, *The Indian Office: Growth and Development of an American Institution, 1865–1900* (Ann Arbor: UMI Research Press, 1979); Lawrence C. Kelly, *The Navajo Indians and Federal Indian Policy, 1900–1935* (Tucson: University of Arizona Press, 1968); Donald L. Parman, *The Navajos and the New Deal* (New Haven: Yale University Press, 1976); Graham D. Taylor, *The New Deal and American Indian Tribalism: The Administration of the Indian Reorganization Act, 1934–45* (Lin-

coln: University of Nebraska Press, 1980); Laurence M. Hauptman, *The Iroquois and the New Deal* (Syracuse: Syracuse University Press, 1981).

32. Loring Benson Priest, *Uncle Sam's Stepchildren: The Reformation of United States Indian Policy, 1865–1887* (New Brunswick, N.J.: Rutgers University Press, 1942), pp. v–vi.

33. Ibid., pp. 3–5, Chapters 8, 10, 18, and 19.

34. Ibid., p. 145 and Part 3. See also Angie Debo, *And Still the Waters Run: The Betrayal of the Civilized Tribes* (Princeton: Princeton University Press, 1940); *The Road to Disappearance* (Norman: University of Oklahoma Press, 1941); *The Rise and Fall of the Choctaw Republic* (Norman: University of Oklahoma Press, 1934).

35. Priest, *Uncle Sam's Stepchildren*, pp. 232, 203–216, Chapters 17 and 18. For more on the questions of rights-based liberalism see Alan Brinkley, *The End of Reform: New Deal Liberalism in Recession and War* (New York: Alfred A. Knopf, 1995).

36. Priest, *Uncle Sam's Stepchildren*, pp. 174–175, 250–252.

37. Interview with Angie Debo in *Indians, Outlaws, and Angie Debo*, prod. Barbara Abrash and Martha Sandlin, Institute for Research in History, 58 mins. (PBS videocassette, 1988); Kenneth McIntosh, "Geronimo's Friend: Angie Debo and the New History," *Chronicles of Oklahoma* 66 (Summer 1988): 164–166; Suzanne H. Schrems and Cynthia J. Wolff, "Politics and Libel: Angie Debo and the Publication of *And Still the Waters Run*," *Western Historical Quarterly* 22 (May 1991): 186; Shirley A. Leckie, *Angie Debo: Pioneering Historian* (Norman: University of Oklahoma Press, 2000). Among the historians who have noted Debo's important contributions are Francis Paul Prucha, "Books on American Indian Policy: A Half-Decade of Important Work, 1970–1975," *Journal of American History* 63, 3 (December 1976): 658; Michael Green, *The Creeks: A Critical Bibliography* (Bloomington: Indiana University Press, 1979); and Patricia Nelson Limerick, who makes amends for not previously acknowledging an intellectual debt to Debo in *Something in the Soil: Legacies and Reckonings in the New West* (New York: W. W. Norton, 2000), pp. 331–332. Leckie's superb biography is the best source of information on Debo's life.

38. Interview with Angie Debo, *Indians, Outlaws, and Angie Debo;* Schrems and Wolff, "Politics and Libel," pp. 186–187; McIntosh, "Geronimo's Friend," pp. 165–167; Leckie, *Angie Debo*, Chapter 2; Heather M. Lloyd, "Biography of Angie Debo," The Angie Debo Papers, Special Collections and University Archives, Oklahoma State University, Stillwater, Oklahoma (hereafter Debo Papers, OSU); Heather Lloyd, "Chronology of Angie Debo's Life," Debo Papers, OSU.

39. Interview with Angie Debo, *Indians, Outlaws, and Angie Debo;* Schrems and Wolff, "Politics and Libel," pp. 186–187; McIntosh, "Geronimo's Friend," p. 167; Leckie, *Angie Debo*, pp. 36–40. For a thorough assessment of women's status in the American historical profession see Jacqueline Goggin,

"Challenging Sexual Discrimination in the Historical Profession: Women Historians and the American Historical Association, 1890–1940," *American Historical Review* 97, 3 (June 1992); Bonnie G. Smith, *The Gender of History: Men, Women, and Historical Practice* (Cambridge: Harvard University Press, 1998).

40. Schrems and Wolff, "Politics and Libel," 188–189; McIntosh, "Geronimo's Friend," pp. 167–172.

41. Angie Debo, "Edward Everett Dale: The Teacher," in Arrell M. Gibson, ed., *Frontier Historian: The Life and Work of Edward Everett Dale* (Norman: University of Oklahoma Press, 1975), pp. 26–35; McIntosh, "Geronimo's Friend," 167–171; Schrems and Wolff, "Politics and Libel," 187–189; Dorman, *Revolt of the Provinces,* pp. 170–171; Edward Everett Dale, "A History of the Ranch Cattle Industry in Oklahoma," (Ph.D. diss., Harvard University, 1920); Edward Everett Dale, *Cherokee Cavaliers* (Norman: University of Oklahoma Press, 1939); Edward Everett Dale, *Tales of the Tepee* (Boston: D. C. Heath, 1920); Edward Everett Dale, *The West Wind Blows* (Oklahoma City: Oklahoma Historical Society, 1984). For a revealing discussion of Debo's relationship with Dale see Richard Lowitt, "Dear Miss Debo: The Correspondence of E. E. Dale and Angie Debo," *Chronicles of Oklahoma* 77, 4 (Winter 1999–2000). Lowitt is perhaps less sympathetic to Debo's plight than to Dale's difficulty in dealing with his rather willful student.

42. Angie Debo, "Edward Everett Dale," pp. 23–34; Leckie, *Angie Debo,* pp. 26–28; Dorman, *Revolt of the Provinces,* pp. 170–171; Hoxie, *A Final Promise,* p. 242; Hoxie, "Curious Story of Reformers," pp. 220–221.

43. Interview with Angie Debo, *Indians, Outlaws, and Angie Debo;* Schrems and Wolff, "Politics and Libel," p. 189; McIntosh, "Geronimo's Friend," pp. 169–172; Angie Debo, *The Rise and Fall of the Choctaw Republic* (Norman: University of Oklahoma Press, 1934), pp. x, 291.

44. McIntosh, "Geronimo's Friend," pp. 172–173; Leckie, *Angie Debo,* p. 47; Grant Foreman, *Pioneer Days in the Early Southwest* (Cleveland: Arthur Clark, 1926); Grant Foreman, *Indians and Pioneers: The Story of the Southwest before 1830* (New Haven: Yale University Press, 1930); Grant Foreman, *Indian Removal: The Emigration of the Five Civilized Tribes* (Norman: University of Oklahoma Press, 1932); Grant Foreman, *Advancing the Frontier, 1830–1860* (Norman: University of Oklahoma Press, 1933); Grant Foreman, *Beginnings of Protestant Christian Work in Indian Territory* (Muskogee, Okla.: Star Printery, 1933); Grant Foreman, *Five Civilized Tribes* (Norman: University of Oklahoma Press, 1934); Grant Foreman, *Sequoyah* (Norman: University of Oklahoma Press, 1938); Stanley Clark, "Grant Foreman," *Chronicles of Oklahoma* 31 (Autumn 1953); Edmunds, "Native Americans, New Voices," p. 722; Debo, *The Road to Disappearance,* p. 104 and Dedication.

45. Debo, *Rise and Fall of the Choctaw Republic,* p. xii.

46. Ibid., pp. 111–112, 131, Chapters 4 and 5.
47. Ibid., pp. 163, 220, and Chapter 9.
48. Ibid., p. 290, Chapters 11 and 12. For more on the "disappearing" Indian see Edmunds, "Native Americans, New Voices"; Berkhofer, *The White Man's Indian;* and Klein, *Frontiers of Historical Imagination.*
49. Annie Abel-Henderson, "Review of *The Rise and Fall of the Choctaw Republic,*" *American Historical Review* 40, 4 (July 1935): 795–796; Anna Lewis, "Review of *The Rise and Fall of the Choctaw Republic,*" *Mississippi Valley Historical Review* 21, 3 (December 1934): 409–410; "Report of the Chattanooga Meeting," *American Historical Review* 40, 3 (April 1936): 456.
50. Interview with Angie Debo, *Indians, Outlaws, and Angie Debo;* Angie Debo, *And Still the Waters Run: The Betrayal of the Five Civilized Tribes* (Princeton: Princeton University Press, 1991 [1940]).
51. Debo, *And Still the Waters Run,* p. 24.
52. Ibid., pp. 24–26.
53. Ibid., pp. 31, 127–128, 91.
54. Ibid., pp. 91, 85, 92, and Chapters 3 and 4.
55. Ibid., pp. 7, 325–326, 341–342.
56. Ibid., p. viii.
57. Interview with Angie Debo, *Indians, Outlaws, and Angie Debo;* Debo quoted in Schrems and Wolff, "Politics and Libel," p. 203.
58. Debo quoted in Schrems and Wolff, "Politics and Libel," p. 203; interview with Angie Debo, *Indians, Outlaws, and Angie Debo.*
59. Brandt and Wardell quoted in Schrems and Wolff, "Politics and Libel," pp. 189–193; interview with Angie Debo, *Indians, Outlaws, and Angie Debo.* I am much indebted to Suzanne Schrems and Cynthia Wolff for their excellent research and analysis of these events in "Politics and Libel"—the best discussion of Debo's efforts to publish *And Still the Waters Run.* Debo's conviction that Dale was behind the squelching of her manuscript at the University of Oklahoma Press may have been nurtured by some sense that Dale did not seem to extend himself as far as he might have in helping her secure an academic appointment. In 1937, she asked Dale, who was then chairman, to consider her for a vacany in Oklahoma's history department. Dale replied that she was unqualified for the job because the department wanted to recruit a specialist in Hispanic America. See Lowitt, "Dear Miss Debo," pp. 389–390; and Leckie, *Angie Debo,* pp. 77–78.
60. Interview with Angie Debo, *Indians, Outlaws, and Angie Debo;* McIntosh, "Geronimo's Friend," pp. 171–172; Leckie, *Angie Debo,* p. 86.
61. Interview with Angie Debo, *Indians, Outlaws, and Angie Debo;* Schrems and Wolff, "Politics and Libel," pp. 197–203.
62. Grant Foreman, "Review of *And Still the Waters Run,*" *Mississippi Valley Historical Review* 27, 4 (March 1941): 637, 636; Dan E. Clark, "Review of *And Still the Waters Run,*" *Journal of Southern History* 7, 4 (November 1941): 574.

63. Angie Debo, *The Road to Disappearance* (Norman: University of Oklahoma Press, 1941), p. xi; LeRoy F. Hafen, "Review of *The Road to Disappearance*," *American Historical Review* 48, 4 (July 1943): 827; R. S. Cotterill, "Review of *The Road to Disappearance*," *Journal of Southern History* 8, 3 (August 1942): 432.

4. History, Class, and Culture between the World Wars

1. Caroline Ware, ed., *The Cultural Approach to History* (New York: Columbia University Press, 1940), p. 73; Ware referred to the need for a history that attends to the "inarticulate" on p. 8, for example.
2. Commons's massive history of American labor straddled the Progressive and interwar years. See John Commons et al., *History of Labour in the United States*, 4 vols. (New York: Macmillan, 1918–1935). For a summary of the criticism of early labor history, see Herbert G. Gutman, "Work, Culture, and Society in Industrializing America, 1815–1919," in Herbert G. Gutman, *Work, Culture, and Society in Industrializing America* (New York: Knopf), pp. 9–12.
3. Norman Ware, *The Industrial Worker, 1840–1860* (Boston: Houghton Mifflin Co., 1924), p. xvii.
4. Ibid., p. xi. For a respectful critique of the limits of *The Industrial Worker* from the vantage point of recent labor history see Walter Licht, "Norman Ware's *The Industrial Worker* Revisted: Reflections on Recent Writings in Early American Industrialization," *Radical History Review* 36 (1986): 137–148. David Montgomery discusses the preoccupations of early historians of labor in "The Conventional Wisdom," *Labor History* 13, 1 (Winter 1972).
5. N. Ware, *Industrial Worker*, pp. x–xi.
6. Ibid., Chapter 4, "The Degradation of the Worker."
7. Ibid., pp. xviii–xix, 19–22.
8. Ibid., pp. 22–23, Chapters 14 and 15.
9. Fred E. Haynes, "Review of *The Labor Movement in the United States, 1860–1895: A Study in Democracy*," *Mississippi Valley Historical Review* 16, 2 (September 1929): 288; Warren B. Catlin, "Review of *The Labor Movement in the United States, 1860–1895*," *American Economic Review* 19, 4 (December 1929): 705–706; Norman J. Ware, *The Labor Movement in the United States, 1860–1895: A Study in Democracy* (New York: D. Appleton and Co., 1929). For a contemporary discussion of Ware's interpretation and the Knights of Labor see Leon Fink, *Workingmen's Democracy: The Knights of Labor and American Politics* (Urbana: University of Illinois Press, 1983).
10. Ibid., pp. 198, xiv–xv.
11. Ibid., pp. 47–55, 71–79, 111–114.
12. "Interview with Caroline Ware: Women in the Federal Government Project," 27–29 January 1982, transcript, Schlesinger Library, Radcliffe College (hereafter cited as "Ware Interview—WFGP"), pp. 1–2, 7A–8, 1–4; Ellen Fitz-

patrick, "Caroline Ware and the Cultural Approach to History," *American Quarterly* 43, 2 (June 1991): 177–180.

13. Fitzpatrick, "Caroline Ware and the Cultural Approach to History," pp. 179–180.

14. Author's interview with Caroline Ware, 18 April 1989; "Ware Interview—WFGP," p. 25; Bryn Mawr College, *The Summer School for Women Workers in Industry at Bryn Mawr College, June 15 to August 10, 1921; Bryn Mawr Daisy,* 8 June 1922, pp. 1–2; "Concerning the Bryn Mawr Summer School," 10 July 1922, Box 159, Caroline F. Ware Papers, Franklin Delano Roosevelt Library, Hyde Park, New York (hereafter cited as Ware Papers); Alice Kessler-Harris, *Out to Work: A History of Wage-Earning Women in the United States* (New York: Oxford University Press, 1982), pp. 243–244; *The Women of Summer: The Bryn Mawr Summer School for Women Workers, 1921–1938* (documentary film); Richard Altenbaugh, *Education for Struggle* (Philadelphia: Temple University Press, 1990).

15. Author's interview with Caroline Ware, 18 April 1989; "Ware Interview—WFGP," pp. 27–28; Oxford University File, Box 131, Ware Papers.

16. Author's interview with Caroline Ware, 18 April 1989; Merle Curti to author, 27 November 1989; Ware, *Cultural Approach to History,* pp. 10–11.

17. Fitzpatrick, "Caroline Ware and the Cultural Approach to History," pp. 183–184; Herbert Heaton, *A Scholar in Action* (Cambridge: Harvard University Press, 1952), p. 44; Edwin De Turck Bechtel, Lecture Notes for Economics 11 (Professor Gay), Harvard University Archives, Cambridge, Mass.; Edwin Francis Gay, "The Rhythm of History," *Harvard Graduates' Magazine* 32 (September 1923): 1–16; Blanche E. Hazard, *The Organization of the Boot and Shoe Industry in Massachusetts before 1875* (Cambridge: Harvard University Press, 1921); "Ware Interview—WFGP," pp. 30–31.

18. Caroline F. Ware, *The Early New England Cotton Manufacture: A Study in Industrial Beginnings* (Boston: Houghton Mifflin Co., 1931), p. 17. This book was a modest revision of Ware's doctoral dissertation, completed in 1925; see Caroline F. Ware, "The Industrial Revolution in the New England Cotton Industry," (Ph.D. diss., Radcliffe College, 1925).

19. C. Ware, *Early New England Cotton Manufacture,* pp. 3, 11–12, 17–18, and Chapter 1. For evidence of Ware's influence see Alan Dawley, *Class and Community: The Industrial Revolution in Lynn* (Cambridge: Harvard University Press, 1976); Thomas Dublin, *Women at Work* (New York: Columbia University Press, 1979); Jonathan Prude, *The Coming of the Industrial Order* (New York: Cambridge University Press, 1983); Alexander Keyssar, *Out of Work: The First Century of Unemployment in Massachusetts* (New York: Cambridge University Press, 1986); Herbert G. Gutman and Donald H. Bell, *The New England Working Class and the New Labor History* (Urbana: University of Illinois Press, 1987).

20. C. Ware, *Early New England Cotton Manufacture,* pp. 11–14, 236.

21. Ibid., pp. 11–12, 65.
22. Ibid., pp. 240–242.
23. Ibid., p. 268 and Chapters 9 and 10.
24. Ibid., pp. 290–294.
25. Ibid., pp. 60, 297.
26. Ibid., pp. 297–298.
27. Delmar Leighton, "Review of *The Early New England Cotton Manufacture,*" *American Economic Review* 21, 2 (June 1931): 317–318.
28. Gordon S. Watkins, "Review of *The Industrial Worker, 1840–1860,*" *Political Science Quarterly* 40, 2 (June 1925): 310–311.
29. Ibid., p. 311; Lester Burrell Shippee, "Review of *The Armies of Labor: A Chronicle of Organized Wage-Earners,*" *Mississippi Valley Historical Review* 7, 2 (Spring 1920): 157–158. See also the report of papers by Selig Perlman and Frank Carleton delivered at the 1919 meeting of the American Historical Association in John Franklin Jameson, "The Meeting of the American Historical Association at Cleveland," *American Historical Review* 25, 3 (April 1920): 381–382.
30. Arthur B. Darling, "The Workingmen's Party in Massachusetts, 1833–1834," *American Historical Review* 29, 1 (October 1923): 81–85. See Gutman, "Work, Culture, and Society," pp. 10–11, for the limits of Commons's work. Modern labor historians have echoed Darling's criticism of Commons's narrow view of the workingmen's parties but do not share Darling's views of class. See Prude, *Coming of the Industrial Order;* and Cynthia Shelton, *The Mills of Manayunk: Industrialization and Social Conflict in the Philadelphia Region, 1787–1837* (Baltimore: Johns Hopkins University Press, 1986).
31. Elinor Pancoast, "Review of *The Industrial Worker, 1840–1860,*" *Journal of Political Economy* 35, 5 (October 1927): 712–713; Carter Goodrich, "Review of Edward Berman, *Labor Disputes and the President of the United States,*" *American Historical Review* 30, 2 (January 1925): 404–405.
32. Ella Lonn, "Fields for Research in the South after Reconstruction," *Annual Report of the American Historical Association for the Year 1921* (Washington, D.C.: Government Printing Office, 1926), p. 197; "Thirty-Sixth Annual Meeting of the American Historical Association," *Annual Report of the American Historical Association for the Year 1921,* p. 40.
33. David Y. Thomas, "Review of Rhodes, *History of the United States,*" *Mississippi Valley Historical Review* 7, 1 (June 1920): 84–85.
34. Ibid., p. 85; Lester Burrell Shippee, "Review of Rhodes's *History of the United States,*" *Mississippi Valley Historical Review* 8, 1–2 (June–September 1921): 136.
35. "Review of Rhodes, *History of the United States from Hayes to McKinley, 1877–1896,*" *Journal of Negro History* 5, 3 (July 1920): 386–387.
36. "Review of *The McKinley and Roosevelt Administrations, 1897–1909,*" *Journal of Negro History* 8, 3 (July 1923): 348.

37. John Higham, *History: Professional Scholarship in America* (Baltimore: Johns Hopkins University Press, 1989), p. 192; Marcus L. Hansen, "The History of American Immigration as a Field for Research," *American Historical Review* 32, 3 (April 1927): 509, 505; *Dictionary of American Biography,* s.v. "Hansen, Marcus Lee," pp. 278–279.

38. Jacqueline Goggin, *Carter G. Woodson: A Life in Black History* (Baton Rouge: Louisiana State University Press, 1993), pp. 200–204; Carter Woodson, *A Century of Negro Migration* (Washington, D.C.: Association for the Study of Negro Life and History, 1918). For an excellent discussion of early work on the black migration by African American social scientists see Francille Rusan Wilson, "Segregated Scholars: Black Labor Historians, 1895–1950" (Ph.D. diss., University of Pennsylvania, 1988), especially Chapter 3.

39. Henderson H. Donald, "The Negro Migration of 1916–1918," *Journal of Negro History* 6, 4 (October 1921): 386–388, 485; Ernest Kaiser, "Review of *From Slavery to Freedom,*" *Journal of Negro Education* 31, 4 (Autumn 1962): 469; Purvis Carter, "At Freedom's Edge: Black Mobility and the Southern White Quest for Racial Control, 1861–1915," *Journal of Negro History* 78, 1 (Winter 1993): 32–33. See also Alrutheus A. Taylor, "The Movement of Negroes from the East to the Gulf States, 1830 to 1850," *Journal of Negro History* 8, 4 (October 1923); and Woodson, *A Century of Negro Migration.* Donald later wrote *Negro Freedman* (1952), a work of history appropriately derided by August Meier as "inept and anti-Negro"; see Meier, "A Scholar Discovers the Negro World," *Journal of Negro Education* 29, 1 (Winter 1960): 102.

40. Donald, "Negro Migration," pp. 486, 492–494.

41. Arnett G. Lindsay, "The Economic Condition of the Negroes of New York prior to 1861," *Journal of Negro History* 6, 2 (April 1921): 194–195.

42. T. R. Davis, "Negro Servitude in the United States," *Journal of Negro History* 8, 3 (July 1923): 278.

43. Elizabeth Ross Haynes, "Negroes in Domestic Service in the United States," *Journal of Negro History* 8, 4 (October 1923): 423–424.

44. Kathleen Bruce, "Slave Labor in the Virginia Iron Industry," *William and Mary College Quarterly Historical Magazine,* 2nd Series, 7, 1 (January 1927): 24, 26–29; *National Cyclopedia of American Biography,* s.v. "Bruce, Kathleen," pp. 224–225.

45. C. Vann Woodward, *Thinking Back: The Perils of Writing History* (Baton Rouge: Louisiana State University Press, 1986), p. 23.

46. Woodward, *Thinking Back,* pp. 20–21; Daniel Singal, *The War Within: From Victorian to Modernist Thought in the South, 1919–1945* (Chapel Hill: University of North Carolina Press, 1982); Sterling A. Brown, "Unhistoric History," *Journal of Negro History* 15, 2 (April 1930): 134.

47. Woodward, *Thinking Back,* pp. 20–21; Dewey Grantham, *The South in Modern America* (New York: Harper Collins, 1994), pp. 142–143 and

Chapter 6; Singal, *The War Within;* Howard W. Odum, *Southern Regions of the United States* (Chapel Hill: University of North Carolina Press, 1936); Rupert Vance, *Human Factors in Cotton Culture* (Chapel Hill: University of North Carolina Press, 1929); Rupert B. Vance, *Human Geography of the South* (North Carolina: University of North Carolina Press, 1932); *Dictionary of American Biography,* s.v. "Odum, Howard Washington," Supplement 5; Brown, "Unhistoric History," p. 160; Rupert B. Vance, "Review of *I'll Take My Stand,*" *Mississippi Valley Historical Review* 18, 1 (June 1931): 116–117. For a superb discussion of work in southern women's history written by southern women historians during the interwar years, see Anne Firor Scott, *Unheard Voices: The First Historians of Southern Women* (Charlottesville: University of Virginia Press, 1993).

48. Vance, "Review of *I'll Take My Stand,*" pp. 116–117.
49. *Dictionary of American Biography,* s.v. "Odum, Howard Washington"; Grantham, *The South in Modern America,* p. 143; Woodward, *Thinking Back,* pp. 10–13.
50. Hinton Rowan Helper, *The Impending Crisis of the South: How to Meet It* (New York: Burdick Brothers, 1857), pp. 28, 32; Ulrich B. Phillips, "The Central Theme in Southern History," *American Historical Review* 34, 1 (October 1928): 33; Paul H. Buck, "The Poor Whites of the Ante-Bellum South," *American Historical Review* 31, 1 (October 1925): 41.
51. Buck, "The Poor Whites of the Ante-bellum South," pp. 41–42.
52. Ibid., pp. 44–46.
53. Ibid., pp. 47, 49.
54. Ibid., pp. 49–52, 54. Some ten years later, in his book *The Road to Reunion, 1865–1900* (Boston: Little, Brown, and Co., 1937), Buck so celebrated the rise of the New South, with at best a gloss over the "price" paid for reconciliation, that the study only deepened C. Vann Woodward's "despairing perceptions of the received wisdom about the South's past that prevailed around 1937." Woodward, *Thinking Back,* p. 26.
55. Paul Lewinson, *Race, Class, and Party: A History of Negro Suffrage and White Politics in the South* (New York: Oxford University Press, 1932); *Contemporary Authors,* s.v. "Lewinson, Paul," 127: 275; A.C.C., "Review of *Race, Class, and Party,*" *Mississippi Valley Historical Review* 20, 1 (June 1933): 131–132.
56. Woodward, *Thinking Back,* pp. 29–31; C. Vann Woodward, "Tom Watson and the Negro in Agrarian Politics," *Journal of Southern History* 4, 1 (February 1938): 14; C. Vann Woodward, *Tom Watson: Agrarian Rebel* (New York: Macmillan, 1938).
57. Woodward, "Tom Watson and the Negro," pp. 14–17. See also W. M. Brewer, "Poor Whites and Negroes in the South since the Civil War," *Journal of Negro History* 15 (January 1930); and Avery Craven, "Poor Whites and Negroes in the Ante-Bellum South," *Journal of Negro History* 15 (January 1930).

58. Woodward, "Tom Watson and the Negro," pp. 17–21; Woodward, *Tom Watson.*

59. Ibid., pp. 24–25, 31; Woodward, *Thinking Back,* pp. 35–41. See also the essays in John Herbert Roper, ed., *C. Vann Woodward: A Southern Historian and His Critics* (Athens: University of Georgia Press, 1997).

60. John Herbert Roper, "Introduction: The Historian," in Roper, ed., *C. Vann Woodward,* pp. 1–7; Michael O'Brien, "From a Chase to a View: The Arkansan," in Roper, ed., *C. Vann Woodward,* pp. 235–238; David Potter, "C. Vann Woodward: Pastmaster," in Roper, ed., *C. Vann Woodward,* pp. 267–269; M. E. Bradford, "The Strange Career of C. Vann Woodward," in Roper, ed., *C. Vann Woodward,* pp. 255–256.

61. Woodward, "Tom Watson and the Negro," pp. 26, 30–31; Woodward, *Thinking Back,* pp. 36–37 and Chapter 2; Bertram Wyatt-Brown, "The Sound and the Fury: Woodward Thinking Back," in Roper, ed., *C. Vann Woodward,* p. 49.

62. Roger W. Shugg, *Origins of Class Struggle in Louisiana* (University: Louisiana State University Press, 1939), pp. ix–x, 21–24, and Chapter 2.

63. Ibid., pp. 29–34, 51, and Chapter 3.

64. Ibid., pp. 78–79, 116, 156.

65. Ibid., pp. 197–98, 212–217, 231, and Chapters 7–9.

66. Paul H. Buck, "Review of *Origins of Class Struggle in Louisiana,*" *American Historical Review* 46, 3 (April 1941): 681–682; Fred Shannon, "Review of *The Coming of the Civil War,*" *American Historical Review* 48, 3 (April 1943): 588. See also Jefferson Davis Bragg, "Review of *Origins of the Class Struggle in Louisiana,*" *Mississippi Valley Historical Review* 26, 4 (March 1940): 579–580.

67. Frank L. Owsley, "Review of *Origins of Class Struggle in Louisiana,*" *Journal of Southern History* 6, 1 (February 1940): 116–117; August Meier and Elliott Rudwick, *Black History and the Historical Profession* (Urbana: University of Illinois Press, 1986), pp. 103–104; L. D. Reddick, "Review of *Origins of Class Struggle in Louisiana,*" *Journal of Negro History* 25, 1 (January 1940): 116–117.

68. Howard K. Beale, "On Rewriting Reconstruction History," *American Historical Review* 45, 4 (July 1940): 808–809, 813.

69. Paul H. Buck, "The Genesis of the Nation's Problem in the South," *Journal of Southern History* 6, 4 (November 1940): 460–461.

70. James C. Bonner, "Profile of a Late Ante-Bellum Community," *American Historical Review* 49, 4 (July 1944): 663–664.

71. Ibid., pp. 665, 667.

72. Ibid., pp. 667–670, 672–675, 678–680.

73. Jesse Dunsmore Clarkson, "Escape to the Present," *American Historical Review* 46, 3 (April 1941): 559.

74. Carter Woodson, "The Negro Washerwoman, a Vanishing Figure," *Journal of Negro History* 15, 3 (July 1930): 269–272.

75. Meier and Rudwick, *Black History and the Historical Profession,* pp. 79–83, 102–104; Lorenzo T. Greene and Carter G. Woodson, *The Negro Wage Earner* (Washington, D.C.: Association for the Study of Negro Life and History, 1930); Sterling D. Spero and Abram L. Harris, *The Black Worker* (New York: Columbia University Press, 1931); Wilson, "Segregated Scholars," pp. 326–328; Emmett E. Dorsey, "Review of *The Black Worker,*" *Journal of Negro History* 16, 3 (July 1931): 340–341.

76. Abram Harris, *The Negro as Capitalist* (Philadelphia: American Academy of Political and Social Science, 1936). Harris quoted in Broadus Mitchell, "The Negro as Capitalist," *Journal of Negro History* 22, 1 (January 1937): 97–98. For the best discussion of Harris's views and career see Wilson, "Segregated Scholars," pp. 320–332, 394–404.

77. Marcus W. Jernegan, *Laboring and Dependent Classes in Colonial America, 1607–1783: Studies of the Economic, Educational, and Social Significance of Slaves, Servants, Apprentices, and Poor Folk* (Chicago: University of Chicago Press, 1931); "Review of *Laboring and Dependent Classes in Colonial America,*" *Journal of Negro History* 17, 2 (April 1932): 232–233; Norman J. Ware, "Review of *Laboring and Dependent Classes in Colonial America,*" *American Economic Review* 22, 3 (September 1932): 483; Arthur M. Schlesinger, "Review of *Laboring and Dependent Classes in Colonial America,*" *Mississippi Valley Historical Review* 19, 1 (January 1932): 107–108.

78. Abbot Smith, "The Transportation of Convicts to the American Colonies in the Seventeenth Century," *American Historical Review* 39, 2 (January 1934); Abbot Smith, "The Indentured Servant and Land Speculation in Seventeenth Century Maryland," *American Historical Review* 40, 3 (April 1935): 472; Abbot Smith, *Colonists in Bondage: White Servitude and Convict Labor in America, 1607–1776* (Chapel Hill: University of North Carolina Press, 1947).

79. Abbot Smith, "Indentured Servants: New Light on Some of America's 'First' Families," *Journal of Economic History* 2, 1 (May 1942): 40; Oscar Handlin, "Review of *Colonists in Bondage,*" *William and Mary Quarterly,* 3rd Series, 5, 1 (January 1948): 109–110.

80. Lorenzo Greene, *The Negro in Colonial New England, 1620–1776* (New York: Columbia University Press, 1942); Richard B. Morris, *Government and Labor in Early America* (New York: Columbia University Press, 1946); Marcus Jernegan, "Review of *Government and Labor in Early America,*" *Journal of Economic History* 7, 2 (November 1947): 271; see also John E. Pomfret, "Review of *Government and Labor in Early America,*" *Journal of Southern History* 12, 4 (November 1946); Charles MacLean Andrews, "On The Writing of Colonial History," *William and Mary Quarterly,* 3rd Series, 1, 1 (January 1944): 36–37.

81. Vera Shlakman, *Economic History of a Factory Town: A Study of Chicopee, Massachusetts,* Smith College Studies in History 20, 1–4 (October 1934–July 1935; rpt. New York: Octagon Books, 1969), pp. 59–60, 98, 210, 226.

82. Ellen Schrecker, *No Ivory Tower: McCarthyism and the Universities* (New York: Oxford University Press, 1986), pp. 169–170; Herbert G. Gutman and Donald H. Bell, eds., *The New England Working Class and the New Labor History* (Urbana: University of Illinois Press, 1987), pp. x, xii.

83. Constance McLaughlin Green, *Holyoke, Massachusetts: A Case History of the Industrial Revolution in America* (New Haven: Yale University Press, 1939).

84. Samuel Rezneck, "The Depression of 1819–1822, a Social History," *American Historical Review* 39, 1 (October 1933): 28, 30–32, 46–47.

85. Almont Lindsey, "Paternalism and the Pullman Strike," *American Historical Review* 44, 2 (January 1939): 272, 277–282, 289.

86. Harry J. Carman, "Terence Vincent Powderly—An Appraisal," *Journal of Economic History* 1, 1 (May 1941): 84–85, 87.

87. Harvey Wish, "Altgeld and the Progressive Tradition," *American Historical Review* 46, 4 (July 1941): 814–817.

88. C. Ware, *Cultural Approach to History*, p. 7.

89. Ibid., pp. 8–9.

90. The Editors, "Educating Clio," *American Historical Review* 45, 3 (April 1940): 505.

91. C. Ware, *Cultural Approach to History*, pp. 15–16.

92. Editors, "Educating Clio," p. 516; *Contemporary Authors* s.v. "Capers, Gerald Mortimer," 70: 70–71; Jesse D. Clark, "Escape to the Present," *American Historical Review* 46, 3 (April 1941): 525–529. Schuyler's remarks are quoted and summarized in Clark, "Escape to the Present," p. 529.

5. The Myth of Consensus History

1. John Higham, "The Cult of the 'American Consensus': Homogenizing Our History," *Commentary* 27, 2 (February 1959): 100; Roy F. Nichols, "Postwar Reorientation of Historical Thinking," *American Historical Review* 54, 1 (October 1948): 78–81.

2. Nichols, "Postwar Reorientation," p. 81.

3. Higham, "The Cult of the 'American Consensus,'" pp. 93–94.

4. Ibid., pp. 94–97. See also Higham's earlier pass at this subject, "Anti-Semitism in the Gilded Age: A Reinterpretation," *Mississippi Valley Historical Review* 43, 4 (March 1957): 561–562.

5. Higham, "The Cult of the 'American Consensus,'" pp. 94–95, 100; John Higham, "Beyond Consensus: The Historian as Moral Critic," *American Historical Review* 67, 3 (April 1962).

6. For more on consensus history see John Higham, *History: Professional Scholarship in America* (Baltimore: Johns Hopkins University Press, 1989), pp. 221–224 and Chapters 6 and 7; Peter Novick, *That Noble Dream: The "Objectivity Question" and the American Historical Profession* (Cambridge, U.K.: Cambridge University Press, 1988), Chapter 11, esp. pp. 333–335, 415–417; Irwin Unger, "'The New Left' and American History: Some Recent

Trends in United States Historiography," *American Historical Review* 72, 3 (April 1967); Barton Bernstein, ed., *Towards a New Past: Dissenting Essays in American History* (New York: Pantheon, 1968), pp. v–xiii; and a recent overview by David Oshinsky, "The Humpty Dumpty of Scholarship," *New York Times,* 26 August 2000, pp. A17, A19. Paul Buhle, ed., *History and the New Left: Madison, Wisconsin, 1950–1970* (Philadelphia: Temple University Press, 1990) does an excellent job of tracing the continuity between the work of several important historians in the 1950s and the New Left.

7. Arthur Mann, "Review of *The Liberal Tradition in America,*" *William and Mary Quarterly,* 3rd Series, 12, 4 (October 1955): 655; Arthur M. Schlesinger, Jr., *The Vital Center: The Politics of Freedom* (Boston: Houghton Mifflin Co., 1949); Higham, "Anti-Semitism in the Gilded Age," p. 562.

8. Higham, "Beyond Consensus," p. 625; Mann, "Review of *Liberal Tradition,*" pp. 653–654; Stow Persons, "Review of *The End of Ideology,*" *American Quarterly* 12, 3 (Autumn 1960): 428. John Higham moderated somewhat his earlier portrait of consensus history in a 1962 essay for the *American Historical Review* entitled "Beyond Consensus." In that article Higham noted the emphasis on pluralism among many consensus historians and admitted that "a lively critical impulse" had survived despite the dominance of conservative views; see pp. 615–619. Despite this admission, Irwin Unger resurrected Higham's starker 1959 statement only to demonstrate its inadequacy in Unger's 1967 *American Historical Review* essay "The 'New Left' and American History," pp. 1240–41. Still, both men emphasized the overwhelming political conservatism and moral neutrality of postwar historiography.

9. For the best treatment of this subject see Ellen Schrecker, *No Ivory Tower: McCarthyism and the Universities* (New York: Oxford University Press, 1986) and Novick, *That Noble Dream,* especially Chapters 10 and 11.

10. Chester McArthur Destler, "Western Radicalism, 1865–1901: Concepts and Origins," *Mississippi Valley Historical Review* 31, 3 (December 1944): 335–338, 343–348; Chester McArthur Destler, *American Radicalism, 1865–1901: Essays and Documents* (New London: Connecticut College, 1946).

11. Destler, "Western Radicalism," pp. 351–353, 356.

12. Ibid., pp. 361–364, 360, 358, 364, 366.

13. Ibid., pp. 366–368.

14. Louis M. Hacker, "Review of *American Radicalism, 1865–1901,*" *American Historical Review* 52, 4 (July 1947): 757–758.

15. Edgar Eugene Robinson, "Review of *The Shaping of the American Tradition,*" *American Historical Review* 53, 1 (October 1947): 117–119.

16. Townsend Scudder, "Review of *Critics and Crusaders: A History of American Protest,*" *American Historical Review* 53, 1 (October 1947): 120.

17. George D. Harmon, "Review of *Land of Liberty: Being an Informal History of the Common People and Their Heroes,*" *American Historical Review* 53, 3 (April 1948): 550–551.

18. R. B. Nye, "American Radicals: Some Problems and Personalities," *Ameri-*

can *Historical Review* 63, 1 (October 1957): 154–155; Donald R. McCoy, *Angry Voices: Left-of-Center Politics in the New Deal Era* (Lawrence: University of Kansas Press, 1958); Fred Shannon, "Review of *Angry Voices,*" *Journal of Southern History* 25, 2 (May 1959).

19. Daniel Aaron, *Writers on the Left: Episodes in American Literary Communism* (New York: Harcourt, Brace and World, 1961); Robert M. Hutchins, *Freedom, Education, and the Fund: Essays and Address, 1946–1956* (New York: Meridian, 1956); Thomas C. Reeves, *Freedom and the Foundation: The Fund for the Republic in the Era of McCarthyism* (New York: Knopf, 1969); Victor S. Navasky, *Naming Names* (New York: Penguin, 1981), p. 326; William Peden, "Review of *Writers on the Left,*" *Journal of Southern History* 29, 2 (May 1963): 276.

20. H. C. Peterson and Gilbert C. Fite, *Opponents of War, 1917–1918* (Madison: University of Wisconsin Press, 1957); C. Vann Woodward, "Review of *Opponents of War,*" *American Historical Review* 63, 1 (October 1957): 155–156.

21. Herbert Solow, "Review of *William Sylvis, Pioneer of American Labor,*" *American Historical Review* 51, 4 (July 1946): 731.

22. Ray Ginger, *The Bending Cross: A Biography of Eugene Victor Debs* (New Brunswick: Rutgers University Press, 1949); David A. Shannon, "Review of *The Bending Cross,*" *American Historical Review* 55, 3 (April 1950): 641–642; W. M. Brewer, "Review of *The Bending Cross,*" *Journal of Negro History* 34, 4 (October 1949): 469.

23. Murray B. Seidler, *Norman Thomas: Respectable Radical* (Syracuse: Syracuse University Press, 1961), p. 162; Frederick I. Olson, "Review of *Eugene V. Debs: Socialist for President,*" *Mississippi Valley Historical Review* 49, 4 (March 1963): 724; Martin Ridge, *Ignatius Donnelly: The Portrait of a Politician* (Chicago: University of Chicago Press, 1962); Don K. McKee, "Daniel De Leon: A Reappraisal," *Labor History* 1, 3 (Fall 1960); Robert E. Doherty, "Thomas Hagerty, the Church, and Socialism," *Labor History* 3, 1 (Winter 1962).

24. Richard Drinnon, *Rebel in Paradise: A Biography of Emma Goldman* (Chicago: University of Chicago Press, 1961); Robert K. Murray, "Review of *Rebel in Paradise: A Biography of Emma Goldman,*" *Mississippi Valley Historical Review* 49, 1 (June 1962): 158–159.

25. Murray, "Review of *Rebel in Paradise,*" pp. 159–160; Robert H. Bremner, "Review of *Rebel in Paradise,*" *Journal of Southern History* 28, 3 (August 1962): 378–379.

26. Karl Obermann, *Joseph Weydemeyer, Pioneer of American Socialism* (New York: International Publishers Co., 1947); Jonathan Grossman, "Review of *Joseph Weydemeyer, Pioneer of American Socialism,*" *Journal of Economic History* 8, 2 (November 1948): 238–239.

27. Chester McArthur Destler, "Review of *Joseph Weydemeyer, Pioneer of American Socialism,*" *American Historical Review* 53, 2 (January 1948):

399; Harvey Klehr and John Earl Haynes, *The American Communist Movement: Storming Heaven Itself* (New York: Twayne, 1992), p. 100.

28. Destler, "Review of *Joseph Weydemeyer,*" p. 399.

29. Hal Draper, "Joseph Weydemeyer's 'Dictatorship of the Proletariat,'" *Labor History* 3, 2 (Spring 1962): 208–209; Joseph Weydemeyer, "The Dictatorship of the Proletariat," *Labor History* 3, 2 (Spring 1962): 214–217.

30. Carl Wittke, *The Utopian Communist: A Biography of Wilhelm Weitling, Nineteenth Century Reformer* (Baton Rouge: Louisiana State University Press, 1950); Carl Wittke, *Refugees of Revolution: The German Forty-Eighters in America* (Philadelphia: University of Pennsylvania Press, 1952); Arthur E. Bestor, Jr., "Review of *The Utopian Communist,*" *American Historical Review* 56, 1 (October 1950): 148–149; Arthur Eugene Bestor, *Backwoods Utopias: The Sectarian and Owenite Phases of Communitarian Socialism in America, 1663–1829* (Philadelphia: University of Pennsylvania Press, 1950).

31. Alice Felt Tyler, "Review of *Backwoods Utopias,*" *American Historical Review* 55, 4 (July 1950): 923–925; Alice Felt Tyler, "Review of *Refugees of Revolution,*" *American Historical Review* 58, 1 (October 1952): 134–136.

32. Vera Shlakman, "Review of *The Uprooted: The Epic Story of the Great Migrations That Made the American People; Refugees of Revolution: The German Forty-Eighters in America,*" *Journal of Economic History* 13, 2 (Spring 1953): 241–242.

33. Ibid., pp. 242–243.

34. Ibid., p. 244.

35. Howard H. Quint, *The Forging of American Socialism: Origins of the Modern Movement* (Columbia: University of South Carolina Press, 1953), p. vii; Harry Laidler, "Review of *The Forging of American Socialism,*" *American Historical Review* 59, 4 (July 1954): 955.

36. Howard H. Quint, "Julius A. Wayland, Pioneer Socialist Propagandist," *Mississippi Valley Historical Review* 35, 4 (March 1949): 585–589, 591; William A. Glaser, "Algie Martin Simons and Marxism in America," *Mississippi Valley Historical Review* 41, 3 (December 1954): 419–434.

37. Harry W. Laidler, "Review of *The Forging of American Socialism,*" *American Historical Review* 59, 4 (July 1954): 955–956; T. D. Seymour Bassett, "Review of *The Forging of American Socialism,*" *Mississippi Valley Historical Review* 40, 3 (December 1953): 553–554. See also William T. Doherty, Jr., "Review of *The Forging of American Socialism,*" *Journal of Southern History* 20, 1 (February 1954): 136–137.

38. David A. Shannon, "Review of *The American Socialist Movement, 1897–1912,*" *Journal of Southern History* 19, 3 (August 1953): 402–403; Howard H. Quint, "Review of *The American Socialist Movement,*" *Mississippi Valley Historical Review* 40, 1 (January 1953): 158–160.

39. Harry W. Laidler, "Review of *The American Socialist Movement, 1897–1912,*" *American Historical Review* 58, 3 (April 1953): 658–659.

40. David A. Shannon, *The Socialist Party of America: A History* (New York: Macmillan, 1955); David A. Shannon, "The Socialist Party before the First World War: An Analysis," *Mississippi Valley Historical Review* 38, 2 (September 1951): 269–282, 288; Howard Quint, "Review of *The Socialist Party of America*," *Mississippi Valley Historical Review* 42, 4 (March 1956): 771; Stow Persons, "Review of *The Socialist Party of America*," *American Historical Review* 61, 3 (April 1956); William D. Miller, "Review of *The Socialist Party of America*," *Journal of Southern History* 22, 2 (May 1956).

41. Donald Drew Egbert and Stow Persons, eds., *Socialism and American Life*, 2 vols. (Princeton: Princeton University Press, 1952); George Harmon Knoles, "Review of *Socialism and American Life*," *Mississippi Valley Historical Review* 39, 4 (March 1953): 808.

42. Grady WcWhiney, "Louisiana Socialists in the Early Twentieth Century: A Study of Rustic Radicalism," *Journal of Southern History* 20, 3 (August 1954): 315–317.

43. McWhiney, "Louisiana Socialists," pp. 319–20, 325–27, 334, 336.

44. M. S. Venkataramani, "Norman Thomas, Arkansas Sharecroppers, and the Roosevelt Agricultural Policies, 1933–1937," *Mississippi Valley Historical Review* 47, 2 (September 1960): 225–246.

45. Stow Persons, "Review of *The Roots of American Communism*," *Mississippi Valley Historical Review* 44, 3 (December 1957): 572–573; Howard H. Quint, "Review of *The Roots of American Communism*," *American Historical Review* 63, 1 (October 1957): 153–154; Max M. Kampelman, "Review of *The American Communist Party*," *American Historical Review* 64, 4 (July 1959): 976; C. E. Ayres, "Review of *The Social Basis of American Communism*," *Journal of Southern History* 28, 3 (August 1962): 382–384. John L. Shover's more nuanced study of the Communist Party's efforts to address the farm crisis, "The Communist Party and the Midwest Farm Crisis of 1933," *Journal of American History* 51, 2 (September 1964), likewise concluded that the party never fully understood the American farmer.

46. Wilson Record, *The Negro and the Communist Party* (Chapel Hill: University of North Carolina Press, 1951); Walter White, "Review of *The Negro and the Communist Party*," *American Historical Review* 57, 1 (October 1951): 193–194; Emmett E. Dorsey, "Review of *The Negro and the Communist Party*," *Mississippi Valley Historical Review* 39, 3 (December 1952): 589; Rayford Logan, "Review of *The Negro and the Communist Party*," *Journal of Southern History* 17, 4 (November 1951): 574–575.

47. Vaughn D. Bornet, "Historical Scholarship, Communism, and the Negro," *Journal of Negro History* 37, 3 (July 1952): 310, 304–309, 317.

48. Ibid., pp. 311–317.

49. Ibid., pp. 323, 304, 312.

50. Vernell Olivier, "Pre-Marxist Russian Radicals and the American Civil War," *Journal of Negro History* 38, 4 (October 1953): 428–429, 437; Harvard Sitkoff, *The Struggle for Black Equality* (New York: Hill and Wang, 1981),

pp. 17–18; Ellen Schrecker, *Many are the Crimes* (Boston: Little, Brown, 1988), pp. 389–95; Wilson Record, *Race and Radicalism* (New York: Cornell University Press, 1964); Gerald Horne, *Black and Red: W. E. B. Du Bois and the Afro-American Response to the Cold War, 1944–1963* (Albany: State University of New York Press, 1986).

51. John C. Miller, *Crisis in Freedom: The Alien and Sedition Acts* (Boston: Little, Brown, and Co., 1951); Max Savelle, "Review of *Crisis in Freedom,*" *Mississippi Valley Historical Review* 39, 3 (December 1952): 550; Fred Rodell, "Review of *Crisis in Freedom,*" *William and Mary Quarterly* 9, 2 (April 1952): 271–272.

52. Rodell, "Review of *Crisis in Freedom,*" pp. 271–272. Savelle, "Review of *Crisis in Freedom,*" pp. 550–553.

53. James Morton Smith, *Freedom's Fetters: The Alien and Sedition Laws and American Civil Liberties* (Ithaca: Cornell University Press, 1956); Adrienne Koch, "Review of *Freedom's Fetters,*" *Mississippi Valley Historical Review* 44, 2 (September 1957): 344; Marshall Smelser, "Review of *Freedom's Fetters,*" *American Historical Review* 62, 1 (October 1956); James Morton Smith, "The Sedition Law, Free Speech, and the American Political Process," *William and Mary Quarterly* 9, 4 (October 1952): 497–498.

54. Leonard Levy, *Legacy of Suppression: Freedom of Speech and Press in Early American History* (Cambridge: Harvard University Press, 1960); Harold M. Hyman, *To Try Men's Souls: Loyalty Tests in American History* (Berkeley: University of California Press, 1959). See also the following responses to these books: Robert E. Brown, "Review of *Legacy of Suppression,*" *Journal of Southern History* 27, 2 (May 1961): 239–240; Harold Hyman, "Review of *Legacy of Suppression,*" *American Historical Review* 66, 2 (January 1961): 471–472; John A. Schutz, "Review of *Legacy of Suppression,*" *Mississippi Valley Historical Review* 47, 3 (December 1960): 488–489; James Morton Smith, "Review of *Legacy of Suppression,*" *William and Mary Quarterly* 20, 1 (January 1963): 156–159; Leonard Levy, "Review of *To Try Men's Souls,*" *William and Mary Quarterly* 17, 4 (October 1960): 565–567; Charles A. Barker, "Review of *To Try Men's Souls,*" *American Historical Review* 65, 4 (July 1960): 914–915.

55. Robert K. Murray, "Communism and the Great Steel Strike of 1919," *Mississippi Valley Historical Review* 38, 3 (December 1951): 446, 448–455, 457.

56. Ibid., pp. 464–466, 446–447.

57. Robert K. Murray, *Red Scare: A Study in National Hysteria, 1919–1920* (Minneapolis: University of Minnesota Press, 1955); John M. Blum, "Review of *Red Scare,*" *Mississippi Valley Historical Review* 42, 1 (June 1955): 144–146; John M. Blum, "Nativism, Anti-radicalism, and the Foreign Scare, 1917–1920," *Midwest Journal* 3 (Winter 1950–51); Selig Adler, "Review of *Red Scare,*" *American Historical Review* 61, 1 (October 1955): 149.

58. John Higham, *Strangers in the Land* (New Brunswick: Rutgers University

Press, 1955); Donald Johnson, *The Challenge to American Freedoms* (Lexington: University of Kentucky Press, 1963); Sidney Fine, "Anarchism and the Assassination of McKinley," *American Historical Review* 60, 4 (July 1955): 777–799; Philip Taft, "The Federal Trials of the IWW," *Labor History* 3, 1 (Winter 1962): 57–91. See also Harry N. Scheiber, *The Wilson Administration and Civil Liberties, 1917–1921* (Ithaca: Cornell University Press, 1960); Robert D. Ward, "The Origin and Activities of the National Security League, 1914–1919," *Mississippi Valley Historical Review* 47, 1 (June 1960); James Weinstein, "Anti-war Sentiment and the Socialist Party, 1917–1918," *Political Science Quarterly* 74, 2 (June 1959), and John Braeman, "World War One and the Crisis of American Liberty," *American Quarterly* 16, 1 (Spring 1964).

59. William Preston, Jr., *Aliens and Dissenters* (Cambridge: Harvard University Press, 1963). For an excellent discussion of this book and the larger literature of which it is a part, see Braeman, "World War One," an essay that exemplifies the concerns postwar historians raised about political repression.

60. Preston, *Aliens and Dissenters*, pp. 274–275; Theodore Saloutos, "Review of *Aliens and Dissenters*," *American Historical Review* 69, 2 (January 1964): 484.

61. John W. Caughey, *In Clear and Present Danger: The Crucial State of Our Freedoms* (Chicago: University of Chicago Press, 1958); Irving Dilliard, "Review of *In Clear and Present Danger*," *American Historical Review* 64, 2 (January 1959): 412; Carl Wittke, "Review of *In Clear and Present Danger*," *Mississippi Valley Historical Review* 45, 2 (September 1958): 354–355; Celia Lewis, Vera Shlakman, and Louis Jaffee, "Academic Freedom in a Time of Crisis," New York Teachers Union, Local 555, April 1948, p. 10; Daniel Bell, ed., The New American Right (New York: Criterion Books, 1955); Richard Hofstadter, *Anti-Intellectuals in American Life* (New York: Knopf, 1963); Richard Hofstadter, *The Paranoid Style in American Politics* (New York: Knopf, 1965).

62. For a thoughtful discussion of these issues that reaches somewhat different, though largely complementary, conclusions see Jonathan M. Wiener, "Radical Historians and the Crisis in American History, 1959–1980," *Journal of American History* 76, 2 (September 1989) as well as Herbert Aptheker's illuminating response, "Welcoming Jonathan Wiener's Paper, with a Few Brief Dissents," *Journal of American History* 76, 2 (September 1989).

63. Robin D. G. Kelley, "Interview with Herbert Aptheker," *Journal of American History* 87, 1 (June 2000): 152. For an eloquent description of an individual historian's discovery of Aptheker, and of Aptheker's treatment by professional historians, see Robin D. G. Kelley, "Afterword," *Journal of American History* 87, 1 (June 2000). For recent appreciations of Aptheker see also Herbert Shapiro, ed., *African American History and Radical Historiography: Essays in Honor of Herbert Aptheker* (Minneapolis, Minn.: MEP Pubs., 1998);

Gary Y. Okihiro, ed., *In Resistance: Studies in African, Caribbean, and Afro-American History* (Amherst: University of Massachusetts Press, 1986).

64. Herbert Aptheker, *American Negro Slave Revolts* (New York: Columbia University Press, 1943); Avery Craven, "Review of *American Negro Slave Revolts,*" *Journal of Economic History* 5, 1 (May 1945): 75–77.

65. Herbert Aptheker, *The Negro in the Civil War* (New York: International Publishers, 1938); J. G. de Roulhac Hamilton, "Review of *American Negro Slave Revolts,*" *American Historical Review* 49, 3 (April 1944); B. I. Wiley, "Review of *The Negro in the Civil War,*" *American Historical Review* 45, 1 (October 1939): 244.

66. Lewis McMillan, "Review of *American Slave Revolts,*" *Mississippi Valley Historical Review* 30, 4 (March 1944): 598–599; W. M. Brewer, "Review of *American Slave Revolts,*" *Journal of Negro History* 29, 1 (January 1944): 87–90; Kenneth W. Porter, "Communications," *American Historical Review* 50, 1 (October 1944): 210–212.

67. Kelley, "Interview with Herbert Aptheker," pp. 155–156, 158; Herbert Aptheker, "An Autobiographical Note," *Journal of American History* 87, 1 (June 2000): 158; Staughton Lynd, "The Bulldog Whitewashed: A Critique of the Investigation of Herbert Aptheker's Nonappointment at Yale University," in Herbert Shapiro, ed., *African American History and Radical Historiography* (Minneapolis: University of Minnesota Press, 1998).

68. Philip S. Foner, *Business and Slavery: The New York Merchants and the Irrepressible Conflict* (Chapel Hill: University of North Carolina Press, 1941); Arthur C. Cole, "Review of *Business and Slavery,*" *Mississippi Valley Historical Review* 29, 3 (December 1942): 435–436; Avery Craven, "Review of *Business and Slavery,*" *American Historical Review* 47, 4 (July 1942): 889–890; William O. Lynch, "Review of *Business and Slavery,*" *Journal of Southern History* 7, 4 (November 1941).

69. "Philip S. Foner, Labor Historian and Professor, 84," obituary, *New York Times,* 15 December 1994; Foner, *Business and Slavery,* p. viii; *Contemporary Authors,* s.v. "Foner, Philip," 3: 203–204; Schrecker, *No Ivory Tower,* pp. 43, 82; Ronald C. Kent, Sara Markham, David R. Roediger, and Herbert Shapiro, *Culture, Gender, Race, and U.S. Labor History* (Westport, Conn.: Greenwood Press, 1993); Philip S. Foner, *The Complete Writings of Thomas Paine,* 2 vols. (New York: Citadel Press, 1945); Harry Hayden Clark, "Review of *The Complete Writings of Thomas Paine,*" *American Historical Review* 51, 4 (July 1946): 725; Philip S. Foner, *The Life and Writings of Frederick Douglass,* 3 vols. (New York: International Publishers, 1950); Kenneth Stampp, "Review of *The Life and Writings of Frederick Douglass,*" *American Historical Review* 58, 1 (October 1952): 138–139.

70. Philip Foner, *History of the Labor Movement in the United States from Colonial Times to the Founding of the American Federation of Labor* (New York: International Publishers, 1947); Philip S. Foner, *History of the Labor Move-*

ment in the United States, Vol. II, From the Founding of the American Federation of Labor to the Emergence of American Imperialism (New York: International Publishers, 1955); Lloyd G. Reynolds, "Review of *History of the Labor Movement,*" *Journal of Economic History* 8, 2 (November 1948); Clarence D. Long, "Review of *History of the Labor Movement,*" *American Historical Review* 54, 3 (April 1949): 632–633; Leslie H. Fishel, "Review of *History of the Labor Movement,*" *Journal of Negro History* 41, 4 (October 1956): 355; Joel Seidman, "Review of *History of the Labor Movement,*" *Labor History* 6, 3 (Fall 1965); Wiener, "Radical Historians," p. 409.

71. William Appleman Williams, *The Tragedy of American Diplomacy* (Cleveland: World Publishing Co., 1959); William Appleman Williams, *The Contours of American History* (Cleveland, Ohio: World Publishing Co., 1961); Buhle, *History and the New Left*; Wiener, "Radical Historians," pp. 407–410.

72. Janet Whitney, *Abigail Adams* (Boston: Little, Brown and Co., 1947); Stewart Mitchell, ed., *New Letters of Abigail Adams* (Boston: Houghton Mifflin, 1947); James B. Hedges, "Review of *Abigail Adams* and *New Letters of Abigail Adams,*" *American Historical Review* 53, 3 (April 1948); Louise Hall Tharp, *The Peabody Sisters of Salem* (Boston: Little, Brown and Co., 1950); Stewart Mitchell, "Review of *The Peabody Sisters of Salem,*" *American Historical Review* 55, 4 (July 1950).

73. Ruth Painter Randall, *Mary Lincoln: Biography of a Marriage* (Boston: Little, Brown and Co., 1953); Harry Carman, "Review of *Mary Lincoln,*" *American Historical Review* 58, 4 (July 1953): 945–947. See also Sydney Greenbie and Majorie Barstow Greenbie, *Anna Ella Carroll and Abraham Lincoln: A Biography* (Manchester, Maine: Falmouth Publishing House, 1952); and Harold E. and Ernestine Briggs, *Nancy Hanks Lincoln* (New York: Bookman Associates, 1952).

74. Avery Craven, "Review of *Mary Lincoln,*" *Mississippi Valley Historical Review* 40, 3 (December 1953): 537–539; Albert D. Kirwan, "Review of *Mary Lincoln,*" *Journal of Southern History* 19, 4 (November 1953): 537–538.

75. Lillian O'Connor, *Pioneer Women Orators: Rhetoric in the Ante-bellum Reform Movement* (New York: Columbia University Press, 1954); David Mead, "Review of *Pioneer Women Orators,*" *Mississippi Valley Historical Review* 41, 3 (December 1954): 513–514; Mary Earhart, *Frances Willard* (Chicago: University of Chicago Press, 1944); John Krout, "Review of *Frances Willard,*" *Mississippi Valley Historical Review* 32, 1 (June 1945): 115–117.

76. Giraud Chester, *Embattled Maiden: The Life of Anna Dickinson* (New York: G. P. Putnam's Sons, 1951); James Harvey Young, "Anna Elizabeth Dickinson and the Civil War: For and Against Lincoln," *Mississippi Valley Historical Review* 31, 1 (June 1944); Louise M. Young, "Review of *Embattled Maiden,*" *American Historical Review* 58, 1 (October 1952); Mildred E. Danforth, *A Quaker Pioneer: Laura Haviland, Superintendent of the Under-*

ground (New York: Exposition Press, 1961); J. Welford Holmes, "Review of *A Quaker Pioneer*," *Journal of Negro History* 46, 3 (April 1961): 199–201; Louis Filler, "Review of *The Heart Is Like Heaven: The Life of Lydia Maria Child*," *Journal of American History* 52, 1 (June 1965): 154–155.

77. Edward Wagenknecht, *Harriet Beecher Stowe: The Known and the Unknown* (New York: Oxford University Press, 1965); Paul C. Nagel, "Review of *Harriet Beecher Stowe*," *Journal of American History* 52, 2 (September 1965): 392–393; Johanna Johnston, *Runaway to Heaven: The Story of Harriet Beecher Stowe* (Garden City, N.Y.: Doubleday, 1963); Edna Burke Jackson, "Review of *Runaway to Heaven*," *Journal of Negro History* 49, 1 (January 1964): 68–69.

78. Esther Popel Shaw, "Review of *Victorian Cinderella*," *Journal of Negro History* 33, 1 (January 1948): 99–101.

79. Pauli Murray, *Proud Shoes: The Story of an American Family* (New York: Harper & Brothers, 1956); Edgar Allan Toppin, "Review of *Proud Shoes*," *Journal of Negro History* 42, 1 (January 1957): 67–69; Emma Gelders Sterne, *Mary McLeod Bethune* (New York: Alfred A. Knopf, 1957); Charles Walker Thomas, "Review of *Mary McLeod Bethune*," *Journal of Negro History* 43, 1 (January 1958): 62; Sadie Daniel St. Clair, "Myrtilla Miner: Pioneer in Teacher Education for Negro Women," *Journal of Negro History* 34, 1 (January 1949).

80. Emery Battis, *Saints and Sectaries: Anne Hutchinson and the Antinomian Controversy in the Massachusetts Bay Colony* (Chapel Hill: University of North Carolina Press, 1962); Raymond P. Stearns, "Review of *Saints and Sectaries*," *American Historical Review* 69, 3 (April 1964); Earl Wesley Fornell, *The Unhappy Medium: Spiritualism and the Life of Margaret Fox* (Austin: University of Texas Press, 1964); Sydney Ahlstrom, "Review of *Unhappy Medium*," *Journal of American History* 52, 2 (September 1965): 393–394.

81. Allen F. Davis, "The Social Workers and the Progressive Party, 1912–1916," *American Historical Review* 69, 3 (April 1964): 671–688; Allen F. Davis, "The Women's Trade Union League," *Labor History* 5, 1 (Winter 1964): 16–17; Archie Green, "The Death of Mother Jones," *Labor History* 1, 1 (Winter 1960): 68–80.

82. James T. Patterson, "Mary Dewson and the American Minimum Wage Movement," *Labor History* 5, 2 (Spring 1964): 134; Dorothy Rose Blumberg, "'Dear Mr. Engels': Unpublished Letters, 1884–1894 of Florence Kelley (-Wischnewetzky) to Friedrich Engels," *Labor History* 5, 2 (Spring 1964); Dorothy Rose Blumberg, *Florence Kelley: The Making of a Social Pioneer* (New York: Augustus M. Kelley, 1966).

83. Arthur Marvin Shaw, "Mrs. Jefferson Davis at Fortress Monroe, Virginia," *Journal of Southern History* 16, 1 (February 1950); Mary Boykin Chesnut, *A Diary from Dixie,* ed. Ames Williams (Boston: Houghton Mifflin, 1949); Wendell Holmes Stephenson, "Review of *A Diary from Dixie*," *American*

Historical Review 55, 3 (April 1950): 629–630; John Q. Anderson, ed., *Brokenburn: The Journal of Kate Stone, 1861–1868* (Baton Rouge: Louisiana State University Press, 1955); Mary Elizabeth Massey, "Review of *Brokenburn,*" *Mississippi Valley Historical Review* 42, 2 (September 1955): 331–332; Phoebe Yates Pember, *A Southern Woman's Story: Life in Confederate Richmond,* ed. Bell Irvin Wiley (Jackson, Tenn.: McCowat-Mercer Press, 1959); Kate Cumming, *Kate: The Journal of a Confederate Nurse* (Baton Rouge: Louisiana State University Press, 1959); John Edmond Gonzales, "Review of *A Southern Woman's Story,*" *Journal of Southern History* 26, 3 (August 1960); Patience Pennington, *A Woman Rice Planter,* ed. Cornelius O. Cathey (Cambridge: Harvard University Press, 1961); Franklee G. Whartenby, "Review of *A Woman Rice Planter,*" *Journal of Economic History* 22, 2 (June 1962).

84. Frances Anne Kemble, *Journal of a Residence on a Georgian Plantation in 1838–1839,* ed. John A. Scott (New York: Knopf, 1961); Weymouth T. Jordan, "Review of *Journal of a Residence on a Georgian Plantation,*" *Journal of Southern History* 27, 4 (November 1961): 547; Jerome W. Jones, "Review of *Journal of a Residence on a Georgian Plantation,*" *Journal of Negro History* 46, 4 (October 1961): 261–262; John A. Scott, "On the Authenticity of Fanny Kemble's *Journal of a Residence on a Georgian Plantation in 1838–39,*" *Journal of Negro History* 46, 4 (October 1961).

85. Ray Allen Billington, ed., *The Journal of Charlotte Forten: A Free Negro in the Slave Era* (New York: Dryden Press, 1953); Ray Allen Billington, "A Social Experiment: The Port Royal Journal of Charlotte L. Forten, 1862–1863," *Journal of Negro History* 35, 3 (July 1950): 233–264; Charles Walker Thomas, "Review of *The Journal of Charlotte Forten,*" *Journal of Negro History* 38, 3 (July 1953): 343; Edwin Adams Davis, "Review of *The Journal of Charlotte Forten,*" *Mississippi Valley Historical Review* 40, 4 (March 1954): 743–744; Elsie M. Lewis, "Review of *The Journal of Charlotte Forten,*" *Journal of Southern History* 19, 2 (May 1953): 237–238.

86. Pearl M. Graham, "Thomas Jefferson and Sally Hemings," *Journal of Negro History* 46, 2 (April 1961): 89–90, 99–103.

87. Morris U. Schappes, "Ernestine L. Rose: Her Address on the Anniversary of West Indian Emancipation," *Journal of Negro History* 34, 3 (July 1949): 344–355; Frederick B. Tolles, *Slavery and "the Woman Question"* (Haverford, Pa., and Boston: Friends Historical Association and Friends Historical Society, 1952); Majorie L. Felton, "Review of *Slavery and 'the Woman Question,'*" *Journal of Negro History* 37, 4 (October 1952): 455–457; Gerda Lerner, "The Grimké Sisters and the Struggle against Race Prejudice," *Journal of Negro History* 48, 4 (October 1963); Gerda Lerner, *The Grimké Sisters of South Carolina* (Boston: Houghton Mifflin, 1967).

88. Eleanor Flexner, *Century of Struggle* (Cambridge: Harvard University Press, 1959); Gertrude B. Rivers, "Review of *Century of Struggle,*" *Journal of Negro History* 44, 4 (October 1959): 370–371.

89. Aileen Kraditor, *The Ideas of the Woman Suffrage Movement, 1890–1920* (New York: Columbia University Press, 1965); Anne Firor Scott, "After Suffrage: Southern Women in the Twenties," *Journal of Southern History* 30, 3 (August 1964): 317–318.

Epilogue

1. Richard Hofstadter, *The Progressive Historians* (New York: Vintage, 1970), p. xv; John Higham, *History: Professional Scholarship in America* (Baltimore: Johns Hopkins University Press, 1965), pp. 245–251; Peter Novick, *That Noble Dream: The "Objectivity Question" and the American Historical Profession* (Cambridge, U.K.: Cambridge University Press, 1988), Chapter 13; Thomas C. Cochran, "Economic History, Old and New," *American Historical Review* 74, 5 (June 1969): 1561–62; Paul Buhle, *History and the New Left: Madison, Wisconsin, 1950–1970* (Philadelphia: Temple University Press, 1990), pp. 25–28; Ian Tyrrell, *The Absent Marx: Class Analysis and Liberal History in Twentieth Century America* (New York: Greenwood Press, 1986), pp. 103–106, Chapters 5 and 6.
2. John Hope Franklin, "The New Negro History," *Journal of Negro History* 42, 2 (April 1957): 95–96.
3. Ibid., pp. 92–96.
4. Ernest Kaiser, "Review of *From Slavery to Freedom: A History of American Negroes; The Negro in the United States: A Brief History; A Pictorial History of the Negro in America; Africa's Gift to America; The People that Walked in Darkness,*" *Journal of Negro Education* 31, 4 (Autumn 1962): 468; Robert Livingston Schuyler, "Review of *The American Historian: A Social-Intellectual History of the Writing of the American Past; Essays in American Historiography: Papers Presented in Honor of Allan Nevins,*" *Journal of Southern History* 27, 2 (May 1961): 237; James A. Barnes, "The Fifty-Third Annual Meeting of the Mississippi Valley Historical Association," *Mississippi Valley Historical Review* 47, 2 (September 1960): 284; Schuyler, "Review of *The American Historian,*" p. 237; Clarence L. Ver Steeg, "Review of *The British Empire before the American Revolution,*" *Journal of American History* 53, 2 (September 1966): 343; see also Gene Wise, "Political 'Reality' in Recent American Scholarship: Progressives versus Symbolists," *American Quarterly* 19, 2, Part 2, Supplement (Summer 1967): 305.
5. Donald R. McCoy, "Underdeveloped Sources of Understanding in American History," *Journal of American History* 54, 2 (September 1967): 270; Buhle, *History and the New Left,* pp. 22–29, 51–53; Harold Cruse, "Americanizing the Radical Program," *Studies on the Left* 3 (Winter 1963). Pioneers in quantitative history early expressed their collective sense that they were opening up an entirely new way of doing history. See John R. Meyer and Alfred A. Conrad, "Economic Theory, Statistical Inference and Economic History," *Journal of Economic History* 17 (December 1957); Jerome M. Clubb and

Howard W. Allen, "Computers and Historical Studies," *Journal of American History* 54 (December 1967); Cochran, "Economic History, Old and New," pp. 1561–2; Robert P. Swierenga, "Computers and American History: The Impact of the 'New' Generation," *Journal of American History* 60, 4 (March 1974): 1045–70; Allan Bogue, "United States: The 'New' Political History," *Journal of Contemporary History* 3 (January 1968).

6. These figures are based on a word search using JSTOR through fifteen leading professional history journals, including the *American Quarterly, American Historical Review, Journal of American History, Journal of Economic History, Journal of Negro History, Journal of Southern History,* and the *William and Mary Quarterly.* Some of the boom in the 1980s may be attributed to the lag time between submission and publication of essays and reviews in major historical journals.

7. Richard C. Wade, "The Sixtieth Annual Meeting of the Organization of American Historians," *Journal of American History* 54, 2 (September 1967): 363–364; Irwin Unger, "The 'New Left' and American History: Some Recent Trends in United States Historiography," *American Historical Review* 72, 4 (July 1967): 1237–63; Eugene D. Genovese, "Letter to the Editor," *American Historical Review* 73, 3 (February 1968): 993–995; Novick, *That Noble Dream,* pp. 424–427 and Chapter 13.

8. Unger, "The 'New Left' and American History," pp. 1237–42, 1246, 1261.

9. Ibid., pp. 1257, 1259–62.

10. Eugene D. Genovese, "Letter to the Editor," *American Historical Review* 73, 3 (February 1968): 993–995.

11. Barton Bernstein, ed., *Towards a New Past: Dissenting Essays in American History* (New York: Vintage Books, 1969), pp. v–vi.

12. Ibid., pp. vi–vii.

13. Ibid., pp. vii–ix.

14. Ibid., pp. ix–xiii.

15. Ibid., p. x; Jesse Lemisch, "The American Revolution Seen From the Bottom Up," in Bernstein, ed., *Towards a New Past,* pp. 4–6, 29; Eugene D. Genovese, "Marxian Interpretations of the Slave South," in Bernstein, ed., *Towards a New Past,* pp. 90–125. Lemisch references the work of Herbert Aptheker in his notes; see, for example, Lemisch, "The American Revolution," p. 39, n. 74. Staughton Lynd offered a respectful appraisal of Beard and a challenge to Beard's critics in his essay, "Beyond Beard," in Bernstein, ed., *Towards a New Past,* pp. 46–64.

16. Aileen S. Kraditor, "Review of *Towards a New Past,*" *American Historical Review* 74, 2 (December 1968): 531; Jesse Lemisch, "Letter to the Editor," *American Historical Review* 74, 5 (June 1969): 1766–68; Aileen Kraditor, "Letter to the Editor," *American Historical Review* 74, 5 (June 1969): 1768–69; David Donald, "Review of *Towards a New Past,*" *American Historical Review* 74, 2 (December 1968): 532–533. See also Irwin Unger's surprisingly mild response to the book: Irwin Unger, "Review of *Towards a New Past,*" *Journal of American History* 55, 2 (September 1968): 369–371.

17. James H. Hutson, "An Investigation of the Inarticulate: Philadelphia's White Oaks," *William and Mary Quarterly,* 3rd Series, 28, 1 (January 1971): 21; Jesse Lemisch and John K. Alexander, "The White Oaks, Jack Tar, and the Concept of the 'Inarticulate,'" *William and Mary Quarterly,* 3rd Series, 29, 1 (January 1972): 110–111.

18. For a thoughtful analysis of the distinction between the sort of social history Merle Curti advanced in the 1950s and the subsequent "new social history" see James A. Henretta, "The Making of an American Community: A Thirty-Year Retrospective," *Reviews in American History* 16, 3 (September 1988).

19. Lawrence Veysey, "The 'New' Social History in the Context of American Historical Writing," *Reviews in American History* 7, 1 (March 1979): 5–8; Robert E. Gallman, "Some Notes on the New Social History," *Journal of Economic History* 37, 1 (March 1977): 5; Robert Forster, "Achievements of the Annales School," *Journal of Economic History* 38, 1 (March 1978); Michael McGiffert, "American Puritan Studies in the 1960's," *William and Mary Quarterly,* 3rd Series, 27, 1 (January 1970): 58; James Henretta, "Social History as Lived and Written," *American Historical Review* 84, 5 (December 1979); Darrett Rutman, "Comments on 'Social History as Lived and Written,'" *American Historical Review* 84, 5 (December 1979); Carl N. Degler, "Remaking American History," *Journal of American History* 67, 1 (June 1980); Mark Kaplanoff, "The Emperor's New Clothes," *Reviews in American History* 9, 1 (March 1981); Daniel Joseph Singal, "Beyond Consensus: Richard Hofstadter and American Historiography," *American Historical Review* 89, 4 (October 1984); Thomas Bender, "The New History— Then and Now," *Reviews in American History* 12, 4 (December 1984); Morris B. Katz, "Review of *Ordinary People and Everday Life,*" *Journal of Economic History* 45, 3 (September 1985); Joyce Appleby, "A Different Kind of Independence: The Postwar Restructuring of the Historical Study of Early America," *William and Mary Quarterly,* 3rd Series, 50, 2 (April 1993).

20. C. Vann Woodward, "The Future of the Past," *American Historical Review* 75, 3 (February 1970): 721. For a stimulating and nuanced discussion of the dynamics of historiography see Robert F. Berkhofer, Jr., *Beyond the Great Story: History as Text and Discourse* (Cambridge: Harvard University Press, 1995).

21. Richard Hofstadter, *The Progressive Historians* (New York: Vintage Books, 1968), p. xv.

22. Ibid., p. xiv. Higham also made note of these parricidal tendencies in John Higham, "Review of *The Past before Us,*" *American Historical Review* 86, 4 (October 1981) when he observed, "Although our historiography is overtly self-critical, at a deeper level does it not function as an elaborate form of boundary maintenance? I suspect it does, and not only vis-à-vis the world outside our professional networks. Historiography also articulates the self-consciousness of successive generations of scholars. It enables a newly ascendant generation to define itself by distinguishing its own efforts from those of its predecessors" (p. 807).

Index

Aaron, Daniel: *Writers on the Left,* 198–199

Abbott, Edith, 60; *Women in Industry,* 58

Abel, Annie Heloise, 83–85, 96, 133; "The History of Events Resulting in Indian Consolidation West of the Mississippi," 83; "Indian Reservations in Kansas and the Extinguishment of Their Title," 83; "The Indians in the Civil War," 84; *The Slaveholding Indians,* 84; *The American Indian as Participant in the Civil War,* 107

Abolitionism, 93, 230, 231, 236–237. *See also* Slavery

Adams, Abigail, 229

Adams, George Burton, 65–66, 69

Adams, Herbert Baxter, 19

AFL. *See* American Federation of Labor

African Americans: and Du Bois, 14, 44, 45, 92–93; and Sloane, 18; and Jameson, 21; and Phillips, 64; and Beard, 74–75; and Progressive era historiography, 91–97; and Milling, 111; and Native Americans, 112–113, 114; and colonial America, 113; and Rhodes, 158; and Woodson, 159; and migration, 159–160; and industrialism, 160–161; and labor, 160–163, 173, 178–179, 181–182; and Lindsay, 161; and Helper, 167; and Watson, 169, 170–171; and Woodward, 169, 170–171; and Shugg, 173; and cap-italism, 179; and economy, 179–180; and Debs, 200; and Ginger, 200; and communism, 212–215; and Johnston, 231; and women, 232; and Franklin, 240–241; recognition of, 252

Agriculture: and cotton, 26, 46, 47, 62, 150, 152, 165; and McMaster, 31; and Du Bois, 45; and Progressive era, 54; and Beard, 71, 73; and Libby, 72; and Native Americans, 130; and N. Ware, 145–146, 147; and C. Ware, 151; and Thomas, 157; and Socialism, 166, 210, 211; and South, 168, 173; and Watson, 169; and Woodward, 170

Ahistoricity, 53, 247, 248

Ahlstrom, Sydney, 232–233

Alden, John Richard: *John Stuart and the Southern Colonial Frontier,* 107

Alien, 220. *See also* Immigration

Alien and Sedition Acts, 193, 215–216

Alien Registration Act, 220

Amateurs, 29–43, 90

Ambler, Charles, 107–108

American Baptist Missionary Society, 136

American Civil Liberties Union, 219

American Federation of Labor, 147, 155, 179, 206. *See also* Labor

American Historical Association, 13

American Historical Review, 33, 91, 97

American Revolution, 25–26, 28, 46, 88–89, 193, 215–216, 247, 248

People, common: and new history, 3, 4; and Progressive era, 5–6; and industrialism, 15; and Sloane, 16–17; and Jameson, 19, 24, 27, 28; and McMaster, 31; and Eggleston, 36; and Turner, 48–49, 67; and Beard, 71; and Roosevelt, 87, 88; and Becker, 89; and interwar historiography, 141–142; and labor, 143–144, 178; and N. Ware, 144; and Shugg, 173; and South, 173, 176; and sources, 176; and Jernegan, 180; and Bancroft, 261n5. *See also* Culture; Social history; Society

People's Party, 169, 196

Persons, Stow, 211; *Socialism and American Life,* 209

Peterson, H. C.: *Opponents of War, 1917–1918,* 199–200

Phillips, Ulrich B., 59, 63–64, 80, 93, 167, 223; "The Origin and Growth of the Southern Black Belts," 63; *American Negro Slavery,* 64, 92

Pilgrims, 37. *See also* Colonial America; Religion

Pittsburgh Survey, 59

Plains Indians, 103. *See also* Native Americans

Planters/plantation, 73, 172, 173, 175. *See also* Slavery; South

Politics: and Sloane, 16, 17; and Jameson, 20, 21, 23, 24; and McMaster, 31; and Eggleston, 33, 42, 43; and Turner, 48, 61, 68–69; and Seligman, 54–56; and Hart, 61; and Phillips, 63, 64; and G. B. Adams, 65; and Beard, 70, 71; and J. H. Robinson, 70; and Becker, 88; and Debo, 130–131; and Native Americans, 130–131; and C. Ware, 153; and N. Ware, 154; and Rhodes, 157, 158; and Lewinson, 168; and Reconstruction, 168; and Woodward, 168, 169–170

Politics, contemporary: and 1960s historiography, 1–2; and American Historical Association, 13–14; and Jameson, 20, 21, 22, 27; and Populism, 28–29; and McMaster, 31; and Du Bois, 47; and Progressive era, 52, 60; and Seligman, 57; and Phillips, 64; and Turner, 68; and Beard, 73, 75; and McLaughlin, 73; and Semple, 78, 79; and Paxson, 82; and interwar period, 99; and Milling, 110;

and Native Americans, 115, 117, 120, 121; and Downes, 117; and Gates, 117; and Priest, 121; and Woodward, 171; and post–World War II period, 193; and Fite, 200; and Peterson, 200; and communism, 215–216; and Levy, 217; and Blum, 218; and radicalism, 220; and Graham, 236; and race, 236; and Unger, 242; and Genovese, 244; and Bernstein, 245–246. *See also* Society, contemporary

Populism: and Jameson, 27; and capitalism, 28–29, 195; and Libby, 71–72; and South, 168; and Woodward, 168, 169; and Shugg, 171; and post–World War II period, 193; and radicalism, 194, 195, 196; and Marxism, 195; and Wayland, 207; and socialism, 210; and Hofstadter, 221

Porter, Kenneth, 113–114, 115, 225

Potter, David: *People of Plenty,* 189, 190

Poverty, 115–116, 133, 134, 165, 166, 167, 168, 177, 210. *See also* Economy

Powderly, Terence, 184

Prejudice, 180, 181. *See also* Discrimination; Racism

Present, 49, 83, 97. *See also* Politics, contemporary; Society, contemporary

Presentism, 7, 68, 75, 117, 191, 217, 244, 248

Preston, William, Jr.: *Aliens and Dissenters,* 220–221

Priest, Loring: *Uncle Sam's Stepchildren: The Reformation of United States Indian Policy, 1865–1887,* 121–124

Professionals, 29, 31

Progress, 5, 31, 41, 42–43, 54

Progressive era: and new history, 4–5, 52–53, 240, 249; and Beard, 8, 69; and Becker, 8; complexity of, 8; and Turner, 8, 67, 69; and interwar period, 10, 98, 99; and contemporary politics, 52, 60; and industrialism, 53, 54; and economy, 53–54, 89; and democracy, 60; and Semple, 78; and social history, 85–86, 89; and immigration, 89–90; and women, 90–91; and Higham, 189; and consensus history, 191, 192; and radicalism, 194, 196; and McCoy, 241–242; and Bernstein, 245; and Hofstadter, 251

Protestantism, 108, 136, 210. *See also* Religion